# THE
## *Qualitative*
# DISSERTATION

### SECOND EDITION

*To all those students who have
enriched our lives and thinking by sharing
their scholarly journey with us
and
To all those students who are about to
embark on their dissertation journey*

# The Qualitative Dissertation

### Second Edition

## a guide for Students and Faculty

# Maria Piantanida
# Noreen B. Garman

#### Foreword by Frances Schoonmaker

CORWIN
A SAGE Company

*For information:*

Corwin
A SAGE Company
2455 Teller Road
Thousand Oaks, California 91320
(800) 233-9936
Fax: (800) 417-2466
www.corwinpress.com

SAGE Ltd.
1 Oliver's Yard
55 City Road
London EC1Y 1SP
United Kingdom

SAGE India Pvt. Ltd.
B 1/I 1 Mohan Cooperative
   Industrial Area
Mathura Road, New Delhi 110 044
India

SAGE Asia-Pacific Pte. Ltd.
33 Pekin Street #02-01
Far East Square
Singapore 048763

Printed in the United States of America.

*Library of Congress Cataloging-in-Publication Data*

Piantanida, Maria.
The qualitative dissertation : a guide for students and faculty / Maria Piantanida, Noreen B. Garman.—2nd ed.
      p. cm.
Includes bibliographical references and index.
ISBN 978-1-4129-5107-4 (cloth : acid-free paper)
ISBN 978-1-4129-5108-1 (pbk. : acid-free paper)
   1. Dissertations, Academic. 2. Research—Methodology.
I. Garman, Noreen B. II. Title.

LB2369.P48 2009
808.′02—dc22                              2008042302

This book is printed on acid-free paper.

09   10   11   12   13   10  9  8  7  6  5  4  3  2  1

| | |
|---|---|
| *Acquisitions Editor:* | Debra Stollenwerk |
| *Associate Editor:* | Julie McNall |
| *Production Editor:* | Cassandra Margaret Seibel |
| *Copy Editor:* | Adam Dunham |
| *Typesetter:* | C&M Digitals (P) Ltd. |
| *Proofreader:* | Theresa Kay |
| *Cover Designer:* | Scott Van Atta |

# Contents

# List of Exemplars, Sample Reference Lists, Figures, and Reflective Interludes

# *Foreword*

**Frances Schoonmaker, Professor**
*Teachers College, Columbia University*

It is not surprising to find Piantanida and Garman's book entering into a second edition. When I first read *The Qualitative Dissertation,* I found myself wishing I had been fortunate enough to have it in hand when I wrote my own dissertation some twenty years ago. Almost all of the issues that undermine confidence in doing the dissertation, delineated by Piantanida and Garman, are old friends to me. They did not remain behind with the completion of the dissertation but reappear in every research project I undertake! So while the book is directed to beginners, *The Qualitative Dissertation* is not just for beginners. While it is imminently practical, it is not a recipe book. It repeatedly drives home the point that qualitative research is careful, thoughtful, rigorous, much more than technique, and it can be a liberating process.

Piantanida and Garman's message about research is one that the broader educational research community needs to consider at this point in history. While the evolution of research has opened an array of rich modes of inquiry, the political context for research within the United States represents an indifferent closing to a century of growth and development within the educational research community. In the early days of the 20th century, the behavioral sciences provided the model for researchers. Unprecedented developments in the traditional disciplines of knowledge, as well as in science and technology, brought the promise that human problems, including those of the school, could be studied and ameliorated. Much of the research that was produced in those early years attempted to provide scientific proofs for justification of what were thought to be best practices (Bolin, Sawyer, & Borrego-Brainard, 1998). By the 1950s, the "descriptive-correlational-experimental loop" (Rosenshine & Furst, 1973, p. 122) had "achieved the status of orthodoxy" in the United States (Bellack, 1978, p. 1). Students made research choices on the basis of what colleges and universities honored, leading to hundreds of studies that, while methodologically correct, were trivial and failed to illuminate practice. Education then, as now, was far too complex to be viewed through one research lens.

Increased awareness of the complexity of teaching and learning led to critiques of the traditional research paradigm from within the research community in the 1970s. However, for the most part, these criticisms reflected a preoccupation with methods and "*the myth of methodology,* the notion that the most serious difficulties which confront behavioral science are 'methodological,' and that if only we hit upon the right methodology, progress will be rapid and sure" (Kaplan, cited in Bellack, 1978, p. 16)—a myth *The Qualitative Dissertation* dismisses immediately. Reid (1979), directing his attention to curriculum research, argued that experimental work has largely been based on the assumption that solutions to curriculum problems will come from reducing them to procedural problems rather than addressing them as "uncertain practical problems" (p. 202). In the name of efficiency, problems are treated as if they have technical solutions leading to a situation where the problems that are addressed are those for which some procedural techniques exist rather than those that matter most (p. 203). This has meant that curriculum theorizing, research, and development were seen as specialized tasks to be done only by those schooled in technique. Furthermore, a professional literature emerged "that had meaning only to those enculturated into the community of researchers with their own discourse and methods of translating and evaluating information" (Ornstein, 1995, p. 2).

But by the close of the 1970s, a variety of methodologies drawn from sociological and philosophical perspectives appeared as a counterpoint to quantitative, experimental work. Researchers interested in the applications of social sciences methodologies to schools opened the way for researchers interested in understanding teaching from the perspective of teachers and students through description and analysis of classroom events as perceived and interpreted by those participating in them (Snyder, Bolin, & Zumwalt, 1992). Researchers entered into the ambiguity of classrooms, schools, and contexts inhabited by students, accepting the multiple perspectives of those involved.

As Piantanida and Garman point out, the field of qualitative research has grown to include a rich array of discourses. Today, the qualitative researcher not only takes into account the perspectives of participants but also is directly involved as researcher (Cochran-Smith & Lytle, 1999). Methodologies in which teachers can participate, guide, or initiate have the advantage of producing knowledge about practice that is easy to understand and directly applicable. Whereas much of the research *on* teaching had the effect of demeaning practice, emergent forms of inquiry have emphasized the teacher's professional discretion in matters of curriculum and teaching and resetting a social agenda for schools, challenging the structures of oppression that exist within schools and communities. While liberating to the researcher who is interested in exploring educational issues and events, the complexity of choice can be daunting.

The simplistic view of educational research that existed at the dawn of the 20th century is understandable. New ways to apply principles of research to educational practice were being invented and the kinks worked out. It is baffling to see it reemerge today in public policies that privilege quantitative perspectives through funding or high stakes testing as the criteria of successful schooling.

The art and science of research—quantitative and qualitative—is now more deeply and broadly understood within the educational research community. More than ever, "heterogeneity in educational scholarship" is needed in order to understand both the science and poetry of the human events that surround teaching and learning (Berliner, 2002, p. 20). Yet scholars—including those embarking on a dissertation—must be able to articulate the rationale for their choices within a social and political arena in which simplistic views are more welcome. For the student or seasoned researcher who chooses to enter the ambiguous world of qualitative research, Piantanida and Garman help to demystify the process. They provide ample resources to guide the researcher in formulating a cogent argument for choice of genre and their justification within a broader public arena.

Underlying the practical suggestions, array of exemplars, and case suggestions that Piantanida and Garman offer is an assumption that research can be more than a project. In the broadest and fullest sense, research, as they describe it, is a way of being-in-the-world that claims discursive deliberation as "a driving force and sustaining energy."

# REFERENCES

Bellack, A. A. (1978). *Competing ideologies in research on teaching.* (Uppsala Reports on Education No. 1). Uppsala: Uppsala University, Department of Education.

Berliner, D. C. (2002). Educational research: The hardest science of all. *Educational Researcher, 31*(8), 18–20.

Bolin, F. S., Sawyer, R. D., & Borrego-Brainard, M. (1998). Methods of inquiry in supervision. In G. R. Firth & E. F. Pajak (Eds.), *Handbook of research on school supervision* (pp. 25–40). New York: Macmillan.

Cochran-Smith, M., & Lytle, S. L. (1999). The teacher research movement: A decade later. *Educational Researcher, 28*(7), 15–25.

Kaplan, A. (1964). *The conduct of inquiry.* San Francisco: Chandler.

Ornstein, A. C. (1995). Teacher effectiveness: A look at what works. *Peabody Journal of Education, 70*(2), 2–23.

Reid, W. A. (1979). Practical reasoning and curriculum theory: In search of a new paradigm. *Curriculum Inquiry, 9*(3), 187–207.

Rosenshine, B., & Furst, N. (1973). The use of direct observation to study teaching. In R. Travers (Ed.), *Second handbook of research on teaching* (pp. 122–183). Chicago: Rand McNally.

Snyder, J., Bolin, F. S., & Zumwalt, K. K. (1992). Curriculum implementation. In P. Jackson (Ed.), *Handbook of research on curriculum* (pp. 402–435). New York: Macmillan.

441038833 - 000

# FULFILLMENT CENTER

1101 Business Parkway South
Westminster, MD 21157

SHIP TO: DON CRANE
2649 DESERT ROSE DR
LANCASTER CA 93536
United States Of America

| PAGE NO. | 1 |

| ORDER NO. | DS295784 |

| DATE | 1/20/14 |

SHIP VIA: USPS TRACKING # eVS

SHIPMENT NO. 9115001

| SHIP | Line | Item Description | Ord | Purchase Order No. |
|------|------|------------------|-----|--------------------|
| 1 | 001 | DISSERTATION JOURNEY A PRACTICAL AND COM | 1 | |
| 1 | ... | TOTAL QUANTITY FOR ORDER ... | 1 | |
| | | END OF ORDER    1/20/14    14:45:54 | | |

Item Number
9781412977982

Your satisfaction is our #1 priority, so we make it simple for you: 30 Day, from shipping date, money back guarantee-100% refund on the book purchased. To be eligible for a refund, you must return the item in the same condition you received it - Videos, DVD's, audio, and computer software purchases, returned opened and not in the original packaging are non-refundable. Shipping fees are non-refundable.

In order to receive your refund, please enclose a brief note stating the reason for your return with the items that you are returning. Send the item(s) back to us so we receive them undamaged within 30 days of shipping. We do not accept packages marked return to sender. Postage fees incurred due to packages sent return to sender, refused, undeliverable or deemed to have an insufficient address by the carrier will be deducted from the buyers refund. Shipping and handling charges, for returning the item, are the responsibility of the buyer. A 20% restocking fee will be assessed to all items received returned after 30 days of ship date.

Please ship all returns to:

**SuperBookDeals**
**Ref:[transaction or order number]**
**1101 Business Parkway, South**
**Westminster, MD 21157**

**Tips for returning: Be sure to purchase tracking and/or insure when shipping your package! Tha way if it is lost or damaged you will still get money back from the shipping company. Also, please allow your return enough mail delivery time to reach us within the 30 day period.

DON CRANE
2649 DESERT ROSE DR

LANCASTER CA 93536

VIA: TLBM

SHIPPER NO. —

PKG. ID#
9241999984227159 62120

9115001

DON CRANE
2649 DESERT ROSE DR
LANCASTER CA 93536
United States Of America

Return Label

ORDER # DS295784

DON CRANE
2649 DESERT ROSE DR
LANCASTER CA 93536
United States Of America

**Fulfillment Center**
**1101 Business Parkway South**
**Westminster, MD 21157**

SOE9115001

# *Preface to the Second Edition*

## GENESIS OF THE BOOK

The seeds for the first edition of *The Qualitative Dissertation* were planted in 1980, before the term *qualitative research* had entered the mainstream discourses of educational inquiry. At that time, we, the authors, shared an interest in understanding what it would mean to do an "alternative" dissertation—one that would not follow the precepts of quasi-experimental research that was so dominant at our university back then. Because so few references were available in the educational literature to guide our thinking, we formed a dissertation study group in which to cultivate our understanding of what came to be called *qualitative research*. Since then, the study group has evolved through several generations, providing an exceptionally fertile context for our learning about the intricacies of dissertation work. In addition, our understanding has been enriched and challenged by a number of experiences including teaching a two-semester course on the nature of doctoral study, developing and teaching a research oriented master's program for practicing teachers, teaching an introductory course on qualitative research, participating in two qualitative research discussion groups that are flourishing in Pittsburgh, participating in the growing number of qualitatively-oriented research sessions at national conferences, working with several doctoral students from Australia, and coediting a book on the dissertation experience of study group members (Garman & Piantanida, 2006). Together, these experiences serve as the context within which this second edition of *The Qualitative Dissertation* took root and grew.

Perhaps the most powerful lesson we have learned from our experiences is the capacity for some educational practitioners to embrace a life of study and scholarship. Certainly, this has not been the case for all doctoral students that we have met. Nor has it been the case for all students who have spent time with our study group. But what strikes us as remarkable is the number of teachers and administrators who have entered the group with very little understanding of what it means to do research and, through work on their dissertations, have come to embody scholarly habits of mind.

In recent years, the purpose of the dissertation within doctoral educational has received renewed attention, as for example, by The Carnegie Initiative on the Doctorate and the American Educational Research Association. We are heartened by such deliberations, which are reaffirming the importance of the dissertation in preparing a new generation of scholars. At the same time, however, we are troubled by assumptions that seem to perpetuate a traditional dichotomy between academic researcher/scholar and practice-based professional. Despite several decades of discourse in which practitioner-generated knowledge gained recognition and credibility, the assumption that practitioners are consumers, not producers, of knowledge still lingers. We recognize that not all practitioners embrace the identity of scholar. Yet our experience persuades us that more than a few practitioners long for an intellectual life that goes beyond compliance with federally mandated accountability measures and the efficient implementation of prepackaged instructional materials. This second edition of *The Qualitative Dissertation* arises from our desire to affirm and support those who are striving to embrace the identity of scholar-practitioner.

## PURPOSE OF
## *THE QUALITATIVE DISSERTATION*

Internalizing the identity of scholar-practitioner requires more than the simple acquisition of specific research techniques (e.g., interviewing, content analysis). It entails reforging one's sense of self, one's way of being in the world. We believe that the dissertation can serve as a crucible within which such a transformation of self can take place. Just as alchemists sought to transmute metals into gold by burning away impurities, aspiring scholars must often burn away a number of misconceptions and dysfunctional assumptions in their quest for a scholarly identity. This is never an easy endeavor. As the subtitle of *The Qualitative Dissertation* suggests, this book is meant as a guide to this potentially transformative process.

By *guide* we do not mean an instruction manual on qualitative research methods. Nor do we mean a recipe, formula, or template for preparing dissertation-related documents (e.g., proposal, final report). Rather, we call attention to issues and questions that arise as students struggle to learn about qualitative dissertation research. Often, it seems to us, this struggle proceeds on two interconnected levels represented by the following questions:

- What does it mean to do a dissertation?
- What does it mean to do qualitative research?

There is no simple or single answer to either question. Indeed, there will be as many answers as there are individuals who struggle to make meaning of the dissertation and qualitative research. So the challenge facing aspiring practitioner-scholars is orienting themselves to the learning associated with—necessitated by—serious engagement with these overarching questions.

The prospect of this learning can be quite daunting. Where do I start? What do I read? What questions am I supposed to think about? What is expected of me? Where do I turn for help? Lying beneath these rather action-oriented concerns is a substratum of more introspective questions. Who am I as a practitioner, researcher, and scholar? Who am I striving to be? What am I bringing to this dissertation process? What do I believe about the nature of knowledge and how knowledge is generated? What role do I see for myself in this knowledge-generating enterprise? In our experience with thoughtful doctoral students, a dynamic and productive tension seems to arise from the interplay between the two types of questions. Our purpose in *The Qualitative Dissertation* is to encourage readers to probe these tensions—using practical issues to surface issues of worldview and issues of worldview to inform the decisions associated with crafting and conducting a qualitative dissertation.

# AUDIENCE FOR *THE QUALITATIVE DISSERTATION*

Clearly, we hope that *The Qualitative Dissertation* will be useful to those who are about to embark on the dissertation journey. But we recognize that students begin this journey with different professional aspirations and levels of preparation. Some, for example, may be aiming for faculty positions where they will be expected to pursue a robust research agenda, possibly teach research methods courses, and ultimately guide thesis and dissertation research. Others may also plan to pursue academic careers, but in colleges where responsibility for teaching takes precedence over research. Still others may come to doctoral study with a desire to remain in positions in public or private schools. Regardless of an individual's specific aspirations, we contend that doctoral study carries with it an obligation for scholarship. The students we meet in our doctoral-level courses often express surprise when we say this. Typically, they see themselves as practitioners who are temporarily reentering the role of student in order to enhance their knowledge and skills or to obtain a credential for career advancement. *Scholars* are the people they study. The idea that they, too, might someday be viewed as scholars can be quite startling. For readers who resonate with this sense of surprise, the book invites you to consider what it means to hold the highest degree in the land.

Students also arrive at the dissertation with varying degrees of familiarity with research methods. Some may have extensive coursework; others relatively little. Some may have worked as assistants on research projects; others may have been principal investigators on projects of their own; still others may have had no prior experience in conducting research. Given such variation in levels of preparation, it is impossible for *The Qualitative Dissertation* to meet the specific needs of all prospective readers. We do, however, believe that the dissertation represents a particular research genre that differs from large-scale, publicly or privately funded research projects as well as from casual inquiries into matters of personal or professional curiosity. Further, the dissertation is not merely a longer version of a course-based research paper. Nor is it an arbitrary (and consequently meaningless) academic hoop as it is all too often portrayed. Given this, *The Qualitative Dissertation* can be useful to readers who want to understand more clearly what it means to engage in a substantive inquiry as an unfunded, individual researcher who is, in all likelihood, also working full time in a professional capacity.

Although most of our experience has been with professionals in the field of education, we have had opportunities to work with students from other fields, including genetic counseling, health-related professions, library and information sciences, public health, and social work. Many of the dissertation issues faced by these working practitioners echo those expressed by teachers and school administrators. It is our hope, therefore, that *The Qualitative Dissertation* may be useful to readers outside the field of education.

Given the historic moment in which readers are embarking upon their dissertation journey, *The Qualitative Dissertation* may serve another important purpose. Beginning in the mid-1970s and continuing for over three decades, scholars in education (as well as many other disciplines and professions) have struggled to articulate the nature of *qualitative research* against a centuries-long backdrop of positivist science. Sometimes characterized as the *paradigm wars,* battles have been waged on many fronts—the epistemological, the methodological, the political, and the linguistic to name a few.

One might think after all of this effort, a state of clarification would have been achieved. This has not happened, nor is it likely to. So newcomers to the discourses of qualitative research can find the language quite disorienting—especially those who are trying to articulate ideas that do not conform to the precepts of postpositivism. We have encountered two variations of this struggle for language and understanding. In some instances, those with formal schooling in quantitative research methods are trying to relate what they already know to a view of research that may at times seem quite similar and at times quite foreign. In other instances, individuals with little or no previous research training may be struggling to understand new ideas against a vaguely conceived caricature of "science." *The Qualitative Dissertation* is grounded in an interpretive view of qualitative research and, as such, offers a counterpoint to many of the dissertation books that are embedded in a postpositivist tradition. Hopefully, this difference in epistemological context will help those who are engaged in either variation of the struggle for language.

As the subtitle of the book suggests, faculty are another potential audience for *The Qualitative Dissertation.* Here again, individual readers may vary in their need for a guide to guiding dissertations. Some faculty may be in the early stages of chairing dissertations and be drawing primarily from their own experience of the dissertation writing process. If the advice and guidance they received is not proving helpful to the students whom they are now advising, they may be searching for ways through an impasse. Conversely, senior faculty who have guided many quantitative studies may be wondering what, if any, differences arise in the course of a qualitative study. Finally, as we have exchanged dissertation-advising stories with colleagues, it seems that many of us have encountered students who have trouble getting into or carrying through to the end of the dissertation process. It is our observation that impediments to progress often lie less in an understanding of method than in unspoken anxiety about what the dissertation represents. In making some of these anxieties more explicit, we hope to create spaces where students and faculty can talk about the often symbolic meanings associated with the dissertation.

## OUR INTERPRETIVE PERSPECTIVE

Before turning to the organizational structure of *The Qualitative Dissertation,* we feel it is important to make explicit the perspective from which we view qualitative dissertation research. First, we identify most strongly with an interpretive tradition in qualitative research grounded in the arts and humanities rather than the natural or social sciences. This orientation was both foreshadowed and strengthened by our formal study of literary criticism. Second, our most intensive and productive work has been with women doctoral students who share our proclivity for interpretive ways of knowing. Third, as noted in our opening comments, the students with whom we have worked most closely are educational practitioners, most of whom remained in practitioner roles after completing their degree. This experience has contributed to our understanding of the interplay between theory and practice as well as the role of the dissertation in nurturing a scholarly stance in practitioners. Fourth, our thinking about qualitative dissertations has been informed most deeply by our experiences in working with doctoral students as they struggle to conceptualize their dissertations. The views put forward in this book reflect, not some sweeping treatise on qualitative research writ large, but lessons we have learned as we have inhabited deliberative spaces with students.

## ORGANIZATION OF *THE QUALITATIVE DISSERTATION:* DIFFERENCES BETWEEN THE FIRST AND SECOND EDITIONS

One decision confronting every qualitative researcher is choosing which ideas to place in the foreground and which to place in the background. These *writerly decisions* are made more manageable once one has an organizing principle for whatever text one is crafting. In the first edition of *The Qualitative Dissertation,* we used the concept *cycles of deliberation* as the organizing principle. Throughout the book, we stressed the iterative nature of the deliberative process and suggested that progress on the dissertation occurred as students move recursively through successive cycles of understanding. Although recursive deliberation remains central to our view of good dissertation research, in this second edition we wanted to bring into clearer relief the concept of *self as instrument of inquiry* and the centrality of constructing texts in interpretive inquiry.

From our interpretive perspective, research is a process of meaning-making that is embodied within the *self* of the researcher. What questions one chooses to study, what procedures one chooses to follow, what interpretations one makes of "data," what knowledge claims one offers—every aspect of a study is constructed from the perspective of an individual self situated within a particular psycho-socio-cultural, historical, political, and epistemological context. Given this, learning to become a qualitative researcher is not simply a matter of acquiring and applying a reified set of methods or techniques. It entails cultivating oneself as an *instrument of inquiry.* In structuring the second edition of *The Qualitative Dissertation,* we have placed more emphasis on encouraging doctoral students to relate concepts of qualitative research to their own experiences, beliefs, talents, and sensibilities. This has led to several new features in the individual chapters as well as some reorganization of the book as a whole and revisions of individual chapters.

### Overall Organization of the Book

First, the contents of the book have been organized into four sections. Section One, Facing the Dissertation Journey, comprises four chapters aimed at cultivating a mindset for entering into the learning and dissertation process: In Chapter 1, "Coming to *Study,*" we suggest that adopting a stance of study toward learning about qualitative research will help one prepare to engage in qualitative research. In Chapter 2, "On the Deliberative

Nature of the Dissertation," the connection between a stance of study and deliberation is explored. Chapter 3, "Meanings of the Dissertation," challenges the dysfunctional notion that the dissertation is simply an academic hurdle to be surmounted. Chapter 4, "Facing the Dissertation," focuses on the shift from thinking about the dissertation in some vague way to committing oneself to the task that lies ahead.

The five chapters in Section Two, Preparing for the Dissertation Journey, focus on conceptual issues associated with one's sense of self as an instrument of inquiry. These issues come into play throughout the dissertation process and for this reason they serve as a backdrop to the more specific planning issues that arise in the course of planning, proposing, and conducting a qualitative dissertation. In Chapter 5, "Orienting Oneself to Interpretive Inquiry," we provide a brief orientation to different worldviews that underlie various approaches to qualitative research. Chapter 6, "Situating Oneself in the Inquiry," looks more closely at the concept of self as instrument of inquiry. In Chapter 7, "Rethinking the Concept of Method," we introduce the notion of *research genre* as an alternative to the more narrow conception of *method* as data collection and analysis techniques. Chapter 8, "Rethinking the Concept of Data," presents an argument for the concept of *text* as more congruent than *data* in an interpretive approach to qualitative research. Chapter 9, "Moving From the Experiential to the Theoretic," focuses on the crafting of "experiential text" as a way of contextualizing the phenomenon under study and the knowledge claims that will be put forward about the phenomenon.

The chapters in Section Three, Entering Into and Living Through the Dissertation Journey, call attention to more practical issues of moving through the dissertation process. Chapter 10, "Developing Ideas for the Dissertation Proposal," revisits and elaborates issues related to honing a topic for one's dissertation. Chapter 11, "Crafting an Interpretive Dissertation Proposal," considers the organization of the proposal. In Chapter 12, "Proposing the Dissertation Study," issues related to moving the proposal into a public space are addressed. Chapter 13, "Living With the Study," is characterized as a two-part phase that is punctuated by a pivotal "aha moment" in which the researcher comes to see the central thesis that provides theoretic coherence to the dissertation. The issue of moving the dissertation document into public purview is explored in Chapter 14, "Entering Into Public Discourse: The Dissertation Meeting." Chapter 15, "Life After the Dissertation," offers some concluding reflections on readjusting to postdissertation life. In the Afterword we share some concluding thoughts about the meaning of the dissertation and our hope that *The Qualitative Dissertation* will help students to shape an inquiry that is personally and professionally meaningful.

Section Four contains six case studies that we discuss in relation to new features in this second edition.

## New Features

Each chapter in Sections One through Three includes two features that were not present in the first edition of *The Qualitative Dissertation*. One is a list of key concepts. Our aim in the chapters is not to give definitive definitions or explanations of these concepts. Rather, we strive to orient novices to the complex and often confusing discourses that surround these important concepts. The second feature is a series of reflective interludes. Each interlude poses questions that are meant to encourage readers to relate the key concepts to the context of their lives and their sense of self as a researcher. Hopefully, students will begin writing responses to the questions early in their doctoral program and continue to revise them periodically as their thinking evolves. (Faculty might consider using the questions as a basis for class discussion.)

As in the first edition of *The Qualitative Dissertation*, we illustrate key concepts and issues with examples drawn from the work of students. Short exemplars are interspersed throughout the chapter narratives. There are, however, six much longer examples, which we refer to at various junctures throughout the book. To facilitate ease of reference, these case examples have been consolidated into Section Four: Case Examples of Interpretive Dissertations. The following chart offers a brief orientation to these Case Examples.

| Example | Author | Genre | Phenomenon | Context |
|---------|--------|-------|------------|---------|
| 1 | Micheline Stabile | Practice-based heuristic | Educational inclusion | Planned and spontaneous encounters with professionals, parents, and individuals with disabilities |
| 2 | Lynn Richards | Personal narrative | Creative dramatics | Second-grade, public school classroom for one school year |
| 3 | Patricia McMahon | Personal narrative | Reflection and deliberation in writing | Community college composition course for one academic semester |
| 4 | Kathleen Ceroni | Literary criticism | Teacher empowerment in school reform | Pennsylvania Lead Teacher Initiative |
| 5 | Jean Konzal | Arts-based Readers Theater | Parent involvement in school reform | Public school district in New England town |
| 6 | Joan Leukhardt | Conceptual case study | Adolescent girls' interest in science | Science program for gifted adolescent females |

Readers might find it useful to gain an overall sense of these case examples by reading through them before starting the chapters in Section Two and then referring to them in relation to specific issues.

Another new feature of this revised edition is the inclusion of sample reference lists that may serve as starting points for further reading on particular aspects of qualitative research (e.g., interviewing, data analysis, textual interpretation, various research genre). Rather than embedding these illustrative citations into various sentences, which makes them difficult to spot, we have listed the author's name and date of publication in boxes.

The full citation is provided in the References at the end of the book. Hopefully, this feature will make it easier for readers to locate references of potential relevance to their learning. We want to emphasize that these references serve only as starting points. The number of books and articles about qualitative research has been growing exponentially. It is virtually impossible to keep abreast of all the new publications. So in citing various sources throughout *The Qualitative Dissertation,* we have been guided by two principles. First, we have included those that have informed our thinking in particularly helpful ways. Even though some of these are older—perhaps now classic—references, they remain useful because of the power of the ideas that are presented. Second, we have included references that may be helpful in pointing readers to bodies of discourse related to their particular projects. These references are in no way exhaustive, but rather might serve as starting points for further exploration. We encourage students to establish a system for tracking newly emerging resources that can help them to shape their dissertation.

The index has also been revised so that it connects to the key concepts introduced in each chapter. We have included in the index the names of authors whose work we cite to make it easier to locate such passages. Authors whose work is referenced only in the exhibit boxes have not been included in the index. A listing of exhibit boxes is included after the table of contents to facilitate locating the list of references on particular aspects of qualitative dissertation research (e.g., genre, interviewing, interpreting text, writing).

A final change has been the elimination of a section containing "think pieces." Information from think pieces in the first edition has been woven into the chapter narratives to better integrate the *experiential, discursive,* and *theoretic texts* that compose *The Qualitative Dissertation.*

Maria Piantanida
Noreen B. Garman
*Pittsburgh, Pennsylvania*
*January 2009*

# *Acknowledgments*

We are indebted to members of our dissertation study group, whose commitment to scholarship has engendered our deep belief in the personal meaning and value of the dissertation process. As each member has engaged with the dissertation in her own unique way, we have gained important insights into the challenges and rewards of engaging in interpretive inquiry. The lessons learned as we have tried to support their dissertation work have made this book possible.

We are also indebted to many colleagues who have supported and encouraged our thinking about qualitative dissertation research. They extend our deliberative community beyond the walls of our own university and have connected us to exciting discourses occurring elsewhere in the country and around the world. Among those who have contributed so much to our thinking are Robert Donmoyer, Michael Gunzenhauser, Patricia Holland, Stephen Koziol, Janet Miller, William Pinar, William Schubert, and Peter Willis.

## PUBLISHER'S ACKNOWLEDGMENTS

Corwin gratefully acknowledges the contributions of the following reviewers:

Kimberly L. King-Jupiter, PhD
Associate Dean and Associate Professor
College of Education
Lewis University
Romeoville, IL

Anne L. Pierce, PhD
Associate Professor of Fine Art and
  Director of Humanities
Hampton University
Hampton, VA

Jennifer Reeves, PhD
Director of Institutional Research and
  Athletic Administration
Fischler School of Education and
  Human Services
Nova Southeastern University
Fort Lauderdale, FL

Deborah M. Seymour, PhD
Director
Laureate Education, Inc.
Baltimore, MD

# *About the Authors*

**Maria Piantanida,** PhD, is an adjunct associate professor in the School of Education at the University of Pittsburgh and Carlow University. As a curriculum consultant, she has worked with a variety of programs for health and human services professionals. For her efforts to catalyze research among hospital-based educators, she received the 1989 Distinguished Author Award and the 1987 Distinguished Achievement Award from the American Society for Healthcare Education and Training. In 2007, she received the Distinguished Adjunct Faculty Award from Carlow University.

**Noreen B. Garman,** PhD, is a professor in the Administrative and Policy Studies Department at the University of Pittsburgh School of Education. Previously, she directed the University's Institute for International Studies in Education and the Social and Comparative Analysis in Education Program. A former high-school English teacher and recent Fulbright scholar, Garman has published journal articles and chapters in the fields of clinical supervision, curriculum studies, and qualitative research. From 1994 to 1997, she directed programs for teacher-education planning and development in Bosnia and Herzegovina. She has served on more than 70 dissertation committees during her career, and in 1994, she received an award from the American Educational Research Association, "For Mentoring Women and Activism in Women's Issues." In 2007, she received the Provost's Award for Excellence in Mentoring.

The authors' collaborative relationship spans more than three decades, first as student and teacher, then as doctoral candidate and advisor, and now as colleagues. With backgrounds in literary theory, literary criticism, and curriculum studies, they bring an interpretive perspective to qualitative research in education, exploring modes of inquiry that are particularly well suited to practice-based dissertation research. As cofacilitators of a qualitative dissertation study group, they have worked with about 100 educational practitioners (teachers and administrators from elementary, secondary, and collegiate settings) using a variety of research methods including grounded theory, case study, heuristic inquiry, personal narrative, and arts-based research. Individually and as coinstructors, they have taught graduate courses on qualitative research as well as courses to orient students to inquiry-centered, deliberative study at the masters and doctoral levels. Through this work, Piantanida and Garman have gained a deep appreciation for graduate students' struggles to develop a mind-set compatible with qualitative research. Together, they have given numerous presentations and workshops on qualitative dissertation research at local, national, and international conferences.

# SECTION ONE

*Facing the
Dissertation Journey*

# 1

# *Coming to* Study

---

## Key Concepts

| | |
|---|---|
| Communities of Discourse | Studying Qualitative Research |
| Study | Will to Study |
| Stance of Study | |

---

## TOWARD A *STANCE OF STUDY*

Efforts to explain the dissertation process run the risk of stripping away its messiness and creating the impression of a neat, orderly sequence of discrete steps. Within an idealized model, one first plans the study by identifying or choosing a topic and then selecting a research method that "fits one's question." During the implementation phase, data are first collected, then analyzed and displayed, then interpreted, and reported. Each step of the process appears to have a clear beginning and end.

In working with nearly 100 doctoral candidates on qualitative dissertations, we have never witnessed such a neatly executed process. Nor have we encountered students who, having mastered the skills of qualitative research, came to the dissertation ready to apply them. This causes us to ponder two questions:

- *What* must one learn in order to do a qualitative dissertation?
- *How* must one approach learning qualitative dissertation research?

There are, of course, no definitive or universal answers to these two questions, for both the *what* and the *how* will depend a great deal upon the individual embarking on a qualitative dissertation journey. We do, however, believe that no matter where one starts or what one brings to the journey, it is helpful to think of learning in a way described by John Holt (1976):

> Another common and mistaken idea hidden in the word "learning" is that learning and doing are different kinds of acts. Thus, not many years ago I began to play the cello. I love the instrument, spend many hours a day playing it, work hard at it, and mean someday to play it well. Most people would say that what I am doing is "learning to play" the cello. Our language gives us no other words to say it. But these words carry into our minds the strange idea that there exist two very different processes: (1) learning to play the cello; and (2) playing the cello. They imply that I will do the first until I have completed it, at which point I will stop the first process and begin the second; in short, that I will go on "learning to play" until I have "learned to play" and that then I will begin "to play."
>
> Of course, this is nonsense. There are not two processes, but one. We learn to do something by doing it. There is no other way. (p. 13)

We resonate with Holt's contention that we learn by doing. Yet how might this be possible if one is not yet formally or officially doing one's dissertation? The answer, we believe, lies in how one approaches learning about qualitative research. To explain what we mean, we turn to the concept of *study.*

Curriculum scholar William Pinar (2006), paraphrasing the work of Robert McClintock, observes:

> While one's truths—academic knowledge grounded in lived, that is subjective and social experience—cannot be taught, McClintock (see 1971, 169) underscores they can be acquired through the struggle of study, for which everyone has the capacity, but not necessarily the will. (p. 120)

Several points about this perspective are worth underscoring. First is the contention that one's truths can be acquired but not taught. This calls for critical reflection on one's assumptions about and expectations of teacher, student, and the limitations of learning within traditional academic classes. While faculty in their capacity as classroom teachers may impart valuable information about research and the dissertation, only a learner can grapple with the *meaning* of such information in relation to her or his own understandings.

Second, *study* connotes a shift in stance. "Tell me what I need to know and do?" must give way to, "What am I committed to understanding, and how do I engage with the world to pursue this commitment?" On the face of it, such a shift may seem quite attractive, perhaps even simple. Yet over the years, we have encountered more than a few students for whom embracing a *stance of study* was quite difficult. The difficulty, we speculate, relates to the point that not everyone necessarily has *the will to study.* To illustrate what we mean, let us consider the kinds of questions students often pose when asked their reasons for enrolling in our introductory course on qualitative research:

- How do I do a qualitative interview?
- How can I analyze my data? Should I use a software package to do this?
- Can I do a mixed-method study?
- If I'm doing a qualitative study, can I include numbers?
- How do I triangulate my data?
- How many subjects do I need for a qualitative study?
- How can I use ethnography (or case study or grounded theory) for my dissertation?

### Sample Reference List 1.1

#### Interviewing

Douglas, 1985

Fontana & Frey, 2003

Fontana & Prokos, 2007

Holstein & Gubrium, 1995

Kvale, 1996

McCracken, 1988

Mishler, 1986

Rubin & Rubin, 1995

Seidman, 2006

Tripp, 1983

Questions framed this way imply an expectation for straightforward, practical answers that are readily available from a knowledgeable source: "Yes, you can do that and here's how it is done." Or, "No, you can't do that, but here is what you can do instead." This expectation for definitive answers works against a stance of study.

Even a fairly perfunctory search of literature on qualitative research methods will turn up multiple resources on any of these questions. There are, for example, a number of books devoted exclusively to interviewing (see Sample Reference List 1.1) or data analysis (see Sample Reference List 1.2), as well as numerous references on research methods like ethnography, case study, or grounded theory (see Sample Reference List 7.5). Reading more than a few of such references makes it clear that different authors approach interviewing, data analysis, ethnography, and so on in different ways. Understanding the reasoning behind and significance of these differences requires time and diligent effort. It requires *study*.

Yet educational practitioners who are pursuing a doctorate often work in arenas where efficiency is highly valued and rewarded. Pressure to do more with less continually mounts. Workloads increase exponentially. Solutions to problems need to be found and put into place as quickly as possible. "Putting out fires" is not an occasional emergency, but a way of life. Successful acclimation to such a culture often engenders a stance of performing, doing, solving, and acting. If this *stance of doing* is carried into a doctoral program, then successful learning may be seen as the acquisition of specific information that pays off in greater efficiency in the workplace or in the expeditious completion of academic tasks. An unquestioned valuing of efficiency is not conducive to a stance of study.

For many, letting go of a mindset that places a premium on efficiency may be easier said than done. *Study* entails a prolonged engagement with complex ideas. It requires a tolerance for ambiguity and an appreciation of multiple positions on complicated issues. The goal is not an efficient winnowing away of "extraneous" or "irrelevant" information so that correct action can be taken. Rather, it is a quest for deeper, more nuanced understanding of dilemmas for which there is no correct action, only difficult trade-offs among less than ideal alternatives. This form of study calls not just for an openness to new ideas but also for a recognition of one's own assumptions. At the most fundamental level, these are assumptions about one's self and one's way of relating to others and to the world. The "subject" of study is as much oneself as external bodies of knowledge or information about a particular question. It is, as Pinar (2006) and McClintock (1971) suggest, coming to understand one's own truths, and this understanding often entails profound and humbling insights. A *stance of study*, then, is not for the faint of heart.

This brings us back to the question, "How can one learn by doing if one is not yet doing the dissertation?" It is our contention that embracing a stance of study toward learning qualitative research helps one to cultivate the sensibilities eventually needed to undertake a qualitative dissertation.

## ENTERING INTO THE STUDY OF QUALITATIVE RESEARCH

**Sample Reference List 1.2**

**Qualitative Data Analysis & Interpretation of Text**

Coffey & Atkinson, 1996

Corbin & Morse, 2003

Dalute & Lightfoot, 2004

deMarrais, 1998

Gott & Duggan, 2004

Hodder, 2003

Kezar, 2003

Madriz, 2003

Maranhao, 1990

Miles & Huberman, 1994

Morse, 1994

Peshkin, 2000

Riessman, 1996

Wolcott, 1994

In our experience, it is not unusual for students to approach the idea of qualitative research expecting to learn a specific method. Letting go of this expectation is an important step toward entering into the *study of qualitative research*. It is useful to think of *qualitative research* as a shorthand descriptor that is used in casual conversation and even in the formal literature to connote a wide range of ideas. Some authors, for example, use the term to differentiate linguistic data from numeric data. Other authors use the term to distinguish studies conducted within naturally occurring contexts from those conducted within the controlled environment of a laboratory. Still others are alluding to a set of assumptions about the ways in which legitimate knowledge is generated. Given this, it is not very productive to ask, "What *exactly* does qualitative research *really* mean?" Rather, it is useful to ask, "What are the meanings associated with qualitative research, and how do these various meanings contribute to my own sense of self as an evolving qualitative researcher?" *Studying qualitative research* with this question in mind allows one to learn by doing, because understanding the connotations associated with any concept is integral to the process of a qualitative dissertation.

Probing beneath the casual use of the term *qualitative research* takes one into a complex and often-confusing body of literature. To begin orienting oneself, it is useful to consider several questions when reading an article or book about qualitative research:

- When was the piece written?
- From what disciplinary perspective is the author writing?
- What method (or genre) of qualitative research is the author discussing?
- What philosophical assumptions underpin this author's thinking?

*Historical Context.* Writing in 2003, Denzin and Lincoln (2003b) described qualitative research as being in its seventh historical moment and posit that

> the history of qualitative research is defined more by breaks and ruptures than by a clear, evolutionary, progressive movement from one stage to the next. These breaks and ruptures move in cycles and phases, so that what is passé today may be in vogue a decade from now, and vice versa. (p. 611)

By 2005, when the third edition of the *Handbook* was published, Denzin and Lincoln suggested that the field of qualitative research was already shifting from an eighth to a ninth moment. Thus, placing a book or article within a historical context can help one to understand not only what point the author is making but why he or she felt it was necessary to make given the conversations occurring at that particular moment. For example, educational philosopher Jonas Soltis (1984) wrote an article called "On the Nature of Educational Research," which he opens with the comment, "I have been bothered by the fact that I have been unable to place the many and vastly different languages and logics that people call educational research into a coherent conceptual framework" (p. 5). He then proposed three descriptors—*empirical, interpretive,* and *critical*—as a conceptual frame for distinguishing among fundamentally different philosophical approaches to educational research. Without taking the date of publication into account, one might think Soltis's observation about the lack of a conceptual framework still pertains or that his framework is the only one available. Since 1984, however, many authors have proposed a variety of frameworks for describing different approaches to educational research (e.g., Barone, 1995; Barone & Eisner, 1997; Crotty, 1996, 2003; Creswell, 2007; Eisner, 1993, 1997; Oldfather & West, 1994; Paul, 2005; Sipe & Constable, 1996). Soltis's article still has significance, because it reflects an important moment in the history of educational research, and it helped to frame a previously disjointed conversation. In addition, the way Soltis explains the philosophical underpinnings of empirical, interpretive, and critical inquiry are still informative. But his piece cannot be taken out of its historical context and quoted as though it offers a definitive description of educational research. The same can be said for any resource that students might turn to in their quest to understand qualitative research.

*Disciplinary Context.* In addition to placing an article or book in its historical context, it is useful to recognize the discipline within which an author is writing. At one time, most discussions of qualitative research were embedded in the social sciences where fieldwork required an alternative to laboratory-based methods of inquiry. In the late 1970s and early 1980s, those who wanted to conduct qualitative research in education typically turned to the social sciences to inform their thinking. This was an understandable connection for those who wanted to study educational processes as they occurred "naturally" within school settings and needed an alternative to the more experimentally oriented research of educational psychology. Since then, however, a great deal has been written about qualitative research within the field of education itself. Qualitative research that serves the purposes of social science scholars may or may not usefully serve the purposes of education researchers, especially those who are trying to understand the nuances of educational practice. To read all literature on qualitative research as though it is addressing a uniform and universal set of intellectual questions can be counterproductive.

It is important to note, for example, that as some educational scholars were turning to the social sciences for qualitative research methods, others were turning to the arts and humanities. Over time, the literature on qualitative research in education encompassed both threads of discourse—one grounded in scientific ways of knowing and the other grounded in aesthetic ways of knowing. Understanding this difference in disciplinary background can be crucial in sorting out what form of qualitative research an author is discussing and to what extent an author's thinking may be helpful to one's own form of qualitative research.

The importance of disciplinary perspective also came into play as we worked with students from fields other than education. In one instance, a doctoral student in social work was quite interested in doing a qualitative dissertation but feared that this would not be acceptable within her profession. It was not particularly relevant or useful for us to say, "But qualitative research is quite well accepted in education." Instead, the student undertook a review of research literature in the field of social work. There she found a small, but growing, discourse on qualitative research from which she could argue for the legitimacy of this type of study. The same situation arose for students in the fields of genetic counseling, information sciences, and rehabilitation sciences. Our point is simply this: It is important to become conversant with the literature on qualitative research within one's discipline, profession, or field of study. With this as a base, it is possible to branch out into other discourses to gain additional insights.

Entering into the study of qualitative research without an appreciation of disciplinary differences, one runs the risk of at least two problems. First, drawing indiscriminately from a variety of fields can lead to a hodgepodge of ideas rather than a coherent rationale for one's approach to qualitative research. Second, overlooking literature about qualitative research in one's own discipline or field runs the risk of naiveté.

Before leaving this brief discussion about the disciplinary contexts of qualitative research, one other point is worth raising: In a postmodern era, an excessive fixation on disciplinary boundaries can be seen as quaintly old fashioned or rigidly narrow minded. Creative researchers may draw from multiple disciplinary sources to inform their thinking and their inquiries. We are not arguing for exclusivity at the expense of cross-disciplinary deliberation or creative modes of inquiry. We are arguing for an understanding of the intellectual roots and traditions from which one is drawing. When ideas from multiple traditions are blended intentionally and thoughtfully, much can be gained. When they are patched together out of ignorance, the credibility of qualitative research can be jeopardized.

*Methodological Context.* Qualitative research is an umbrella descriptor encompassing a wide range of methods (or genres). So when approaching an article or book, it is important to consider what method an author is discussing. Some authors might write as though there is a generic form of qualitative research or a common set of procedures that cuts across all forms of qualitative research. We do not find this view particularly useful. Again, we are not advocating for an arbitrarily rigid demarcation among methods. We are, however, suggesting that it is useful to recognize that different methods exist, and each of these methods has a history. Further, these histories reveal different variations within any given method. Ethnography, for example, has one of the longest histories in educational research, and it would be a mistake to think there is only one way to conceptualize and conduct an ethnographic study. The same can be said for a host of other methods including grounded theory, narrative, case study, and action research.

Often, variations in a particular method may stem from an author's disciplinary perspective. For example, robust discourses about grounded theory continue within sociology (its discipline of origin) as well as in education, psychology, nursing, counseling, and other fields that have adapted the method to their own needs and purposes. What any particular author has to say about grounded theory, then, will be shaped at least in part by the disciplinary context within which he or she is writing. The same can be said of other methods falling under the descriptor *qualitative research.* Beyond disciplinary and methodological contexts, however, is another consideration—philosophical context.

*Philosophical Context.* Perhaps one of the most surprising and disconcerting aspects of entering into the study of qualitative research comes when a student, looking for practical guidance on specific techniques, is suddenly plunged into a consideration of philosophical assumptions. These assumptions, while interconnected, can be grouped into three clusters under the headings of *epistemology, ontology,* and *axiology.* Epistemology refers to assumptions about the nature of knowledge, the nature of truth, and the methods that generate legitimate claims of knowledge and truth. Assumptions about knowledge and truth are connected to assumptions of ontology—what we take to be real and our way of being in and relating to the world. Assumptions of axiology address what we value as reality, knowledge, and truth.

As mentioned above, assumptions of science and scientific research dominated much of educational research for most of the 20th century. By the dawn of the 21st century, challenges to the primacy of scientific ways of knowing had created space for educational research that draws from traditions grounded in the disciplines of philosophy, history, rhetoric (e.g., Angus & Langsdorf, 1993; Covino, 1994; Edwards, Nicoll, Solomon, & Usher, 2004; Roberts & Good, 1993), literary theory (e.g., Petrey, 1990), literary criticism (e.g., Abrams, 1989; Fahnestock & Secor, 1991; Juhl, 1980), linguistics, humanities (Bullough, 2006), and the arts (Barone, 1995, 2000, 2001; Eisner, 1991, 1993, 1997). Today, these various traditions are robustly represented and still debated in the discourses of educational research (as well as in federal policy). Becoming attuned to these fundamentally different worldviews is an important aspect of studying qualitative research in two ways. It helps in sorting through ideas being presented in the literature. And, more importantly, it helps in sorting through the type of research one wants to conduct.

## COMMUNITIES OF DISCOURSE

The important point to take from the preceding comments is that different scholars in different fields with different philosophies hold different views of qualitative research. Many scholars associated with the disciplines serving educational research (e.g., sociology, anthropology, political science, psychology) began to think of social science as "dialects of language which provide heuristic fictions for supposing the world is this way or that way" (Popkewitz, 1984, p. vii). We return to this idea later, but for now it is important to understand that conceptions of qualitative research are formed, debated, and advanced within communities of discourse. It is through a community of like-minded scholars within a common field that knowledge is generated through the various notions of discourse (Sills & Jensen, 1992). It is also the case that discourse communities have various means of critiquing the knowledge claims of their members through review processes. Those who formally represent the review process (e.g., dissertation committee members, journal editors, reviewers of conference paper proposals) serve as gatekeepers and often decide what is acceptable as legitimate qualitative research.

In the following chapters we raise many issues that doctoral students with an interest in qualitative research must consider in order to locate and engage with *communities of discourse* that will further their capacity for scholarship.

## A WILL TO STUDY

As we conclude this first chapter, let us return to Pinar's (2006) point that not everyone has a *will to study.* In some ways, it is easy to attribute a lack of will to more pressing demands on one's time, energy, and attention. For overextended educational practitioners, this is no small consideration. Yet we have been privileged to work with a number of practitioners who, despite the pressure of professional and personal commitments, have been drawn to study qualitative research.

We cannot say with any certainty what makes the difference between those who choose a stance of study and those who do not. We speculate, however, that a desire for engagement with ideas—their own and others—is deeply compelling to some doctoral students. Micheline Stabile and Marilyn Llewellyn,[1] two members of our study group, exemplify very different approaches to learning qualitative research (Exemplar 1.1). What they had in common was a deep commitment to their own learning, a capacity for engagement with complex ideas, and a will to study.

---

**EXEMPLAR 1.1    Exhibiting a Stance of Study**

Shortly after joining our dissertation study group, Micheline and Marilyn recounted stories about learning to ski. Micheline registered for an introductory course that began with a series of lectures in an auditorium, continued with skill training in the gym, and finally moved to preliminary practice on the beginners' slopes. Marilyn, after a brief introductory lesson on the beginners' slope, hopped on a ski lift, rode to the top of a mountain, and suddenly found herself careening down an advanced slope with the dawning realization that perhaps she had not fully mastered all the nuances of skiing—most notably, techniques for stopping.

Their respective approaches to learning the craft of qualitative research paralleled their approaches to skiing. Micheline proceeded cautiously, wanting to understand as fully and explicitly as possible what she was going to be doing and why. Marilyn plunged in and began reviewing discourses related first to a study on peace education, then to a study on education and social justice, and finally to a study on spirituality and pedagogy.

*(Continued)*

Although Micheline and Marilyn represent two very different learning styles, they illustrate a range of approaches that students might take in tackling the learning associated with doing a qualitative dissertation. Because it is impossible to acquire all of the information one needs at the outset of the dissertation journey, the questions posed in the Reflective Interludes provide frameworks for pursuing multiple avenues of learning. If started early and updated periodically, responses to the Reflective Interlude questions allow students to gather—incrementally—the information and resources needed to undertake the journey.

We emphasize *incrementally* because, in our experience, students who flounder in the dissertation process may have assumed that they can master qualitative research by taking one methods course, reading a how-to dissertation guide, or pressing a perceived expert for specific answers to procedural questions. Often, we receive calls from students like Ginny who have heard of our interest in qualitative research. With great urgency, Ginny pleaded for a meeting to discuss her study. Although she still had quite a few pre-dissertation requirements to complete, she frantically latched onto each shred of information as though it were an intellectual life preserver. The simplistic and erroneous conclusions she drew from what we viewed as conversation openers took our breath away. At some point in the conversation, we were overwhelmed by the image of a swimmer caught in an undertow, desperately flailing against powerful currents she could not remotely begin to control. The learning necessary to enter into and complete a qualitative dissertation requires a modicum of calmness in which deliberation can occur. Adopting a stance of study from the outset of doctoral work can serve one well.

From our perspective, the dissertation affords a not-to-be-missed opportunity to deliberate about matters of educational importance and, through deliberation, to come to new understandings of oneself. In the next chapter, we take a closer look at the deliberative and recursive nature of dissertation research.

**Reflective Interlude 1.1**

## What Am I Bringing to the Study of Qualitative Research?

- What prompts my interest in qualitative research?
- What has informed my understanding of the historical moment in which I am studying and engaging in qualitative research?
- What do I envision learning about qualitative research? What is the basis for this vision?
- What background in research am I bringing to the study of qualitative research?
- What research methods courses have I taken?
- To what research-oriented journals do I subscribe?

- To what research-oriented professional associations do I belong?
- What research-oriented conferences do I attend?
- What books on qualitative research have I read?
- How many qualitative dissertations have I read, and what methods did the authors use? With which of these methods did I feel a sense of affinity?
- Given my responses to the preceding questions, how would I characterize my willingness and desire to enter into the study of qualitative research?

## NOTE

1. Throughout *The Qualitative Dissertation,* we draw upon our experiences with students to illustrate the concepts and issues we are discussing. When we introduce individuals using a full name, we are doing so with their permission. Information about these individuals appears throughout the book and offers what we consider to be positive examples of learning associated qualitative research. When individuals are referenced only by a first name, these are pseudonyms.

# 2

# *On the Deliberative Nature of the Dissertation*

During an introduction to a qualitative research class, we were discussing the importance of *deliberation* when one class member remarked, "I think deliberation is important, but as an administrator, I don't have the luxury for a lot of deliberation. I have to make decisions on the firing line, and there's just no time for a lot of talking about problems." Other class members nodded, seemingly in agreement.

This view of deliberation as endless discussion and rumination can keep one from entering productively into the study of qualitative research. This is problematic because doctoral study in general and the dissertation process in particular entail a *deliberative mode of knowing*. Over the years, we have encountered students who exhibit tremendous variation in their capacity for *deliberation*. Using composite characterizations, we portray some of the ways in which students manifest an inclination or disinclination for deliberation. Following these illustrative examples, we contrast a mind-set of *encapsulation* to that of *deliberation*. We end the chapter by exploring the recursive and discursive aspects of deliberation.

# VARIATIONS IN DELIBERATIVE INCLINATION

In Chapter 1, we offered a caution to those seeking quick and ready answers to the question, "What is qualitative research?" Tremendous amounts of time, energy, and money can be consumed in a fruitless quest for a straightforward explanation of a complex field of study. Several years ago, for example, Hazel came to the first meeting of an introductory course on qualitative inquiry and proudly informed other students that she had purchased the textbook on how to do qualitative research. Because we relied on a variety of articles rather than a single, required textbook for the course, we were puzzled by this assertion until she pulled from her briefcase a newly purchased copy of Denzin and Lincoln's (1994) *Handbook of Qualitative Research* (which has gone through two additional editions, the second being divided into three separately titled volumes; see Denzin & Lincoln, 2003a, 2003b, 2003c, 2005). No matter how many times we explained that the *Handbook* introduced a number of different approaches to qualitative research, Hazel clung to the belief that it contained *the* formula for doing a qualitative study.

Although Hazel's misconception was somewhat extreme, it typifies a nondeliberative mind-set that is problematic if one wants to enter seriously into the study of qualitative research. Quite a different mind-set was exhibited by Marjorie Logsdon and Micheline Stabile. Marjorie entered her doctoral program while she was teaching English at an all-girls Catholic high school. Throughout her doctoral coursework, she pursued her interest in feminist issues until a focus for her dissertation—issues of authority and feminist pedagogy—began to emerge. Marjorie further refined her thinking about these issues through her comprehensive examination and ultimately her dissertation (Logsdon, 2000, 2006).

During the first year of her professional life, Micheline, a public school administrator, had developed a deep and abiding concern for children who are labeled failures by school systems even as their special educational needs are not being met by those systems. Therefore, she was both surprised and troubled when, 20 years later, she felt herself resisting the mandate for special education inclusion sweeping through her district. When we began to work with Micheline, she was trying to make sense of what felt like a major anomaly in her professional beliefs and commitments. Gradually, she shaped a study that allowed her to deliberate more carefully and systematically about the problematics inherent in educational inclusion (Stabile, 1999, 2006).

The contrast between Hazel's mind-set and those of Marjorie and Micheline is quite striking. On one hand is a steadfast inability to let go of preconceptions, a need for certainty, and a desire for simple answers. On the other is a willingness to grapple deeply with one's truths in light of practice-based, policy-based, and research-based *discourses*. Between these two very different mind-sets lies tremendous variation in students' inclination for deliberation. We offer the following characterizations not to demean students, but as a cautionary note for those who may be struggling to understand what it might or might not mean to deliberate.

*Daphne—The Academic Gadfly.* Daphne enjoyed talking about herself and her own ideas. She was deft at turning conversations into monologues, often focusing on obscure ideas, arcane information, or her own exotic international experiences. Regardless of the topic under consideration, Daphne quickly jumped in with an anecdote that simultaneously conveyed a sense of "been there, done that" and launched into a harangue about her favorite subject—the subjugation of women by patriarchal power structures. Although she talked with great enthusiasm about doing her dissertation, she never settled on a topic, dug into the literature, or drafted a single page of a research proposal. For whatever reason, Daphne had a greater need to put forward her own ideas than to step back and critically examine them.

*Alan—The Academic Hurdler.* Alan approached his doctoral work as a series of academic hurdles. For him, the shortest distance between two points was a straight line to be traversed as quickly as possible. Having completed his coursework, Alan bragged to other students about "managing" his dissertation committee to preclude what he perceived to be unnecessary and arbitrary impositions on his time. Interestingly, Alan took about as long to complete his study as other students who started their research at the same time, yet he seemed reluctant, almost embarrassed, to share his dissertation with professional colleagues once it was finished.

*Ray—The Teflon Syndrome.* Although less blatantly manipulative than Alan, Ray also subscribed to the academic-hurdle view of the dissertation and longed to finish as quickly as possible. Unable or unwilling to engage deeply with ideas, he skimmed the surface of any subject under consideration, including the topic of his dissertation.

*Angie & Eric—Collecting the Doctoral Ticket.* As members of an introductory class in qualitative research, Angie and Eric seemed to have breezed through earlier coursework without giving much thought to the implications of concepts or issues being studied. They conveyed an aura of "psyching out" instructors' expectations and delivering products that might meet the letter, but not the spirit, of assignments. When discussing their program of studies, they seemed to view it as a collection of courses and accumulated credits rather than a well-reasoned agenda for their own learning. When Angie and Eric described their reasons for pursuing a doctorate, they focused on extrinsic rewards, relishing the prestige associated with the title or anticipating the opportunities for salary and job advancement. Angie and Eric exhibited little patience with "all this talk," viewing discussions with fellow students and instructors as a waste of time.

*Priscilla—Laboring in Isolation.* While Angie and Eric remained disengaged from deliberation, Priscilla made great sacrifices in order to labor over her dissertation. In the process, however, she increasingly isolated herself from committee members and colleagues. Her isolation, in turn, seemed to fuel a growing sense of bitterness over a perceived lack of support for or appreciation of her scholarly endeavors.

*Bethany—Now What Do They Want?* Bethany typified a number of students who seem unable to find a generative balance between their ideas and the ideas of others. Bethany would take notes during meetings with her committee, but when she sent a revised draft, none of the faculty comments would have been addressed. In fact, the new version would represent a radical departure from anything she had already written. In some instances, the changes were tantamount to a new study. Although faculty comments had been intended to help Bethany refine and develop the ideas she had put forward, we speculate that she interpreted them as, "I haven't done what they want me to. I have to change my study."

Over the years, we have pondered what might account for such variation in student inclination for deliberation. We offer the concept of *encapsulation* as a way of framing the struggle that educational practitioners may experience as they return to the world of academia.

## ENCAPSULATION
## VERSUS DELIBERATION

It is not uncommon for professionals who decide to return to formal studies to experience a state of mind we refer to as *encapsulation*. As professionals for a number of years, they are used to being in the mode of "performing" their professional duties. As students, they are expected to "inquire," to, in essence, change their learning proclivities. Labaree (2003) characterizes the ensuing struggle as a twofold cultural conflict:

> One [conflict] derives from potential differences in worldview arising from the nature of teaching as a practice and the nature of educational research as a practice. The other derives from possible struggles over the kind of education one needs in order to become an effective educational researcher. (p. 16)

Assumptions about the kind of education one needs are embedded within a powerful form of knowledge we characterize as *scholastic folklore* (Garman, 1985). Practitioners who return to the academy in pursuit of a doctorate may harbor tacit expectations of the way formal teaching and learning are supposed to be. At the same time, they may harbor feelings of resistance, often expressed as, "This is not the *real* world." A tension can arise from two conflicting role images—one, the professional, and the other, the student.

The professional self looks for direct role-learning cues, those ideas and methods thought of as practical and useable in one's own work world. Meanwhile, the student self looks for traditional teacher cues to find out what one is *supposed to get out of class involvements*. In this frame of mind, the primary sources of information that students can accept are their own professional experiences (taking place elsewhere) and a teacher's expectations as described in course documents (e.g., syllabi, objectives, assigned readings, evaluation procedures). Students can become trapped between these two roles. As long as they are mentally encapsulated by their own scholastic folklore, their level of learning is impoverished. The powerful force that causes one to search for cues to what one is supposed to understand is the same force that blocks personal inquiry and the self as instrument of learning. It impedes the search for insight and meaning that can lead to knowledge regarding one's own world. *Encapsulation*, then, can be construed as the self lost in the tension between the professional role and the student role that manifests in a form of estrangement and keeps one from a deliberative frame of mind.

As professionals enter more deeply into graduate study and become more socialized into the role of learner, they may become less frustrated by the lack of immediate relevance to their world of work. More important, many students begin to find relationships between their academic and professional worlds. However, the conditions of encapsulation remain. The structure of coursework encourages students to focus most of their energies on interpreting and meeting the expectations set by instructors. As one professor lamented, "These students continually want to be told what to do for the class, even after I've explained the expectations. It's a shame they can't be more independent learners."

Formal graduate programs and courses in the United States generally are not organized so that students can be independent learners. However, when doctoral students move into the dissertation experience, they become independent learners whether they are ready or not. Deliberation becomes imperative as students are expected to move from a coursework mode of learning to a deliberative mode.

## ON THE NATURE OF DELIBERATIVE LEARNING

*Deliberation* is commonly used to describe how groups proceed when making a decision. A jury, for example, deliberates in order to weigh evidence and render a verdict. Congressional committees deliberate on the need for and potential consequences of potential legislation. Doctoral students, in concert with their dissertation committee, deliberate on potential topics for and avenues of inquiry. Deliberation, then, occurs in socially constructed ways as ideas are developed through reading, talking, and writing. Inherent in this process is an exchange of views—some of which may be in concert with one another, and some of which may be in conflict. Typically, ideas become more robust and more refined as contrasting positions are advanced and explored. Thus, one's thinking is advanced through the vigorous (and rigorous) expression of stances and counterstances.

This engagement with others in the exploration of ideas is no mere academic exercise. It is the very heart of inquiry—whether qualitative or quantitative. Like our illustrative students above, those who remain in an encapsulated state of mind resist (either explicitly or implicitly) entering into a *deliberative mode of learning*. Whether deliberation is associated with face-to-face discussions or a more solitary engagement with literature, this mode of learning involves seeking information from diverse sources, carefully weighing the ideas, and thoughtfully acting on the results. For the doctoral student, we are suggesting that a *deliberative mode of learning* can be portrayed as a *recursive process* in which learners *question, listen, think,* and *act.*

## ON THE RECURSIVE NATURE OF DELIBERATION

One of the unfortunate side effects of discrete academic courses is the imposition of arbitrary timeframes on learning and thinking. At the end of each semester, a course concludes; required products are turned in and evaluated; a grade is received, and the student moves on to the next set of discrete experiences. In some ways, the time limitations of this academic routine can be quite comforting. Whether one's work receives a high or low grade, the experience is over and the course products can be filed or discarded as one chooses. In a sense, each semester begins as a blank slate upon which new course expectations are inscribed. Disrupting the rhythms of academic performance can be quite disconcerting, and this is what happens when students are asked to shift into a deliberative mode of learning.

Nowhere did this discomfort become clearer to us than with a group of graduate students enrolled in a five-semester, inquiry-centered, team-taught master of arts in educational praxis program. At first tentatively, then plaintively, and finally angrily, these students asked, "When are we going to be finished with this paper?" *This paper* represented the earliest expression of ideas that would eventually be shaped into a thesis. From a faculty perspective, *this paper* would undergo successive iterations during the next four-and-a-half semesters as it evolved into a final document. From the students' perspective, the lack of closure and lack of a grade were both disorienting and frustrating. They interpreted comments and questions about their ideas as fault-finding criticisms, not as efforts to engage with them in deliberation.

It might be easy to dismiss the students' response as a master's-level reaction to an unfamiliar and unexpected form of learning. Unfortunately, we encounter a similar response among students enrolled in a two-semester course intended to introduce them to doctoral study. At both levels of graduate study, the recursive nature of deliberation can be disconcerting or, worse, debilitating.

In framing productive questions, one is actively seeking information or commentary about his or her preconceived ideas. In a deliberative mode, listening requires one to set aside judgmental filters in order to hear more deeply what is being presented. Thoughtful reasoning helps the learner sort the significant from the trivial. Most important, however, is the action—what one does with the information presented. *Action* here implies a way of thinking in order to advance an inquiry. This may mean further conceptualization, consideration of new ideas, and revision of current thinking. In the deliberative mode, ideas are treated as momentary conclusions that are always subject to revision and extension. To act, then, is to revise, to produce a next draft of one's thinking and writing. The recursive nature of deliberation calls for a continual revisiting of ideas through questioning, information gathering, listening, thinking, and acting, albeit not necessarily in that order.

## ON THE DISCURSIVE
## NATURE OF DELIBERATION

In Schools of Education, as well as other places in the academy, discussion is viewed as one of the most valued of all class events. There is a popular assumption that when students exchange ideas, either among themselves or with the instructor, important learning is taking place. Doctoral students who are familiar with and adept at such class discussion might assume they are well prepared for the discursive aspects of deliberation. This may not necessarily be the case.

While class discussion might be an example of deliberation, it might also be an example of conversation—individuals talking with and at each other. Within the context of academic coursework, discussions are often organized and directed by the instructor. This tends to focus attention on the assignment for the class rather than on inquiry into a question. Indeed, there is a kind of knowledge generating that comes from such course-based conversation. As people put forward ideas, others may choose to agree or disagree. In many cases, group discussion can help members become more aware of each other and begin to develop a respect for the diversity of a group. This is an important result, but it should not automatically be equated with deliberation. In the exchange of ideas, group members are often focused on being respectful or promoting their own experiences. Wrestling openly with ideas at the edge of one's knowledge tends not to occur within the time constraints and syllabus-driven discussions of academic courses. This changes as students move into the dissertation process and their own thinking becomes the focus of deliberation.

Inevitably, thinking through complex issues to shape a viable study entails working and reworking ideas. Preliminary ideas grounded in personal experience undergo revision and refinement as one reviews formal bodies of literature. Idiosyncratic interpretations of experience may be challenged by others whose perspective of the same or similar events is quite different from one's own. Critiques of documents typically call for another round of reading and writing. If this recursive process is construed as false starts, blind alleys, or failures, frustration can escalate. Recognizing from the outset that discourse and deliberation are nonlinear processes that are advanced through the contestation of ideas can do much to alleviate excessive anxiety.

## VULNERABILITY OF DISCURSIVE DELIBERATION

In closing this discussion, we raise a final point for consideration: Repeatedly, we are reminded of the fragility of *discursive deliberation* between student and advisor. On one hand, these deliberations must be intellectually tough, challenging ill-formed ideas or poorly conceived studies. On the other hand, excessive or heavy-handed feedback can undermine students' confidence, causing them to abandon potentially good studies, or worse, the entire dissertation venture. Maintaining productive deliberation requires some risk taking and a great deal of trust on the part of both student and advisor. We are still haunted by the possibility that we missed some important cue from students in the following situations:

> One student came to us, intrigued by the overrepresentation of adopted children in special education. Her review of literature indicated that unlike many other professions (e.g., law, medicine, social work, psychology, public welfare), special education had neither a robust nor long-standing discourse on adoption. She had begun to build a case for generating such a discourse but vacillated between looking at infant or older-child adoptees. At one point, when she was leaning toward infant adoptees, she formulated an intent for her study that rested upon flawed assumptions. Calling this to her attention seemed to precipitate a conceptual paralysis that persisted until personal commitments caused her to relocate to another area of the country. As far as we know, she never completed a dissertation.

Kristen, a high school vice principal, was torn between her own desire to counsel students so they could become more engaged learners, and organizational expectations that she would function as the school's disciplinarian. Our suggestion that she might craft a study around this very dilemma seemed to engender a similar paralysis. After sitting silently through a number of study group meetings, she eventually dropped out of the group and avoided individual contact with her advisor.

Both of these students were extremely bright, capable practitioners. Both had potentially meaningful and doable studies. We still wonder if something we said or did not say—some missed cue—short-circuited the process of discursive deliberation. Such experiences remind us of the vulnerability associated with thinking aloud with others.

Inherent in the recursive nature of deliberation is an expectation to share ideas that are in formation. Whether this takes the form of informal discussion, formal presentations, or written papers, this expectation can be quite daunting for practitioners and students who assume that competence lies in demonstrating what one already knows. Sharing one's uncertainties, groping for words to express vaguely understood ideas, wallowing publicly in confusion—these aspects of deliberation can engender feelings of vulnerability, incompetence, and embarrassment. Years of conditioning may lead one to hide these "unacceptable" feelings by waiting to share ideas only after they are well honed and fully developed. Adopting this self-protective approach is, perhaps, the most dysfunctional response one can make to the intellectual uncertainties of the inquiry process. Sternberg and Horvath (1995), in exploring the concept of expert teaching, posit that "Whereas novices and experienced nonexperts seek to reduce problems to fit available methods, true experts seek progressively to complicate the picture, continually working on the leading edge of their own knowledge and skill" (p. 13).

Working on the edge of one's knowledge and skill implies entering new conceptual territory, pushing beyond the comfort zone of one's assumptions, challenging one's understanding of self, others, and the nature of one's field of study. Making one's thinking public and subjecting it to the scrutiny of others, while potentially unnerving, are integral to the discursive nature of deliberation.

In an effort to diffuse the anxiety of sharing ideas in formation, we suggest that students write think pieces. A *think piece* is a semiformal document that is more structured and public than an entry in a personal or professional journal, yet less polished than a formal paper or publishable article. Generally, think pieces focus on a particular idea, concept, issue, problem, or question that the author is beginning to explore. Whether one starts by describing some problematic aspect of practice or some nebulous idea catalyzed by reading literature, framing a piece of writing as a *think piece* conveys three messages: (1) This is where I currently am in my thinking about a subject; (2) I recognize that my thinking is somewhat constrained and/or limited; and (3) I want to engage in conversation that will help me identify avenues for broadening and/or deepening my thinking about the subject. Think pieces can be written at any time in a learning or inquiry process as a way of engaging others in deliberation when one has reached an impasse in one's understanding of an issue or question. Serving as a focal point for deliberation, successive drafts of think pieces provide a space for bringing together reflections on experience and insights from the literature. The point of the writing and deliberation is for the author to get hold of the meanings he or she is trying to formulate and to test the merits of those meanings through the give and take of ideas with faculty, fellow students, and professional colleagues.

### Reflective Interlude 2.1

## What Is My Capacity for Deliberation?

- What is my reaction to the concept of *encapsulation?* In what ways do I mediate my own intellectual interests with those of faculty within academic courses, members of my dissertation committee, and/or colleagues in professional settings?
- How would I characterize my inclination for deliberation? How would faculty, my advisor, and colleagues characterize my engagement in deliberation? What learning might arise as I reflect upon these characterizations? What implications for learning arise?
- What is my reaction to Sternberg and Horvath's (1995) idea that expert practitioners are working at the leading edge of their knowledge?
- How might the dissertation process help me work at the leading edge of my knowledge?
- How comfortable am I in thinking aloud with others? What experiences have contributed to my comfort or discomfort? How might I continue to practice such discursive deliberation?
- What is my process for moving from *discussing* my ideas to *writing* about them?
- What type of response do I expect from others when I share my writing?
- What is my process for using responses to my writing to advance my thinking?
- Given my responses to the preceding questions, how would I characterize my inclination and capacity for deliberation? What might I do to enhance this capacity?

# 3

# *Meanings of the Dissertation*

---

## Key Concepts

Dissertation Folklore

Doctoral Candidate

Dysfunctional Stereotypes

Pacing of the Dissertation

Stewardship of the Disciplines

Stewardship of the Professions

Support for the Dissertation

---

Typically, doing a dissertation is a once in a lifetime experience—and an experience that is relatively rare in the population at large. So doctoral students may understandably approach the dissertation with vaguely formed notions of what this work entails. Further, the familiar structure of academic courses that are planned and conducted by faculty suddenly disappears as one moves from doctoral student to doctoral candidate. Lack of familiarity coupled with a sense of mystery around this "unstructured" process can activate whatever latent anxiety students may bring to the dissertation. We have seen this anxiety manifest as- debilitating bewilderment or frenzied activity as students search desperately for ways to make sense of this amorphous thing called THE DISSERTATION.

A not uncommon response to this anxiety is to seek advice from other students or recent graduates of doctoral programs. Although talking with peers can offer both reassurance and useful advice, it can also connect students with a body of *dissertation folklore* rife with misinformation and *dysfunctional stereotypes*. Circulating like urban legends of the academic world are stories of unreasonable advisors who force students to jump through an endless series of arbitrary hoops; committee politics in which students are sacrificed in the ego wars of rival faculty; the plight of hapless students who fail to find the right advisor to get them through the process with minimal hassle; the real-world irrelevance of this empty academic ritual; the inescapable misery inherent in doing research; and on and on. Is the dissertation process, as these horror stories suggest, inevitably and only about power, empty ritual, paying dues, and getting by? Or are there other stories to be told? We believe there are. Hopefully, the perspectives shared in this chapter (and throughout *The Qualitative Dissertation*) will encourage students to recognize dysfunctional stereotypes, which we define as any view that denigrates the value of the dissertation and/or diminishes a student's capacity for deliberation. We hope that students will find ways to engage with their dissertation that are personally and professionally meaningful.

While the meaning of the dissertation will undoubtedly vary from student to student and even from institution to institution, it is important to note that there is a renewed academic interest in the purpose of doctoral education and the role of the dissertation within the doctorate. We begin, therefore, with a brief account of discourses aimed at re-visioning doctoral education. Following this, we liken commitment to the dissertation to commitment to running a marathon and consider issues of pacing and support necessary to stay the course.

## RENEWED INTEREST IN THE DOCTORATE AND DISSERTATION

At the beginning of the 21st century, a strand of discourse emerged focusing renewed attention on the purpose of doctoral education and the role of dissertation research within the doctorate. In 2001, the American Educational Research Association (AERA) devoted an issue of the *Educational Researcher* to the theme "research for doctoral students in education," in which three scholars (Metz, 2001; Page, 2001; Pallas, 2001) offered their thoughts on the following questions:

> Can prospective scholars be prepared to appreciate and learn from the presence of epistemological controversy and diverse perspectives? How might graduate programs in education develop researchers who have the capacity to appreciate and perhaps use multiple perspectives and methodologies?
>
> Given the finite amount of time in graduate school, and students' needs to (a) become expert enough in a given domain/method to say something new and different, and (b) be able to make a thoughtful match between research problem and perspective/methodology, how should we organize research preparation in doctoral study, and to what end? Is it even realistic to consider preparing researchers to use multiple methodologies and to work from different perspectives? (Young, 2001, p. 3)

The purpose and meaning of doctoral education received further scrutiny when, "In 2001, The Carnegie Foundation undertook a five-year project—The Carnegie Initiative on the Doctorate (CID)" (Golde, 2006, p. 6). Education was one of six disciplines invited to participate in the project whose participants reached the following conclusion:

> We propose that the purpose of doctoral education, taken broadly, is to educate and prepare those to whom we can entrust the vigor, quality, and integrity of the field. This person is a scholar first and foremost, in the fullest sense of the term—someone who will creatively generate new knowledge, critically conserve valuable and useful ideas, and responsibly transform those understandings through writing, teaching, and application. We call such a person a "steward of the discipline." (Golde, 2006, p. 5)

This emphasis on scholarship and stewardship may come as a surprise to educators (particularly those in public education) who are pursuing doctorates but have no intention of leaving their current practice to pursue careers in the academy. (It may also be shocking to those who have bought into the dysfunctional stereotype of the dissertation as nothing more than an academic hoop.) Indeed, the nature of research preparation that is necessary and appropriate for doctoral-level practitioners has been a subject of debate (Anderson, 2002; Eisenhart & DeHaan, 2005; Evans, 2007; Golde, 2000, 2006, 2007; Golde & Walker, 2006; Labaree, 2003; Metz & Page, 2002; Richardson, 2006; Shulman, 2007; Shulman, Golde, Conklin, Bueschel, & Garabedian, 2006; Young, 2001). At the heart of the debate lie issues concerning the nature and legitimacy of practitioner research. Although we are in no position to resolve such a long-standing and complex debate, this book is based on the premise that practitioners should not *de facto* be seen only as informed consumers of research. If *scholarship* and *stewardship* represent ways of being in the world, then practitioners as well as academicians have the potential for embodying both. This book is intended for those who want to develop their capacity for scholarship and stewardship through thoughtful engagement in their dissertation research. Having the dissertation serve this transformative purpose requires much learning that can be quite challenging. (See Sample Reference List 3.1 for illustrative readings on teacher/practitioner research.)

**Sample Reference List 3.1**

**Teacher/Practitioner Research**

Almy & Genishi, 1979

Anderson, 2007

Anderson & Herr, 1999

Boehm & Weinerg, 1997

Burnaford, Fischer, & Hobson, 2001

Christensen & James, 2008

Clark et al., 1996

Clarke & Erickson, 2003

Cochran-Smith & Lytle, 1999

Cohen, Stern, & Balaban, 1997

Dana, 2003

Evans, 2007

Genishi, 1992

Hatch et al., 2005

Hitchcock & Hughes, 1989

Kincheloe, 1991

Ladson-Billings, 2005

Mohr et al., 2003

Richardson, 1994

Ritchie & Wilson, 2000

Robinson & Lai, 2006

Thompson, 2007

Zeichner, 1999

**Reflective Interlude 3.1**

### What Does the Dissertation Mean to Me?

- What meanings do I associate with the dissertation?
- What sources of information have I relied on to inform my understanding of the dissertation?
- How systematically have I gathered information to inform my understanding of the dissertation?
- What information about the dissertation requirements in my institution have I read?
  - What do these documents say about the purpose of the dissertation in my institution?
  - What do these documents say about the acceptability of qualitative research methods?
  - Does my school offer an outstanding dissertation award? If so, what criteria are used to judge the dissertations? What dissertations have won the award? How many of these dissertations have I read?
- Have I spoken with faculty in my school or department about their views of the dissertation?
  - What was their dissertation experience like?
  - What research approaches did they use for their dissertations, and why did they choose those particular approaches?
  - What do they think makes a good dissertation?
  - When serving as dissertation advisors, how do they see their roles and what expectations do they have of their advisees?
  - When serving as members of a dissertation committee, how do they see their roles and what expectations do they have of the candidate?
- What folklore circulates in my school or department about the dissertation? How much credence do I want to place in this folklore?
  - What are the sources of this folklore?
  - How is the folklore perpetuated?
  - What have I done to evaluate the merits of the folklore as reliable information upon which to base decisions about my dissertation?
- What does being a steward of a discipline or profession mean to me?
- In what ways am I or might I be a steward of my discipline or profession?

## STAYING THE COURSE OF THE DISSERTATION

For many years, Pittsburgh hosted a 26-mile marathon. Although we had seen snippets of the race on television, actually joining the throngs of cheering spectators on one exceptionally hot and humid May morning had a powerful emotional impact. The out-pouring of support for those who chose to run this grueling race was a palpable force along the crowded streets. Support came in various forms. Outreached hands offered fruit, energy bars, and cups of water and juice. Garden hoses provided cooling showers. But most compelling of all were the shouts of encouragement. Some clearly came from family and friends who called by name to specific runners. Most, however, came from strangers as encouragement was directed to the runners' numbers, often to someone whose energy seemed to be flagging. And the air was filled with general shouts of "You can do it," "Go for it," "You're more than half-way there," "You're looking good," and "Keep it up." The runners themselves did not break stride, make eye contact, or give any indication that the messages of encouragement penetrated their fierce concentration. Yet surely they must have been sustained in some measure by the tunnel of supportive energy through which they ran.

Even as we were caught up in the excitement of the moment, we contemplated the parallels to the dissertation. Clearly, some individuals are drawn to the challenge of the marathon, whereas others are not. Yet even those who would never dream of running a marathon themselves may care about the success of those who do choose to run. There is something compelling about watching the struggles and, hopefully, triumphs of those who are willing to undertake an extraordinary challenge. And although no one can run the race for someone else, a great deal can be done to encourage and support that effort. We use this marathon analogy to raise two important issues of dissertation research—pacing oneself through the process and mobilizing support.

## Pacing

Understandably, students want some sense of how long it takes to complete a dissertation. Unfortunately, this is impossible to predict since it varies in large part depending on the amount of time and intensity of conceptual effort a student is willing and able to devote to the dissertation. Thus, the length of time it takes to complete a dissertation will vary depending on the individual's commitment of time, competing responsibilities, expenditure of effort, concentrated deliberation, and readiness for "the race." Despite individual variations, several markers can be used to gauge progress—for example, completing a qualifying examination, receiving approval of one's research proposal, and defending one's final document. (Several resources provide advice on issues related to moving through doctoral study and the dissertation. See, for example, Brazziel, 1992; Burgess, Sieminski, & Arthur, 2006; Finn, 2005; Geiger, 1997; Golde, 2000; Ogden, 2006; Roberts, 2004.)

It is our contention that moving from one marker to the next depends less on what one is *doing* than on what one is coming to *understand*. Forward movement occurs as the conceptual structure and content of the inquiry become increasingly clear and coherent. Markers for this form of progress are far more nebulous. How then, does one set a pace and keep to it? We suggest immersion in a process of deliberation focused on four overarching and interconnected themes:

- Evolving one's sense of self as researcher
- Clarifying and contextualizing the intent of one's inquiry
- Understanding the logics and procedures of one's inquiry
- Conceptualizing, representing, and warranting the inquiry and its results

Although these are presented as a list, it does not matter which theme catalyzes the deliberative process. What is crucial is attending to the interplay among issues related to all four themes. Sometimes, this can feel like skipping around without focus or like blindly shuffling pieces of an unsolvable puzzle. But exploring connections among the various issues is what finally allows one to move more deeply into the dissertation process and eventually through it. The questions posed in the Reflective Interludes for each chapter offer a structure for entering into an exploration of these themes. By revisiting and revising one's responses to the questions, it is possible to incorporate new understandings and thereby evolve one's thinking on all four themes.

## Mobilizing Support

As with running a marathon, support for the dissertation can take many forms, from enthusiastic cheering to careful coaching. Sometimes, family and friends want to be supportive, but because they have never experienced the dissertation process, they are at a loss as to how to be helpful.

One student, whose family was probably trying to express an interest in her work, experienced considerable anxiety and embarrassment when they asked, "How's the dissertation going? Are you almost finished?" It seems that her brother-in-law, who had done a traditional scientific study, took a week off from work, rented a hotel room, and came out at the end of seven days carrying his laptop computer and a completed dissertation. Lurking beneath the seemingly supportive questions may have been a more corrosive and debilitating message, "What's wrong with you that you can't get it done?" Helping family and friends to understand the nature of a qualitative inquiry may help them to understand more realistically the length of time such studies can take. In addition, by brainstorming a wish list of desired help (e.g., emotional/psychological support, support for learning about qualitative research, financial support, and support with tasks of daily living), students can identify specific needs and begin to form a support team.

Sometimes, support (or the lack of support) comes from unexpected places. We are reminded of one student who did not mention her husband in her acknowledgments. Throughout the dissertation process, he had continually undermined her efforts. It was her mother-in-law who offered the most tangible support, providing extra child care, doing grocery shopping, and preparing meals that could be quickly reheated. As this anecdote illustrates, it is not only the student who is invested in the dissertation. Over time, we have come to see that friends, relatives, and colleagues may also take more than a passing interest in one's dissertation.

Although intentional undermining of another person's dissertation is probably rare, well-meant but misplaced assistance can create obstacles. For example, one member of our study group, a highly committed school administrator, finally came to the difficult decision to take a leave of absence so that she could concentrate on the final conceptualization and writing of a highly complex dissertation. Her leave was scheduled to begin July 1, but her supervisor "generously" suggested that she should feel free to continue wrapping up loose ends past this date. What appears on the surface to be a helpful suggestion to alleviate work-related pressure might actually be detrimental. There are always loose ends to tie up, and delaying the start of this conscientious employee's leave of absence could throw off her pacing, break her concentration, and erode the precious and limited time available to finish the dissertation.

Students who band together in support groups but spend most of their time relating dissertation horror stories or commiserating about "meaningless academic hoops" are also caught in a potentially debilitating dynamic. There is a fine line between complaining about a difficult undertaking and a sense of support arising from the camaraderie of a shared challenge.

On more than one occasion, we have met students who seem ready, willing, and able to embark on a marathon. Yet they have been advised by family, friends, and even faculty to avoid the race. This advice is rarely blatant, but more often takes the form of comments such as, "Remember, the dissertation isn't your life's work. Do something small and manageable. Do *that* ambitious study once you've got the doctorate." While this has the ring of good common sense, it glosses over an important point. How often does one have the motivation and opportunity to undertake a project as intensive as a dissertation? Is it likely that one will be inclined to devote time and energy to a major research endeavor once life returns to normal?

Without prompting undue paranoia, we encourage students to think about the people who may have a vested interest either in the student's abandoning the race or staying the course. Avoiding the former can be liberating; surrounding oneself with the latter can be tremendously sustaining.

## Reflective Interlude 3.2

### How Prepared Am I to Stay the Course of the Dissertation?

- Given the meanings I ascribe to the dissertation, what time and energy am I willing to commit to the process?
- What are the implications of this commitment in terms of pacing myself through the process?
- Who has a vested interest in my completing the dissertation? What do they represent in terms of support?
- What resources are available to support me through the dissertation?
  - What are my sources of financial support?
  - What are my sources of emotional support?
  - What are my sources of deliberative support?
  - What are my sources of technical support?
  - What are my sources of support for my personal responsibilities?
  - What are my sources of support for my professional responsibilities?

# 4

---

# *Facing the Dissertation*

---

## Key Concepts

Cheerleader Mentality

Counterproductive Dichotomy

Deliberative Curiosity

Dissertation Jitters

Dissertation Puddles

Human Dilemma Puddle

Practitioner Intervention Puddle

Facing the Dissertation

Precommitment Anxiety

Receding Horizon Phenomenon

Vendetta Mentality

---

A s students near the end of their doctoral coursework, the prospect of *facing the dissertation* becomes more immediate. Although the dissertation requirement should come as no surprise, committing to it—intellectually and emotionally—can require some adjustment.

Over the years, we have met a number of students for whom the dissertation seems to have symbolic meanings apart from its academic purpose as a demonstration of scholarly ability. An experience that Maria had more than 25 years ago lingers as a vivid reminder of the emotional undercurrents that may be swirling beneath the task of the dissertation. Physically, the student in Exemplar 4.1 seemed unable to face the dissertation—perhaps an outward manifestation of difficulty in committing to the dissertation. Avoiding such commitment is understandable if a student does not have a growing sense that "I can do this."

---

**EXEMPLAR 4.1    The Emotional Power of the Dissertation**

Several years after completing my dissertation, I conducted a workshop on practice-based research at the hospital where I worked. Among the participants was a nurse who had completed all of her doctoral courses and, as she put it, "needed to gear up for the dissertation." She claimed that the workshop was energizing, and she had regained her enthusiasm for finishing the degree.

Periodically, we would meet in the hospital corridors, and in an effort to be supportive, I would ask, "How's the dissertation going?" Inevitably, she replied, "I'm going to be meeting with my advisor and get started. It's just that work keeps me so busy right now, I'm having trouble finding time for it."

After several of these exchanges, I began to notice that when I posed my question about her dissertation, my colleague's eyes would sort of roll up under her eyelids; she would avert her face, almost speaking to me over her shoulder. With that realization, I stopped asking. But the image of her contorted face continued to haunt me. Eventually, I came to speculate that it was the dissertation—not me—that she couldn't bear to face. How painful, I thought, to be paralyzed—unable to move either forward into the dissertation process or to walk away from it.

*Authors' Commentary.* Over the years, we have met a number of students who appear to be stuck in this fashion. Often, they seem to fade away until one day, we suddenly say, "I wonder what ever happened to so-and-so." From our perspective, it is regrettable if students passively avoid the dissertation until they run out of time. In essence, they make a decision through their inaction. Are they, we wonder, haunted by a sense of unfinished business, or worse, failure? We know of two instances in which students seemed to make a deliberate and well-reasoned decision to remain all-but-dissertation. In one case, the demands and rewards of fatherhood seemed to override the importance of the dissertation. In the other case, the student talked quite explicitly about his distaste for writing and his feeling that he was already doing what mattered to him professionally. Whatever benefit might accrue from holding the title of doctor was not worth the personal turmoil of writing. These two individuals seemed at peace with their decision not to complete the dissertation. Feeling trapped into doing a dissertation is not likely to be a productive or satisfying experience. If one chooses to move in some other personal or professional direction, we hope they and their family and friends take time to mark this transition. Choosing to stop or change direction need not be a sign of weakness, failure, or quitting. Indeed, having the wisdom to know one's own mind and the courage to act on that knowledge is cause for celebration. (Those who are interested in understanding the experience of students who do not complete their doctorate, Golde, 2000, offers an interesting perspective.)

Therefore, under the heading of *Precommitment Anxiety,* we explore several issues that seem to affect students' confidence in tackling the dissertation. In our experience, as students begin to face the dissertation, they tend to think first in terms of potential topics.

Practitioners often draw upon personal work experience as a source of topics. In a section called "Deliberations About Topic," we use a puddle metaphor to alert students to both the value of drawing from one's practice and the potential pitfalls of doing so. A posture of *deliberative curiosity* is suggested as a safeguard.

# PRECOMMITMENT ANXIETY

In previous chapters, we have mentioned *academic folklore,* which imbues the dissertation with an aura of mystery. Students may not know the details of doing a dissertation, but they know that it is a BIG DEAL. The sense of importance and mystery associated with the dissertation can generate considerable anxiety that, in turn, may undermine even the most able students' sense of confidence. A number of issues seem to contribute to this sense of *dissertation jitters.*

At a workshop for students who had been avoiding the dissertation for several years, we asked participants to write a reflection on "what comes to mind when you think about doing the dissertation." A content analysis of these writings yielded a set of weighty issues that can contribute to predissertation anxiety including the following:

- Impact on lifestyle/quality of life
- Financial factors
- Payoffs/value
- Commitment, ownership, sacrifices
- Conflicting obligations and priorities
- Support
- Committee factors/relationships
- Time/energy factors
- Discipline/pacing
- Avoidance behaviors
- Performance/competence issues
- Emotional reactions

Such issues can create a vulnerability to several pitfalls.

## The Infinitely Receding Horizon Phenomenon

For at least some students, the dissertation is a distant aspect of doctoral work. Vaguely, they know it is something they will eventually have to get to, but like Scarlett O'Hara, they'll think about it tomorrow. The tendency to put off thinking about the dissertation came more fully to our attention as we read the passage in Exemplar 4.2, an excerpt from a student think piece on the meaning of the dissertation. No matter how imminent the dissertation becomes, it always seems to be receding, like the shimmering horizon at the end of a long, straight highway.

**EXEMPLAR 4.2    The Receding Horizon Phenomenon**

Hard to believe that I am at the point in my academic career that I am giving serious thought to my comprehensive examination. It seemed (and to some extent still seems) like such a long way off. Just another step in the process, I believed, when I first heard the word *comps* posed to me in casual conversation by fellow classmates. Casual conversation as bantered about when asking, "Where are you in the process?" And getting answers like, "I'm in the process of completing my comps." or "I just finished my comps"—to me that just meant they were pretty close to finishing up. As I reflect now, I'm not sure what it was I thought they were close to finishing—their coursework; their actual dissertations? All I can say I thought for sure was that they were a step closer to "finishing."

Now as I draw closer to this stage of the comprehensive examination myself, I am giving much thought as to what it really does mean and what it is I'll "have to do." In discussions with my advisor, I'd have to say that it is still not crystal clear.

I am still thinking in terms of the fact that it is a long way off for me though my Intro to Qualitative Research class has been putting the whole notion of actually writing a dissertation much more into perspective. Given the fact that I have only two more classes to go before completing my coursework, I'm getting a bit antsy about not having a topic just yet. It is only within the last two weeks that I have seriously thought about the direction my inquiry will take to find that topic of mine.

*Authors' Commentary.* Note the student's tendency to persist in seeing doctoral requirements as a long way off, even though she has only two more courses to complete. She may sustain the illusion of distance by shifting her focus from the more imminent requirement (the comprehensive examination that is the initial focus in this writing) to the more remote dissertation. Making this shift may postpone the task of coming to grips with the comprehensive examination, which, she says, "is still not crystal clear."

We wonder if the expectation for crystal clarity may be indicative of a desire for her advisor to supply a precise description of the comprehensive examination. If such a set of instructions is not forthcoming, will the student perpetuate the folklore about the mystery surrounding doctoral requirements or see it as an opportunity to engage with her advisor in discussion and deliberation?

## Counterproductive Dichotomy

This *receding horizon phenomenon* may be reinforced when students dichotomize their doctoral program into coursework and dissertation. Some students, as illustrated in the following comment, tend to manage their anxiety by maintaining a very narrow focus:

I have approached the whole doctoral degree as "a need to know" process. By that I mean I think about the next step when I need to take it. In the beginning of my pursuit of the degree, I never looked at the catalog to determine how many credits I would need to take. If I had looked to see that it would take 90 credits to complete the degree, I may not have gone any farther. I know from talking to persons with the doctoral degree that a dissertation is part of the process, and that was enough to scare me.

An overly narrow fixation on the dissertation may heighten students' anxiety by obscuring intermediate steps (e.g., qualifying examinations, the research proposal) that move students into the process. Awareness of these requirements, however, is no guarantee of understanding their relationship to each other or their significance for the inquiry process. This seems especially true when such requirements are seen as meaningless academic hurdles intended only to complicate life and impede attainment of one's degree.

## Painful Fussing

Another issue that arises during this time of transition is raised in an e-mail from Micheline, whom we have already introduced. Micheline and Marilyn had set up a standing library night to provide some structure and accountability for their inquiry process. Over time, they had invited other students to join them, and the following note refers to a conversation with Ted, a recent addition to the library group:

> Maria, your note about rescuing others from the struggles of the dissertation brings up an interaction that I had last night at the library with Marilyn and Ted. Ted seems in such misery over how to get a focus for his study, a pain all too familiar to me. I think of the place Ted is—at the very beginning—as probably the most frustrating, anxiety-provoking, miserable, unpleasant, and painful part of this whole process. It elicits such empathy in me. At any rate, as I sat listening and trying to respond to Ted's machinations for over 45 minutes during what was supposed to be library time, Marilyn joined in. Actually in her attempt to rescue me from rescuing Ted, she became ensnared. Micheline

We, too, are familiar with this impulse to rescue students from the pain of their machinations—an impulse prompted by a mixture of initial empathy and growing impatience as we begin to wonder, "Why don't you just get on with it?" For some students, a reluctance to commit to a particular topic or focus delays their progress in facing the dissertation.

## Inner Doubts

A reflection written by Pam Krakowski, another study group member, provides some insight into another issue related to facing-the-dissertation, an issue that can prolong the painful fussing:

> Up to this point [the second night of a qualitative research course], I had never read a dissertation. In my mind, I imagined these foreboding, black-bound books to be boring, full of hard to decipher statistics, and having little relevance

to classroom practice. I picked up one of the dissertations and read the title, *Pictures in Our Minds: A Narrative Study of Creative Dramatics as Pedagogy in Elementary Classroom Content Areas* [Richards, 1996]. It intrigued me, and so I borrowed it.

That night, instead of watching television, I sat down to read the dissertation. I found that I could not put it down. It read like a story and was full of accounts that I could relate to as a teacher. I kept asking myself, "Are you really allowed to do this?" I couldn't believe that a teacher was allowed to write about her classroom—or creative dramatics—or even a narrative. That evening I felt a sense of relief—yes, maybe even I could write a dissertation. Up to now, the whole process seemed daunting to me.

Students who have been socialized into projecting an image of confidence may not share their inner doubts and fears about tackling the dissertation. Interestingly, the dissertation that Pam found so reassuring was written by Lynn Richards, who wrote the following recollection several months after completing her doctorate:

For the past seven years, I had worked steadily towards my goal of completing a doctoral degree in the field of education. The traditional university requirements of coursework, preliminaries, and competency exam had provided markers of my progress along the academic way. As I left the comfortable deadline-driven role of student and began my role as an independent researcher and scholar, I was often disturbed by an overwhelming sense of inadequacy and an embarrassing lack of direction. Although I had chosen my topic of dissertation inquiry—creative dramatics—and had been gathering information about narrative as a method of inquiry—I knew little of how to weave the two together in the construction of an acceptable dissertation.

The anxiety voiced by Pam and Lynn is more common among students than we had ever imagined. Often, students who outwardly appear confident are secretly wracked with fears. In fact, to us, Lynn had seemed to progress through the process with amazing aplomb. We were stunned when she shared the following story several months after masterfully defending her study:

Shortly after I had asked the study group for help structuring my overview proposal, I received a box in the mail from an anonymous sender. It was full of expensive books addressing qualitative research design. I was certain that the study group had taken up a collection in an attempt to educate such an unsophisticated, unscholarly elementary school teacher as myself. I was so disturbed by the image of my own academic incompetence that I sat on the floor of my bedroom closet and wept. (Recounted in Richards, 2006, p. 25)

A major aspect of facing the dissertation is letting go of potentially debilitating doubts and fears or finding ways not to ignore—but to diffuse—them. Although a certain amount of empathy from friends and faculty is certainly called for and welcome, support for prolonged wallowing in anxiety is counterproductive. From our perspective, the most useful way for students to ease into dissertation commitment is through writing. Often, the most comfortable place to begin writing is through consideration of potential topics for study.

## DELIBERATIONS ON TOPIC

### Getting in Touch With a Topic

In the halls of academe, "Have you *found* a topic yet?" is a common query directed toward those nearing the end of their doctoral coursework. "*Choose* a manageable topic" are common words of advice. Such comments tend to focus attention outward, suggesting that topics can be stumbled across or selected from an existing buffet of options.

An alternative is to talk about *shaping* a dissertation. This notion stems from our belief that novice scholars have within themselves embryonic images that can be fashioned into credible and worthy studies. The task is not to *look for* or *choose* a topic, but rather to get in touch with these nebulous, inner images and to bring them into clearer relief.[1]

What, then, is a starting point for this shaping process? Because our focus is on interpretive and practice-based qualitative research, we suggest that one's experience offers a fertile context for potential topics. Often, we meet practitioners who come to the dissertation from one of two stances—outrage over some perceived inadequacy or zeal for some perceived intervention. We represent these as two variations of *dissertation puddles*.

### The Human Dilemma Puddle

The earliest expressions of a dissertation topic are often couched in terms of a desire to take corrective action toward some person, situation, or event (see Figure 4.1).

Not uncommonly, such expressions are tinged with indignation or outrage over some perceived affront or injustice. One young woman remains a vivid example of this approach to the dissertation.

**Figure 4.1**    Human Dilemma Puddle

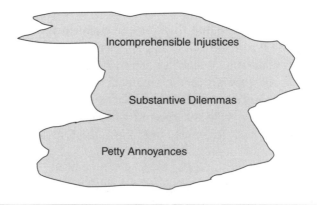

Incomprehensible Injustices

Substantive Dilemmas

Petty Annoyances

When asked about her topic, she stated quite vehemently, "I want to develop a course to teach college administrators how to communicate." Upon further probing, she described her work situation where a supervisor had encouraged staff members to suggest ways to improve their department. When suggestions were made, however, the supervisor ignored them and maintained the status quo, predictably resulting in lower employee morale. The young woman was personally affronted that her suggestions had been dismissed and had concluded that supervisors in general do not know how to communicate effectively with their employees. Her solution was to use her dissertation to design a communication skills training program that could rectify this perceived managerial incompetence.

Another example comes from the arena of health education, where we cannot keep track of all the students who define the *problem* for their research as a lack of organizationally sponsored wellness programs. In so many words, they say:

> My work organization doesn't have a stress-management program. We know that work-related stress can cause all sorts of problems—risk of heart attack, absenteeism, and lower productivity. For my study, I want to design and implement a stress-management program.

Such intentions do not constitute viable dissertation research. Yet giving this feedback risks fueling even greater vehemence about the need to make others see that a problem exists. Over the years, we have come to realize that these rather naïve comments often represent the earliest attempts to articulate an incipient research topic. This brought us to the notion of the *human dilemma puddle.*

In the course of their personal and professional lives, practitioners often find themselves immersed in perplexing and confusing circumstances. Many times, it is difficult to pinpoint the source of their consternation, but a nagging feeling persists—something is wrong, something doesn't make sense. The *human dilemma puddle* is meant to convey a fundamental assumption—that is, embedded within this amorphous conglomeration of troublesome and troubling experiences are often important dilemmas that warrant serious study.

As Figure 4.1 illustrates, these human dilemmas range from the petty to the profound. Petty annoyances are irksome or frustrating but essentially trivial. As irritating as they might be, in the scheme of the universe, such dilemmas seem inconsequential (e.g., Why won't my supervisor listen to me? Why won't my company sponsor a stress management course?).

At the opposite end of the spectrum are the virtually incomprehensible dilemmas of human existence (e.g., violence in the schools, inequities in schooling, racial prejudice, and social oppression). Most of us shake our heads and wonder, "How can such things happen? How can this be?" Some students come to the dissertation with a desire to ameliorate such human ills through their research.

In the middle ground lie substantive dilemmas usually embedded in the student's practice. These dilemmas are often characterized by a vehement, even angry, desire to fix something, take corrective action, or improve a situation. Underlying the specific circumstances are often basic questions—for example, What is going on here? What does all this

**Figure 4.2**    Practitioner Intervention Puddle

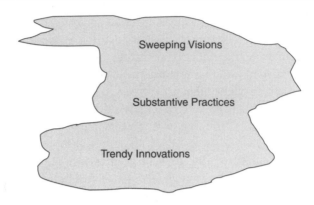

mean? What can be done? What should be done? Action-oriented and focused on issues of substance, such dilemmas have the potential to be consequential and meaningful, not just to the researcher but also to other practitioners and scholars.

## The Practitioner Intervention Puddle

If outrage is the stance represented by the human dilemma puddle, zeal is the stance of the *practitioner intervention puddle* (see Figure 4.2).

At the trendy-innovation end of the continuum, this stance manifests as wide-eyed wonder over some relatively narrow innovation—often a particular technique, program, or model. Students convey a "Gee whiz! Ain't it great!" attitude and want their dissertation to convince the rest of the world to embrace their particular intervention. Illustrative of this situation was a student who had recently been involved with a health promotion program in which a mobile van toured through communities whose citizens would not otherwise have access to wellness services. With unbridled enthusiasm, she wanted to write her dissertation as a grant proposal to obtain funding to replicate this service in other parts of the state.

Students operating from this stance often have a missionary zeal for promulgating their innovation throughout the educational community. Encouragement to tie their study to underlying theoretical issues may be perceived as disinterest or dismissal of their topic, which, in turn, might push them toward the resentments of the dilemma puddle.

At the opposite end of the intervention continuum are students who want their dissertations to catalyze sweeping educational or social reform. Underlying such grandiose visions is often a deep-seated commitment to an educational principle or philosophy. Such students remind us of Robert Kennedy's eloquent statement, "Some men [sic] see things as they are and ask why; I dream of things that aren't, and ask why not." Lurking within the students' sweeping visions are intimations of what might be.[2]

The middle of the intervention puddle encompasses an array of substantive methods or techniques that students may be using in their practice. Typically, these students are well-regarded practitioners who have an intuitive sense of what works. They approach the dissertation with a sincere and heartfelt desire to explain their practice for the benefit of others.[3]

## The Role of Outrage and Zeal

Tierney and Lincoln (1994), in discussing the teaching of qualitative research, comment that

> when we study our own culture, we need to create a subjective distance so that we do not merely record data from an insider's point of view. Indeed, as Margaret Mead has noted, "If a fish were to become an anthropologist, the last thing it would discover would be water" (in Spindler 1982, p. 4). (p. 111)

The sense of outrage or zeal can serve as a catalyst for helping us to "notice the water." What others have taken for granted or overlooked can be brought to conscious awareness by the sense of outrage or wonder. This awareness can be a starting point for shaping a study. The challenge for both students and their advisors is to slosh around in the puddle long enough to tease out, to bring into relief, a viable study.

Periodically, we encounter students who are well into their dissertations but seem to have little enthusiasm for or ownership of their research. They may have been stuck in the process for several years and are having trouble bringing their project to closure. When we explore their situation, it is not uncommon to discover that early in the process, the student had been sloshing around in the profound dilemma or sweeping reform part of the puddle and had been given the well-intentioned advice to choose a smaller, more manageable project or to change topics entirely. (Sadly, we meet far fewer students who have been advised to abandon a trivial problem or trendy innovation in favor of a more substantive issue.)

We have begun to speculate that such students bog down in the process because they are working against their own resistance. Having had no opportunity to come to grips with their original idea, they harbor regrets about the study that might have been or resentment about doing "someone else's study." Ironically, it often seems that either the student or the advisor—or both—was so anxious to get on with the study that insufficient time was devoted to bringing embryonic ideas into sharper focus. The price for expediency in choosing a topic may be paid in the time it takes to complete the dissertation.[4]

The sloshing process entails a movement from simplistic reaction toward a posture of *deliberative curiosity.* Without such movement, students can fall into traps illustrated by the continuum in Figure 4.3. Unchecked outrage can lead to a *vendetta mentality,* using the dissertation for personal vindication (e.g., "I'm going to prove just how wrong and unfair you are!"). Unbridled zeal can lead to the *cheerleading mentality* (e.g., "My dissertation will prove just how wonderful my intervention is!"). Adequate and appropriate sloshing can convert outrage or zeal into deliberative curiosity, which in turn provides intellectual and emotional fuel to sustain an inquiry. Reflective Interlude 4.1 suggests an exercise that is meant to support intellectual sloshing in one's nebulous ideas for the dissertation.

**Figure 4.3**   Postures Toward the Dissertation

| Vendetta Mentality | Deliberative Curiosity | Cheerleading Mentality |

## MOVING FROM NEBULOUS IDEAS TOWARD A STUDY

**Reflective Interlude 4.1**

### Sloshing Around in the Dissertation Puddle

To prepare for this reflective activity, have on hand plenty of paper (large sheets of newsprint are ideal) and colored markers or pencils. Find a quiet place with lots of space to spread out your materials. Close your eyes, take some deep breaths, and spend several minutes clearing your mind. Visualize a puddle (some students report seeing a pond, stream, or even a swimming pool) lying before you. Notice its qualities and then imagine yourself entering the puddle. Note how it feels and what images come to mind. When you are ready, use the colored markers to draw the puddle, yourself in relation to the puddle, and any features or images that came to mind. As you draw, feel free to add new images and details that come to mind. During the drawing phase, try to concentrate on visual images. Avoid thinking in terms of words and sentences. Let the images guide you.

Once you have finished drawing the images associated with your puddle, you can write notes on what the images mean to you. This can be done as a private journal entry. Sharing the drawing and the meanings associated with it can serve as a basis of discussion within a class, study group, or conference with an advisor.

For a more verbal approach to surfacing ideas for your dissertation, you might respond to the types of questions suggested by the authors in the following books: Robert Nash (2004). *Liberating Scholarly Writing: The Power of Personal Narrative,* pages 57–59; and Wayne C. Booth, Gregory G. Colomb, & Joseph M. Williams (2003). *The Craft of Research* (2nd ed.), pages 40–49.

Regardless of whether you try an imagistic or verbal approach to teasing out a topic, we (like the authors of the suggested texts) encourage you to think about topics, issues, problems, and concerns that matter to you. Without passion for one's topic of investigation, research becomes a tedious and empty exercise.

The transition from early sloshing to a well-conceptualized research proposal entails considerable work. In calling attention to the process of facing the dissertation, we hope to engender a greater tolerance for the messiness and anxiety associated with bringing the embryonic images of a study into clearer relief. Giving sufficient time for these early deliberations can help to safeguard against jumping too quickly into a vaguely conceived study for which there is little enthusiasm. At the same time, however, it is important not to become bogged down in a swamp of possibilities—never making a commitment to forward movement. As we have watched students try to chart a course between premature closure and failure to commit, we have been troubled by two unproductive patterns.

One pattern consists of an endless shuffling and reshuffling of ideas. Although students caught in this pattern may generate multiple documents or engage in endless conversations about the dissertation, their thinking remains scattered. It is as if they are working on a 5,000-piece jigsaw puzzle by continually sliding individual pieces around in a random fashion rather than trying to fit pieces together. In some instances, all this activity generates an aura of frantic intellectual flailing; in other instances, there is an aura of helpless floundering. The key to helping such students move toward the dissertation in a more deliberative way continues to elude us.

A second troubling pattern can be characterized by the old saying, "A little knowledge is a dangerous thing." This pattern is exemplified by students who conclude that they know what qualitative research is after only a preliminary introduction to this field of study. The certitude expressed in the following comment does not bode well for a *stance of study* or *deliberative curiosity:*

In this course, I learned what qualitative research is, why it is important, what is distinctive about it, what its merits are, and the form it can take in regards to methods and how to analyze qualitative data. Qualitative research has six key features . . .

Far more congruent with qualitative inquiry is the deliberative posture suggested in the following comment:

So what have I learned during this course? I have learned that others have paved the way for me; the struggle I face is within me. I have learned that others are willing to share—advice, a shoulder, a critical review; I need to learn to ask for help. I have learned that qualitative research speaks to me; I need to continue to find and strengthen my own voice. I have learned that a peer group is an effective learning tool for me—professionally and personally. . . . I have learned that professors have an interest in my growth and development; acceptance and internalization of that interest is necessary for me to develop more fully and deeply. I have learned that being uncertain or unsure may be uncomfortable but is an okay place to be—for others; I need to learn that I, too, can be unsure or uncertain and be free with those feelings. I have learned that others share some of the same fears I face; facing fear is what is important. I have learned that I believe I have a place within the realm of qualitative research; developing self-confidence with this realization must continue.

The realizations expressed in this student's comments (as with the comments of the student in Exemplar 4.3) open up avenues for deeper learning—for entering into the study of qualitative research, for engaging in deliberation. When we see this focus and intensity of conceptual grappling, we know that students have begun to embark on the dissertation journey.

**EXEMPLAR 4.3     Deliberative Posture Toward Learning About Qualitative Research**

One of the major things I learned in this course is something I have to relearn time and time again. I couldn't find the originator of this quote but it's one that has affected me profoundly for some time because of its simplicity and power. "There is only one thing that is certain, and that is that nothing is certain."

I learned that qualitative research could be described in a similar fashion. It's one thing and many things. We can be sure that it's not quantitative research, but we wouldn't want to define it that way and that definition wouldn't be an informing one (nor would it be absolutely true since some aspects of qualitative and quantitative research overlap). The definition that best explains qualitative research changes as the debate about it continues and the doers of the research continue their work. In essence, we can't confine things that are so multifaceted and ever changing to a neat, tidy definition. Nor can we define them in reaction to a preexisting concept in a compare and contrast manner.

I've learned not to anticipate but to explore, and that the rigidity that I abhor but allowed to take over my life and thoughts, plans, and behavior was not productive and, more importantly, wasn't necessary. I learned to my surprise that there are a wide variety of types of dissertation work being done . . .

What I've also learned is that although exaggerated somewhat by my personal neurosis, the anxiety I've been experiencing in this process is no different than what virtually every other student in the doctoral program has/is experiencing.

I must add that I have learned an entirely new way of looking at processes, one that allows for a different kind of examination, a kind that's not so polarized and constricted. Not so either/or. Along with this, however, I've learned that applying a more flexible way of analyzing things can be complicated and just outright difficult because it inherently requires new kinds of thinking that may wind up all over the map. This kind of thinking requires more care and focus. It's the kind that could easily take researchers (and students) off on tangents from which they have to pull back and focus on the most important pieces before losing sight of the issue at hand . . .

The course handout, "Thinking About Qualitative Dissertation Research," best illustrates the new way of thinking I'm describing. For example, taking a stiff question like, "What methodology should I use?" and turning it into an informing one like, "What methods allow me to fulfill the intent of my study and address my guiding questions?" is a major shift for me. These are questions that reside in two different worlds of thought, one that represents existing and one that represents living.

## NOTES

1. For students who are working on major research projects under the mentorship of a senior investigator, *choosing a topic* may be an appropriate description for the process. In these circumstances, students may have the opportunity to choose among several potential subsets or spin-offs of the overall project.

2.   Students who approach the dissertation from this perspective may be inclined to ground their research in the critical theorist tradition. Brenton Prosser (1999), for example, completed a critical study of attention deficit disorder with intent to promote social and educational change. Jo Victoria Goodman (2003) took a critical-theory stance toward studying the curriculum implications of discourses following the September 11 terrorist attacks. Those who want to read further about critical theory might begin their exploration with Crotty (1996, 2003), Fay (1987), Kincheloe (1991, 2005), Kincheloe & McLaren (2003), Macey (2000), Wexler (1991), and Willis (2007).

3.   We have been privileged over the years to work with a number of students who have done exceptionally fine dissertations grounded in their practice (Blackford, 1997; Ceroni, 1995; Conlan, 2006; Goodman, 2003; Goodwin, 1983; Grubs, 2002; Harris, 1995; Hazi, 1980; Holland, 1983; Knapp-Minick, 1984; Konzal, 1995; Krakowski, 2004; Leukhardt, 1983; Llewellyn, 1998; Logsdon, 2000; McMahon, 1993; Milne, 2000; Prosser, 1999; Richards, 1996; Sanida, 1987; Stabile, 1999; Willis, 1998; Wojecki, 2004). In no way do we mean to imply that these are the only good practice-based dissertations that have been done. Indeed, students are encouraged to talk with their advisors about exemplary qualitative dissertations that have been completed at their own university. We mention these dissertations at this juncture in the writing because several of them are used throughout the book to illustrate various aspects of qualitative inquiries.

4.   Over the years, we have gained an ever-deepening appreciation of the fragility of these early deliberations. It has been sobering to learn—sometimes years after the fact—that conversations we meant to be exploratory and affirming of students' interests were experienced by students as critical and demoralizing. Part of the difficulty, we suspect, lies in the multilayered nature of these deliberations. Even as students are sorting through potential ideas for the dissertation, they may be learning what it means to deliberate and be deciding how safe it is to share their thinking, particularly their disagreements, with individuals who are perceived as authority figures.

# SECTION TWO

---

*Preparing for the Dissertation Journey*

# 5

# *Orienting Oneself to Interpretive Inquiry*

---

**Key Concepts**

| | |
|---|---|
| Axiology | Knowledge Claims |
| Connoisseurship | Ontology |
| Discernment | Phronesis |
| Enlightened Eye | Research Tradition—Interpretivism |
| Epistemology | Research Tradition—Postpositivism |
| Heuristic Theory | Scientism |
| Ideal Theory | Warrant |
| Intimate Studies | Worldview |

---

U p to this point in the book, much of what we have said about the dissertation process can be related to both quantitative and qualitative studies. Readers might understandably be wondering, "Just what is the difference between these two types of studies?" It would be very nice if we could offer a clear, concise definition that would distinguish between these forms of research. But that would be misleading. The term *qualitative research* has been used in so many different ways that it does not convey very precisely the nature of a study. Granted, we and others still use the term as a convenient shorthand for a constellation of very complex ideas. Coming to grips with what it means to do a qualitative dissertation requires probing beneath the shorthand to understand the nature of *knowledge claims* one is putting forward. In this chapter we explore worldview issues that underlie the nature of knowledge claims in interpretive educational research.

# A QUESTION OF LEGITIMACY

It is generally assumed that the primary purpose of educational research is to create new knowledge. Educational researchers (including doctoral candidates) conduct inquiries in order to have something to say about the state of educational affairs, to understand educational conditions, and to improve educational practice, policy, and institutional patterns (e.g., Bodone, 2005; Firestone & Riehl, 2005; Ladson-Billings & Tate, 2006; Maxwell, 1992). As a result of carrying out an inquiry, the researcher claims to have found out something new about a particular aspect of education. In reporting the results of the inquiry, the researcher makes public, for a particular audience, what he or she has come to know. The function of the written report (e.g., dissertation) is not only to inform readers about what knowledge the researcher is claiming, but also to persuade them of its legitimacy. Consider, for example, the following conversation between Noreen and Marcy, a research assistant working in the research and evaluation department of a large urban school district.

"My assignment," Marcy said,

> was to develop a survey of opinions our staff held about the personnel department. It seems that there had been some dissonance between the personnel department and the rest of the staff. The board of directors asked for clarification of the issues. Well, I didn't really know what the nature of the disagreements was. I didn't know much about what the personnel department did either, so I began to talk with people. I did formal interviews; I had conversations over lunch with people from both groups; I talked to people in the elevators. I listened to their stories about important incidents. By the time I constructed the items for the survey, I knew more about the personnel department and the situation with staff than I ever imagined. It was rich stuff. Somehow, when I began to put it into abstract form for the items of the survey, though, it was lifeless and didn't really get to the heart of the matter.

When Noreen asked why Marcy felt she couldn't use the rich data for her research results instead of findings from the survey, Marcy responded,

> My boss really only believes that quantitative data is full-blown, or maybe, *hard*, research. If I report the results of all the narrative data, that would only be my own interpretations. The survey would verify that the respondents really hold certain views. It would be more objective. I'm really frustrated, though, because the findings on the survey really don't get to the heart of the matter. They just don't get to the heart of the issues.

Embedded in this anecdote are taken-for-granted assumptions that legitimate (reliable and valid) knowledge is established through scientific investigation, and quantification is the means for legitimate proof. As Polkinghorne (1997) points out, during "the heyday of positivism,"

> a true knowledge statement has logical certitude because it was the product of a formal process. As was the case with mathematical solutions, the validity of research conclusions were understood to be independent of both the person making the claim and the audience to whom the claim was presented. (p. 7)

The pervasiveness of this view of legitimate knowledge still lingers, even for students who may have little or no formal training in research methods. However, as suggested by the anecdote in Exemplar 5.1, students often have at least an intuitive sense that the knowledge claims of qualitative dissertations may be problematic. Moving beyond such vague misgivings requires at least some understanding of *worldview*.[1]

## CONSIDERATIONS OF WORLDVIEW

While *worldview* comprises the totality of one's beliefs, for research purposes the most relevant beliefs are those of ontology, epistemology, and axiology.

*Ontology,* as Crotty (2003) explains, "is the study of *being*. It is concerned with 'what is,' with the nature of existence, with the structure of reality as such" (p. 10). Not only does ontology refer to our beliefs about reality, but also to our way of "being in the world," our way of relating to the world. *Epistemology* refers to beliefs about what we take to be true and what counts as knowledge. It also encompasses beliefs about how knowledge and truth are determined. *Axiology* refers to beliefs about what forms of knowledge are valuable and what modes for determining knowledge are valued. Axiological beliefs also shape values related to ways of being in and relating to the world and others.

---

**EXEMPLAR 5.1    Intimations of the Problematic Nature of Qualitative Knowledge Claims**

---

On the first night of an introductory course on qualitative research, we were trying to give students a preliminary sense of research conducted within the context of educational practice.

"Imagine," we suggested,

that we wanted to understand this class. One approach would be to understand it in terms of observable, verifiable facts—size of the room; arrangement of chairs; the number, gender, and nationality of students; the nature of interactions among students and instructor; who talks; who remains silent; and similar "objective" features. Through the use of audio- and videotapes or multiple observers, we could then create a description that corresponds as closely as possible to this observable reality of "the class." What we might come to understand through this approach is something of the classroom environment/composition. It would not, however, give us much insight into your experience of it. To understand the class in that sense, we might take another approach—asking each of you to describe what led you to register for the course, how you feel about being here, what you are learning, which materials and class activities are useful, and which questions are emerging from your deliberations. We would now have 18 different sets of qualitative data. The issue becomes, What do we do with this stuff, and how can it help us to understand the class? For example, we couldn't generalize from your reactions to all doctoral students in education, or even to all students here at the university. We—

"Yes, that's right," one student interrupted. "Who would even care what the 18 of us thought?"

"How would you summarize or present what the 18 of us were thinking?" asked another. "I mean, how would you go from all that to something more general?"

In a nutshell, these students began to touch on the most troubling issue of qualitative research—the nature and value of knowledge generated through small, in-depth, context-bound inquiries. If such *intimate studies* do not yield reliable and valid scientific generalizations, then what form of knowledge is generated, and what makes it of value and legitimate?

Various ontological, epistemological, and axiological beliefs are embedded within long-standing traditions of philosophical discourse. It is likely that educational practitioners have neither the time nor inclination to undertake a formal study of philosophy as part of their dissertation journey. Nevertheless, the crux of understanding the difference between *quantitative* and *qualitative* research in education lies in understanding assumptions about the nature of the world, of human beings, and of one's relationship to both. As Schwandt (2007) observes:

> Rather than conceiving of the difference between so-called qualitative and quantitative inquiry in terms of tools and methods, students of qualitative inquiry might be better served by examining the differences (and similarities) among epistemologies for qualitative inquiry—for example, the epistemologies of empiricism and hermeneutics or empiricist and feminist epistemologies. Epistemologies provide much of the justification for particular methodologies (i.e., the aim, function, and assumptions of method). (pp. 87–88)

Schwandt's examples of epistemological descriptors point to one of the challenges facing students of qualitative research—namely, acquiring a language for recognizing and expressing one's taken-for-granted assumptions. For much of the 20th century, educational research was guided by assumptions that were variously characterized as positivist, post-positivist, empirical, or scientific. Regardless of the descriptor, an underlying assumption held that one could discover objective truths about the nature of things through careful measurement.[2] Hence, *quantitative research* served as a shorthand descriptor for a world-view embedded in the Western European "Enlightenment" of the 17th century.[3] By the latter half of the 20th century, this view of objective, value-free knowledge was subject to critique in many fields, including education. As scholars worked to articulate a different view of knowledge, *qualitative research* served as a convenient counterpoint to *quantitative research* that valued measurement.[4]

Very quickly, however, this loose differentiation between approaches was found wanting. It was too superficial to simply contrast studies on the basis of numeric (quantitative) versus linguistic (qualitative) data. It became increasingly apparent that the difference did not lie in the form of data per se, but rather in what one made of the data. In other words, what sort of *knowledge claims* was the researcher putting forward on the basis of collected data? To illustrate this point, consider the following claim: Frequent standardized testing of children interferes with their learning. Whether a researcher gathered quantitative data via a standardized survey or qualitative data via a semistructured interview, such a general knowledge claim could not be supported by either type of data if it were gathered from a small sample of one classroom, or even one school or district. Put another way, what knowledge claims can be made from small, nonrandom data sets, and what would be the value of such knowledge claims? In short, what constitutes legitimate knowledge?

This question pushed qualitative researchers to articulate more clearly the nature of knowledge claims they were making. This, in turn, led to considerations of ontology, epistemology, and axiology. As mentioned in Chapter 1, Soltis (1984) proposed three descriptors—empirical, interpretive, and critical—for distinguishing among different worldviews. Since then, a great many descriptors have entered the educational research discourses. Lincoln and Guba (1985), for example, introduced the concept of *naturalistic inquiry*. Sipe and Constable (1996) contrast *positivist, interpretivist, critical theory*, and *deconstructivist* perspectives. Paul (2005) expands the number of perspectives of research to nine using the following descriptors—*postpositivism, pragmatism, constructivism, interpretive* and *narrative, arts-based, race-ethnicity-gender, critical theory, ethics-methodology-democracy*, and *poststructuralism*. Crotty (2003) offers another set of descriptors—*positivism, postpositivism, constructionism, interpretivism, symbolic interactionism, phenomenology, hermeneutics, critical inquiry, feminism, postmodernism*, and *poststructuralism*. DeMarrais and LeCompte (1999) cluster theories into three groupings with different epistemological underpinnings: *social transmission theories* (functionalism and conflict theory), *interpretive theories* (phenomenology, symbolic interactionism, ethnomethodology) and *social transformation theories* (critical theory, critical ethnography, postpositivist, postmodern and feminist theory). Schwandt (2003) discusses *interpretivism, hermeneutics*, and *social constructionism* (see also Fosnot, 2005). Some scholars (e.g., Bruner, 1986, 1996; Polkinghorne, 1988; Richardson, 1990, 2003) contrast *scientific* with *narrative* knowing. Eisner (1991, 1993, 1997) and Barone (1995, 2000, 2001) contrast *science-based* with *arts-based* research, a distinction foreshadowed by C. P. Snow in a series of lectures now collected under the title of *The Two Cultures* (see Snow, 1998).

In recent years, these distinctions among philosophical traditions have been further challenged by feminists who critique the traditional privileging of masculine assumptions about knowledge (e.g., Anderson, E., 2007; Dimen, 1989; Elam & Wiegman, 1995; Harding, 2007; Hesse-Biber, 2006; Hesse-Biber & Leavy, 2006; Kleinman, 2007; Olson, 2004; Lather, 2004a, 2004b, 2007; Longino, 2007; Madriz, 2003; St. Pierre, 2000). Other scholars have called for greater awareness and sensitivity to various racial and ethnic epistemologies (e.g., Banks, 1995; Cleveland, 2004; Dei & Johal, 2005; Denzin, Lincoln, & Smith, 2008; Ladson-Billings, 2003; Longino, 2007; Lopez & Parker, 2003; O'Connor, Lewis, & Mueller, 2007; Scheurich & Young, 1997; Stanley, 2007; Tillman, 2002; Tyson, 1998). Still others have challenged epistemological assumptions embedded in a heterosexual worldview (e.g., Christians, 2003; Gamson, 2003). The third edition of *The SAGE Handbook on Qualitative Research* (Denzin & Lincoln, 2005) contains a number of important chapters on epistemology from various ethnic and gendered perspectives.

The prospect of sorting through these various philosophical assumptions can be overwhelming, especially since there is no single definition of the various descriptors.[5] For example, postpositivism may refer to a worldview in which positivist assumptions have been tempered to account for the socially constructed nature of knowledge. Or it may be used more broadly to refer to a wide range of research approaches that have gained prominence in the aftermath of positivism's decline.

One starting point is to recognize that for much of the 20th century research was dominated by an assumption that the social world could and should be studied in the same way as the natural world. Consequently, the ontological, epistemological, and axiological assumptions of "scientific research" dominated thinking about what counts as legitimate research. Flyvbjerg (2001), drawing on the work of philosopher Hubert Dreyfus, offers the following thumbnail sketch of *ideal theory,* which has served as the gold standard for research:

Ideal theory is viewed by Dreyfus as having six basic characteristics that can never be fully realized, but can be approached to varying degrees. Socrates introduced and argued for the first three of these when he said that a theory must be (1) explicit, (2) universal, and (3) abstract. It must be *explicit* because a theory is to be laid out so clearly, in such detail, and so completely that it can be understood by any reasoning being; a theory may not stand or fall on interpretation or intuition. Second, a theory must be *universal* in that it must apply in all places and all times. Third, a theory must be *abstract* in that it must not require the reference to concrete examples.

Descartes and Kant supplemented Socrates' three criteria with two more. A theory must also be (4) *discrete,* that is, formulated only with the aid of context-independent elements, which do not refer to human interests, traditions, institutions, etc. And it must be (5) *systematic;* that is, it must constitute a whole, in which context-independent elements (properties, factors) are related to each other by rules or laws.

Finally, modern natural science has added further a criterion of ideal theory; that it must be (6) *complete* and *predictive.* The way a theory accounts for the domain it covers must be comprehensive in the sense that it specifies the range of variation in the elements, which affect the domain, and the theory must specify their effects. This makes possible precise predictions. Today, it is especially this last criterion which is the hallmark of epistemic sciences. (pp. 38–39)

In terms of education, an ideal theory would allow for the control of instructional inputs to achieve consistently predictable learning outcomes. Since interpretation and intuition must play no part in this causal equation, teachers are seen as inconvenient variables. Teacher-proof curricular materials and scripted lessons are two manifestations of this worldview. So, too, is the quest for "best practices," which can be applied selectively given the variables of a particular educational situation. Despite much effort and huge expenditures of research dollars, such ideal educational theory remains elusive. (See, for example, Berliner, 2002; Burkhardt & Schoenfeld, 2003; Labaree, 1998; 2003.) Flyvbjerg (2001) contends that such ideal theory in the realm of human affairs is unattainable because of

a critical difference between natural and social sciences: the former studies physical objects while the latter studies self-reflecting humans and must therefore take account of changes in the interpretations of the objects of study. Stated in another way, in social science, the object [of study] is a subject. (p. 32)

Those who subscribe to the belief that the natural world and the social world are fundamentally different have challenged the privileged position of postpositivist, ideal theory. Drawing from different philosophical traditions (e.g., phenomenology, hermeneutics, aesthetics, symbolic interactionism, constructivism), such scholars see the consciousness and self-consciousness of human beings as integral to the knowledge generating process. The capacity of humans to make meaning of life events and to exercise a sense of agency in their lives is not considered a confounding variable to be controlled through research procedures. Rather, these interpretive acts of meaning-making lie at the heart of what is to be understood through qualitative—that is, interpretive—research. Thus, *interpretivism* or the *interpretivist tradition,* as Schwandt (2007) explains,

is occasionally used as a synonym for all qualitative inquiry, blurring important distinctions in intellectual traditions. More accurately, the term denotes those approaches to studying social life that accord a central place to *Verstehen* as a method of the human sciences, that assume that the meaning of human action is inherent in that action, and that the task of the inquirer is to unearth that meaning. (p. 160)

It is our contention that small-scale dissertation research conducted by individual educational practitioners is better suited to the task of unearthing the meanings inherent in classroom action than it is to the quest for ideal theory. The knowledge generated through such research is akin to what Flyvbjerg (2001) describes as Aristotle's concept of *phronesis*—"Ethics. Deliberation about values with reference to praxis. Pragmatic, variable, context-dependent. Oriented toward action. Based on practical value-rationality" (p. 57). Inherent in the concept of *phronesis* is a valuing of wisdom that can guide action within the complexities of unfolding experience. In critiquing the limitations of inquiry premised solely on a philosophy of knowledge, Maxwell (1992) argues for a philosophy of *wisdom:*

> The central task of inquiry may be said to be to devote *reason* to the growth of *wisdom*—wisdom being understood to be the desire, the active endeavor, and the capacity to discover and achieve what is desirable and of value in life, both for oneself and for others. (p. 219)

In a postmodern, pluralistic, democratic society, knowing what is of value for oneself and for others is never easy. Knowing what constitutes wise action within contexts of practice is also challenging and requires a posture that Schwandt (2001) characterizes as *responsiveness*. As Schwandt (2001) explains,

> To have the virtue of *phronesis* or responsiveness means that one is capable of using this perceptive capacity to reach a wise judgment. To grasp the importance of relevant details of a case at hand and to apprehend their interrelationships in human affairs requires the power of discernment . . . On one hand, one always attends first and foremost to the concrete or situational particulars of the immediate case. On the other hand, one brings into view principles, goods, criteria, standing comments, and the like. (p. 77)

This capacity for discernment echoes Eisner's (1991) concept of *educational connoisseurship*—that is, the capacity to apprehend and appreciate the nuances of educational practice; the capacity to see with an *enlightened eye*. Interpretive research, then, aims to generate theories that are *heuristic* in nature.[6] Such theories help the researcher and others discern, portray, and interpret more carefully the nuances of experience. (We return to this conception of theory in Chapters 9 and 13.)

This brings us back to the concepts of *ontology, axiology,* and *epistemology.* Axiologically, it is important for doctoral students to consider what forms of knowledge they see as valuable in informing (and perhaps improving) their own educational practice and the state of educational affairs. Ontologically, it is important to consider what they take to be the "reality of educational practice." Is it, for example, a technical craft that values the mastery of techniques or skill sets for the delivery of instruction? Or is education a moral and ethical endeavor in which the wisdom to "do no harm" is valued? Some might argue that this is a false dichotomy and that both forms of knowledge are of value. While this may be true, for purposes of conceptualizing a study, it is useful to sort out what form of knowledge claims one hopes to make by the end of the research process. If one hopes to prove the efficacy of particular instructional techniques or "best practices," then methods consistent with a scientific epistemology and ontology may be called for. If one is seeking insight into the practical consequences (or ethical implications) of educational policy or the meanings that participants ascribe to their educational experience, then methods consistent with an interpretive epistemology and ontology may be more appropriate.

Let us return for a moment to the anecdote recounted in Exemplar 5.1 where students began to ponder the value and legitimacy of knowledge claims emerging from what we characterize as *intimate studies.* In short, what knowledge claims could we make based on the responses of 18 students to our particular introductory course in qualitative research? Here is the gist of the thoughts we shared with the students:

> Over the past three or four years, we've been talking to faculty who are responsible for teaching introductory courses on qualitative research. All of us are struggling to understand how to help students make sense of such an enormous and complex field. At present, three or four different approaches seem to be used. For instance, some faculty assign published examples of really good qualitative research. Other faculty use a single textbook that illustrates a variety of qualitative research methods in education. Still others concentrate on a particular research method, such as case study or ethnography, or a particular methodological issue, such as data analysis or interviewing skills. Our approach is to have you read a variety of articles that will help you develop a framework for making sense of discourses that you might encounter as you continue your studies.
>
> So we might want to understand, "What happens with our approach to introducing qualitative research? How do students experience this type of course? What does it mean to them?" By asking for students' reactions, we might gain deeper insights into how our intentions for the course play out. The aim of our research would not be to *prove* that our approach is better than other approaches, or to say, "This is how all students react to learning about qualitative research." Rather, we would be trying to tease out the issues, questions, concerns, and so on that surface among students. We could use that information to make decisions about the design of our own course. But if we shared that information with other faculty, it might help them make planning decisions for their courses.

As we talked, we saw students nodding thoughtfully, as though our explanation made some sense. Essentially, we provided a conceptual frame for making sense of the data—a phenomenon to be studied within a particular context for purposes of informing the thinking of a particular discourse community. So, in this example, the frame consisted of a pedagogical dilemma (introducing qualitative research) within an educational context (a doctoral level course) with potential relevance to a particular audience (faculty engaged in similar teaching). Similarly, the conceptual frame for each dissertation is created by the student-researcher as he or she situates the "What?" "So what?" and "Who cares?" of the study within broader discourses. Without a well-reasoned and clearly articulated conceptual frame for the study, it is exceptionally difficult to engage in an interpretive knowledge-generating process.

Exemplar 5.2 illustrates what can happen when students with a newfound enthusiasm for qualitative research encounter those who value postpositivist or scientific research. On one hand, the physician's disdain for qualitative research may represent a mismatch of worldviews. On the other hand, it is possible that he may have been reading a study that lacked a clear and persuasive conceptual framework. If so, his negative critique of the study may have been entirely justified. Unfortunately, however, he used this one flawed study as a *warrant* for dismissing an entire research tradition. If the physician had encountered a poorly conceptualized and conducted quantitative study, would he have limited his critique to the study itself and still seen value in the broader tradition of postpositivist research? We raise this speculation, because we have seen similar reactions among faculty colleagues like the one who commented at the end of a dissertation meeting, "If *this* is qualitative research, then I don't want to serve on any more committees for qualitative dissertations." Our intent is not to discourage students from undertaking qualitative dissertation research, but to reinforce the importance of understanding the nature of *knowledge claims* that can persuasively say something of relevance beyond the circumscribed context in which a phenomenon is studied.[7]

Generating knowledge from such intimate studies entails a movement from the particular to the general, from the concrete to the abstract, from the idiosyncratic to the universal—in short, from the situational to the conceptual. The movement from the situational to the conceptual is a highly interpretive process dependent upon the researcher's capacity for making meaning from his or her research experience. For this reason, the researcher is not seen as a detached, objective observer of events. Rather, the researcher is actively engaged in an intersubjective and intrasubjective process of interpreting the meaning of events. It is in this sense that intimate qualitative studies fall within the tradition of interpretive, rather than postpositivist, inquiry.

---

**EXEMPLAR 5.2    A Student's Reflective Musings on Research Worldview**

I was really excited when I registered for this class [Introduction to Qualitative Research]. I was really looking forward to it, then I made an egregious error—I told a work colleague what I was studying this semester and got lambasted. POW!

You see, the doctor I work with is one of this country's most respected researchers in my field. He has published hundreds of peer-reviewed research articles in some of the most prestigious journals in medicine. He was the editor of a peer-reviewed journal that was "ruined" by qualitative research. He snarled, "There is no such thing as qualitative research. It is an oxymoron. I cannot believe that a journal would publish an article citing interviews with earthquake survivors who all say 'it was terrible' and call that research!" I really like and respect this doctor, so his critique really took the wind out of my sails.

*Authors' Commentary.* Time and time again, we hear similar anecdotes from students. We try to point out that such critics of qualitative research are often members of a different discourse community (or that they may have a valid criticism of shoddy qualitative research). Yet it is difficult for novice researchers to ignore such voices when the speaker is a member of one's field of study, a respected colleague, a mentor, or even a member of one's dissertation committee.

Student responses to such remarks vary. At one extreme are those who lapse into an "ain't it awful" state of perpetual complaining that feeds the folklore about the unacceptability of qualitative dissertations. Others, however, use such comments as a spur to their own thinking and writing.

Repeatedly, students have told us that voices of harsh critics like this physician echo in their ears each time they sit down to write some facet of their study. Some find it debilitating and second-guess the "acceptability" of every word they write. Others use the imagined criticism to clarify issues that they need to think through more carefully.

Because ontological, axiological, and epistemological assumptions are among our most deeply held beliefs, it is very difficult to recognize them through casual musing. As Exemplar 5.2 illustrates, unexpected and possibly painful critiques by others may serve to bring one's assumptions to the surface and precipitate a crisis of understanding. Approaching the dissertation with only vague and unexamined impressions of what constitutes legitimate scientific research runs the risk of *scientism* (e.g., Lather, 2004b) resulting in a study that fails to meet the criteria of either good quantitative or good qualitative research. It is for this reason that we urge students to watch vigilantly for indicators of the worldview and knowledge claims that are shaping their understanding of research.

Dan, for example, taught high school science. He enrolled in our introductory course on qualitative research because he thought he might gather some qualitative data about his students' reactions to studying science. From the first class to the last, Dan kept asking, "How can I be certain that the qualitative data will be reliable and valid?" Given Dan's field of study, his beliefs about what constitutes "real research" were understandably embedded in the inquiry tradition of the natural sciences. As much as he struggled, he could not reconcile contextually grounded data from his students with broader truth claims of science. This was a strong indicator of Dan's worldview and offered him a good starting point for shaping a study within a more postpositivist tradition.

Sometimes students talk about "choosing" a worldview. Jesse, a newcomer to qualitative research, continually talked about selecting the worldview that would fit the problem to be studied. This circumvented a more introspective posture that might have helped him to understand how the assumptions constituting his own worldview shape his understanding of "the problem" in the first place. Other students will ask if it is possible to change one's worldview. A book edited by Heshusius and Ballard (1996) offers insightful accounts by noted researchers and evaluators of their transition from positivist to more interpretivist worldviews. Tananis (2000, 2006) coined the term *epistemorph* to describe her own struggle to shift from positivist to interpretivist worldview and to explore the issues that arose in this process. (See also Piantanida, Tananis, & Grubs, 2004.)

Because scientific epistemology and ontology are so entrenched in Western culture, it often takes quite a bit of time and effort to gain even glimmers of insight into assumptions that can exert their grip throughout the dissertation process. It can be useful to consider what forms of knowledge one is drawn to. For example, some individuals are drawn to and value knowledge that is orderly, has a reasonable degree of certainty, shows causal or correlational relationships, and allows for prediction. This form of knowledge is assumed to be generated through scientific methods that meet criteria of objectivity, reliability, validity, and generalizability. Research aiming toward this form of knowledge places great emphasis on procedures and procedural precision. Replicability of results when following the same procedures is important. It assumes that we can get to the essence of a phenomenon by reducing it to its component parts and eliminating the extraneous or confounding variables so that we are left with the most relevant or central variables. Valid knowledge holds up across contexts.

Other individuals are drawn to ambiguity and seek understandings that are provisional and tentative. Knowledge is assumed to be subjective (or intersubjective) as it is inevitably constructed within contexts and shaped from socio-historical-political-gendered, ethnic, and/or racial perspectives and positions. Perceived patterns within and across contexts are considered *heuristic,* not causal or correlational. While attention to research procedure is important, procedural precision and replicability are less important than diligence in seeking out multiple perspectives and the quality of insight brought to bear on the data.

Such thumbnail sketches of the difference between postpositive and interpretive views of research serve only as a starting point for gaining insight into one's worldview. Repeatedly, we have seen students come to the deepest understanding of their own worldview as they struggle to generate knowledge claims from their data. It is in this part of the process that the full import of procedural decisions sinks in as students come to grips with what their data represent, what claims can be warranted by the data, and how the data and claims can be portrayed. Although this reckoning often comes late in the process, it is never too soon to begin grappling with worldview issues as suggested by the questions in Reflective Interlude 5.1.

Hopefully, this brief consideration of worldview has called into question the postpositivist assumption of a researcher's detached objectivity. In the next chapter, we look more closely at the role of the researcher in generating interpretive knowledge claims.

## Reflective Interlude 5.1

### How Can I Come to Understand the Worldview Through Which I Am Conceptualizing and Conducting My Dissertation Research?

It is difficult to explore one's worldview in the abstract. Here are three suggestions for beginning to surface, name, and examine the ontological, epistemological, and axiological assumptions that may be shaping your dissertation.

1. Return to any notes that you have made about potential topics for your dissertation during previous reflective interludes. If you have already generated potential questions for study or statements of intent, look closely at the language you have used to express your thinking. Does your language suggest that you are trying to prove the efficacy of a particular technique, strategy, or program? Are you assuming that what you do as a practitioner can or should bring about predetermined outcomes in others? Are you interested in best practices?

Please note that it is not uncommon for students who are interested in more interpretive work to use more postpositivist language early in the learning process. It is a default language for many. So here are some questions to ask yourself:

- Am I comfortable with this language or does it make me uneasy?
- Do I value order and certainty in my educational practice or am I energized by the spontaneity arising from interactions with and among students?
- Do I see ambiguity as a problem to be eliminated or as a condition to be explored and understood?
- Do I believe that educational outcomes can and should be predictable or that each learner makes meaning of educational experiences in his or her own way?
- Do I believe that what I do as a teacher directly effects what students learn, or do I see my own efforts as one among many influences that shape learning?

*(Continued)*

(Continued)

2. As you read literature on your topic, take special note of articles and books to which you are drawn. What do you find appealing about the reference? Is it the research results, or the method used, or the theoretic perspective? Try to analyze the assumptions that underpin these pieces. Those with which you resonate are likely to point toward your worldview.

3. As you read literature on research methods, take special note of the language used by various authors. See if you can differentiate language that is more expressive of postpositivism from that which is more interpretive (or critical, or postmodern, etc.). When you encounter articles or books that click with you, that help to clarify something that has been puzzling or confusing you, look carefully for assumptions that underpin the authors' views. Similarly, when an article or book leaves you scratching your head and saying, "Huh?" take note of the underlying assumptions. These can help you to begin sorting out the assumptions you are bringing to your research project.

- What counts as legitimate knowledge? Must legitimate knowledge be scientific knowledge?
- In what ways is legitimate knowledge generated?
- If I assume that legitimate knowledge must be objective, reliable, and valid, upon what basis do I make this assumption?
- If I assume that legitimate knowledge can be subjective or intersubjective, upon what basis do I make this assumption?
- When studying a phenomenon, how should I position myself in relation to that which I want to know or understand?
- Is knowledge of the human world generated through the same methods as knowledge of the natural/physical world?
- What do I take to be real; what is the nature of reality; what are the possibilities and limits of knowing reality?
- What is my way of being in the world; how is it that I want to be in relationship with others?
- Upon what bases do I construct my understanding of the world and of others?

## NOTES

1.   In grappling with what it means to do legitimate research, it is useful to consider differences between a modern versus postmodern worldview. See, for example, Anderson, 1990; Angus & Langsdorf, 1993; DeMarrais & LeCompte, 1999; Freeman, deMarrais, Preissle, Roulston, & St. Pierre, 2007; Howe, 1998; Scheurich, 1997; St. Pierre, 2002a, 2002b.

2.   Logical positivism, as a philosophy of science, dominated the research thinking of the physical sciences from the 1920s to 1950s. Schrag (1992) contends that this philosophy enjoyed about a 30-year life "before the weight of criticisms of their doctrines caused its internal collapse" (p. 5). The vestiges of positivism still remain in many discourses on educational research.

3. For accounts of the rise of positivist science see Crosby (1997). Crosby discusses the epochal shift to quantitative perception in Western European thought during the late Middle Ages and Renaissance. This shift, he contends, made modern science, technology, business practice, and bureaucracy possible. By the 16th century, more people were thinking quantitatively in Western Europe and eventually this way of thinking gained dominance throughout the world. Crosby's work helps to explain the quantitative mind-set that we hold even today as a dominant way of thinking. Other useful references on this point are Flyvbjerg (2001), Heshusius & Ballard (1996), and Shapin (1996).

4. Within the discourses on qualitative research there are scholars who take the position that distinguishing between *qualitative* or *quantitative* is neither necessary nor useful. Other scholars argue, as we do, that these approaches are fundamentally different and must be understood as distinctive traditions. For a brief introduction to these positions, see Ercikan & Roth, 2006; Salomon, 1991; Yanchar & Williams, 2006.

5. It can be helpful to consult dictionaries such as *The Penguin Dictionary of Critical Theory* (Macey, 2000) and *The Sage Dictionary of Qualitative Inquiry* (Schwandt, 2007). Neither of these dictionaries offers precise definitions. Rather, they help to put key concepts into a historical perspective by relating the concept to an evolving school of thought. With these brief summaries as a preliminary orientation, students might then be in a better position to pursue additional resources to gain the in-depth understanding needed to conceptualize their inquiries. Other dictionaries that offer overviews of important concepts include Blake & Hanley (1995) and Bullock, Stallybrass, & Trombley (1988). See also Given (2008), *The SAGE Encyclopedia of Qualitative Research Methods*.

6. The concept of *heuristic* is important in qualitative research. The *Fontana Dictionary of Modern Thought* (Bullock, Stallybrass, & Trombley,1988) offers the following definition: "In social science, the term is used especially to characterize conceptual devices such as ideal types, models, and working hypotheses which are not intended to describe or explain the facts, but to suggest possible explanations or eliminate others" (p. 382). In brief, it is a conceptual representation of a phenomenon that conveys the complexity of the phenomenon in a way that makes it more accessible for discourse, deliberation, and inquiry. In the scientific tradition, hypotheses are one form of heuristic. In the arts and humanities, heuristics might take the form of visual or verbal images or metaphors.

7. Since 2000, the debate about what constitutes legitimate educational research has resurfaced with a renewed intensity. Although echoes of the old argument tinge the new rhetoric, the debate seems to have shifted from the academic to the political realm. Fueled by the passage of No Child Left Behind and the publication of the National Research Council's (2002) report, *Scientific Research in Education,* these debates center around policy mandates for scientifically-based educational methods, a hegemonic reprivileging of scientific educational research, and contested conceptions of science. (See, for example, Barone, 2001; Denzin & Giardina, 2006; Eisenhart & Towne, 2003; Jacob & White, 2002; Lather, 2004a, 2004b, 2007; Lather & Moss, 2005; Maxwell, 2004; Mayer, 2000, 2001; Shavelson & Towne, 2002; Slavin, 2002, 2004; St. Pierre, 2002.) It goes beyond the scope of this book's purpose to analyze the contested positions on the question of what constitutes legitimate educational research. Rather, we want to alert doctoral students to the debates so that they can carefully consider what it means to propose and conduct a defensible qualitative dissertation within this contentious milieu.

# 6

---

# *Situating Oneself in the Inquiry*

## Key Concepts

Disciplinary Perspective            Resonance

Positionality                       Self as Instrument

Reflection—Conceptual               Stance

Reflection—Introspective            Theoretical Sensitivity

Reflection—Recollective             Voice

Within a postpositivist epistemology, reliable and valid knowledge claims are assumed to be researcher independent as well as generalizable across contexts. Ideal scientific theories strive to articulate universal laws that endure across time. In contrast, interpretivist epistemology assumes that knowledge claims are researcher dependent and provisional within particular contexts. In recent years this has led to an almost formulaic recitation of the researcher's *positionality*—his or her gender, ethnicity, sexual orientation, socioeconomic status, professional role, and other attributes of position or perspective that might influence how the meaning of events is construed. Our intention is not to be dismissive of such descriptions of one's position in relation to the phenomenon under study. Quite the contrary, the position and perspective of the researcher is so important it deserves more than perfunctory attention. Therefore, we begin this chapter with a discussion of the researcher as an *instrument of inquiry*. This is followed by a brief consideration of the role of *reflection* in interpretive inquiries as well as attention to *voice* and *stance*. A final consideration in this chapter is the role of *disciplinary perspective* in shaping the researcher's understanding of the phenomenon under study.

# SELF AS INSTRUMENT OF INQUIRY

When novice interpretive researchers are trapped in a postpositivist notion that rigorous techniques for data collection lie at the heart of the inquiry, they can invest a great deal of energy in deciding whether to use questionnaires, audio- or videotapes, interviews, focus groups, or other techniques for gathering and recording information about experiences related to the intent of the inquiry. However, these are only ancillary tools in interpretive inquiries. At the heart of interpretive inquiry is a researcher's capacity for encountering, listening, understanding, and thus "experiencing" the phenomenon under investigation. Rather than assuming the traditional stance of a detached and neutral observer, an interpretive inquirer, much like a tuning fork, resonates with exquisite sensitivity to the subtle vibrations of encountered experiences. As Eisner (1991) observes, "The self is the instrument that engages the situation and makes sense of it. It is the ability to see and interpret significant aspects. It is this characteristic that provides unique, personal insight into the experience under study" (p. 33).

In discussing the nature of creativity, psychoanalytic theorist Rollo May (1975) offers another way of thinking about the capacities associated with the *self as instrument:*

> The receptivity of the artist must never be confused with passivity. Receptivity is the artist's holding him- or herself alive and open to hear what being may speak. Such receptivity requires a nimbleness, a fine-honed sensitivity in order to let one's self be the vehicle of whatever vision may emerge. . . . It requires a high degree of attention, as when a diver is poised on the end of the springboard, not jumping but holding his or her muscles in sensitive balance for the right second. It is an active listening, keyed to hear the answer, alert to see whatever can be glimpsed when the vision or words do come. It is a waiting for the birthing process to begin to move in its own organic time. It is necessary that the artist have this sense of timing, that he or she respect these periods of receptivity as part of the mystery of creativity and creation. (pp. 80–81)

While Eisner and May are writing about an aesthetic sensibility, a similar perspective was offered by the two scholars who formulated grounded theory as a research method in sociology. They used the concept of *theoretical sensitivity* to describe the wisdom that researchers bring to an inquiry (Glaser, 1978; Glaser & Strauss, 1967). Even though they are writing in the field of sociology and their use of masculine pronouns is somewhat dated, their conception of *theoretical sensitivity* helps to further illuminate the concept of *researcher as instrument of inquiry:*

> Once started, theoretical sensitivity is forever in continual development. It is developed as over many years the sociologist thinks in theoretical terms about what he [sic] knows, and as he queries many different theories on such questions as What does the theory do? How is it conceived? What is its general position? What kinds of models does it use? Theoretical sensitivity of a sociologist has two other characteristics. First, it involves his personal and temperamental bent. Second, it involves the sociologist's ability to have theoretical insight into his area of research, combined with an ability to make something of his insights. (Glaser & Strauss, p. 46)

Some students erroneously assume that they should not mention any background information because doing so will show that they are biased. By pretending no prior involvement in the focus of a prospective study, they hope to demonstrate objectivity. This notion is sometimes reinforced by erroneous messages from advisors who do not understand the nature of interpretive research. For example, an international student had begun to conceptualize a dissertation that would examine issues that students from China confront as they adjust to higher education in the United States. Upon hearing this, a professor said, "But you can't study that! You're a Chinese woman studying in the United States." Similarly, when Pam Krakowski (2004, 2006) shared the idea of studying her own pedagogy with other art educators, several of them responded, "That's not a good idea. You couldn't be objective about your own teaching." Such comments are indicative of a postpositivist, science-based research tradition. They are not applicable in an interpretive study, which is one example of why it is so important for doctoral students to understand the epistemological and ontological contexts of their proposed study.

Developing oneself as instrument entails taking a careful look at what one brings to an interpretive inquiry. The Reflective Interludes suggested throughout *The Qualitative Dissertation* are meant to encourage greater self-awareness and self-disclosure. By this we do not mean that students are obliged to bare their souls or engage in pseudo-psychoanalysis. Rather, it means cultivating a heightened awareness of one's worldview, experiences, preconceptions, biases, current knowledge, and so on, and recognizing how these may expand or constrict one's capacity for being open to and resonating with the experience of the study. Exemplars 6.1 and 6.2 illustrate two facets of developing self as instrument—acknowledging one's relationship with potential participants in the study and acknowledging one's personal (possibly traumatic) experience with the phenomenon under study.

Integral to the notion of *self as instrument* is a capacity for reflection. Through reflection, the interpretive researcher *resonates* with both the specific and the significant aspects of contextualized experience. To understand what this means, it is helpful to consider, albeit briefly, the notion of reflection. (See also Piantanida, in press.)

---

### EXEMPLAR 6.1    Developing Self as Instrument: Developing a Capacity to Listen

As I finished my doctoral coursework, I had the opportunity to become the first Resident in Education at a large urban teaching hospital. Patterned after the concept of medical residencies, this position was intended to provide an intensive learning experience for educators who wanted to practice in hospital settings. At the time, this was a fairly new arena of practice for educators, and part of my responsibility was to articulate what contribution educators might make to the hospital. In order to understand the role, I visited other educators in health care facilities around the city. From this experience, I had tremendous respect for some of my peers, and complete disdain for others. So when I began to formalize plans for my dissertation, I knew there were certain people I should interview for my study of hospital-based education, but I couldn't stand the thought of talking to them. As I worked and reworked the statement of intent for the study, I kept imagining myself transcribing certain interview tapes and wanting to throw up. Finally, I came to an intent for the study that moved me out of this terribly judgmental place. Inside, I felt genuinely curious to hear from each and every person. For me, this was the moment I moved from a self-serving stance to a posture of inquiry. That freed me to proceed with the study. I still had my own views and beliefs about education. But they would no longer result in an immediate rejection of perspectives that didn't match my own.

### EXEMPLAR 6.2    Developing Self as Instrument: Issues of Vulnerability and Authenticity

For her dissertation, Carol was contemplating a case study of learning disabilities among nursing students. As she talked, it was clear that she felt passionately about this issue and, as a nurse educator, felt that certain instructional supports were essential for these students. Several faculty with whom she had met for guidance on doing a case study sensed that her interest stemmed from a personal struggle with attention deficit. When some gentle prodding confirmed this was indeed the case, the following conversation ensued between Carol and Maria.

"Carol, you might begin by writing your own story, explaining what brings you to this study."

"But," Carol protested, "wouldn't telling my story make the study biased? Wouldn't the results be more acceptable if I research the issue in a more detached, depersonalized way?"

"Another—more interpretive—way to look at the issue of your personal experience is that it allows you to resonate more deeply and fully with the information you gather from participants in your study. Rather than contaminating the study, your perspective can help you to make more sensitive, more powerful, interpretations."

"Yes," Carol reluctantly conceded. "But I'm not sure I want my story to be in the dissertation."

"Writing your story doesn't automatically mean you have to include it in the dissertation," Maria countered. "It allows you to see more clearly the biases and preconceptions you are bringing to the study. Once you know that, you can make a conscious choice about whether to share the biases directly through your story or indirectly through a more descriptive summary. Either way, the study becomes more authentic, because you acknowledge the position from which you are studying the issue."

*Authors' Commentary.* Although Carol kept insisting that she wanted to do an interpretive inquiry, she brought to the dissertation at least a vaguely held notion that *real* research is objective. Also embedded in her comments is the assumption that her personal

*(Continued)*

//// Exemplar 6.2 (Continued)

experience will contaminate the study, and that distancing herself from the study will somehow neutralize the effects of the trauma she had experienced as a student with a learning disability. (The belief that it is somehow possible to separate ourselves from our life experiences presents some thorny ontological questions. To begin exploring such questions, see Heshusius, 1994.)

Carol's reluctance to share her personal story touches on another issue, what we have come to see as a "dark side" of interpretive inquiry. The stance of self as instrument requires a degree of vulnerability. Upon further discussion, Carol acknowledged experiencing discrimination at the hands of insensitive teachers. Telling her story entailed making public the pain of humiliation engendered by this discrimination.

Thus, the suggestion that Carol write her story was meant to discharge some of the heretofore unspoken pain that underlies the intent of the study. It was hoped that this would help her shift from a crusading stance to a more deliberative posture of inquiry. That said, there is a danger of pressing students to reveal more of themselves than they feel comfortable doing. So the issue of self-disclosure requires considerable care on the part of both student and committee members.

### Reflective Interlude 6.1

**In What Ways Am I Developing Myself as an Instrument of Inquiry?**

- What has been my reaction to the idea of *self as instrument* of inquiry? Does it seem jarring or exciting? Does it engender skepticism or curiosity?
- What does my instinctive reaction to the idea of *self as instrument* of inquiry tell me about my worldview—about my epistemological assumptions?
- Has any of my coursework or professional experience helped me to develop a capacity for active listening? Can I find or create opportunities for further enhancing my capacity for active listening?
- When I look at the ideas represented in my dissertation puddles, what have I done to broaden and deepen my understanding of them?
- What strategies do I use to challenge my own interpretation of events, to gain different perspectives, to recognize my biases and prejudices, to surface and recognize my taken-for-granted assumptions?

## CONCEPT OF REFLECTION

We confess some reluctance about introducing the concept of reflection because in some circles it has been trivialized to the point of cliché. Yet with the publication of Donald Schön's book *The Reflective Practitioner* in 1983, the notion of *reflection* resurfaced as an important thread in the discourses of education and educational research. Schön draws from the work of John Dewey, in particular his notion of "education as reconstruction of experience" in *Democracy and Education* (1916). Dewey suggests that although experience is the context from which learning emerges, it is the act of reconstructing *the meaning* of experience that actually yields learning. Reconstructing the meaning of experience is the interpretive act at the heart of interpretive inquiry. Although we do not want to reduce reflection into discrete subcomponents, it can be helpful to think about reflection as encompassing the following aspects:

*Recollective Reflection:* In this form of reflection, researchers resonate with the situational aspects of encountered experience, recalling the specific details of what happened, when it occurred, and who was involved. In this sense, *reflection as recollection* is a matter of giving an account of experience.

*Introspective Reflection:* In this form of reflection, researchers look within, examining their own mental and emotional responses to encountered experience. A word of caution is in order here, for this aspect of reflection seems to conjure up images of touchy-feely, highly emotive, self-confessional writing. When students try self-consciously for such a "feeling" effect, the results can seem quite solipsistic—little more than a litany of the researcher's likes and dislikes, a self-serving justification of preconceptions, or a judgmental pronouncement about the rightness and wrongness of others' points of view. At their best, however, introspective reflections can yield insights and questions that move the researcher's thinking beyond specific details to the significant aspects of encountered experience. (In Exemplar 6.1, Maria's account of her own judgmental biases toward colleagues and her struggle to work through those biases is an example of how introspective reflection can help a researcher to cultivate greater theoretical sensitivity.)

*Conceptual Reflection:* In this form of reflection, researchers begin to connect their recollective and introspective reflections with broader theoretical concepts and issues. Instead of relying on their immediate or instinctive interpretation of events, researchers begin to draw upon formal and informal discourses to (re)construct the meaning of experiences in relation to the purpose of their inquiry. In *conceptual reflection,* interpretive researchers are resonating simultaneously with the specific experiences of the study, with existing discourses, and with the phenomenon under study.

On more than one occasion, students have remarked that they engage in quite a bit of reflection—ruminating on the events of their day as they drive home, take a shower, work out at the gym, or engage in various household tasks. While such ruminations may serve as useful starting points for reflection, they are often too casual or haphazard to support a rigorous inquiry. Creating stable records of one's reflections through writing supports the recursive nature of the inquiry process by allowing the researcher to revisit and critique ideas over time. Keeping a personal-professional journal (Holly, 1989; Janesick, 1997, 1998; Street, 1990, 1995) is an excellent strategy for developing a disciplined approach for tracking one's recollections, introspective musings, and evolving insights. Our work with several students has also alerted us to the importance of considering multiple modalities for engaging in reflection. Wendy Milne (2000, 2006), for example, describes her process of sketching ideas not only to record experiences but also to generate conceptual reflections. Meath Conlan (2006) uses "doodling" as a mode of processing impressions and information. After an initial rejection of these visual images by a more traditionally minded faculty supervisor, Meath found a deliberative community that affirmed the importance of his drawing, which then figured prominently in his final dissertation. The point to keep in mind is that reflection should not be considered some vague notion but rather an integral part of how we make meaning of our experiences. Claiming one's own proclivities for meaning-making and integrating those proclivities into one's inquiry process can add depth and richness to an interpretive dissertation. Before responding to the questions in Reflective Interlude 6.2, it might be useful to review the Case Examples in Section Four to get a feel for the rigorous reflection associated with dissertation research.

### Reflective Interlude 6.2

#### What Is My Capacity for and Mode of Reflection?

- Do I have a systematic process for recording significant events?
- What is the nature of this process and how does it fit into the routines of my life?
- What type of process or processes do I engage in when I am trying to sort out an experience, to figure out what happened, or discern what something meant?
- In what ways do the lenses through which I see experiences shape my interpretations of their meanings:
  - Gender
  - Sexual orientation
  - Race, ethnicity
  - Socioeconomic status
  - Political ideology
  - Profession and professional experience
  - Personal history
  - Worldview (epistemology, ontology, axiology)

## STANCE AND VOICE

The discussion in this chapter is meant to highlight the importance of thinking through one's relationship with that which is under study. Too often, we see students default to a vaguely held belief that a researcher must assume a detached, objective stance and write in a neutral, depersonalized voice. The following comments made during a dissertation meeting flag a classic carryover from this science-based approach to research. One faculty committee member commented,

> I found this dissertation to be one of the best I've read in a long time. I'm troubled by it, but I really liked it. It read almost like a novel in places. I really like it . . . but I'm troubled by the first person references. I tell my students, *Never* use "I."

A second member then said that he found the writing to be refreshing, but that the candidate was lucky to have committee members who were sympathetic to her approach. "Not all faculty," he added, "would be so understanding."

The idea that the candidate is lucky and that the dissertation is acceptable only because of a sympathetic committee misses the point. The student was working within an interpretive tradition of personal narrative and would have created an epistemological and ontological inconsistency by writing in the third person. Thus, the difference in addressing the researcher's relationship to that which is researched goes back to issues of ontology, epistemology, and axiology. From a postpositive perspective and the quest for ideal/scientific theory, it is assumed that knowledge exists apart from the researcher. As mentioned above, an interpretive perspective assumes that knowledge is *positional*—that is, generated by individuals within specific contexts and from particular positions. Within the interpretive perspective, then, writing in the first person is one way to make explicit the positional nature of the knowledge claims. (For additional perspectives on the issue of voice, see, for example, deMarrais, 1998; Hargreaves, 1996; Knoeller, 1998; Tierney & Lincoln, 1997.)

Schwandt (1999), in arguing for the relational nature of understanding, draws upon the work of existential philosopher Hans Georg Gadamer to distinguish among three different stances that a researcher might take.

> The first is to try to discover the typical behavior of the Other and to make predictions about others on the basis of experience. We thereby form what we call knowledge of human nature. Here, we treat the Other as an object in a free and uninvolved way, much as we would any other object in our experiential field. (p. 458)

This stance is reflective of a worldview that assumes understanding of human beings and human affairs can be attained through the same methods as knowledge of the physical world. In a second way of understanding, Schwandt goes on to explain, "the interpreter claims to know the Other from the Other's point of view, and even to understand the Other better than she understands herself" (p. 458).

As qualitative research gained in legitimacy, a number of researchers stated the intent of their study as "giving voice" to a silenced or marginalized group (e.g., minority students, homeless individuals, individuals with mental disabilities). Many such studies seemed to be premised upon this second view of understanding in which a researcher could come to know others and thus speak for them. Although experienced researchers soon began to recognize the problematic nature of such claims of understanding the Other, we encounter many doctoral students who believe their studies will represent the views of others. Often, this belief manifests in teacher comments such as "I know what my students like," or "I want to show that students really learn through this instructional technique." The implication is that a teacher can gain some degree of certainty about students as Other. Such a stance of certitude is challenged by the third form of understanding, which

> requires an openness to experience, a willingness to engage in a dialogue with that which challenges our self-understanding. To be in a dialogue requires that we listen to the Other and simultaneously risk confusion and uncertainty both about ourselves and about the other person we seek to understand. (p. 458)

Notice this third view of understanding brings us back to the *self as instrument* of inquiry, which entails a capacity to resonate with experience and with Other. Of particular importance is the idea of "challenging our self-understanding," because in practice-based research, professionals are calling into question what they think they already know. Sternberg and Horvath's (1995) view of expert practitioners working "at the leading edge of their own knowledge and skill" (p.13) offers a way to think about the potential value of intimate studies carried out within specific contexts of educational practice. Presumably, those who have attained a high level of expertise are familiar with the knowledge base of the profession. They are familiar with literature, "best practices," and nuances of classroom life. In short, they have already worked hard to heighten their theoretical sensitivity. Knowing a great deal of what is possible to know, they are still willing to call that knowledge into question for themselves. In doing so, they open themselves to confusion and uncertainty, creating the possibility of transforming their *way of being* educational practitioner. Such transformations, when they happen, represent a reforging of one's ontological stance. With a different stance, new perspectives, new insights, and new understandings might be gained—the type of wisdom that Flyvbjerg (2001) and Schwandt (2001) associate with Aristotle's notion of *phronesis*. It is this type of understanding, of wisdom, that is shared through interpretive dissertations and in the process might allow others to discern more carefully the intricacies of practice and to see new possibilities for their way of being in practice.

### Reflective Interlude 6.3

**What Is My Response to the Idea That I Am Not Only an Instrument of Inquiry but That My Understandings Are Also the Subject of Inquiry?**

- What is my response to the idea of experts working on the leading edge of their knowledge and skill? How does this view of expert teaching (or administering or other educational practice) fit with my reasons for pursuing a doctorate? Was I assuming that the purpose of doctoral education was to add more techniques and methods to my educational toolbox? Did I enter doctoral study expecting to find solutions to existing problems? Does it surprise or perplex me to think that a purpose of doctoral education and the dissertation is to learn a process for studying problems more deeply; to complicate my understanding of educational practice?
- Revisit your responses to the Reflective Interlude question on worldview in light of the discussion about stance. Ask yourself, What assumptions about the relational nature of understanding are reflected in my responses? Which of the three forms of relationship between researcher and researched seem embedded in my responses on worldview? If I am interested in conducting an interpretive inquiry, to what extent will I need to challenge and rethink my initial assumptions about the objective and/or subjective nature of legitimate knowledge?

As may be apparent, this type of practice-based, interpretive inquiry exudes an auto-biographical quality. That is one reason why writing in the third person would be disingenuous. The dissertation author is representing the understandings that he or she has gained through the inquiry. Writing in the first person is one way of acknowledging the position and perspective from which such interpretive knowledge claims have been generated and are offered. Bullough and Pinnegar (2001) offer a number of extremely important guidelines for enhancing the quality of autobiographical writing in self-study research. Of particular importance is the connection between personal experience and broader discourses:

> It is the balance between the way in which private experience can provide insight and solution for public issues and troubles and the way in which public theory can provide insight and solution for private trial that forms the nexus of self-study and simultaneously presents the central challenge to those who would work in this emerging area. (p. 15)

One of the ways in which to begin making such connections between the private and the public is to consider the *disciplinary perspective* one may be bringing to a study.

## Reflective Interlude 6.4

### With What Stance and Voice Am I Writing?

How do I imagine situating myself in relationship to that which I am studying? For example, which of the following stances or combination of stances might I assume?

- Distant, objective, observer
- Relational, participant, subjective, intersubjective, collaborative/cooperative, intimate
- Teacher, professional, practitioner
- Scholar, inquirer
- Citizen
- Advocate, cheerleader, zealot
- Expert
- Skeptic, critic, connoisseur

In what tone of voice do I imagine writing? For example,

| | |
|---|---|
| Reflective | Argumentative |
| Contemplative | Critical |
| Thoughtful | Temperate |
| Curious | Fair |
| Tentative/speculative | Humorous/ironic |

*(Continued)*

(Continued)

| | |
|---|---|
| Passionate | Serious, earnest |
| Dispassionate | Invitational |
| Authoritarian | Assertive |
| Didactic | Certain |
| Strident | Polemical |

What type of stances and what kind of voices are apparent in my current professional and academic writings?

## DISCIPLINARY PERSPECTIVE

Within the academy, disciplines are branches of instruction and learning characterized by formal, theoretical bodies of knowledge. These branches reflect the ways in which humans strive to comprehend various aspects of the world (e.g., the physical, social, emotional, mental, spiritual).[1] Academic disciplines (e.g., natural sciences, social sciences, arts and humanities, philosophy and religion) reflect these major quests for human understanding. Within the various disciplines are long-standing traditions of ways of coming to know the world and human experience within it. Beginning at the undergraduate level and intensifying at the graduate level, students become socialized into their chosen discipline's ways of thinking. Successful students learn not only bodies of existing knowledge but also what questions occupy the attention of scholars in their discipline, what constitutes legitimate forms of knowledge, and what research methods are credible.

Education is a particular form of human experience, and those striving to understand its nature have drawn from various discipline-based ways of knowing to guide their research. For example, those with an interest in the social and cultural aspects of schooling have drawn from sociology and anthropology. Those with an interest in human behavior and learning have drawn from psychology, biology, and, more recently, neurosciences. Those with an interest in schools as public institutions have drawn from economics and political science. Those with an interest in the moral and ethical nature of education have drawn from philosophy and theology.

As the field of education has matured, a number of educational theorists and researchers have argued that it, too, can be viewed as a discipline in its own right (e.g., Belth, 1965). Richardson (2006) outlines three schools of thought on the disciplinary status of education:

> The first suggests that since education borrows from and combines with other, more traditional, disciplines and often focuses on practice, it should not be

called a discipline but a field of study or a second-level discipline. Using the same rationale (that many areas within education bring together a traditional discipline within an educational frame), the second school of thought calls education an "inter-discipline." And because education has its own set of problems, questions, knowledge bases, and approaches to inquiry, a third school of thought pushes for accepting education as a discipline. (p. 253)

It is useful for doctoral students to ask themselves which of these views on the disciplinary status of education they hold. Do they, for example, want to claim the stance of a social scientist working knowledgeably within the traditions of sociology or anthropology? Do they want to claim the stance of artist, philosopher, or historian working within the traditions of the arts and humanities? Or do they want to claim the stance of educator who understands and draws upon traditions of research that fit the nature of education as a particular human enterprise? The question of disciplinary perspective, however, may not be as clear-cut as the preceding questions imply. Many skillful educational researchers are drawing from multiple disciplinary traditions. Indeed, it is not uncommon for doctoral students in education to have completed a discipline-based bachelor's and/or master's degree. Some doctoral programs require formal study in a cognate area. As Reflective Interlude 6.5 suggests, it is useful to consider any formal grounding one might have in discipline-based inquiry, rather than contemplating *research tradition* in some vague or abstract way. (So, too, is considering what counts as knowledge within specific content areas, e.g., math, science, history, language arts. See, for example, Kelly, Luke, & Green, 2008.)

Considering disciplinary orientation can be helpful in sorting through the wealth of literature that is now available on qualitative research. Authors of various texts are writing from disciplinary perspectives and publications are often geared to scholars in particular disciplines. Recognizing these differences can help students locate information about qualitative research that is likely to be most useful for their work. At times, it may be useful to draw upon references from disciplines and fields of study outside of education. Brickman (1982) and Flood (1979), for example, write about qualitative research in relation to history; Alasuutari (1995) writes about researching culture; Crotty (1996) writes about phenomenology in nursing research; and Fischer (2006) writes about qualitative empirical research in psychology. Sometimes, such references provide important insights into qualitative research, and so they should not be overlooked. Yet care should be taken to link these insights to educational research, and the growing body of literature related directly to research in education should play a central role in students' deliberations (e.g., Best & Kahn, 2006; Bresler & Ardichvili, 2002; Cohen, Manion, & Morrison, 2007; Conrad & Serlin, 2006; Crossley & Watson, 2003; Gall, Gall, & Borg, 2007; Lowe, 2006; McGinty, 2000; McMillan & Schumacher, 1997, 2006; Opie, 2004; Suter, 2006). Again, it is important to review such books with an eye toward their underlying epistemological stance in order to find those references most relevant to one's own research plans.

Also important in considering self as instrument of inquiry are various talents one might draw upon in conducting a study. We turn to this aspect of interpretive research in the next chapter.

**Reflective Interlude 6.5**

**What Disciplinary Perspective(s) Am I Bringing to Bear on My Study of Education?**

Do I see myself as a social scientist or as an educator engaged in research?

When I enter into my study will I claim the stance of educator, or social scientist, or subject-matter specialist? What are the implications of my stance for the way in which I conduct my study, the discourses to which my study will contribute, and the nature of the knowledge I will generate through my study?

What formal grounding do I have in the arts, humanities, social sciences, or other disciplines that may be influencing my thinking about the nature of education, the nature of my educational practice, and the types of issues and questions about education that interest me?

In what ways has my prior education socialized me into seeing certain forms of research as "legitimate"?

What ways of knowing might I want to draw upon for my dissertation, and what will be the rationale for doing so?

What is my perspective on the question of education's status as a discipline or field of study? Upon what am I basing this perspective?

# NOTE

1. Those who want to explore the notion of academic disciplines might start with Phenix (1964), Roberts & Good (1993), and Vidich & Lyman (1994).

# 7

Rethinking the
Concept of Method

## Key Concepts

Conventions of a Genre                    Mixed Method

Method as Technique                       Research Genre

Method as Logic-of-Justification          Self-Conscious Method

## FROM METHOD AS
## TECHNIQUE TO RESEARCH GENRE

Over the past 30 years, the number of books on planning a dissertation has been steadily increasing. So, too, has the number of books on qualitative research. (See Sample Reference Lists 7.1 and 7.2 for illustrative listings of both the former and latter resources.) In fact, sorting through the wealth of resources that are now available can be quite daunting. This is one reason we stress the importance of understanding one's own research proclivities. Because the residue of postpositivism often operates as a default conception of research, we offer an interpretivist perspective as a contrast. To begin shifting one's mindset from a postpositivist to an interpretive perspective, it is useful to consider a distinction that Smith and Heshusius (1986) made between two different ways of thinking about method:

Method can be characterized in at least two ways. The most commonly encountered meaning is *method as procedures or techniques.* In this case the term invokes the kinds of "how-to-do-it" discussions long found in introductory textbooks on quantitative inquiry and, more recently, in a number of basic textbooks on qualitative inquiry . . . The second characterization of *method is as "logic-of-justification."* . . . The focus here is not on techniques but on the elaboration of logical issues and, ultimately, on the justifications that inform practice. . . . This conceptualization involves such basic questions as, What is the nature of social and educational reality? What is the relationship of the investigator to what is investigated? And How is truth to be defined? (p. 8; italics added)

The idea of *logic-of-justification* may be disconcerting to those who equate qualitative research with a specific technique of data collection (e.g., interviews) or data analysis (e.g., coding). Clinging to this equation impedes the type of learning needed to conceptualize and conduct an interpretive dissertation. By analogy, if one wants to play football, one needs to learn more than passing or blocking. *Understanding football* comprises a complex constellation of rules that govern what counts as legitimate and successful play. A very different constellation of rules governs what counts as legitimate play in other sports, such as baseball, soccer, hockey, or golf. The descriptor *qualitative research* can be considered analogous to *ballgames.* Particular types of qualitative research—what we call *research genres* (e.g., case study, grounded theory, ethnography, action research, narrative)—can be considered analogous to specific sports. Each has its own conventions and internal logic.

If we move from the realm of sports to that of literature, the distinctions among various genres may not be as widely or readily recognized. Even so, many individuals are able to distinguish a play from a poem, a short story from a novel, a documentary from a science fiction film. Here, too, each type of literary work has certain characteristics of form that distinguish it as a particular genre. Creating a movie script entails one set of conventions that is quite different from creating a collection of poems or essays.

## Sample Reference List 7.1

### Dissertation Research

**PLEASE NOTE:** Some of these books may be more suitable for guiding traditional, postpositivist dissertations; others may have a chapter or section devoted to qualitative research; still others may have qualitative research as their primary focus. If possible, it would be advisable to check the table of contents before purchasing any of these guides.

Allison & Race, 2004

Biklen & Casella, 2006

Bryant, 2004

Castetter & Heisler, 1984

Davis & Parker, 1979

Fitzpatrick, Secrist, & Wright, 1998

| | |
|---|---|
| Glatthorn, 2005 | Ogden, 2006 |
| Herr & Anderson, 2005 | Paltridge & Starfield, 2007 |
| Locke, Spirduso, & Silverman, 2007 | Roberts, 2004 |
| Lunenburg, 2007 | Rudestam & Newton, 2007 |
| Manheimer, 1973 | Smyth, Hattam, & Shacklock, 1997 |
| Mauch & Birch, 1983 | Sternberg, 1981 |
| Meloy, 2002 | Thomas, 2003, 2007 |

It is our contention that each *genre* of qualitative research, like various forms of ball-games and literary works, embodies its own set of conventions. These conventions have evolved over time within particular philosophical and disciplinary traditions. Language specific to the genres has evolved to express the conventions. Football, for example, uses a language of *downs, goalposts, holding, kickoff,* and *referees,* while baseball uses a language of *strikes, home runs, bases, outs,* and *umpires.* The language for discussing a poem differs from the language for discussing novels. Those who want to understand a particular genre of qualitative research need to understand the language used to discuss the conventions of that genre. *Going into the field,* for example, falls within the language of ethnographic inquiry. *Meditation* falls within the language of spiritual inquiry. To talk as though *going into the field* is a defining characteristic of all qualitative research genres would be comparable to saying that all ballgames are defined by *running bases.*

It is possible that some readers are thinking, "Yes, but one could say that all ballgames share a common characteristic in that they all use equipment." While this is true, such a general commonality offers little insight into how the game is played. In other words, the logics of the game are not made clear or explicit at that level of generality. Learning to "do" a qualitative dissertation entails drawing upon the conventions of a genre to construct the logic-of-justification. Just as no one would expect to master the conventions of any particular ball game by reading one or two books, it is unrealistic for doctoral students to think they will master the conventions of a particular research genre without devoting themselves to the serious study of the genre. As Exemplar 7.1 suggests, serious study takes time, so the earlier one becomes immersed in literature on qualitative research the better.[1]

As students begin to appreciate this perspective, several questions immediately arise: How do I know which genre to study? Which one should I choose? Where do I find a list of all my options along with some guidelines for choosing the best one for my study? Shouldn't the choice of "method" be based on the research question I am asking? On one hand, these seem like perfectly reasonable questions. But let us push beneath them by extending our sports analogy just a little further. How did Tiger Woods decide to play golf? Did he consider the full range of sports available to him and then use a set of objective criteria to decide upon golf as his sport of choice? Did Wayne Gretzky or Mario Lemieux peruse the same list of sports options and select hockey? Did Michael Jordan settle on basketball through such a process?

///  EXEMPLAR 7.1    Understanding One's Research Proclivities

In the spring of 1997, Maria and two members of our dissertation study group participated in a day of academic celebration sponsored by our school of education. During
a panel presentation about various types of study groups, a faculty member asked,
"I've been trying for a long time now to understand the difference between quantitative and qualitative paradigms. I'd like to know, especially from the students' point of
view, how long did it take you to learn the qualitative paradigm?" A study group
member who had completed a dissertation in 1993 responded, "I don't think it was so
much a matter of learning a paradigm as understanding more clearly the paradigm
I've always worked in."

*Authors' Commentary.* In our experience, it takes doctoral students about a year to a year
and a half to understand their research proclivities well enough to explain the logics of
their study in a well-reasoned proposal. This is a year or so from the point at which one
seriously enters into the study of qualitative research.

Again, we can imagine some readers thinking, This comparison is totally unfair. First,
these sports figures are virtuosos; they knew as children that they had a talent for a particular sport. Besides that, they had chances to develop their innate talents. And, there are
lots of athletes who play more than one sport as children and even in high school, then
choose to concentrate on a particular sport when they play college ball. Given this, why is
it so unrealistic for us to want to choose from a list of options—especially when research
is an area that we know so little about?

Sadly, we concede that those of us who grow up in the United States are far more likely
to be aware of the range of sports genres than we are of research genres. Given the residue
of positivism and the pervasiveness of postpositivist assumptions about knowledge,
other modes of knowing were, for many years, obscured.[2] Since the mid-1970s, however,
this has no longer been the case, and doctoral study provides opportunities for students
to raise their awareness of multiple research traditions and genres. A growing number
of books are collections of a variety of research genres (see Sample Reference List 7.3).
Sample Reference List 7.5, at the end of this chapter, offers a sampling of references on
particular genres.

Because one might spend a professional lifetime developing expertise in any one of
these genres, imagining that one can master all—or even several—of the possibilities
prior to embarking on a dissertation can be counterproductive. Therefore, although an
awareness of various qualitative genres is prudent, concentrating on one or two approaches
is probably more feasible and productive for doctoral students facing the dissertation.
Shaping one's study entails determining which genre might be most relevant. Often, this
is determined more by one's instinctive proclivities for coming to know than by the topic
or question to be studied.

# CLAIMING ONE'S RESEARCH GENRE

Conventional wisdom holds that one chooses one's research method based on the question to be studied. In one sense this is true. Yet we contend that an affinity for a particular research genre (and beyond that research tradition) predates any specific decisions about strategy, method, or technique. In all likelihood, this fundamental choice is based on an elusive mix of personal orientation, worldview, interests, and talents. To return to our sports analogy, we occasionally see an athlete who plays two professional sports. Michael Jordan's foray into baseball is a notable example and provides an interesting object lesson. Despite Jordan's superb physical conditioning, his mental discipline, and his willingness to master new skills, in the end he achieved only moderate success in baseball and ultimately returned to the sport for which he was uniquely talented.

## Sample Reference List 7.2

### Qualitative Research

**PLEASE NOTE:** Some of these books may approach qualitative research from a more traditional, postpositivist worldview; others may offer multiple perspectives. If possible, it would be advisable to check the table of contents before purchasing any of these guides.

Bessant, Hill, & Watts, 2003

Bogdan & Biklen, 1992

Brizuela, Stewart, Carrillo, & Berger, 2000

Cohen, Manion, & Morrison, 2007

Conrad & Serlin, 2006

Crabtree & Miller, 1992

deMarrais, 1998

Ely, Anzul, Friedman, Garner, & McCormack Steinmetz, 1991

Glesne & Peshkin, 1992

Golden-Biddle & Locke, 2006

Hammersley, 1989

Hesse-Biber & Leavy, 2006

Kamberelis & Dimitriadis, 2005

LeCompte, Milroy, & Preissle, 1992

Lichtman, 2006

Marshall & Rossman, 2006

Mason, 2002

Maxwell, 2004, 2005

Maykut & Morehouse, 1994, 2004

Mazzei, 2007

McCullough, 2004

McLaughlin & McIntyre, 2006

Miller & Fredericks, 1996

O'Donoghue & Punch, 2004

Page, 2000

*(Continued)*

(Continued)

| | |
|---|---|
| Rossman & Rallis, 2003 | Somekh & Lewin, 2005 |
| Schram, 2003 | Stephens, 2007 |
| Schratz, 1993 | Van Maanen, 1983 |
| Sherman & Webb, 1988 | Willis, 2007 |
| Silverman, 2004 | Willis & Neville, 1996 |

Similarly, we contend that doctoral students are more suited to engage in some modes of inquiry than in others. They bring to the dissertation a fundamental orientation for learning and knowing. Their worldview draws them to particular types of phenomena, causes them to ponder certain types of questions, and inclines them toward a particular research genre. Professional experience and expertise equip them with important and potentially useful skills.

### Sample Reference List 7.3

**Collections of Readings on Qualitative Research Genres**

Conrad & Serlin, 2006

Creswell, 2007

Denzin & Lincoln, 1994, 2003a, 2003c, 2005

Eisner & Day, 2004

Fischer, 2006

Green, Camilli, & Elmore, 2006

Jaeger, 1997

Kamberelis & Dimitriadis, 2005

Lancy, 1993

Moustakas, 1994

Patton, 2001

Rose, 2007

Short, 1991

Tobin & Kincheloe, 2006

Van Maanen, Dabbs, & Faulkner, 1982

Willis, Smith, & Collins, 2000

Consider, for example, the dissertation crafted by Marilyn Llewellyn (1998) around the concept of spirituality as pedagogy (Exemplar 7.2). For quite some time, Marilyn pondered which research genre could most appropriately frame her study and which logic-of-justification could guide her thinking. Working within a scientific tradition and using a scientific research genre (e.g., a quasi-experimental study) to gain insights into the nuances of a spiritual pedagogy struck Marilyn as a logical inconsistency. Genres grounded in the arts and humanities (e.g., personal narrative, autobiography) or social sciences (e.g., case study, ethnography)—although possibilities—did not feel quite right. As Marilyn struggled with this issue and tried to imagine how she would carry out the study, the notion of spiritual inquiry gradually came into focus.

In all likelihood, the language in Exemplar 7.2 may strike many readers not only as unfamiliar but also completely inappropriate for a research endeavor. We chose this example precisely for its power to challenge preconceptions. To understand how spiritual inquiry can be considered legitimate, it is important to place this research genre into a personal context and research tradition. It is relevant to know that Marilyn has an extensive background in theological studies, is a member of a religious community, and lives her commitment to spirituality on a daily basis. Furthermore, she draws upon the writings of recognized scholars in theology and philosophy to connect her study to a long and respected tradition of spiritual inquiry. The language that Marilyn uses to create the logic-of-justification for her inquiry comes not from the scientific tradition but from philosophical and theological traditions. Working in an interpretive, rather than postpositive, tradition also allows Marilyn to draw upon her knowledge of hermeneutics and humanistic curricula.

Most of the ideas that appear in the conceptual outline in Exemplar 7.2 were present from the outset of Marilyn's thinking about her dissertation. During her early deliberations, however, Marilyn could not see the interconnections among the various ideas. Nor did she think to draw upon her existing store of knowledge about contemplation, meditation, *kairos,* and so on. By entering into ongoing deliberation—with herself and others—Marilyn slowly began to tap into her knowledge, using it to express what she wanted to study, why the study would be important, and the mode of inquiry she would follow. At this point, she was able to claim a tradition and genre that gave her a clearer sense of how she could proceed.

---

%%% **EXEMPLAR 7.2    Crafting a Study Consistent With One's Worldview, Personal Orientation, and Unique Talents**

*Dissertation Title.* Bringing Forth a World: Spirituality as Pedagogy

*Intent of the Study.* To articulate a personal understanding of spirituality as pedagogy and to portray the transformative possibilities in being and learning together in such a way as to make them accessible to other educators who are interested in spirituality as pedagogy.

Guiding Research Questions:

1. What brought me to the study of spirituality as pedagogy?

2. What life events have helped to shape my spirituality and pedagogy?

3. How is my spirituality and pedagogy manifested in "Bringing Forth a World"?

4. Through a series of meditative writings, how can I generate and articulate deeper understandings of spirituality as pedagogy?

5. How can I portray essential lessons of spirituality as pedagogy?

*Research Genre—Spiritual Inquiry.* As I entered into this inquiry, a language emerged that allowed me to best express the ways that I engaged in this process. The inquiry process itself came to embody the spiritual. *Kairos,* contemplation, meditative writings, and exegesis comprise the spiritual inquiry. In constructing the inquiry in this way, I drew on a language and created a context for the inquiry that was faithful to what was under study. (For a more detailed account of Marilyn's process of claiming her inquiry genre, see Llewellyn, 2006.)

---

Rene offers an interesting contrast to Marilyn. The impetus for Rene's inquiry into school restructuring stemmed from her involvement in a special reform effort at a local school district. Formally trained as a program evaluation specialist, having well-honed skills in the systematic collection of extensive qualitative data, and having access to a setting rich with complexity, Rene was ideally positioned to ground her study within a genre of evaluation. Unfortunately, Rene approached her dissertation with a fixation on research techniques and a disinclination toward deliberation. Consequently, she did not take time to consider how she could best use her background to guide her study. In the end, her dissertation contained several significant conceptual flaws stemming from disconnections between her procedures and the knowledge claims she put forward.

It is our contention that the earlier one begins exploring various research genres, the better able one will be to identify those that are most compatible with one's way of making meaning of experience. The questions suggested in Reflective Interlude 7.1 offer a starting point for such explorations.

---

**Reflective Interlude 7.1**

**To What Research Genres Am I Drawn?**

- As a child, what subjects did I most enjoy in school? What did I find enjoyable about them?
- What drew me to the field of education? What drew me to my particular subfield within education?
- As an undergraduate, in what fields did I major and minor? What drew me to these fields? What did I enjoy about them?
- What led to my choice of a graduate program; what did I enjoy about my graduate studies?
- As I read the research literature in my field, what forms of research do I find particularly exciting, enlightening, meaningful?
- As I think about the scholars in my field, whose work do I admire and find useful? In what research genres do these scholars work?
- What type of research can I imagine myself doing?
- What form would I like my dissertation to take? What form or forms can I imagine for my dissertation?

---

## CONVENTIONS OF A GENRE AND LOGIC-OF-JUSTIFICATION

Let us return once again to our sports analogy to explore the relationship between *research genre* and *logic-of-justification*. The logic-of-justification within a particular form or genre of research is akin to the strategies that coaches lay out for winning a game. Coaches have tremendous leeway in shaping their strategies as long as they adhere to the underlying logic and rules of the game. For example, a football coach is at liberty to use many different plays to achieve a first down, but dribbling the ball down the field is not among them. Developing the logic-of-justification for a qualitative dissertation in education entails an understanding of conventions within a particular genre. The conventions of narrative inquiry, for example, are different from the conventions of quasi-experimental research. Similarly, the conventions of ethnography differ from those of biographical or historical research. At this point, however, our sports analogy becomes strained beyond the point of usefulness. While sports tend to be governed by very explicit and precise rules, the conventions of any given research genre tend to be more fluid. So, even within a particular genre (e.g., case study, narrative, ethnography), different conventions might pertain within different disciplines or fields of study. Case studies, for example, take different forms in education, medicine, law, and business. Similarly, the conventions of a genre may change over time just as new scholars push the forms in new directions.[3]

Thus, it is important to realize that understanding the conventions of a genre is not the same as looking for rules to follow in order to properly conduct a study. The genre of grounded theory offers a particularly powerful illustration of this point. Since Glaser and Strauss (1967) published *The Discovery of Grounded Theory*, a robust and, at times, acrimonious debate has arisen about what constitutes the "real" method. Students who approach this contentious literature in the hope of finding the "right" way of doing grounded theory are likely to be frustrated because no resolution of the disagreements is in sight. Recognizing that a debate is in progress, understanding the epistemological and methodological pressure points that are being contested, and sorting through which ideas might best guide one's study are more productive uses of a student's time than trying to figure out what rules must be followed in order to do "real" grounded theory.

If the conventions of a genre do not offer prescriptive formulas for conducting research, then what do they offer? The answer lies in Smith and Heshuisus's (1986) distinction between method as technique and method as logic-of-justification. The conventions of a given genre provide the starting point for constructing the logic-of-justification for one's study.

# CONSTRUCTING A LOGIC-OF-JUSTIFICATION

In an interpretive dissertation, the researcher is obliged to go beyond descriptive answers to the *what, when, how,* and *who* questions of the study. Embedded in these descriptions should also be explanations of *why.* For example, it is not unusual for us to read something like, "I'm going to do a qualitative study. I plan to interview teachers at my high school." This may be followed by myriad details about how the teachers will be recruited and selected; where the interviews will be conducted; how long each interview will last; whether the interview will be taped, and so on. What remains unaddressed is the purpose of the study—what it is the student wants to understand—which is crucial for providing a logic-of-justification for more fundamental questions such as the following:

- What is meant by *a qualitative study,* and why is that an appropriate study to do?
- Why is it appropriate to use an interview to collect information from teachers?
- What interviewing conventions will be followed, and why are those particular conventions appropriate?
- Why is it appropriate to interview teachers from one's own school, and what rationale will be used to determine which teachers and how many?
- What purpose is served by taping the interviews, and what do these interviews represent as a form of knowledge?

Addressing these types of *why* questions in a substantive way entails an understanding of the research traditions (e.g., postpositivism, interpretivism) and the research genres (e.g., ethnography, grounded theory, narrative, case study, arts-based) in which the researcher is situating the study. This is where the conventions of a genre come into play, offering a rationale for the procedural choices that the researcher is making. For example, two-hour interviews with 15 teachers are unlikely to provide the breadth and depth of data usually associated with the extensive fieldwork of ethnography. Yet interviewing 15 teachers who had participated in a particular educational project might be very congruent with the conventions of case study. If the interviews are conducted as part of a narrative study, some experts would insist that the interviewees should have an opportunity to review and approve the transcripts; other experts would not. Immersion in the literature on a particular research genre allows for a twofold understanding of (a) the conventions associated with the genre and (b) variations among conventions within a genre.

This understanding allows a doctoral student to offer a persuasive rationale for the procedures of his or her study. Within an interpretive tradition, there is likely to be one rationale for the procedures by which the researcher will capture the details of experiences within a particular context. There is likely to be another rationale for how the researcher will theorize from and about this contextually grounded experience. The conventions of a research genre allow the researcher to warrant these interpretive moves.

Kilbourn (1999) characterizes the ability to articulate the conventions that one is following as *self-conscious method* and argues for this attribute as a key criterion for judging the quality of a dissertation:

> It [self-conscious method] should betray the author's sensitivity to concerns of epistemology, to concerns about the connection between method and meaning. An author should be aware of the bearing of method on what the study has to offer in ways that move beyond glib nods to the horrors of positivism or the abuses of narrative. The author should explicitly demonstrate an awareness of his or her role as a writer with a biography. The author should, in some way, make clear her or his sensitivity to the conceptual and methodological moves made during the conduct of the study and in the presentation of the study as a readable document. The author should show an awareness of the bearing of those moves on the overall integrity of the work, should be able to give *good reason* for making them. (p. 28)

---

**Criterion for Judging Interpretive Dissertations**

**Self-conscious method**—Providing explicit rationales for conceptual and methodological decisions within the conventions of one's research genre; making visible one's process for thinking through the interconnected facets of the inquiry; understanding the epistemological and ontological implications of one's decisions; providing a persuasive logic-of-justification

---

Seale (1999), while cautioning against an over fixation on epistemological awareness, nevertheless suggests that "methodological discussions of the quality of research, if they have any use at all, benefit the quality of research by encouraging a degree of awareness about the methodological implications of particular decisions made during the course of a project" (p. 475).

This focus on methodological awareness echoes Smith and Heshusius's (1986) argument for conceiving of method as *logic-of-justification*. From our perspective, these logics make clearer the procedures used to move from the situational to the conceptual. To a great extent, the persuasiveness of a dissertation rests upon the researcher's ability to articulate his or her logic-of-justification in a clear and cogent manner. Of critical importance is the extent to which the procedures fit with the knowledge-generating assumptions embedded in the genre claimed for the study. Mismatches between these assumptions and the research procedures create logical inconsistencies or conceptual flaws that compromise the credibility of the study.

Constructing a logic-of-justification—coming to self-conscious method—are exceptionally difficult aspects of conceptualizing and conducting an interpretive study, especially in places where postpositivist language operates as the default mode for discussing qualitative research. Before turning to this issue of language in the next chapter, we want to address an issue that has surfaced in the last few years—the issue of *mixed method*.

## THE CONCEPT OF MIXED METHOD

The concept of *mixed method* has gained increasing prominence since the early 1990s (see Sample Reference List 7.4). As is the case with so many other concepts in qualitative research, *mixed method* has multiple meanings that, from our perspective, tend to undermine its usefulness in constructing a coherent, interpretive logic-of-justification. In its narrowest sense, *mixed method* is often used to refer to studies that combine numeric and linguistic data. In such instances a *mixed data* study might be a more apt descriptor. Perhaps one of the questions most frequently asked by students in our introductory course on qualitative research is, If I do a qualitative study, can I include numbers? When asked to elaborate on what they have in mind, students typically respond that they are thinking of supplementing a survey with several interviews. When pushed a bit further, students are seldom talking about *survey* as a research genre with its own conventions. Rather, they are using it in a more casual way to mean a written questionnaire, which is likely to include numbers in the form of rating scales. So the issue is not whether one can mix numbers with interview data. The issue is how either form of data would serve the intent of the study within a given genre. If survey research is viewed as a postpositivist genre with conventions for statistical sampling as well as for the validation of questionnaires, it is likely that the researcher is seeking more generalizable knowledge claims. What purpose, then, would be served by qualitative data from a few supplemental interviews? As Richardson (1994) suggests, the incorporation of the qualitative data often devolves into "human filler"—snippets of comments meant to illustrate a point that has presumably already been warranted by the quantitative data. If a study is not going to conform to the statistical sampling conventions of survey research as a genre, then one is likely to be considering a more intimate, interpretive study. In that case, the researcher might be gathering multiple forms of data to gain a more robust picture. A small, purposeful sample of individuals might be asked to complete a questionnaire to provide some standardized demographic information and then be interviewed to probe more deeply into the nature of their experience. These multiple forms of "mixed data" might serve to warrant different conceptual points within a given genre such as grounded theory

——————  ——————

### Sample Reference List 7.4

**Mixed Method**

Creswell, 2002

Creswell & Plano-Clark, 2007

Johnson & Christensen, 2007

Johnson & Onwuegbuzie, 2004

Mertens, 2005

Morgan, 1998

Morse, 1991

Opie, 2004

Tashakkori & Teddlie, 2003

Taylor, 2005

Thomas, 2003

Yanchar & Williams, 2006

or case study or narrative. Within an interpretive tradition, we see no value in referring to multiple forms of data as *mixed method*. We urge students to think very carefully about the epistemological implications of simply adding some "quantitative data" to create an aura of legitimacy. If generalized knowledge claims are being put forward without adequate attention to issues of statistical sampling, simply calling it *qualitative research* will not magically transform it into a legitimate study.

Another way in which mixed method may be used is to refer to multiple sources of data. For example, a study may call for gathering perspectives on an issue from different groups (e.g., teachers, students, and parents; doctors and patients; social workers and clients). Again, we see no advantage to labeling this *mixed method*, because the conventions of many genres (both postpositivist and interpretive) provide for the collection of information from multiple sources. The more fundamental and important question is the purpose to be served by the data from multiple sources. In a postpositive tradition, the aim may be to "triangulate" perspectives—to seek corroboration of the "facts" of an event or consensus on an issue. In an interpretive tradition, however, the aim is often to push for diverse perspectives to enrich the possible interpretations of an event. Being able to articulate what purpose is served by data from each source is part of constructing the logic-of-justification.

A third way in which we hear *mixed method* being used is to describe multiple techniques for collecting data. This sense of the term is often connected with the first two as, for example, the use of a written questionnaire and interview with one group of study participants, or a combination of classroom observation of students and questionnaires with principals, or individual interviews with teachers and focus groups with parents. We suspect that those who define *method* as technique are more likely to find the concept of *mixed method* to be useful. However, when *method* is seen as logic-of-justification then the conventions within a genre are likely to provide a more than adequate rationale for mixing multiple techniques for collecting multiple forms of data from multiple sources. For example, within the genre of case study, a researcher might (1) collect and analyze archival records documenting a series of meetings that led to the adoption of a particular policy, (2) interview individuals who participated in the meetings, (3) distribute questionnaires to those responsible for implementing the policy, and (4) hold focus groups with those who were to benefit from the policy. All of these forms and sources of data collection can be justified under a single genre of case study and would not need to be considered a mixed method.

Still another meaning of *mixed method* is the combination of multiple research genres. A common variation of this is a mixing of narrative and grounded theory. When considered carefully, the researcher has often equated *narrative* with the collection of stories and has equated *grounded theory* with a procedure for coding data from the stories. From our perspective, this is an impoverished understanding of both *narrative* and *grounded theory* as research genres. Embedded within the genre of narrative are conventions for interpreting the meaning of stories. Grounded theory as a genre for theorizing from experience comprises far more than procedures for coding. And certainly the conventions of grounded theory would allow for the collection of stories as a form of data. We would make a similar critique of a simplistic mixing of "narrative" and "ethnography," or "case study" and "survey." It is quite possible that thoughtful researchers might have very important reasons for drawing upon multiple research genres within the frame of a given study. But to do so naively without an understanding of what can be accomplished within the frame of a given genre is, it seems to us, the antithesis of self-conscious method.

A final justification for *mixed method* is expressed by the seemingly reasonable argument that there is a value in understanding complex phenomenon from multiple worldviews. There is no way to refute the merits of this position. Nor would we want to. We do, however, offer a cautionary consideration. It is one thing to undertake such a "mixed method" study—or more accurately multi-study project—as part of a well-funded, team effort. It is quite another to attempt such an effort as a doctoral student who may be working full time and in the process of learning how to do research. One reason for engaging in a comprehensive review of existing literature is to bring multiple streams of research to bear on one's dissertation topic. In this way, it is possible to illuminate the topic from multiple research traditions while setting the stage for the particular approach to one's dissertation. Students who are wedded to the importance of studying a topic from multiple worldviews might also consider teaming with one or more peers to undertake companion dissertations.

For convenience, we used the term *data* to explore the difficulties we see associated with the concept of *mixed method*. In the next chapter, we invite readers to recognize the concept of *data* as part of postpositivist language and to consider an alternative concept of *text* as more congruent with interpretivism. We contend that crafting text lies at the heart of constructing an interpretive dissertation, and the conventions of a particular genre guide the writing process.

## Sample Reference List 7.5

### Various Qualitative Research Genres

**PLEASE NOTE:** The references cited here should be considered only as starting points for more thorough and exhaustive searches that would be appropriate for a dissertation.

*Action Research.* Altrichter, Feldman, Posch, & Somekh, 2007; Birmingham & Wilkinson, 2003; Cahnmann-Taylor & Siegesmund, 2007; Carson & Sumara, 1997; Coghlan & Brannick, 2004; Crockett, 2006; Greenwood & Levin, 2007; Hendricks, 2006; Herr & Anderson, 2005; Kemmis & McTaggart, 1988; Koshy, 2005; McNiff, Lomax, & Whitehead, 2003; McNiff & Whitehead, 2006; McTaggart, 1997; Mertler, 2006; Phillips & Carr, 2006; Reason & Bradbury, 2006; Sagor, 2005; Schmuck, 2006; Stringer, 2007; Taylor, Wilkie, & Baser, 2006; Whitehead & McNiff, 2006; Whyte, 1991

*Appreciative Inquiry.* Preskill & Catsambas, 2006; Reed, 2007

*(Continued)*

(Continued)

*Arts-based Research/Aesthetic Inquiry (Including the Literary, Visual, and Performing Arts).* Barone, 1995, 2000, 2001; Barone & Eisner, 1997; Diamond & Mullen, 1999; Finley & Knowles, 1995; Milne, 2000, 2006; Mullen & Finley, 2003; Norris, 2000; Stout, 2006; Sullivan, 2005

*Autobiography/Self-Study.* Bullough & Pinnegar, 2001; Mitchell, O'Reilly-Scanlon, & Weber, 2004; Samaras, 2006

*Biography.* Clough, Goodley, Lawthom, & Moore, 2004; Davies & Gannon, 2006; Kridel, 1998

*Case Study.* Hamel, 1993; Hancock & Algozzine, 2006; Merriam, 1997; Mullen, 2005; Stake, 1995, 2003; Yin, 1993, 2003

*Discourse Analysis.* Rogers, Malancharuvil-Berkes, Mosley, Hui, & Joseph, 2005

*Essay (Personal, Philosophical, Speculative).* Logsdon, 2000, 2006; Piantanida, 2006; Schubert, 1991

*Ethnography.* Alasuutari, 1995; Atkinson, 1990; Clough, 1998; Daly, 1997; Denzin, 1997; Eisenhart, 2001; Erickson & Stull, 1997; Fetterman, 1998; Gordon, 2002; Jackson, 1987; McCall, 2003; Mienczakowski, 1995; Noblit, 1999; Noblit, Flores, & Murillo, 2004; Spindler, 1982; Spindler & Hammond, 2006; Stewart, 1998; Tedlock, 2003; Van Maanen, 1995; Woods, 1996 (See also the journal *Ethnography and Education.*)

*Focus Groups.* Krueger & Casey, 2000; Morgan, 1996; Stewart, Shamdasani, & Rook, 2007

*Grounded Theory.* Annells, 1996; Charmaz, 2003; Corbin, 1998; Corbin & Strauss, 1990; Glaser, 1978, 1992, 1994, 1998; Glaser & Strauss, 1967; Grubs, 2006; Miller & Fredericks, 1999; O'Connor, Netting, & Thomas, 2008; Piantanida, Tananis, & Grubs, 2004; Rennie, 1998; Stern, 1980, 1994; Strauss & Corbin, 1998

*Hermeneutic Inquiry.* Caputo, 1987; Kerdeman, 1998; Palmer, 1969; Smith, 1991

*Heuristic Inquiry.* Douglass & Moustakas, 1985; Moustakas, 1990, 1994; Stabile, 1999, 2006

*Memoir.* Zinsser, 1995

*Mythopoetic.* Haggerson, 1988; Holland & Garman, 1992; Leonard & Willis, 2008

*Narrative.* Barone, 1992; Beverley, 2003; Bochner, 1997; Brodsky, 1987; Bruner, 1986; Brunner, 1994; Burdell & Swadener, 1999; Carter, 1993; Casey, 1995–1996; Clandinin et al., 2006; Coles, 1989; Conle, 2001; Connelly & Clandinin, 1990, 1991; Hanninen, 2004; Hopkins, 1994; Jalongo & Isenberg, 1995; Josselson & Lieblich, 1993; Lyons & LaBoskey, 2002; Mitchell, 1981; Nash, 2004; Phillips, 1994; Polkinghorne, 1988, 1997; Reason & Hawkins, 1988; Ricour, 1984; Ritchie & Wilson, 2000; Robinson & Hawpe, 1986; Sandelowski, 1991; Webster & Mertova, 2007

*Phenomenology.* Leonard & Willis, 2008; Moustakas, 1994; van Manen, 1984; Willis, 1998; Willis, Smith, & Collins, 2000

*Portraiture.* Dixson, Chapman, & Hill, 2005; English, 2000; Lawrence-Lightfoot & Hoffman Davis, 1997

*Secondary Analysis.* Hammersley, 1997; Hinds, Vogel, & Clarke-Steffen, 1997; Jensen & Allen, 1996; Morse, 1994; Reinharz, 1993; Szabo & Strang, 1997; Thorne, 1998

*Social Cartography.* Goodman, 2003, 2006; Paulston, 1993, 1995, 1996; Paulston & Liebman, 1994

*Spiritual Inquiry.* Huebner, 1995; Llewellyn, 1998, 2006; Macdonald, 1995

---

# NOTES

1.  Some universities require all doctoral students to take at least one or two courses in both quantitative and qualitative research. Others may require a course or two on "ways of knowing" or "disciplined inquiry." This can be a useful instructional strategy for giving students an overall orientation to different research traditions and genres. It would be unwise, however, for students to assume that completing such courses adequately prepares them to implement a particular research method. Using such courses to sort through one's own research proclivities and find a direction for further study may be more productive.

2.  Similarly, given the privileging of standardized curriculum outcomes, "objectivist" assessment measures, and prescriptive pedagogical methods, children's innate modes of knowing may receive little nurturing. The *Reggio Emilia* philosophy of education, for example, holds that there are 100 languages that might be nurtured in children. (See, for example, Edwards, Gandini, & Forman, 1998; Guidici, Krechevsky, & Rinaldi, 2001.)

In an educational system committed to acknowledging and supporting each child's innate ways of knowing, students might reach the later stages of doctoral work with a clearer sense of their own research proclivities. That said, it is possible to increase one's awareness of various research genres and to begin (re)claiming one's own ways of making meaning.

3.  Given the dynamic nature of research genres, the conventions of literary, visual, and performance arts offer a more useful analogy than sports. Over time, for example, what constitutes a novel, play, short story, or poem has changed. The novels of Faulkner, for example, differ from those of Dickens. The poetry of T.S. Eliot bears little resemblance to the sonnets of Shakespeare. Similarly, the images of the impressionists differ from the landscapes of the romantic painters. Likewise, modern dance differs from classical ballet and ballroom dancing. In writing about the evolutionary nature of scientific inquiry, Thomas Kuhn (1970) describes how one model of science replaces earlier, more flawed models. The push for more definitively encompassing theoretic explanations drives not only what questions are investigated but also what constitutes appropriate methods for studying these questions. In the realm of art, however, multiple modes of representation and expression can coexist. Although modern artists or writers or choreographers may no longer follow the conventions of earlier eras, they generally still understand and value what those earlier forms represent. In a sense, earlier forms have made possible new variations and radical departures from what has gone before. This building upon and departing from earlier conventions within a genre is far more characteristic of interpretive genres of research than Kuhn's notion of scientific paradigms.

# Rethinking the Concept of Data

## FROM DATA TO TEXT

Several years ago at the American Educational Research Association (AERA) annual meeting, Noreen attended a session chaired by Jim Scheurich that focused on possible rapprochement between qualitative and quantitative inquiry. The major question of the session was "Could disparate research traditions find similar research space?" During the session words such as *reliability, validity,* and *trustworthiness* became contested terms. After much debate, a member of the audience stood up and said firmly, "One term we all agree on and share is *data*—we all base our truth claims on data." A few people shook their heads, and Noreen found herself adding to the debate by saying, "Well, although we don't dismiss the notion of *data,* we don't find it particularly useful either. We tend to use *text* to name the written responses and results of our various research activities."

To some, distinguishing between *data* and *text* may seem like quibbling over "mere semantics." For interpretivists, however, this distinction points to important assumptions about the possibility of directly encountering and knowing the "reality of human experience." Schwandt (2007), in discussing three ways to think about text in qualitative work, references a poststructuralist understanding of the concept that is relevant to our discussion. Poststructuralists "hold that *everything* (life experiences, events, relationships, activities, practices, cultural artifacts, and so forth) is a text" (p. 289).

Although we may encounter and apprehend the world in preconscious and preverbal ways, the act of expressing these encounters—even to ourselves—imposes a form and meaning upon them. The form and meaning are not inherent in the details of the encounter per se but rather are constituted through acts of interpretation.

Two objections are often raised in response to such a "subjective" form of knowing. First, someone with postpositivist leanings might say, "Well, if you jumped from the top of a 10 story building, there is an indisputable reality waiting for you at ground level. There is such a thing as gravity and that is not just some interpretation." We leave it to philosophers to debate the more subtle arguments for and against this viewpoint. For our purposes, we draw a more practical distinction between phenomena of the physical/natural world and phenomena in the world of human affairs. Representations of the latter are always and inevitably interpretations offered by a particular person with a particular perspective and a particular position. Consequently, these representations are more usefully thought of as *text* than *data.*

A second objection is raised by the specter of unbridled relativism in which any text or interpretation is as "valid" as any other. In terms of dissertation research, this unpleasant prospect raises the troubling question, "Wouldn't any dissertation have to be accepted, because faculty couldn't challenge the validity of the student's uniquely personal interpretation?" This objection assumes that there is no basis for judging the merits of a text, and therefore one text—any text—is as good as the next. Those who take this view may be so immersed in the criteria for judging "scientific knowledge" that they are simply not aware of long-standing discourses related to studying, interpreting, and judging the merits of *text.*

It is our contention that the dissertation is itself a particular form of research text or, if you will, a distinctive genre in its own right. Thus, there are institutional as well as broader scholarly criteria for judging the merits of a dissertation as a text. Further, the conventions embedded within a particular research genre offer touchstones for judging the merits of particular texts—not the least of which is the extent to which the author has worked within the conventions of a genre or offered a rationale (logic) for departing from those conventions. One has to think only of the vehemence with which sports aficionados engage in postgame critiques to gain a sense of how judgments are made about the rigor, elegance, and success with which the conventions of a sports genre have been met. Those familiar with a particular research genre are in a position to offer similarly robust critiques of dissertations as text. As suggested in Chapter 7, a student's ability to articulate the conventions of the genre he or she is following is one criterion for judging the merits of a dissertation text. Throughout this and subsequent chapters we continue to flag additional criteria. Sample Reference List 8.1 offers a starting point for those who want to examine more fully various criteria for judging the merits of qualitative research.

## FORMS OF TEXT

When *everything*, including persons (see Gergen, 1988), is taken to be *text*, doctoral students might understandably wonder, "How does one go from *everything* to a readable and useful document? What goes into the final text of the dissertation proposal and ultimately the dissertation? How do I know what to include and what to leave out?" These are important considerations, and we have found it helpful to think in terms of four forms of *text*.

### Sample Reference List 8.1

### Criteria for Judging Qualitative Research

| | |
|---|---|
| Ball & Forzani, 2007 | Howe & Eisenhart, 1990 |
| Barthes, 1976, 1979 | Jacobson, 1998 |
| Bochner, 2000 | Kilbourn, 1999, 2006 |
| Bullough & Pinnegar, 2001 | Lincoln, 1995 |
| Clough, 2000 | Nielsen, 1995 |
| Denzin, 1997, 2000 | Palmer, 1969 |
| Derrida, 1989 | Phillips, 1994 |
| Duke & Beck, 1999 | Ray, 1986 |
| Eisner, 1991 | Richardson, 2000 |
| Ellis, 2000 | Ricoeur, 1981, 1991 |
| Fish, 1980 | Seale, 1999 |
| Garratt & Hodkinson, 1998 | Stanley, 2007 |
| Geertz, 1973, 1983 | Taylor, 1985 |
| Hostetler, 2005 | |

### Raw Text

*Raw text* refers to all of the information collected in the course of a study including information about the phenomenon under study, the context within which the phenomenon is being studied, the genre of research being followed, and procedures or techniques being used to carry out the study. We elaborate on the concept of *raw text* after briefly describing the other three forms of text.

## Experiential Text

As suggested by the concept of *intimate studies,* interpretive researchers are probing for insights into the meaning of human affairs within particular contexts. Thus, when it comes time to write the proposal and eventually the dissertation, the doctoral student is obliged to craft a text that portrays the phenomenon under study and the context within which the phenomenon is manifest. Creating this *experiential text* entails a process of sifting and sorting through the mass of *raw texts* to select those that most richly depict the phenomenon embedded within a context. Issues related to this form of text are explored more fully in Chapter 9.

## Discursive Text

Embracing a *stance of study* means that one will become immersed in discourses related to the phenomenon under study as well as the research genre and procedures of the study. As is the case with experiential text, the conscientious researcher will accumulate an extensive set of references aimed at broadening and deepening his or her thinking about the inquiry. When it comes time to write the dissertation proposal (and eventually the dissertation), another process of selection occurs.[1] The doctoral student must choose which materials are most germane to the study and craft them into *discursive text.* Given the multiple purposes that discursive text is meant to serve, it is not particularly useful to think about a monolithic body of literature that is presented in one chapter of the proposal and subsequently transferred in toto to the dissertation. Rather, discursive text is woven throughout the proposal and dissertation to create conceptual bridges between idiosyncratic experience and broader conceptual meanings. Thoughtfully crafted discursive text allows the researcher to

- situate one's study within the broader discourses and concerns of one's field of study,
- warrant the conceptual point or argument that one's study is worth doing,
- provide a rationale for the research tradition and research genre that is being proposed,
- explicate a logic-of-justification for the procedures of one's study, and
- broaden and deepen one's insight into the concepts and issues that are emerging through reflections on and interpretations of experiential text.

In Chapter 10, we return to the notion of crafting discursive text to support the need for and importance of one's study. In Chapter 13, we revisit the concept of discursive text as a way of extending and elaborating on the concepts embedded in one's *theoretic text.*

## Theoretic Text

The result of an interpretive inquiry is a thesis—a position or perspective—that the researcher offers as his or her understanding of the phenomenon under study. Rather than presenting objectively verifiable "findings," the dissertation author is crafting a conceptual argument that is warranted by interweaving experiential and discursive texts. In other words, the author is essentially saying, "Having thought carefully and deeply about the issue under study, here are the insights that I have to offer." The persuasiveness of the theoretic text lies less in procedural precision than in the logics and warrants that the researcher puts forward. Although the theoretic text comes to fruition in the dissertation, a doctoral student's capacity to engage in theorizing can be demonstrated in the proposal as he or she makes the case that the study is worth doing. We return to the concept of *theoretic text* in Chapter 13 where, in the process of living with the study, the doctoral candidate authors an integrated text of the dissertation.

We introduce this notion of multiple forms of text at this point because it is important to have a sense of what they represent when one is conceptualizing and writing a proposal for an interpretive dissertation. All too often we see students who focus on details of "data" collection but give little thought to how they will generate knowledge claims from the data. Surrounded by masses of text but having no clear strategy for making meaning of it, students flounder. Therefore, before turning to issues of proposing an interpretive study, we explore issues related to gathering raw texts in this chapter and crafting experiential text in the next.

## FORMS AND SOURCES OF RAW TEXTS

In preparing to carry out an inductive qualitative study, there are no formulaic rules for gathering texts. Rather, researchers are obliged to think creatively about various forms and sources of potentially relevant information that can shed light on the phenomenon under study. A narrow focus on interviews as the sole source of information can blind students to other important sources of information, especially those that may come to light as the study progresses. In addition, inexperienced qualitative researchers often assume that the information gained through interviews will explicitly address the question they are investigating. We suspect this may be one problem underlying the "research" so contemptuously dismissed by the physician in Exemplar 5.2. If the researcher asked earthquake survivors to describe their experience, it is likely they said, "It was terrible." Anyone with a modicum of empathy might have known that without conducting a "study." So what was the researcher really trying to understand and what other sources of information might have been consulted to shed light on the issues that arise in the aftermath of an earthquake? Obviously we cannot know what that researcher had in mind, but we reference this anecdote to underscore the importance of *theoretical sensitivity* in amassing the kinds of raw texts that will allow the researcher to say something substantive about the issue under study.

We use the term *raw text* because these various forms of information represent the raw materials from which the researcher will ultimately craft the *experiential, discursive,* and *theoretic texts* that constitute the dissertation. Raw texts potentially include a wide array of materials including first-hand accounts of experience, archival records, observations, published literature, and real time discourses. During the early stages of thinking about potential topics for a dissertation, students may be drawn intuitively to various texts without having a clear-cut idea of why, how, or when they might be useful. One colleague referred to this as a *pack rat* stage of inquiry, where anything that might eventually be useful is gathered and stored. Through deliberation, the nature of information that will serve the study does become clearer so that by the time the proposal is written, students should be able to explain what types of raw texts they anticipate gathering.

In addition, once students settle on a genre for their inquiry, the conventions of the genre will help to further clarify what materials will be appropriate. For example, within a narrative genre, researchers might logically collect raw texts in the form of stories gathered through interviews, written recollections, or oral histories. An ethnographic study might include prolonged field observations (e.g., Angrosino, 2007; Angrosino & Mays de Perez, 2003) of daily life and special rituals, a collection of cultural artifacts, and interviews with key informants. A grounded-theory study of a national reform initiative might include a review of the Congressional Record detailing the arguments for and against the reform, interviews with the executive directors of agencies charged with responsibility for instituting the reform, focus groups with representatives of key stakeholders to be benefited by the reform, and newspaper editorials to gauge public opinion of the reform. A biographical study of an important educator might include all of that individual's publications, interviews with those who knew the educator at different points in his or her life, and a series of interviews with the educator. Hopefully, these brief examples serve to illustrate the variety of texts that can contribute to a thoughtful investigation of an issue.

## Experiential Accounts as Raw Texts

Raw texts that provide accounts of experience—both the researcher's experience and the experiences of others to whom the researcher may turn for greater insight into the phenomenon under study—might include personal and professional journals, memories, dreams, audiotapes, interview transcripts, responses to open-ended questionnaire items, notes of conversations, anecdotes, poems, visual images (e.g., sketches, doodles, artwork, photographs, videotapes), letters to newspaper and journal editors, newspaper clippings, and other such artifacts of life events and professional practice. Also falling under the umbrella of *raw texts* are published accounts of individuals' experiences. For example, many practitioner-oriented journals publish articles by teachers who want to share instructional strategies that they have found to be successful. Similarly, individuals may publish articles or books describing particularly difficult experiences—for example, coping with a disability, overcoming adversity, or surviving a catastrophe.

Other, often elusive raw texts can be categorized as *fugitive documents* and *archival records.* Our colleague Helen Hazi (1982) used the term *cache of documents* to refer to

> a collection of documents related by topic which contain primary data for analyses. A collection of letters, a series of reports or articles, or a collection of legal documents are examples. Documents in a cache can be analyzed to obtain salient information about an event, person, social scene, or issue. The researcher views the authors in a cache as the equivalent of an anthropologist's informants, whose voices can be released from print for analytic use. Such documents have generally been used as background or supplemental information to help the researcher understand the area of study. These documents, however, can be used as primary data for analysis and interpretation in the research process. (p. 13)

Because she was writing in the early days of qualitative educational research, Helen used the language of data and data analysis that was available to her at the time. But as suggested in the final sentence, such documents are interpreted by the researcher to gain insight into events or issues under study. Examples of fugitive documents include curriculum, instructional, and assessment materials, minutes of meetings, planning documents, and personal correspondence.

## Formal Literature as Raw Text

Generally, published literature is not thought of as raw material for a study. It is our contention, however, that reading literature and taking notes serves to inform the researcher's thinking. Until the researcher draws from these references to make conceptual points, formal literature represents one more type of raw text. In the early stages of thinking about a study, it may be difficult to identify specific bodies of literature to be read or to see how various references fit together. The anecdote in Exemplar 8.1 illustrates the confusion (and anxiety) that can accompany the early stages of accumulating potentially useful literature.

---

### EXEMPLAR 8.1    Immersion in Discourses

When I was in the Henny Penny stage of organizing this comprehensive exam question—you know, the frantic time of darting about screaming, "The sky is falling, the sky is falling"—I jumped from article to article in a frenetic clip, jotted down notes and fragments of ideas, wrote commands on the cover of texts that said, "Get this." I was in the evacuation mode of grabbing things to possess them. I was a mess. I made Henny Penny look catatonic. Then I'd talk to myself. "Slow down," I'd say. "Panicking will get you nowhere." Ok. Ok. I resolved. Begin at the beginning. Read a research proposal or a college text about feminist theory that will serve as a review for you; this will get you focused and maybe uncover a way to go that will be helpful. Satisfied that I at least had not yet been struck by catastrophe, I had found a place where I felt safe. "Ok, I know this," I'd say as I read. "Yes. I understand that." Then I would read the names of scholars seminal to the theory whom I hadn't read, or I'd read bibliographies, and the panic happened all over again. How could I have formed my topic last summer and not have read so and so? How could this one's work be so significant, and I hadn't even heard of her? "What a thrice triple ass am I," I'd say to myself as Caliban did; you don't know this, or you didn't read that. "Abusing myself to myself," I'd start darting about again, practically stopping people on the street to complain that I'd be on Medicare before I even wrote my comp, let alone the dissertation.

Then it hit me. Not the sky, but maybe a piece of it. I had tried to sort through the differing strands of feminism—the liberals, the radicals, the Marxists, the postmoderns, the socialist, the psychological—and make sense of them. I found strands of commonality in feminist pedagogy and discovered who thought what about what—or at least I was beginning to understand. I thought knowledge, gender, subjectivity, authority, the personal, and emancipatory goals were all significant. But everything seemed to overlap. Some scholars had moved from Marxist feminism to postmodern feminism. Some authors declared themselves occupants of a few places—like critical theorist and educationalist—or were in no place or multiple places. Everything seemed to be moving and shifting (except me)—even the focus of major disciplines in feminism. I was quite overwhelmed in trying to understand it all. In fact, there was no way that I could understand it all.

Then, while driving on the turnpike, I started thinking once again about teaching and feminism, and I was trying to once again sort through what the scholars said and through what I knew and what I felt I needed to know—talk about too much world and too little time. I just couldn't seem to narrow my focus to make all of this manageable. But finally, I asked myself what thing or things really bothered me about this teaching change of mine. I thought about the basketball story I had written and the story about W and J. I thought about my English classes and what I struggled with in the past two years. Authority. Authority and problems with what it means, how it is construed, sharing it, losing it, or not claiming it—these issues seemed to be the seat of real trouble for me. Why not think this thing, the comp, through myself? This might be a way in, a way to come to grips with things that had eluded me. And it certainly seemed not only workable but also feminist in approach. Perhaps this will work, I thought, so I began anew.

In urging students to think more broadly about the types of information that can support their studies, we stress the importance of developing strategies for locating references and grappling with the ideas one is encountering. At a logistical level, busy practitioners who are juggling doctoral work with a full-time job and family responsibilities may not relish spending evenings and weekends in the library. Some students form groups and schedule a standing night at the library to counteract the loneliness of this research task. Added benefits of this approach can also include sharing of relevant references and peer coaching on literature-search strategies. This latter benefit seems particularly valuable to those who are unfamiliar with and possibly intimidated by computer-based library catalogues and literature indexes.[2]

Although the latter issues are likely to wane as more computer-oriented and cyber-savvy generations enter doctoral study, we still meet a surprising number of students who rely almost exclusively on card catalogues or ERIC (Education Recourses Information Center) searches for accessing literature. For example, when we first met Melanie, she had completed the draft of her comprehensive examination about women and welfare that contained few references to education. Given that she was pursuing a doctorate in education, we asked about this omission and were told, "There really weren't any studies about that aspect of welfare." Encouraged to check dissertation abstracts, Melanie discovered a number of relevant studies and references that brought into focus the educational significance of her interest in women and welfare. (A more recent variation of limited understanding of reviewing literature occurs among students who rely almost exclusively on Google searches and resources such as Wikipedia for their information.)

Another plus for busy practitioners is the growing number of online journals and digital archives of scholarly references that can be accessed from one's home computer. At the same time, ease of accessibility may give rise to greater difficulty in sorting scholarly wheat from unscholarly chaff. Deliberating with colleagues, faculty, and committee members can be very helpful in evaluating the intellectual and scholarly merits of such information.

## Real-Time Discourses as Raw Text

We use the concept of *real-time discourses* to designate several other important sources of information that can inform students' thinking about their dissertation work. One such source that is crucial for educational practitioners is connection with (if not immersion in) discourses that occur at professional and research conferences.[3] Although time and funding constraints often limit opportunities for travel to professional meetings, the formal proceedings and informal networking associated with these gatherings can safeguard against provincial thinking. Fortunately, the Internet creates possibilities for ongoing dialogue among scholars and practitioners around the world.[4]

In recent years, the Internet has also become an avenue through which raw texts can be gathered from study participants. Sample Reference List 8.2 offers a starting point for those who want to read more extensively about methodological and ethical issues associated with the online collection of texts.

Another form of real-time discourse can help students settle into a context for their study and hone techniques or procedures for gathering raw texts. For example, when students are planning to conduct interviews, create conversations, gather stories, or observe at a particular site, engaging in these activities as early as possible is useful. Sometimes students are surprised at this idea, fearing that collecting texts before their proposal has been approved will somehow contaminate their study. In actuality, these early encounters can provide students with a number of valuable procedural insights. For example, romanticized notions of "telling stories" may fade with the realization that people often tell rather mundane or boring stories about their lives. Even more sobering may be a realization that the student him- or herself has little innate talent for storytelling. Other insights might relate to

- one's own style and ability for conducting interviews or engaging in observations;
- the pros and cons of various approaches to interviewing and/or observation;
- the types of questions or conversational prompts that elicit useful information;
- procedural issues that go beyond the interview or observation, such as organizing and keeping track of information;
- issues of interpretation, such as what meanings can be derived from raw texts; and
- issues of representation, such as how to craft a compelling account of an experience.

Researchers working within an empirical tradition might frame these early efforts as a *pilot study*. Although this can be useful and in some instances may be necessary, the concept of *pilot study* implies more formality and rigidity than may be appropriate or

---

### Sample Reference List 8.2

#### Online/Internet Research

Cooper, 2000

DeLorme, Zinkhan, & French, 2001

Farmer, 2002

Hamilton & Bowers, 2006

Hine, 2004

Johns, 2003

Jones, 1998

Mann & Stewart, 2000

Thomas, Stamler, Lafreniere, & Dumula, 2000

possible. The point is that such real-time discourses can help students to push beyond their preliminary ideas for a study, to develop greater theoretical sensitivity, and to clarify the logic-of-justification for research procedures that will be proposed for the inquiry.

The nature, variety, and amount of raw texts that are necessary for a qualitative dissertation give rise to both worldview and practical issues. Although these issues often come to the fore as one becomes immersed in a study, it is worth considering them as early as possible for at least two reasons. First, it is helpful in planning the procedures for the study and eventually in drafting this part of the proposal. Second, it continues the process of preparing oneself as an instrument of inquiry.

## WORLDVIEW ISSUES

### Epistemological Considerations in Interviewing

Although we have flagged a variety of raw texts that might be gathered for an interpretive study, we recognize that interviews often constitute a major source of insight into the meaning of human experience. Certainly, students who enroll in our introductory course on qualitative research often express a goal of "learning how to do interviews." As we explore what they mean by this, at least two assumptions commonly surface. First is an assumption that there is one right way to do interviews. Second is a concern about making sure they get uniform data from all participants. Both concerns seem to be fueled by vague impressions of objective interviewing procedures drawn from the social sciences. (For an illustrative list of references on interviewing, see Chapter 1, Sample Reference List 1.1.)

If the intent of a study is to find reliable, valid, and predictable commonalities among individuals experiencing a certain phenomenon, then highly structured interviews might be entirely appropriate. For example, at our university, one research center has been conducting large-scale studies of the psychosocial impact of caring for a family member diagnosed with Alzheimer's disease. Extensive and detailed protocols have been developed for interviews to be conducted at 6, 12, and 18 months into the caregiving experience. Several graduate students are hired and trained to do the telephone interviews and code the data. They are expected to not deviate from the protocol. If one student leaves, another is hired and trained. It is the questions that are important, and the student research assistants are conduits for relaying the questions, recording the answers, and entering coded data into the computer. The aim of the study is to find predictable correlations between caregiving experiences and caregiver stress. To tease out and warrant significant correlations, a large sample is needed. In this model, the interviewer needs communication skills that are good enough to establish rapport, secure the interviewees' cooperation, and listen accurately to responses. The notion of *self as instrument* does not pertain to the research assistants conducting the interviews because they are not responsible for interpreting the data.

This model of interviewing, grounded in social psychology, is not usually feasible for the unfunded, intimate inquiries carried out by solitary doctoral students in education. When the intent of a study is to probe deeply into the meanings that participants have made of some experience, then other approaches, such as semi-structured, open-ended, or conversational interviews, may be far more productive. Such approaches do not aim to discover or verify commonalities across experience, but rather strive to get at the unique meaning each individual ascribes to an apparently similar situation (e.g., surviving an earthquake, participating in a curricular innovation, having a disability). Interviewers follow where the interviewee leads without losing sight of the phenomenon that they are trying to understand.

Robin Grubs (2002), for example, wanted to gain deeper insight into the experiences of women (and their partners) who faced a decision to accept or refuse genetic counseling and testing. Because of the women's advanced age, the risk for giving birth to infants with birth defects was heightened, but this commonality was not the focus of the study. Rather, it was the variations of response to this anxiety-producing experience that Robin believed to be of potential value to genetic counselors. Erasing barriers between researcher and participant is often necessary to establish a level of trust where individuals are willing to share such deeply painful or private information. At the same time, this places study participants in a tremendously vulnerable position, relying on the integrity of the researcher to do no harm with the confidences that have been shared. Achieving the capacity to establish such rapport requires a finely developed sense of *self as instrument* and also a finely honed *ethical sensibility.* "Learning to do this type of interview" goes well beyond the technical aspects of formulating a sequence of questions and recording participant responses.

Inevitably, this view of eliciting information from participants raises questions about its reliability and validity. Novices often ask, "If people know what I'm studying, won't they tell me what they think I want to hear? How do I know they aren't lying to me or making things up? What if their version of what happened doesn't match with other people's versions? What if I get a very skewed or limited perspective?" It is one thing for novice researchers to express a desire to do qualitative research, to understand individuals' lived experiences, or to represent the views of marginalized groups. It is quite another to be inundated with masses of raw text and to be haunted by these axiological and ontological questions. There is no simple answer to these issues, but repeatedly, we see students fall into the epistemological trap illustrated in Exemplar 8.2. In short, a researcher elicits comments about a particular situation and then presents the comments as though they "prove" some reality about the situation itself. Yet, if raw texts have been gathered in a way that does not support claims of correspondence between the situation and its representation, readers will have an uneasy feeling that something is just not right. To avoid this trap, researchers must remain focused on the issue under study and think carefully about what the raw texts represent in relation to that issue. (We discuss the concept of correspondence more fully in Chapter 9.)

---

### EXEMPLAR 8.2   Understanding What Raw Text Represents

Not long ago, a colleague who edits an educational journal asked Noreen to review a manuscript that had been submitted for publication. The manuscript contained a number of stories from faculty who attributed their difficulty in obtaining tenure to the fact that they did qualitative research. The editor was clearly troubled by the manuscript and kept asking, "But are these stories really true? The manuscript seems so one-sided. Shouldn't the author have tried to present a more balanced perspective? Quite honestly, the whole piece comes across like the author and her informants are just whining."

"What the paper lacks," Noreen responded, "is any kind of conceptual frame. The author has just strung together a series of faculty anecdotes. Then she takes these anecdotes at face value and implies that they 'prove' that qualitative research is devalued in the academy."

"Exactly," exclaimed the editor. "Shouldn't she have gone out and looked for stories that give other points of view? Maybe stories from people who had a different experience, to give a more balanced picture."

"If her intent is to verify to what extent faculty value or devalue qualitative research, she certainly needs a much broader and more representative sample. But I don't get the sense that she wanted to do that type of post-positivist study. She seems to be on the verge of a more interpretive study."

The editor looked puzzled.

"She could have done a couple of things. For example, she doesn't put these stories in a context. There's no indication of her own role, perspective, or experience with the issue of qualitative research and tenure. As readers, we have no idea how broad or narrow her experience base is. She doesn't make it clear how her own experience—or lack of it—may be shaping her interpretations of the anecdotes.

"Also, she doesn't connect these anecdotes to any particular question or issue that she is researching. So she seems to take the stories at face value rather than using them to provide insight into some broader issue. It leaves me wondering, 'What's her point in sharing these stories?'

"If she were investigating an issue, then she could have probed beneath the surface meanings of the anecdotes. She could have used them as a starting point for speculations or for raising questions. For example, how do these anecdotes reflect folklore about qualitative research and tenure? Going up for tenure is a particularly anxiety-producing time. So she might have connected the anecdotes to larger contextual issues like that. But these connections don't automatically lie in the 'data.' They lie in her ability to draw from her own experience and wisdom to highlight issues that may only be hinted at in the stories.

"The way this is written, she assumes that the statements in and of themselves have significance rather than serving as exemplars of larger issues. She is interpreting people's statements rather than using the statements to illuminate a phenomenon."

## Understanding What Raw Texts Represent

A related worldview issue arises when doctoral students are investigating some aspect of their own practice and have access to a wealth of information. We are reminded of two doctoral students whose interest in portfolio-making led them to conduct a number of workshops for teachers. Over time, they had accumulated a tremendous cache of artifacts from the workshops—materials they had prepared (e.g., objectives, learning activities, handouts) and materials generated by participants (e.g., journal entries, reflective writing, learning portfolios, flip charts with key discussion points, informal and formal evaluations). Both students were interested in shaping dissertations around the phenomenon of portfolio-making. So a key issue was determining what these workshop artifacts represented. The students tended to see these artifacts as proof that their own views of portfolio-making were shared by teachers participating in the workshops. However, this use of the artifacts was not supportable, nor would it have been possible to warrant knowledge claims about the value of portfolios based on an analysis of this information. On the other hand, a great deal of this information could have been used to portray the pedagogical context within which these two students had begun to explore the phenomenon of portfolio-making.

When researchers intend to involve a particular group of people in their study, they often imagine collecting demographic information about the participants (e.g., age, gender, ethnicity, professional role, marital status, socioeconomic status, and other such variables). Moreover, they imagine reporting this information numerically (e.g., the number and percentage of male and female participants, the number and grade of public school students, the number of teachers and principals in a study). In interpretive studies, numeric data may be very helpful in describing the context of the study. For example, the students who wanted to study portfolio-making might have included charts describing the number of workshops conducted, the number of participants per workshop, the gender and professional role of participants, and so on. From such "quantitative" data, they could have warranted the claim, "We have broadened and deepened our own initial thinking about portfolio-making through our interactions with professionals in these workshop settings." Furthermore, they could have warranted a claim that "during our interactions with workshop participants, a variety of issues and concerns about portfolio-making began to emerge. These issues and concerns include . . . " Such statements could have been used to establish the conceptual context from which their dissertation inquiries emerged. They could not, however, claim that teachers value reflective portfolio-making just because a majority of participants gave the workshop very high evaluation ratings. Nor could they claim that their particular workshop was an especially effective strategy for preparing teachers to initiate portfolio-making in their classrooms even if 100% of the participants had stated an intention to use portfolios as a result of taking the workshop.

Thus, *raw texts* represent the materials available to support the researcher's theorizing process. Unlike the ephemeral events that constitute an original experience, raw texts provide a stable record that can be examined and interpreted over time. Raw texts also include records of the researcher's thinking about the issue under study. A variety of techniques can be used to generate these records. In the social sciences, researchers keep extensive and detailed field notes. In grounded theory, researchers do "memo-ing." In narrative, journaling is commonly used. As mentioned earlier, Wendy Milne adapted the concept of an artist's sketchbook to create a visual as well as verbal record of her thinking. As these examples illustrate, the choice of technique can be based on some combination of the researcher's field of study, the research genre of the inquiry, and the researcher's own talents and abilities. Regardless of the particular technique employed, the aim is to keep as thorough and systematic a record as possible of one's reflective thought processes—the insights, questions, speculations, hunches, tentative interpretations, and so on that occur as one conceptualizes, proposes, and ultimately conducts that study.

## PRACTICAL ISSUES

### Acquiring Sufficient Raw Texts

Even when an encountered experience consists of a fairly discrete event, the amount of raw text that might be gathered is substantial. The task becomes truly daunting, however, when the encountered experience (e.g., classroom practice, an educational innovation) occurs over a prolonged time, involves many individuals, or encompasses a large number of discrete yet interconnected events. Thus, one challenge of interpretive dissertations is capturing raw texts as the phenomenon under investigation unfolds within complex and dynamic contexts. The Case Examples in Section Four help to illustrate this challenge. Micheline outlines a variety of raw texts to be gathered including natural, deliberate, and contrived encounters from colleagues, individuals with disabilities, and parents of students with disabilities, observations, meetings, videos, and training and curricular materials (Part 4 of Case Example 1). Lynn describes a multilayered process for gathering texts throughout an entire school year (Part 5 of Case Example 2). Pat limited her study context to a one-semester college composition course, but in the process gathered 65 student portfolios, her own extensive journal, and deliberative exchanges between her and her students (Case Example 3). Kathy tapped into formal records as well as the experiences of teachers in order to understand the lead teacher initiative in Pennsylvania (Case Example 4). By the time Jean finished gathering raw texts related to a reform initiative, she had over 1,000 pages of interview transcripts as well as a cache of artifacts related to the reform efforts (Case Example 5). Joan focused her study on a group of adolescent females who had participated in a specific, science-oriented program for gifted students. Even with such a circumscribed study, she had a wealth of raw texts ranging from scores on standardized tests to collages created by the students (Case Example 6). Hopefully, these few examples illustrate the breadth and depth of raw texts that are amassed to support an interpretive dissertation.

Another important issue in gathering raw texts is determining whether they can realistically be obtained. For example, a researcher might be very interested in the ethical implications of policy decisions made by a school board. Practical concerns in planning such a study might include whether the researcher would have access to (a) board members, (b) the processes that gave rise to the policies, and (c) the documents that capture the deliberations and the final policy. On one hand, many relevant documents might be accessible through public records. On the other hand, getting at the heart of ethics and policy decisions might require access to behind-the-scenes information where the "real" story can be seen. Without access to such confidential information, the study might not be doable no matter how compelling it is.

Bonnie Knapp-Minick (1984), another member of our study group, faced a slightly different issue in accessing information. She wanted to study stereotypes about why women cannot handle management positions. Early on, she concluded that it would not

be possible to ask people directly, "What are your stereotypes about women and management?" Just as physicists must study the location of electrons by tracing their paths,
Bonnie pondered how she might capture the telltale signs of stereotypes. As she told
people about the idea for her study, she began to notice a recurring response. "Wait till you
hear this," people would say. "You aren't going to believe it." This comment would then be
followed by an outrageous anecdote of why a particular woman was not considered for
promotion to a management position. Suddenly, it occurred to Bonnie that these "incred-
ible tales" were the very traces of stereotypes that she had been searching for. The challenge then became initiating a process for gathering such tales. Again, going out and
asking directly for such stories seemed fruitless. In essence, she had to wait for the tales
to come to her. Thus, she portrayed her process as one of *accumulation* rather than *collection* or *gathering*. She told as many friends and colleagues as possible about her interest.
Soon, a trickle of tales turned into a constant stream as her interest spread by word of
mouth. A year after successfully defending her dissertation, she lamented that her only
problem was stopping the flow of tales that still came her way.

### Reflective Interlude 8.1

**What Raw Texts Might Inform My Study?**

- What texts might I need to develop and study the various issues embedded in my dissertation puddle?
- Realistically, will I be able to gain access to these texts?
- What experience do I have in gathering and working with these forms of text?
- What abilities will I need not only to gather these forms of text but also to interpret them?
- In what ways can I begin now to practice the skills associated with gathering and inter- preting the forms of text I am imagining as part of my dissertation?

## Issue—Managing Raw Texts

The issue of managing an ever-mounting mass of information encompasses both
practical and theoretical considerations. In creating a system for managing the raw
texts of a study, it is wise to build upon one's style of organizing information and to
draw upon existing skills. For example, some people "file" material in stacks strewn
across every surface of their workspace. With unerring instincts, they can delve into the
right pile to unearth a desired scrap of paper. Others would go mad with such a chaotic
system and need to have well-organized file drawers with neatly labeled folders. It is
important to take one's style of conceptualizing into account in developing an information management system for the dissertation. A word of caution for the former style is
in order, however. The dissertation may generate more raw text than one is accustomed
to managing in unlabeled piles. Thus, some blend between unlabeled stacks and precise
folders may be prudent.

In this day and age, it is difficult to imagine an information management system that is anything but computer based. Because software programs are evolving so rapidly, it is pointless for us to review and recommend packages that are currently available. However, features to look for include

- options for formatting dissertations according to different reference styles (e.g., APA, Chicago Style, MLA),
- capability of interfacing with word processing programs,
- ease of adding and searching for key words,
- space for entering notes,
- capability of searching and retrieving resources from online databases, and
- options for linking bibliographic records to PDFs.

Becoming skillful in the use of such a program from the outset of doctoral study can be tremendously helpful in building a cumulative, personalized library that can be used for writing course-related papers, the comprehensive examination, the dissertation proposal, the dissertation, and post-dissertation articles. In recent years, workshops on the use of information management programs have become more prevalent both within universities and at national conferences and workshops.

Typically, qualitative researchers draw heavily upon verbal texts. Thus, a word processing or information management program that allows the researcher to store, sort, and retrieve large passages of text is essential. The growing interest in an arts-based research genre has, however, created additional challenges (e.g., storing images of two- and three-dimensional artwork; recording live performances of music, dance, or drama). Fortunately, the technology for digitalizing such nonverbal information is evolving rapidly.

When choosing software, it is important to differentiate between programs that manage information and programs that analyze data. The former allow the researcher to store, index, sort, and retrieve information. The latter do some forms of content analysis, typically associated with postpositivist research in the social sciences. Our own bias is that such programs may have limited utility for an interpretive research genre. On one hand, data analysis programs may facilitate the process of slogging through mounds of raw text. Yet they may lull novice researchers into a sense of false security—especially if researchers rely on the program to reveal the meaning of texts. Therefore, we urge students to talk with faculty and experienced researchers to find out not only what programs they use but also how they use them. If at all possible, novice researchers should see if resources are available in their university's computer support center so that they can actually try out the software to see if it meets their needs.

A good bibliographic program is valuable for managing literature. Such programs should allow researchers to index the content of articles and then to sort and retrieve them based on a variety of parameters (e.g., author, title, key concepts). Also beneficial are bibliographic programs that interface with word processing programs and make it possible to import references as needed into the body of the dissertation and to generate reference lists in a variety of citation styles. Programs are now available that are compatible with Internet searches and allow for the importing of files with articles and other materials.

A basic consideration in qualitative research is cataloguing raw texts as they are collected so that the researcher can readily identify their sources, the nature of the information contained in the raw text (e.g., interview transcript, fugitive document, casual conversation, published document), and where it is stored. It is also useful to note why the researcher thought this information would be useful to the study. Although the relevance of information seems unforgettably obvious at the time it is gathered, its potential significance can fade as the raw texts accumulate.

Developing a system for cataloguing individual accounts of experience intersects with another important issue—ensuring the anonymity of study participants. The form used to submit dissertation proposals to our own institution's research review board illustrates several ways in which this issue has traditionally been handled. Students are asked to check off one of the following options:

- No subject identifiers or linkage codes will be recorded with the information.
- All subject identifiers and linkage codes will be irreversibly stripped from the recorded information after it is obtained.
- Linkage codes will be recorded on the information; however, the individual(s) having access to linkage code information is (are) independent of this research project.
- Subject identifiers and/or linkage codes (i.e., accessible to the involved research investigators) will be retained with the information. *Note: To qualify for exempt status; if subject identifiers and/or linkage codes are retained with the information, any disclosure of the subjects' responses to the survey or interview outside of the research cannot reasonably place the subjects at risk of criminal or civil liability or be damaging to the subjects' financial standing, employability, or reputation* [italics in original].

These options are not particularly applicable in qualitative (especially interpretive) research. The first three options, for example, are grounded in a scientific/empirical tradition. This is signaled by the term *subjects,* which tends to objectify individuals who participate in a study. Researchers working in an interpretive mode tend to use descriptors such as *participant, informant, coinquirer,* or *coresearcher.* A second point is the assumption that the texts have meaning apart from the individual who provided them or the researcher who uses them—thus, the press to strip away identifying information and/or to deny the researcher access to the identifying information.

In an interpretive tradition, where information is contextualized, the researcher's thinking is informed by knowing the participants. Still, there is a need to protect them from potentially harmful consequences arising from their participation in a study. Conventional wisdom recommends the use of pseudonyms when referring to individual participants. This really begs the issue, however, because in many instances, the identity of the participant is very obvious from other descriptive details. For example, in a case study of a particular school district, there will be only one superintendent and a handful of building principals. Changing only the names will do little to preserve anonymity. Yet altering other descriptive details may compromise the authenticity and verisimilitude of the study. These issues are not easily resolved and must be worked through within the guidelines of the institution and principles for the ethical conduct of research. We return to this issue in Chapter 12 in relation to submitting a dissertation proposal for institutional review.

**Reflective Interlude 8.2**

**What Systems Can I Put in Place to Support My Research?**

- What is my current system for keeping track of articles and books that contain information of interest to me? Will this system be adequate for a project as large as the dissertation?
- What modifications in my current system might help to make cataloguing and retrieving texts more manageable?
- Do I have and/or want a computer-based program? If so, what program is most suited to my needs? How can I increase my familiarity with its features and become more proficient in its use?
- What system will I use for storing and protecting any texts that I gather from participants in my study?
- Have I been imagining that I will use a computer program to analyze my "data"? If so, is this a realistic expectation given the type of research tradition/genre in which I hope to work?

## Issue—Preparing Raw Texts for Interpretation

Organizing raw texts so they can be located as needed is one aspect of preparing these materials for interpretation. Another—putting them into a useable format—is often one of the most tedious and time-consuming aspects of the inquiry. For example, if some raw text is in the form of an extensive written questionnaire, who will enter the responses into a computer? Will responses need to be coded before entry, and if so, who will do this work? Can responses be entered on a spreadsheet or optically scanned? If there are responses to open-ended questions, who will type these into the computer? If extensive audiotaped interviews are collected, who will transcribe the interviews? If videotapes are made, who will code and catalogue them? If policy documents are collected, do photocopies need to be made or should they be scanned into a computer?

Procedures for this aspect of managing raw texts have serious implications in terms of cost, time, and rigor of the inquiry. Some students claim that they would never have finished the dissertation had they done this tedious work themselves. Others, however, have done this "drudge" work out of sheer financial necessity. Still others, who could afford to pay a transcriptionist, prefer to do the work themselves, believing that it adds an important level of discipline to the inquiry. For example, some students erroneously think that they can listen to audiotapes and randomly jot down notes on points that strike them as important. Or those working with extensive questionnaire data may be inclined to write brief narrative summaries based on their casual impressions rather than doing a systematic analysis. Such casual approaches to the raw texts compromise the rigor and integrity of the inquiry. Although it can be extremely tedious, working with raw texts at this very basic level can allow the researcher to resonate more fully and carefully with these materials. The Case Examples in Section Four offer some insight into the care with which researchers must work with raw texts. (See Poland, 1995, for additional thoughts on issues related to the quality of interview transcriptions.)

## CHAPTER CONCLUSION

In this chapter, we have tried to give a sense of why it is useful for interpretive researchers to think in terms of *text* rather than *data*. We have also tried to highlight a number of epistemological and practical issues that are important to think through as one conceptualizes a qualitative dissertation. The earlier one begins to think about these issues, the better prepared one will be when it comes time to write a proposal for the dissertation. An important aspect of imagining one's dissertation is having a sense of how one moves from situational details as captured in raw texts to a coherent portrayal of meaning in *experiential text*. Therefore, before turning to issues related to the dissertation proposal, we look more closely in the next chapter at the interpretive turns that allow the researcher to move from the situational to the conceptual.

## NOTES

1.  Depending upon a particular institution's and/or program's requirements for the comprehensive examination, this, too, can represent a major discursive text to be crafted. Advice on writing comprehensive examinations may be included in books on writing dissertations. See also Manus, Bowden, & Dowd, 1992; Miller, 1990.

2.  One fairly simple, yet often overlooked, strategy is establishing a working relationship with a reference librarian. In conversations with reference librarians, we often hear them express a desire to work with students and lament what seems to be an avoidance of their services. Reference librarians can be helpful not only in locating relevant references but also in teaching one how to access and use various indexing systems.

3.  Students who strongly identify with their practitioner role are encouraged to join not only relevant professional associations but also research associations. Relying primarily on newsletters or trade journals for information related to the profession often does not provide insights into the research concerns of the profession. The American Educational Research Association offers a number of divisions and special interest groups through which students can connect with relevant discourse communities and hear cutting edge perspectives on issues of importance in their field of study.

4.  Sometimes students are reluctant to enter into these discourses for fear that someone will "steal" their unique idea. In reality, becoming an active (if junior) member of a discourse community can not only help to clarify an interested audience for one's study, it can also establish one's identity (and hopefully reputation) as a young scholar in a particular field.

# 9

# *Moving From the Experiential to the Theoretic*

| Key Concepts | |
|---|---|
| Coherence | Logical Positivism |
| Concepts | Rigor |
| Correspondence | Text—Discursive |
| Evidence | Text—Experiential |
| Interpretation—Iterative | Text—Theoretic |
| Interpretation—Theoretic | Triangulation |
| Interpretive Warrants | Verisimilitude |
| Logical Certainty | Writerly Decisions |

W e have used the phrase *intimate studies* to suggest that qualitative dissertations in education are often conducted within small, fairly circumscribed contexts. As discussed in Chapter 5, generating knowledge about issues embedded within these contexts entails a movement from the particular to the general, from the concrete to the abstract, from the idiosyncratic to the universal, from the situational to the conceptual—in short, from the experiential to the theoretic. Whereas the context is particular, concrete, situational, and idiosyncratic, an issue of sufficient educational significance bridges into the universal. The movement from the experiential to the theoretic entails the researcher's capacity to resonate with the raw texts that are being accumulated, interpret the texts for meanings related to the issue under study, construct from those meanings a core thesis, and *warrant* the thesis through carefully crafted *experiential, discursive,* and *theoretic text.* In this chapter, we look more closely at the interpretive move from raw texts to experiential texts. The nature of discursive and theoretic texts is discussed more fully in later chapters.

As discussed in Chapter 6, a capacity for recollective, introspective, and conceptual reflection allows researchers to resonate with raw texts and to speculate about potential meanings. As suggested in Chapter 8, amassing sufficient raw texts to support substantive reflection can be quite challenging. Even more challenging, however, is transforming one's reflections into a compelling, coherent experiential text.

## PURPOSE OF EXPERIENTIAL TEXT

As suggested by the concept of *intimate studies,* interpretive researchers are probing for insights into the meaning of human affairs within particular contexts. Thus, when it comes time to write the proposal and eventually the dissertation, the doctoral student is obliged to craft a text that represents the context within which he or she is theorizing. We refer to this representation of context as *experiential text.*

When Wendy Milne and Pam Krakowski first joined our dissertation study group, they would often say, "If only you could come to my class so I could show you what I do. If you could just see the children. . . ." Perhaps their being art teachers gave them a particularly strong need to share their pedagogical practice by *showing* it to others. However, this longing to have others visit their classroom points to the purpose of experiential text within an interpretive dissertation. Metaphorically, because it is not possible to bring everyone to the context of the study, the qualitative researcher brings the context to interested parties. In other words, the dissertation author creates as textured and nuanced a "picture" of the study context as possible.

Creating this experiential text entails a process of sifting and sorting through the mass of raw texts to select those that most richly depict the context. As mentioned in Chapter 8, it is a mistake to think that the raw texts speak for themselves or that a simple compilation of raw texts adds up to an experiential text. Crafting an experiential text is a highly interpretive, demanding, and creative process in which researchers invite their readers to share vicariously in the experiences at the heart of the inquiry. If the experiential text is thin, weak, boring, superficial, simplistic, or narrow, it will not provide a persuasive warrant for much else that the researcher has to say. Bruner's (1986) concept of *verisimilitude* connotes an important quality of a well-crafted experiential text: Events must be rendered with sufficient detail so that they are recognizable as "truly conceivable experience."

I was in the teachers' cafeteria in a suburban middle school, and I overheard an interesting conversation between a teacher and the principal. The previous day, they had attended an all-day workshop about cooperative learning. The principal asked the typical supervisory question, "Well, Grace, how did you feel about the workshop?"

Grace responded, "Well, first of all, I loved getting away from the building and the kids . . . right about now I really needed the break, and the other teachers were interesting to talk to. About the Miller Cooperative Learning Model . . . well, I have some mixed feelings. You know, I do project groups in my class, the kids work together on a project in small groups, and I really like the way it goes . . . but I don't have the groups competing against each other. In the Miller Model, the groups compete against one another. I really don't agree with that."

The principal said, "Well, you know, the Miller Model comes from research. They have hundreds of studies to prove that the competitive model really works better."

Grace said, "Yeah, well, I suppose I can't argue with research, but well, I know what works with my kids." She paused, then said, "You know what really gets me about this stuff . . . every time we have one of these days, we hear about ideas from research and it makes me feel like what I do in my class doesn't really count very much. The message is that we better start doing something from the workshop. And then you come into class with clinical supervision to see whether we're doing it or not."

The principal answered, "Well, I suppose that's what professional development is. All professionals, like lawyers and doctors, keep upgrading their skills as long as they're in practice."

Exemplar 9.1.1 provides an example of a text written by Noreen to capture a situational moment. We invite readers to ask themselves the following questions:

- Is this anecdotal account believable? Does the anecdote bring to mind conversations I have had or have overheard or can imagine taking place?
- Am I able to vicariously share in this experience? In other words, do I feel as though I am in the cafeteria overhearing the conversation myself?

If the response to these questions is yes, then Exemplar 9.1.1 serves to illustrate the quality of verisimilitude.

In crafting experiential text, the researcher's ontological assumptions about the nature of being and reality come forcefully into play. From an interpretive perspective, it is assumed that even when individuals experience the same or similar events, the meanings ascribed to those events are likely to vary. Axiologically, understanding these variations in meaning is what an interpretive researcher values. So the interpretive researcher faces a dual challenge of representing both the event and the range of meanings associated with it.

For example, Grace, in Exemplar 9.1.1, might be among 20, 40, 60, or more teachers who attended the workshop that is being discussed. Each workshop participant would have a response to that shared event—some of which may be similar to Grace's and others of which may be quite divergent. An interpretive researcher crafting an experiential text would need to make a number of *writerly decisions* including which details about the workshop are important to describe and which responses to the workshop are important to represent. Even more challenging, however, is getting to a level of meaning that has some potential significance in relation to the issue under study. To report that some teachers were happy to have a day away from school or enjoyed the opportunity to talk with colleagues is not very compelling. Like stating that earthquake survivors found the experience to be terrible is too superficial a rendering of the experience to support further theorizing. Yet imagine the difficulty of representing 20, 40, 60, or more individual responses to the workshop without losing one's reader in the myriad details.

> **Criterion for Judging Interpretive Dissertations**
>
> **Verisimilitude of Experiential Text**—Well-crafted experiential text is richly textured or nuanced, exhibiting vibrancy and verisimilitude. It will be evocative, inviting readers to enter vicariously into an experience, raising in the readers' mind the question, "How might I have reacted in such a situation?" Experiential texts succeed to the extent that others see the portrayed events as conceivable and believable.

In postpositivist forms of research, the wealth of details is often managed through data displays in the form of tables, charts, graphs, or lists. Such reductive summaries, however, strip away the very nuances that the interpretive researcher is trying to understand. Therefore, the interpretive researcher is challenged to craft experiential text that portrays the nuances. Depending upon the genre within which the interpretive researcher is working, experiential text might take the form of narrative vignettes based on interviews, case reports, stories, conversations, autobiographical memoirs, poetry, dramatic scenarios, and so on. Regardless of the specific form, however, the vibrancy—the verisimilitude—of experiential text contributes to its believability and, in turn, the credibility of the study.

Just as the conventions of a genre guide the gathering of raw texts, they also provide guidance for deriving meaning from them. Within narrative, the conventions of literary interpretation would be useful. Within grounded theory, coding, constant comparative analysis, and memoing would be appropriate. In short, the conventions of the genre provide the logics for what types of raw texts are appropriate and necessary to gather as well as the conceptual processes by which the researcher probes them for meaning. In general, however, it can be helpful to think about two forms of interpretation—*iterative* and *theoretic*.[1]

## MOVING FROM THE EXPERIENTIAL TO THE THEORETIC

### Iterative Interpretation

A researcher's capacity to resonate with experiences—his or her own and those recounted by others—lies at the heart of an interpretive inquiry. Yet to move from the situational to the conceptual, a researcher must begin to connect specific features of the experiential text to the phenomenon under study. In making these connections, the researcher begins to highlight potentially important nuances of the phenomenon.

To illustrate what we mean, we return to Pam and Wendy's longing for others to come to their classrooms and see the children making art. Assuming for a minute that this would be possible, the classroom would encompass a myriad of potentially interesting and possibly significant features. Consequently, there is no guarantee that everyone would discern the same features or understand the importance of what they were seeing. Pam and Wendy would have to direct their visitors' attention to the aspects of art-making that they wanted to highlight. By the same token, as researchers bring the experiential context to their readers, they must make visible the nuances of the phenomenon they are examining in relation to the issue under study.

To achieve the quality of verisimilitude, a skillful interpretive researcher will include many rich details about the situation he or she is describing. Some of these details may serve as background to set the scene; others will be more central to the issue under study. *Iterative interpretation* calls readers' attention to the latter type of detail by briefly summarizing or restating key points.

Returning to the cafeteria conversation between a teacher and her principal, Exemplar 9.1.2 offers an example of an iterative interpretation. Notice how this interpretation distills key features of the situational encounter, and thereby provides a bridge from the details that imbue the account with verisimilitude to a conceptual issue to be examined.

---

### ▨ EXEMPLAR 9.1.2    Example of Iterative Interpretation

In the lunchroom conversation, we hear a teacher's expression of delight in being away from the classroom and the relief from the daily routine of schooling, of being able to converse with colleagues. We learn that she uses her own version of cooperative learning yet questions the external model being offered in the name of research. We hear her trying to say that the workshop format and subsequent supervision diminishes what she does as a teacher. We hear a principal who needs to support his position by appealing to the authority of research. He may, indeed, be frustrated by the skepticism—and, often, resistance—expressed by teachers about their own professional development. (Doctors and lawyers continue to learn without such resistance, he implies.)

---

### Theoretic Interpretation

*Theoretic interpretation* draws out the meanings of a situation and puts those meanings into some sort of perspective. Drawing upon formal discourses and his or her own theoretical sensitivity, a researcher offers *concepts* to advance an understanding of the situation. In Exemplar 9.1.3, notice how Noreen steps outside of the initial text to locate sources that will illuminate the meaning she finds significant about the scenario. This illustrates the point we made above that experiential texts do not add up to something meaningful. The meaning is constructed by the researcher. Concepts offer a way of making sense of what at first glance seems to be a hodgepodge of confusing details; they offer a language for explaining what is going on in the experiential text. This brings us to a question of whether the situational description in Exemplar 9.1.1 is an example of *raw* or *experiential text*. It also helps to illustrate several points about the ways in which ideas are warranted in interpretive dissertations.

## EXEMPLAR 9.1.3    Example of Theoretic Interpretation

The differences reflected in the conversation between the teacher and the principal can be attributed to philosophic considerations, often referred to as different *ways of knowing*. Each of us comes to his or her judgments and actions through philosophic orientations. The term *orientation* refers to the specific ways in which an individual looks at the world. On the surface, it includes the notions of point of view, perspective, and a person's outlook in relation to events and ideas. (We're not convinced that we hold a consistent orientation, but, rather, we suspect it changes depending on the circumstances at hand.)

We are reminded that "underlying every orientation is a definite epistemology, axiology, and ontology" (van Manen, 1977, p. 211). These high-sounding philosophic terms literally mean that a person's orientation is composed of what he or she believes to be true (epistemology), to be valuable (axiology), and to be real (ontology). "An orientation," van Manen says, "has the uncanny quality of encapsulating the person who has learned to adopt it" (p. 211). In supervision, the issue of epistemological legitimacy is a critical one. Each person's orientation provides him or her with rules for legitimacy in action. In the lunchroom conversation, for instance, one can ask, "Where does the legitimacy reside in a particular model of cooperative learning?" The teacher appeals to pragmatic authority when she uses her experience in saying, "I don't believe that competition is the best approach," whereas the principal evokes scientific authority in his claim for legitimacy, responding with "research says . . . "

In this scenario, the stance of the teacher is grounded in her pragmatic sense. She "knows" what works through her years of experience in the classroom. The principal's scientific counterstance may be a result of his concern that the teacher's way of teaching from experience is narrow and habitual, and he would like to see her change her perspective. On the other hand, the principal may be heavily invested in his own position. He was inserviced in a particular teaching model and is linking his version of clinical supervision to this model. Furthermore, in his mind, his clinical supervision skill depends on his "knowing" what good teaching is.

There is a substantial difference between these two positions. They are not mere differences of opinion but, rather, epistemological conflict. That is, the difference grows from what each takes to be true (knowing from experience vs. scientific legitimacy). In this case, it is the principal, as supervisor, who is on shakier ground. His scientific "knowing" about teaching is limited to brief inservice training. He may have been told about the research, but chances are he would not have read the "hundreds of studies" to which he refers. Yet in this scenario, the teacher with a pragmatist stance (I know from experience) and the principal with a scientific, realist counterstance (I've learned what good teaching is from research) are participants in one of the most common dialogues in clinical supervision.

# EXPERIENTIAL TEXT AS A CONTEXT FOR THEORIZING

To begin this discussion, let us reiterate the point that interpretive studies are not trying to prove a causal or correlational relationship between certain variables. Rather, these studies aim for deeper insight into complex human affairs. At the heart of an interpretive dissertation is a thesis—a conceptual argument—developed through multiple lines of reasoning within the conventions of a research genre. Each line of reasoning must be supported—warranted—with persuasive *evidence*.[2] It is the interpretive researcher's obligation to make transparent the conceptual moves that led from the details of the situational to a theoretic interpretation of meaning.

Returning to the scenario in Exemplar 9.1.1, someone operating from a postpositivist perspective might ask, "How can we be certain that this conversation actually took place in exactly this way?" An interpretivist might respond, "What difference does that make?" Here we begin to get at a fundamental ontological difference between the two worldviews.

Currently, there are communities of postpositivist scholars who have modified the rigid rules of *logical positivism*. However, they continue to value knowledge claims that conform as closely as possible to the original notion of *correspondence* between the entity being studied and the representation or portrayal of that entity. This ontological and epistemological view strives for a certainty of knowledge that is a product of logical operations. In other words, it is possible to develop knowledge portrayals that correspond reliably and validly to external reality.

So in the case of the teacher and principal's encounter, a postpositivist would value establishing a correspondence between what happened and Noreen's description of what happened. A procedure such as audio- or videotaping might be used to verify the accuracy of corresponding details.[3]

Polkinghorne (1997), among others, contends that the postpositivist notion of *logical certainty* as a property of legitimate knowledge has been reconsidered. Instead of logical certainty, knowledge is understood to be an agreement reached by communities of scholars. Knowledge is considered to be the best map or description of reality about which the community has reached consensus. In short, knowledge portrayals are no longer considered to correspond with some external reality; rather, they are human constructions of models or maps of reality. As Polkinghorne explains:

> The more evolved models are not necessarily more accurate descriptions of reality, but their use provides a more successful interaction with the world than previous models. Research reports informed by this understanding of knowledge may be presented as arguments or as narrative accounts. (p. 7)

Thus, the postpositivists' notions of knowledge are quite different from the notions of interpretive scholars who understand knowledge as a map or a heuristic portrayal of aspects of self, others, and human affairs.[4] For these scholars, the press in constructing an experiential text is not for correspondence but for *coherence*. (See Exemplar 9.2 for some musings on correspondence and coherence.)

Interpretivists, then, are not making claims about the encounter per se. As in Exemplar 9.1.1, the scenario is used to establish a context for raising a thorny dilemma of instructional supervision—that is, different epistemological stances that can undermine dialogic understanding between teachers and principals. The persuasiveness of the scenario rests upon the quality of verisimilitude. Is it conceivable that a teacher and a principal might have such a conversation? For those who have engaged in or heard such conversations, does the scenario ring true as it calls such encounters to mind? For others, does the scenario allow for a vicarious experience, to understand empathetically what it might have been like to be either the teacher or the principal in the conversation? The persuasiveness of the experiential text rests not on its correspondence to an external reality, but in its power to evoke a responsive chord in readers. On one hand, evocative experiential text will engender an empathetic response. A well-crafted experiential account of an earthquake would evoke a response in readers: "Oh, how terrible." A well-crafted experiential account of an educational situation might evoke a response of "Oh, how difficult." Beyond such empathy, however, a well-crafted experiential text will evoke questions: What would I have done in this situation? What would be a wise response to such a terrible or difficult situation? By evoking such questions, the researcher sets the stage for the theoretic text he or she will ultimately offer. The theoretic text offers concepts—a heuristic map—that help others to discern what was important in the experience and what might constitute wise action. A well-rendered account of an earthquake, for example, might allow instructors of paramedics to create training scenarios to better prepare disaster response teams. A well-rendered account of a special education classroom might allow school board members to better understand the problems of using student performance on standardized tests as the sole indicator of successful teaching. Well-crafted experiential text challenges both researcher and reader to question taken-for-granted assumptions, simplistic interpretations of complex situations, and prescriptive solutions.

> **Criterion for Judging Interpretive Dissertations**
>
> **Coherence of Experiential Text—** There is a cogent conceptual structure embedded in the text. Logical interconnections are warranted with an overall sense of understanding the significance or importance of the experience. There is a unity in the written text that stems from links among its underlying ideas and the development of thematic content.

Let us now return to the question of whether the scenario in Exemplar 9.1.1 is an example of a raw or experiential text. Noreen has a long-standing interest in the nature of instructional supervision and the ways in which teachers and principals engage in this professional process. She has a heightened *theoretical sensitivity* to any experience potentially related to that interest and often takes the time to record situations like the cafeteria conversation. In this "raw" form, she is not making any particular use of a recorded experience. She is simply noting it because it is of interest and may be useful for some future writing project. In this way, it would constitute a raw text.

At the point when Noreen crafts the scenario to serve a particular rhetorical purpose, it is transformed into an experiential text. We say *craft* because the raw notes rarely give a coherent description. At least some writerly decisions are called for—how to set the scene, what details to include and exclude, how to organize the flow of the scenario, how to capture the dialogue, what word choices will contribute to the verisimilitude, and so on. However, the coherence does not lie only in a smooth chronology of the conversation, but in the way the scenario lays the groundwork for the theoretic interpretation. In other words, hints of the dilemma to be explored are embedded in the description. The iterative interpretation, then, serves to call attention to details that signal the theoretic interpretation.

Here again is a powerful illustration of differences in worldview. A postpositivist might cringe at the preceding explanation, saying, "If you are crafting the experiential text to include the conceptual point that you already know you want to raise, then isn't this a circular argument? In essence, you are just seeing what you want to see or saying what you already know." This criticism rests on an axiological assumption that values objective correspondence between an external event and the account of that event. If the point of recording and examining the situational encounter is to make a generalized claim that teachers and principals operate from conflicting epistemological views, then postpositivist concerns about correspondence are important. For the claim of correspondence to be warranted, rigorous procedures for collecting and reporting data must be followed. The axiological and epistemological assumptions of a deductive, postpositivist study are supported by the format of a science report in which a hypothesis or question is laid out along with a rationale for the type of data needed to support or refute the hypothesis or question. The methods section of the report lays out the procedures that were followed to collect the data and the findings section summarizes and displays the data, which either supports or refutes the hypothesis.

In an inductive, interpretive study, however, the rigor lies in a different process. A great deal of raw text must be amassed from a variety of sources, which ideally represent a diversity of responses to the issue or question under study. In the case of the earthquake study in Chapter 5 (Exemplar 5.1), the aim of collecting raw texts in the form of interviews would not have been to confirm that everyone found the experience to be terrible, but to probe for nuanced differences among the survivors' responses to the catastrophe. Perhaps if these nuances had been brought to light, the physician might have been intrigued rather than repulsed by qualitative research. In the case of Exemplar 9.1.1, the question under study might be, "What issues arise when teachers and principals discuss professional development experiences?" The cafeteria conversation then becomes one of many different conversations between teachers and principals that might be recorded and probed for issues related to professional development. The aim is not to look for general patterns, but to look for nuances of difference. In order to bring important nuances to light, the researcher must *resonate* with the raw texts for an extended time. During this time, alternative interpretations are formulated. Interpretations of various texts are compared and contrasted to one another. Individual texts are visited and revisited to see if different aspects of the text become more salient as other aspects recede.

---

**Criterion for Judging Interpretive Dissertations**

**Rigor**—This criterion speaks to the quality of thought that goes into the inquiry. Are the conclusions carefully crafted from sufficiently thick and rich raw text? Was reflection done in a careful and systematic rather than haphazard fashion? Has the analysis and interpretation of experiential text been thorough and exhaustive? Does the researcher avoid solipsistic reasoning? Is there sufficient depth of intellect, rather than superficial or simplistic reasoning?

**Sample Reference List 9.1**

**Writing Qualitative/Interpretive Research**

Adams, 1984

Alvermann, O'Brien, & Dillon, 1996

Ely, Vinz, Downing, & Anzul, 1997

Golden-Biddle & Locke, 2006

Kamler & Thomson, 2006

Meloy, 2002

Rasberry, 2001

Rhodes, 2000

Richardson, 1990, 2003

Stay, 1996

Wallace & Wray, 2006

Welty, 1984

Wolcott, 2001

Even as the researcher works with the experiential texts, he or she is turning repeatedly to discourses that might serve to illuminate various meanings that are being constructed. So, for example, Noreen might turn to the raw texts she has compiled from reading literature to see if there are any references to epistemological conflicts between teachers and principals. If so, she would reread these to see what insights they might provide. If not, she would search for relevant literature. So the purpose of experiential text is not to prove that some phenomenon exists but to open up avenues of thinking to be explored. In conjunction with these explorations, the researcher is writing. The purpose of the writing is not to report what is already understood but to come to know what is important to say about the phenomenon under study. This role of writing in constructing knowledge through the crafting of text is often not well understood by doctoral students who may be under the sway of explicit or implicit postpositivist assumptions about research. Sample Reference List 9.1 offers a starting point for those who want to read more about the centrality of writing as a way of coming to know.

Through the writing of successive drafts, interpretations are proposed, explored, developed, tested, discarded, reformulated, and refined. At times, ideas seem to be coming together into a coherent document. At other times, the ideas seem to fall apart, pushing researchers to gather more raw texts, reexamine the texts at hand, dismantle an existing document, or rethink the major points they are trying to convey. This recursive process begins with one's earliest musings about a study and continues until the dissertation is completed. Typically, one does not fully grasp the thesis to be argued until well into writing what many students believe to be the final draft of their dissertation. In our experience, this "final" draft quite often becomes the next to the last draft. It is only when the student has written his or her way to the end of the dissertation that the full scope of the ideas comes into focus. At that point, the dissertation author can fine-tune the experiential text to portray with as much verisimilitude as possible the context within which his or her thesis has been constructed. Thus, while the experiential text foreshadows the conceptual points that will comprise the core thesis, these points have been identified and explored through an arduous process.

## CHAPTER CONCLUSION

In this chapter, we have tried to give a sense of how interpretive researchers move from raw to experiential text and then begin to probe the meaning of the experiential text through iterative and theoretic interpretation. With this as a backdrop, we now turn to issues related to crafting an interpretive dissertation proposal. In Chapters 10 and 11, we address issues related to the crafting of discursive text in support of the proposal. In Chapter 13, we discuss the crafting of theoretic text and the interweaving of experiential, discursive, and theoretic texts into a coherent dissertation.

---

### Reflective Interlude 9.1

#### How Prepared Am I to Deal With Writing and Interpreting Text?

- What assumptions have I been making about the relationship between events/experiences and the portrayal of those events/experiences in a dissertation? Am I inclined to value correspondence or coherence? What are the implications of this inclination for conceptualizing a study and ultimately writing my dissertation?
- What sort of experiential text am I imagining that I will write for my dissertation?
- What preparation have I had for writing this form of experiential text that has the quality of verisimilitude?
- What talents other than writing (e.g., drawing) do I have that can help me to create vivid portrayals of experience?
- What preparation do I have in interpreting various forms of text?
- What can I do to practice iterative and theoretic interpretation?

---

### EXEMPLAR 9.2    Musings About Correspondence, Coherence, and Authenticity in Qualitative Research

*Authors' Commentary.* Maria wrote this anecdote after attending a 1996 performance of *Inherit the Wind,* a play by Jerome Lawrence and Robert E. Lee based on the Scopes monkey trial. As she was leaving the theater, she began thinking about the "facts" of the trial.

What got me thinking about the facts of the play was the character of William Jennings Bryan, the prosecuting attorney in the case. I had always thought he was a well-regarded jurist and intellectual. Did he *really* espouse creationism? Did Jennings really collapse and die at the end of the trial? Who *was* the defense attorney in the original case? All I could think of was F. Lee Baily. I knew that wasn't right, but I couldn't jar his name loose so that Clarence Darrow's could come to mind. Did H. L. Mencken really cover the story of the trial?

Even as I pondered these questions, I knew they didn't really matter within the context of the drama. The playwrights had no intention of giving a precise, factual account of the trial. (One could always review the court transcripts for that story.) In fact, as the authors' note in the playbill states

> *Inherit the Wind* is not history. The events which took place in Dayton, Tennessee, during the scorching July of 1925 are clearly the genesis of this play. It has, however, an exodus entirely its own.

*(Continued)*

Only a handful of phrases have been taken from the actual transcript of the famous Scopes trial. Some of the characters of the play are related to the colorful figures in that battle of giants; but they have life and language of their own—and, therefore, names of their own.

The collision of Bryan and Darrow at Dayton was dramatic, but it was not a drama. Moreover, the issues of their conflict have acquired new dimension and meaning in the 70 years since they clashed at the Rhea County Courthouse. So *Inherit the Wind* does not pretend to be journalism. It is theatre. It is not 1925. The stage directions set the time as "Not too long ago." It might have been yesterday. It could be tomorrow.

For me, the more compelling question was, "In what ways do the themes of the drama speak of important and enduring human dilemmas?" The play's significance in this sense was underscored by a recent *New York Times* article reproduced on a huge placard in the theater lobby. The article described an attempt by Christian fundamentalists to ban the teaching of Darwinism. (Since 1996, the debate between creationism, intelligent design, and Darwinism has precipitated several legal battles.)

As I reflected on the difference between my questions about the "facts" of the original trial and my musings about the tensions between belief and reason, I began to think about the notion of authenticity in qualitative research. Suddenly, it seemed that I was understanding at a deeper level the distinction between *correspondence* and *coherence*.

Within a postpositivist tradition, authenticity refers to the reliability and verifiability with which an account of an event corresponds to the "real" details of the event (e.g., date, time, place, people, words spoken). Knowledge claims can be made only if certain procedures have been followed to guarantee to the greatest extent possible that the researcher's account matches or corresponds to the event. Thus, data-gathering techniques emphasize "objective" observation and recording of information, such as audio and video recordings, verbatim transcripts, field notes (preferably multiple researchers taking field notes with high degrees of interobserver reliability); a large number of people agreeing that "what we say we saw was what happened." All such techniques are aimed at increasing confidence in the correspondence between an original event and the description or portrayal of it.

Within an interpretive tradition, the concern is not with what *really* happened in the details of the trial. Rather, it asks, "Does the account portray an event in a compelling way—not the event per se—but some profound human dilemma embedded in the event?" Knowledge claims are based on the way in which the researcher gets at and portrays the human dilemma. In the interpretive mode, the issue is not correspondence to some verifiable event. It is in a coherent and authentic rendering of the meaning of the experience in a way that makes clearer the connection between the individual/idiosyncratic and the universal. Thus, in the drama, the fictive characters represent more universally held positions or belief systems regarding the origins of human beings.

I am reminded of the human dilemma puddle and the concerns that some students have about profound or incomprehensible dilemmas of practice. It may not be possible to study such dilemmas empirically (as so many faculty caution students). Yet it may be possible to get at them through interpretive inquiry. And the more authentic expression of a human dilemma may be portrayed more coherently through an aesthetic rather than scientific mode.

# NOTES

1.  When we first began to teach an elective course titled "Interpretive Inquiry," we encountered several students who clearly intended to pursue empirical studies. As we talked about an interpretative worldview in which knowledge is constructed, these students exhibited signs of escalating cognitive dissonance. Despite what appeared to be painful confusion, these students insisted that they needed a course on interpretation. Finally, we realized that they were looking for techniques to use when they reached the step in their empirical studies of "interpreting" data. This notion of interpretation is probably more akin to the notion of data analysis or discussion of findings in science-based studies.

2.  In recent years there has been a renewed interest in the issue of *evidence*, particularly in light of mandates that federal funding be used to support only "evidence-based" instruction. To begin exploring the concept of evidence, see Freeman, deMarrais, Preissle, Roulston, and St. Pierre, 2007; Morse, 2006; Olson, 2004; Slavin, 2002, 2004, 2008. (The 2008 Slavin reference is the lead article in Volume 37, Number 1 of the *Educational Researcher*, which is devoted to the issue of evidence-based research in education. Other articles in the volume are responses to the perspective laid out by Slavin.)

3.  *Triangulation* is one convention of postpositivist qualitative research that aims to increase confidence in the correspondence between an entity and the researcher's description of that entity. Triangulation is based on the idea that the researcher's perception is going to be slanted by his or her angle of vision. So if a researcher can get at least two other angles of vision, there will be a more accurate "fix" on what really happened. (For additional information on triangulation, see Mathison, 1998; Morse, 1991.)

4.  To contrast the notions of *correspondence* and *coherence* it is useful to think about a geographical map. Depending upon the cartographer's purpose for the map and its intended audience, the map may or may not correspond to the topographical "reality" of a given terrain. A map showing the elevation of a geographic area will differ markedly from a street map of the same area, which will differ from a map showing points of interest for tourists. In each of these instances, it is the cartographer's interpretation that determines how he or she will portray the geographical terrain with coherence. The issue of coherence in the experiential texts of educational research is, of course, more complex than that of a geographic map. Geographic terrain offers a somewhat stable reality from which to interpret various properties (e.g., coordinates for the location of a river or specific buildings or the intersection of two streets). Educational phenomena, on the other hand, include cultural properties, time, space, human interactions, and so on that are continually shifting. And what one makes of these phenomena is varied based on the positionality of the interpreter. For this reason, some educational researchers (e.g., Barone, 1992, 1995; Kilbourn, 1999; McMahon, 2000, 2006) argue that experiential texts as representations of educational phenomena are fictive by nature. The texts can never ensure the kind of certainty that those who claim correspondent reality strive to attain.

# SECTION THREE

*Entering Into and
Living Through the
Dissertation Journey*

# 10

# *Developing Ideas for the Dissertation Proposal*

**Key Concepts**

Arena of Practice                    Intent of a Study

Field of Study                       Topic

Immersion in Literature

In Chapter 9, we suggested that both the proposal and the final dissertation comprise *experiential, discursive,* and *theoretic texts* that are crafted through a recursive process of writing, reading, and deliberation with others. The dissertation proposal represents a student's best approximation of what phenomenon will be studied, why the phenomenon is worth studying, and how the phenomenon will be studied. Quite a bit of exploration is necessary to develop the ideas that will ultimately allow the researcher to

- clarify and contextualize the intent of the inquiry,
- construct the logic-of-justification within the conventions of a given research genre, and
- begin to imagine how the knowledge claims of the study will be represented and warranted.

All of the i[...] to help readers develop a mindset conduc[...] pretive dissertation. In this chapter, we sugg[...] e the intent of their studies within broader [...] sues related to crafting the proposal docum[...]

Before proc[...] eread the Case Examples in Section Four to [...] raised below. It may seem a bit strange to [...] s to illustrate points about developing a p[...] roach served several practical needs. Firs[...] nents. Although our files are replete with m[...] leted drafts of research proposals are no[...] rned these documents with comments an[...] d been formally reviewed by the students' [...]

The prop[...] my proposal, I felt like a student. [...] I understood qualitative research[...] here was a lot of anxiety with the[...] lly? It was all just an idea at that p[...] cholar. I owned the study. I knew [...]

The ter[...] r studies makes it difficult to illustrate th[...] ocess of the study. Although a good prop[...] ertation that the student has made up t[...] student's best educated guess about wha[...] to learn more about the study as they w[...] f the study change. This does not mean[...] ath, but rather that the details and nuan[...] coming clearer as the student refines he[...] y. Thus, revisions in the title, statemen[...] unusual manifestation of this recursive[...]

## CLAR[...]IZING THE [...]

As discu[...] eptualizing a dissertation is often to talk [...] imately, in the research proposal, students [...] t clearly indicates not only what is under study but also the purpose and importance of the inquiry. Thinking about potential *topics* in relation to one's *arena of practice* and *field of study* can be a helpful place to begin exploring possibilities.

## Topic

*Topic* refers to the issue, concept, or subject area that might potentially be the focus of the dissertation (e.g., outcomes-based education, school prayer, cooperative learning, financial equity, student retention, democratic schooling, service learning, educational inclusion). Early on, it is not unusual for students to be interested in several different topics. Rather than prematurely choosing one option over another, it is useful to record various possibilities and weigh their merits as one explores the discourses.

Any topic can potentially be framed in a variety of ways depending upon what one is interested in coming to know or understand. When students first begin to articulate an idea for a study, it is not uncommon for them to be torn between several different issues that are embedded within a general topic area, to describe either an overly grandiose or overly narrow focus on the topic, or to shift their focus each time they describe their research interest. Illustrative of early thinking about dissertation topics is the very first writing that Wendy Milne did about her study (see Exemplar 10.1).

---

**EXEMPLAR 10.1    Early Writing That Expresses Competing Possibilities for a Dissertation**

Currently, I have two topics that I am interested in researching. . . . The first topic deals with a process that I believe is quite valuable to children in the art room. I call this process *reflection sheets.* These reflection sheets have taken on many forms but are usually used at the end of a project or unit, and their purpose is to get the students to evaluate and reflect upon their work in the hopes that they will recall their strengths and weaknesses when they begin a new project. Although many art teachers provide reflection sheets to their students, I believe mine have a unique form. Also, those art teachers that do provide reflection sheets often only do so at the middle school or high school level. Another advantage I have in using the reflection sheets is that I keep them from year to year, and I keep the artwork throughout the school year. This enables me to see the growth in the students' drawings as well as their growth in the reflection sheets. Possibly, I feel the need to research this topic because I find that my personal weakness lies in reflecting upon a project that I have completed.

My second topic is the one that I feel most strongly about. It goes something like this. Over the past 10 years the role of the art teacher has drastically changed, but the perception of the art teacher has not. The only people that I see who value art as an equally important subject are my students. My teaching peers, administrators, and parents have verbally stated this view of unimportance or somehow have silently implied that my field is less than important. I find that I frequently express frustration over this lack of respect. However, I am concerned that if I choose this topic it will just sound as if I'm complaining.

*Authors' Commentary.* Notice Wendy's dual focus. On one hand, there is a fairly narrow focus on a particular instructional technique—the use of reflection sheets with elementary school students. With this focus, Wendy runs the risk of the cheerleader mentality. On the other hand, she has a rather grandiose desire to challenge a perceived devaluing of art. This carries the risk of the vendetta mentality. Such widely divergent possibilities often appear in students' early writings. The issue is the students' need to move beyond these vaguely formed notions to a viable dissertation. Embedded in Wendy's writing are two key phrases that suggest avenues for further deliberation. At the end of the first paragraph, Wendy makes a tentative connection between the reflection she expects of her students and her weakness for this type of thinking. This raises the possibility of connecting her ideas to the educational discourses on teacher reflection. At the end of the second paragraph, Wendy expresses misgivings about sounding like a complainer. This provides an entry point for discussing issues of stance and voice. It also hints at potential bodies of discourse that might provide insights into the significance of the study—namely, the discourses on aesthetic knowing and rationales for art education. Through ongoing deliberation, Wendy eventually came to the concept of *reflective art-making,* which served as the centerpiece of her study (Milne, 2000).

For educational practitioners, considering various topics in relation to one's arena of practice allows some ideas to emerge more clearly, while others, of lesser interest, recede into the background.

## Reflective Interlude 10.1

### What Topics Am I Drawn to Study?

- If you completed Reflective Interlude 4.3, review your ideas and ask, "What topic areas are embedded in my reflections? What questions do I have about these topic areas? What do I find interesting or intriguing about these topics?"
- How have I been using my program of studies and coursework to deepen my understanding of potential topics?
- How might I use papers that I have written or will write for courses to delve more deeply into one or more topic of interest?
- Periodically revisit your working list and consider questions like the following:
  - Has my interest in some topics waned?
  - Have other topics become more compelling?
  - What connections can I now see among topics that previously seemed unrelated?
  - What topic or topics, if researched, would lay the groundwork for future inquiries?
  - Given where I am in my thinking and my life, what topics seem more feasible to study?

## Arena of Practice

*Arena of practice* refers to the setting of one's professional practice as well as one's professional role (e.g., public school teacher, 11th-grade English teacher, private school administrator, headmaster, junior administrator, higher education faculty, program evaluator). Both setting and role can be considered in terms of past, present, and future arenas of practice.

As discussed in relation to the dissertation puddles, past and current arenas of practice can give rise to problematic or troubling issues that might be transformed into a viable dissertation topic. A desire to look backward may be associated with either an unresolved problematic work experience or a particularly enjoyable experience that the student wants to revisit. Anticipated changes in setting or role often help to clarify priorities among potential topics as students come to see the dissertation as laying important groundwork for the next phase of their career.

As mentioned earlier, many of the students with whom we work are experienced practitioners; most continue to work full time as they pursue their doctoral degree. For this group, writing about their arena of practice can help them to step back from the situational details and focus on the conceptual issues embedded in their practice. Other students are enrolled in full-time doctoral study. They may be highly engaged in theoretical discourses as portrayed in formal literature but see less clearly how to frame a study that speaks to a particular discourse community. Some full-time students work on faculty-directed research projects and are expected to complete some aspect of the larger study for their dissertation. International students, a special subset of full-time students, may be operating under specific mandates from a government or academic institution that is sponsoring their doctoral study.

Regardless of one's specific circumstances, writing about one's arena of practice is often a less stressful way to begin approaching the dissertation. It is also affirming of one's professional competence at a time when undertaking an unfamiliar and ambiguous activity may be triggering self-doubts and anxiety.

---

### Reflective Interlude 10.2

### In What Ways Might My Arena of Practice Help to Contextualize the Intent of My Dissertation?

- How have my various professional experiences influenced my thinking about education? What educational moments come to mind either because they trouble me or because they affirm some value or belief I have about education? (As you write about your experiences within various arenas of practice, recalling situational details is an important step. But even more important is considering what issues, ideas, questions, and concerns are embedded within those experiences.)

- Practice settings as contexts for inquiry might be considered in two ways:
  - Conceptually, practice settings might provide contexts for thinking about the intent of one's study—for example, how does an issue play out within a particular type of setting?
  - Logistically, practice settings might actually serve as sites or locations for conducting one's research. It can be useful to record ideas about both possibilities, especially when one is in the early stages of conceptualizing the *intent of a study*.

- What professional roles have I held? To what type of professional role do I aspire? How might past, present, or future roles provide a stance or vantage point from which to pursue my research?

## Field of Study

Formulating a meaningful intent for one's study entails an understanding not only of what is of personal interest but also of why and how a topic might be important to a larger community of practitioners and scholars. Immersing oneself in discourses of one's field eventually yields cogent responses to three key questions about the intent of a study— "What?" "So what?" and "Who cares?"

*Field of study* refers to various subsets of education, such as teaching, instruction and learning, curriculum studies, policy studies, administration, supervision, special education, counseling, evaluation, higher education, school law, or international education. Departments, divisions, and programs within a school of education are generally organized around specific fields of study, and matriculation at a university generally implies a commitment to learning bodies of knowledge associated with one's chosen field. Major fields of study, in turn, often include subgroups with more narrowly focused special interests (e.g., language arts education, science education).

Locating oneself within a particular field of study can lead to preliminary connections between personal and private interests and concerns of larger professional and scholarly communities. Potential topics can be evaluated in terms of two important questions: "So what?" and "Who cares?" In other words, who besides the student might find the topic of significance, and how might the student's interest in a topic contribute to some established body of knowledge or discourse?

One dysfunctional bit of dissertation folklore is an assumption that one's committee is the only audience for the study. This may be reinforced by academic structures in which students are conditioned to write term papers that are read only by a course instructor and then filed away. Students who skillfully meet expectations of course instructors may be surprised by the idea that their dissertation is likely to have a broader professional audience. Likewise, they may be disoriented by the dawning realization that the dissertation serves some larger, more public, scholarly agenda, not simply an instructor's course syllabus. As discussed in Chapter 8, becoming involved with professional and scholarly communities allows one to hear and participate in the evolving conversations of one's field. The earlier one engages in such conversations, the more nuanced one's understanding becomes. While reading the published literature in one's field is of paramount importance, so too is tuning into real-time discourses where cutting-edge issues are often under debate.

**Reflective Interlude 10.3**

**With What Discourse Communities Do I Identify?**

- Where and in what ways am I engaged in ongoing conversations with others in my field?
- To which professional and/or research organizations do I belong? What is the nature of my involvement with the organizations? For example, do I attend annual meetings or conferences, serve on committees or task forces, or give presentations?
- What professional organizations are sponsoring conferences and workshops on my topics of interest?
- When I attend professional meetings or conferences in my field of study, who has presented on my topics of interest?
- If you are not a member of the American Educational Research Association, it would be useful to go to the Web site and carefully review the Divisions and Special Interest Groups. Identify those most directly related to your professional setting, role, and topics of interest. Consider which you might join.
- To which listservs and blogs do I belong? Which do I routinely follow? To which do I contribute?
- Who are the noted practitioners and researchers in my field of study? What issues are they writing about? To what extent have I been following their thinking and writing? What strategies can I use to stay current with their work?

## Immersion in Literature on Topic

At the same time one is reflecting on professional experiences that give rise to topics of interest, it is important to become immersed in literature. As mentioned in Chapter 8, notes on books and articles are an important form of *raw text*, and conscientious researchers accumulate an extensive set of references. This prospect can be intimidating, especially if one is uncertain about what literature is worth pursuing. On more than one occasion, we have heard students say, "I don't want to waste time on literature that may turn out to be irrelevant." Or, "I'm afraid of going off on tangents that aren't going to help me get finished." It is important to realize that a certain amount of scouting around in various bodies of literature is necessary for developing one's ideas for the dissertation proposal. Then as the focus of the dissertation begins to coalesce, a more exhaustive review can be completed. As Boote and Beile (2005) contend

A substantive, thorough, sophisticated literature review is a precondition for doing substantive, thorough, sophisticated research. "Good" research is good because it advances our collective understanding. To advance our collective understanding, a researcher or scholar needs to understand what has been done before, the strengths and weaknesses of existing studies, and what they might mean. A researcher cannot perform significant research without first understanding the literature in the field. (p. 3)

Acquiring a thorough and nuanced understanding of literature in one's field requires time and concentrated study. Therefore, the earlier one plunges into the literature, the better. In taking the plunge, it is helpful to keep in mind that exploring literature serves multiple purposes including

- clarifying and refining questions related to one's topic of interest,
- seeing one's own thinking in relation to the thinking of others,
- gaining a historical perspective on the topic within one's field of study,
- seeing the relationship between one's topic and other topics of concern within one's field of study,
- identifying scholars who are studying issues related to one's topic of interest,
- clarifying the conceptual context for studying the topic, and
- gaining deeper insight into the importance of the topic.

## DEVELOPING A MINDSET FOR REVIEWING LITERATURE

Although it may not be possible to know exactly what references will be most relevant or how various references will be incorporated into the proposal, it is important to have a sense of what one is trying to accomplish through *immersion in literature*. Without a sense of purpose, it is easy to become overwhelmed by what one is reading, as illustrated by Marjorie Logsdon's Henny Penny characterization (Exemplar 8.1). Marjorie's struggle to make sense of highly complex discourses on feminism calls attention to three important points about immersion in literature. First, there is inevitably a time of confusion, when it is impossible to put threads of discourse into any meaningful perspective. Just knowing this is typical of the process can help to alleviate a sense of incompetence or panic. Second, if one persists in reading, relationships among ideas and authors begin to emerge. Third, patterns of meaning are not embedded in the literature per se, but are forged in relation to the nagging issues that are pushing and prodding one toward a picture of one's study. It is important to give oneself time to enter into the discourses, to read without necessarily understanding, to read eventually with glimmers of understanding, and finally to read with enough understanding to begin crafting *discursive text* for the proposal. (See Sample Reference List 10.1 for resources on strategies for reading and using literature.)

**Sample Reference List 10.1**

**Strategies for Reading**

Abrams, 1989

Anfara & Mertz, 2006

Bartholomae & Petrosky, 1999

Boote & Beile, 2005, 2006

Brown & Dowling, 2007

Hart, 1999

Locke, Silverman, & Spirduso, 2004

Maxwell, 2006

Montuori, 2005

Shank & Brown, 2007

Wallace & Wray, 2006

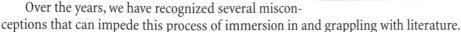

Over the years, we have recognized several misconceptions that can impede this process of immersion in and grappling with literature.

*Misconception—Misinterpretation of "Original Research."* Deterring immersion in literature may be a common bit of folklore—that the topic of one's dissertation must have never before been studied. Repeatedly, we have read preliminary drafts of research proposals that include statements such as the following: "The review of the literature proved that no studies have been done on this topic"; "This topic has not been studied"; "There is nothing in the literature on this topic"; and "Very little has been written on this topic."

For quite some time, we puzzled over this common assertion that the topic had never been researched. Eventually, we came to speculate that it is a misinterpretation of the expectation that the dissertation be an original piece of research.[1] We also speculate that students may avoid immersing themselves in the literature for fear that their topic "has already been done" and that they will be forced to abandon a cherished idea.

To challenge this misconception, we assert, "If nothing has been written on the topic, it probably isn't worth studying."[2] Reviewing literature clarifies where and how one's ideas fit into an evolving discourse about the topic. The notion of *original research* is better understood as "making a meaningful or useful contribution" to the deliberations of a discourse community.

In preparing the research proposal, one must explain not only what one intends to study but also *why* the intended study is worth doing. To make a convincing case for the study, it is important to show how it will fit within and contribute to a body of discourse. Ideally, readings throughout one's course of doctoral study will provide this important context. So, too, will participation in professional organizations as mentioned earlier. Sometimes, professional organizations will publish position papers on critical issues confronting a field. Some professional associations develop research agenda for the field at large. Obtaining copies of such documents can provide useful insights into issues of current concern.

Another strategy for gaining a broad perspective of the discourses within a given field is to consult handbooks, encyclopedias, or other compendia of research related to one's topic (see Sample Reference List 10.2). Reviewing these or similar resources can provide useful insights into the critical issues of concern to a given discourse community.

### Sample Reference List 10.2

#### Handbooks and Encyclopedias

Andrews & Haythornthwaite (2007)—*The Sage Handbook of e-Learning*

Anfara (2007)—*The Handbook of Research in Middle Level Education*

Asamen, Ellis, & Berry (2008)—*The SAGE Handbook of Child Development, Multiculturalism, and Media*

Banks & McGee Banks (1995)—*Handbook of Research on Multicultural Education*

Berliner & Calfee (1996)—*Handbook of Educational Psychology*

Cochran-Smith, Feiman-Nemser, McIntyre, & Demers (2008)—*Handbook of Research on Teacher Education*

Connelly, He, & Phillion (2007)—*The SAGE Handbook of Curriculum and Instruction*

Colwell (1992)—*Handbook of Research on Music Teaching and Learning*

DiStefano, Rudestam, & Silverman (2004)—*Encyclopedia of Distributed Learning*

Eisner & Day (2004)—*Handbook of Research and Policy in Art Education*

English (2006)—*Encyclopedia of Educational Leadership and Administration*

Firth & Pajak (1998)—*Handbook of Research on School Supervision*

Flood, Jensen, Lapp, & Squire (1991)—*Handbook of Research on Teaching the English Language Arts*

Gabel (1994)—*Handbook of Research on Science Teaching and Learning*

Grouws (1992)—*Handbook of Research on Mathematics Teaching and Learning*

Hayden, Thompson, & Levy (2007)—*The SAGE Handbook of Research in International Education*

Husen & Postlethwaite (1985)—*The International Encyclopedia of Education*

Jonassen (1995)—*Handbook of Research for Educational Communications and Technology*

Kelly, Lesh, & Baek (2008)—*Handbook of Design Research Methods in Education*

Lester (2007)—*Second Handbook of Research on Mathematics Teaching and Learning*

Levstik & Tyson (2008)—*Handbook of Research in Social Studies Education*

Mathison (2005)—*Encyclopedia of Evaluation*

Millman & Darling-Hammond (1990)—*The New Handbook of Teacher Evaluation: Assessing Elementary and Secondary School Teachers*

Pinar (2003)—*International Handbook of Curriculum Research*

Runco (2008)—*The Creativity Research Handbook*

Shaver (1991)—*Handbook of Research on Social Studies Teaching and Learning*

Sikula, Houston, & Haberman (1990)—*Handbook of Research on Teacher Education*

Singer, Murphey, & Tennant (1993)—*Handbook of Research on Sport Psychology*

Spodek (1982)—*Handbook of Research on the Education of Young Children*

Tillman (2008)—*The SAGE Handbook of African American Education*

*Misconception—The Blank Slate.* Another disquieting misconception is that qualitative researchers deliberately avoid reading any literature related to their topic as a strategy for counteracting personal bias or subjectivity. This notion is problematic in at least two ways. First, it assumes that objectivity is possible and is the sine qua non of all research. Second, naiveté generally results in shoddy scholarship, not objectivity. Developing one's ideas in relation to formal discourses is crucial for adequately addressing the "So what?" and "Who cares?" of a study.

We are reminded of a student who wanted to study women mentoring women. She proposed doing what she called a phenomenological study and insisted that reviewing literature on mentoring was inconsistent with a phenomenological approach. At the same time, she had no formal grounding in phenomenology, was reading no literature on phenomenology, and seemed singularly unaware that an extensive body of literature on mentoring existed. Despite cautions that naiveté undermines the researcher's credibility, she was convinced that her study would make a unique contribution by calling attention to an unrecognized phenomenon.

Thinking about colleagues, professional associations, and scholars in a particular field of study can personalize the idea of *discourse community* and can underscore the dangers of appearing naive to those who are knowledgeable about the subject of an inquiry.

*Misconception—The Fishing Trip Syndrome.* This misconception is related to the blank slate misconception. Students avoid using literature to frame the intent of their study. They mistakenly think that they will contaminate their study if they indicate any hunches, speculations, or biases that might be guiding their thinking. This creates an impression that they are fishing around in the raw texts, hoping to "catch" something of significance. A well-constructed discursive text will provide a conceptual frame and logic-of-justification for what the researcher is seeking to understand. Micheline, for example, wove together experiential and discursive text to make the case that educational inclusion presented special educators with problematics. Her study then became a way to explore the nature of those problematics. (See Case Example 1.) Lynn (Case Example 2) knew that incorporating creative dramatics into her pedagogy would give rise to dilemmas, just as Pat (Case Example 3) knew she would face pedagogical dilemmas when she initiated a portfolio requirement with her composition students. They crafted experiential and discursive texts to warrant those "going in assumptions" and then illuminated the dilemmas through their inquiry. Kathy (Case Example 4) drew upon personal experience and literature to make the case that promises had been made and broken in the lead-teacher initiative. Jean (Case Example 5) knew that communication between parents and professional educators was fraught with misunderstanding when a reform initiative was launched. Joan (Case Example 6) knew that gifted female students tended to drop out of science courses when they reached adolescence. In each of these cases, they drew upon their professional experience to sharpen their sense of the issue they wanted to study. Then they turned to the literature to see if their personal reaction had sufficient merit to warrant further study. Rather than creating an aura of objectivity, pretending that they had no initial hunches or ideas about the issue would have undermined their credibility. The point to keep in mind is the importance of deliberating with bodies of discourse as a way of testing out one's thinking. In a sense, reading the literature allows a student to ask, "Am I the only one dealing with this issue, or is this an issue that others in my field are dealing with?"

*Misconception—Literature Will Relate Directly to One's Topic.* This misconception came into focus when we worked with an emotional support teacher who was on the verge of burnout. As she described student behaviors that drained her physical and psychic energy, we gave her an article that discussed the concept of *teaching as emotional work.* Puzzled that she never referenced the article in subsequent discussions or writing, we finally asked what she had thought of it. "It was interesting," she replied. "But it didn't really apply to my situation. It was about infants and daycare workers, and my students are much older." Clearly this student misperceived the nature of intellectual work associated with immersing herself in literature—that is, it was incumbent upon her to keep an open mind, to resonate with the possibilities of ideas she was encountering, to connect others' ideas to the ideas she was developing.

While it is useful to begin literature searches with concepts directly related to one's topic, it is often necessary to broaden one's focus, looking for collateral sources that can inform one's thinking. Tracing bibliographies can be a useful strategy for extending one's explorations. This seems to surprise a number of students. "You mean I can do that?" is a common response to the suggestion that students find relevant references by checking the references in articles and books that are particularly meaningful to them. We speculate that a couple of factors may contribute to students' overlooking this obvious strategy. One may be the "academic hoops" mentality, in which compliance with external requirements is the yardstick for completing work. Even at the doctoral level, some students continue to ask, "How long do you want this paper to be? How many references am I supposed to use?" The driving force behind this outlook is getting through a perceived hoop, not deliberative curiosity about a given issue.

*Misconception—The Agree/Disagree Mentality.* Another view of reviewing literature was voiced by Micheline, who had resisted for months the idea of shaping a dissertation around the issue of educational inclusion. Having been told repeatedly that her credentials in special and regular education ideally positioned her to study this issue, she finally blurted out, "But I don't want to have to agree with what others are saying. I disagree with their ideas about inclusion." "But why would you have to?" we responded. By the time she completed her comprehensive examination, Micheline was able to move beyond the original dysfunctional notion that her purpose in reviewing the literature was to decide who is right and who is wrong, with whom she agrees and disagrees. Rather, she used the literature to inform her thinking and thereby to set the conceptual context for her own study. Yet this shift did not occur easily for Micheline, as evidenced by the following comment:

> As a veteran school practitioner, I have always been somewhat skeptical of the researchers who entered my classrooms appearing to be blind to the complexities of life in schools, seeming to recognize only that which is visible, and seeking only to understand that which could be "scientifically measured." Through the years, I have stood alongside of the many teachers under my supervision and have shared their frustration and rage with the hackneyed words, "research says . . . " (Stabile, 1999, p. xxii)

This suspicion of what "research says" is one of the dilemmas that Labaree (2003) flags in his discussion of the preparation of practitioners as researchers:

I argue that the shift from K–12 teaching to educational research often asks students to transform their cultural orientation from normative to analytical, from personal to intellectual, from the particular to the universal, and from the experiential to the theoretical. Embedded in these potential pressures to change is a struggle over the relationship between teaching and research in education and an emergent struggle over the moral responsibility of both kinds of practitioners for education's social outcomes. As a result of this culture clash, students often feel that programs are challenging the legitimacy of their own teacher-based perspective on education, and they often respond by challenging the legitimacy of the proffered research-based perspective. (pp. 16–17)

As suggested both by Labaree's and Micheline's comments, immersion in literature serves a deeper purpose than acquiring information to be used in one's study. It also contributes to the formation of one's identity as scholar and broadens one's understanding of what counts as legitimate knowledge. For scholar-practitioners, this is not a matter of privileging theoretic over experiential knowledge, but rather of understanding and appreciating how each form of knowledge informs the other.[3] The capacity to resonate thoughtfully with both published literature and real-time discourses is crucial when it comes time to craft discursive text that provides a rationale for the intent of one's study. We return to this point in the next chapter as we highlight issues related to writing the proposal document.

> **Criterion for Judging Interpretive Dissertations**
>
> **Insightful Engagement With Discourses**—Discursive text demonstrates a grasp of significant issues confronting one's field of study and connects one's topic to one or more of those issues.

**Reflective Interlude 10.4**

### How Does My Topic Fit Within Evolving Discourses?

- What are major and minor threads of discourse in my field, what scholars are contributing to the various threads, and how does my topic relate to one or more of the threads?
- What is the history and evolution of my field of study? What issues have been of concern during various periods? What issues are of current interest in the field, and how does my topic relate to these issues?
- Where is my topic being discussed (e.g., formal literature, public media, popular press, policy documents)?
- Who is talking about my topic (e.g., practitioners, researchers, policy-makers, general public, special-interest groups)?
- When did the topic become a focal point of discourse (e.g., how long has the conversation about the topic been going on)? Have there been significant shifts in the tenor or focus of the conversation?
- What bodies of literature will help to flesh out my topic? What bodies of literature may be of use later in the dissertation process? What system will I use to keep track of relevant resources?

# NOTES

1. It is likely that the idea of equating *original research* with a "study that has never been done" is a carry over from a paradigm of scientific research. In this paradigm, a researcher is expected to review literature to see how a particular problem has already been studied and to identify gaps in the theory that explains the problem. The gaps offer a focal point for conceptualizing a hypothesis—if X can be shown to be true, there will be further support for the explanatory power of the theory; another piece of the puzzle will be put into place. To increase the certainty that the hypothesis holds true, scientists will often replicate a study hoping that the results will confirm the validity of the hypothesis. Such replication studies would not be considered *original research* because they would not offer new conceptual insight into what constitutes a gap in the theory, a new hypothesis about the problem under study, or a new method for testing a hypothesis. This meaning of *original research* makes sense within a scientific paradigm where knowledge is cumulative, false assumptions are replaced by more accurate assumptions, and the quest is for as great a degree of certainty as empirical evidence can support. Since this is not the nature of interpretive research, this scientific conception of *original research* is not particularly useful or relevant.

2. We recognize that there may be instances where issues have not been adequately recognized or studied. Sexual harassment, for example, came into clearer focus as a topic of study following Anita Hill's testimony at the Clarence Thomas confirmation hearings. Similarly, violence in the schools took on heightened meaning and urgency for study following the tragedy at Columbine High School. Our point is not to deny the possibility that a practitioner or doctoral student may be onto an issue that has not yet received widespread attention. Rather, we stress the danger of assuming that one's own ideas or experiences are so unique that no one else has written about them.

3. Throughout *The Qualitative Dissertation* we have been challenging what we see as a false dichotomy between theory and practice. Authors deMarrais and LeCompte (1999) offer a helpful discussion of several types of theory clustered under the headings of social transmission theories, interpretive theories, and social transformation theories. They explore the influences of these various forms of theories on the purposes of schooling.

# 11

# Crafting an Interpretive Dissertation Proposal

A viable research proposal conveys two overarching messages to members of one's dissertation committee. One, a manageable and worthwhile study is being proposed. Two, the student is capable of conducting the study. Students, particularly those with little or no proposal-writing experience, often express uncertainty about conveying these messages, asking questions such as, "What goes into a research proposal? What does a research proposal look like? How do I write it? How long is it supposed to be?"

Although we believe strongly that the organization of the proposal should serve the conceptual lines of reasoning that the doctoral candidate is constructing, we recognize that institutions may have very specific formats that must be followed. For some students, these formats can help to focus and clarify one's thinking. For other students, the formats may feel confining. If students find themselves in this latter situation, we suggest that they draft the proposal in a way that supports their mode of thinking and expression. Once this draft is in hand, it may be easier to edit it into a university-prescribed format.

As we said earlier, a number of books offer guidance to those writing proposals within a scientific, postpositivist tradition. Therefore, the thrust of the discussion in this chapter is on conceptual issues associated with crafting a proposal for a practice-based, interpretive dissertation. This writing entails drawing upon one's professional context and relevant discourses to forge the structural relationships among the intent of the study, the inquiry process, and the nature of knowledge claims that will be offered at the end of the inquiry. Although the specific format of the proposal may vary to better express the candidate's ideas, the document needs to incorporate several features:

*Title:* Announces in a nutshell the subject of the study and possibly the genre of inquiry

*Introduction:* Orients readers to the purpose, content, and organization of the document and begins to frame the study within experiential and discursive contexts

*The Study:* Provides a concise overview or synopsis of the inquiry

*Statement of Intent:* Communicates the purpose of the study and, ideally, alludes to its significance for a particular audience/discourse community

*Guiding Research Questions:* Lay out the conceptual structure of the entire inquiry

*Rationale for the Study:* Situates the intent of the study within scholarly discourses and persuasively argues that the study is worth doing

*Research Genre and Procedures:* Situates the study within an inquiry tradition and genre and provides a persuasive *logic-of-justification* for each research procedure

*Anticipated Portrayals:* Describes what form of representation the researcher envisions creating to capture the phenomenon under study and to convey the lessons learned from the inquiry

*Tentative Outline of Dissertation Chapters:* Summarizes how the researcher envisions laying out the dissertation document

## TITLE OF THE STUDY

The title of the dissertation conveys the conceptual heart of the study, ideally capturing both what is under study and the research genre to be followed. Consider several titles taken from studies completed by members of our dissertation study group (Exemplar 11.1).

Surprisingly, many students seem to give little thought to a title for their study. Precursors to the research proposal are often untitled, or an early title is retained even though the focus of the study evolves. In a well-crafted title, each word should relate to a key concept in the study. In turn, each concept in the title should be explained in the body of the proposal, and the relationships among the concepts should be made clear. (For an example of this point, see Case Example 1, Part 1 and Case Example 2, Part 1 for additional comments on titles.)

---

### EXEMPLAR 11.1    Examples of Dissertation Titles

1. *The Practice of Hospital Education: A Grounded Theory Study*

2. *An Explication of Human Resources Supervision: A Grounded Theory Study of a Public Alternative High School*

3. *Students in a Special Program for Gifted Female Adolescents: A Conceptual Case Study for Planning Curriculum*

4. *A Hermeneutic Study of Educational Myth: Implications for Clinical Supervision*

5. *A Narrative Study of Three Levels of Reflection in a College Composition Class: Teacher Journal, Student Portfolios, Teacher-Student Discourse*

6. *Promises Made, Promises Broken: A Literary Criticism of the Lead Teacher Experience in Pennsylvania*

7. *Meanwhile Back at the Ranch: A Study of Principals and School Reform*

*Authors' Commentary.* The first five studies have fairly conservative and straightforward titles—stating explicitly what is under study and the research genre (i.e., grounded theory, case study, hermeneutic study, narrative study). In all but Title 4, the research genre also flags the nature of the portrayal to be generated.

The remaining two titles have a more literary quality that reflects the authors' stronger, more explicit orientation to an interpretive mode of inquiry. Students who have sufficient artistic or narrative sensibility to undertake interpretive studies often have at least an intuitive sense of aesthetics. With the more literary phrases in the title, they intend to convey metaphorically or imagistically the insights generated through the inquiry. In crafting a title, it is important not to become so enamored of using artistic or literary wording that the conceptual structure of the study is obscured.

Title 7 is interesting because the final wording emerged after the student had completed a first draft of the dissertation, recognized the document's lack of conceptual coherence, and did a major rewrite to frame the study as a personal narrative. The phrase *meanwhile back at the ranch* captures the central message that the student conveys in the study: While school superintendents are often off campus dealing with external issues affecting a district, building principals remain behind to tend to daily operations.

Also incorporated into Titles 1, 3, and 5 is the context of the study. Over time, we have come to have mixed feelings about including this information in the title. Early on, when many of our colleagues were still leery about qualitative dissertations, this seemed to allay some misgivings by clearly flagging the inquiry as practice based, with no claims for scientific prediction or generalizability. If students could convincingly argue the merits of studying a particular context, committee members seemed satisfied. In some cases, however, including the context seemed to obscure students' understanding of the intent of the inquiry. The context, rather than serving to situate the question under study, became the focal point of the study. In such cases, the "So what?" of the study seemed to get lost, and the dissertation took on a narcissistic quality that contributed little of substance to a broader body of discourse. Yet we are reluctant to state categorically that the context of the study should not be included in the title of the dissertation, because interpretive studies typically yield context-dependent knowledge claims. We flag this as a judgment call that merits explicit deliberation.

# INTRODUCTION TO THE DISSERTATION PROPOSAL

The introductory section of the research proposal accomplishes two major purposes. First, it orients readers to the purpose and organization of the document itself; and second, it begins to frame the study. One reason we are reluctant to prescribe a standard outline for the research proposal is the variety of formats we have seen students use to accomplish these purposes—for example, traditional introductory chapter, preface, prologue, prelude. Decisions about arranging various chunks of information are often shaped by students' style of conceptualizing and writing, the nature of the study, and a narrative flow that feels right.

## Orienting Readers to the Proposal

The first purpose to be accomplished in the introductory section is providing readers with a general orientation to the contents and organization of the research proposal. Some might argue that this is the purpose of the table of contents, but this section of the introduction provides some insight into the thinking behind the organization. Micheline, for example, began her document with a section titled "Summary" that described the intellectual purpose served by the proposal and its organization. This was followed by a table of contents and then by Chapter 1 (see Case Example 1, Part 2; see also the tables of contents included in Case Examples 2, 4, and 5). Other proposals begin more conventionally with "Chapter 1:

Introduction." This, in turn, may begin with a subsection titled "Background to the Study." The point to keep in mind is the importance of letting readers know what to anticipate in the proposal document itself. This is especially important when students are not following the conventions of a scientific proposal.

Robin Grubs (2002, 2006), for example, was crafting a proposal for a grounded-theory study, the first qualitative dissertation to be undertaken in her highly science-oriented program. She worked very hard to craft a proposal that would signal the more interpretive approach she planned to take with her dissertation. Just as Robin was getting ready to circulate her document to her committee, one member offhandedly mentioned, "I assume you've followed the format used to prepare grant proposals for the National Institutes of Health (NIH)." This precipitated a temporary panic, because the proposal did not remotely resemble a typical NIH grant submission. Robin coped with the shock of this comment in several ways. First, she checked with her committee chair, with whom she had been deliberating, and confirmed that her chair understood and supported the format of her proposal. Next, she carefully reviewed her introductory paragraphs, making sure she explained not only how the proposal was organized but also why that organization was appropriate given the inquiry tradition and research genre of her study. Finally, she sorted through and articulated assumptions that might be underpinning her committee member's comment. Once Robin understood where he was coming from, she made sure that she was able to articulate her own assumptions. She circulated the document as written and successfully defended her proposal two weeks later. At the end of the meeting, one committee member commented that Robin's document was among the most clearly written and conceptualized dissertation proposals he had read. This positive outcome was due in large part to the clarity with which Robin had framed her study.

## Framing the Study

Framing the study entails giving readers an overall sense of what the study is about, why it is significant, and how it will be conducted. Although each of these issues is developed more fully in subsequent sections of the research proposal, the introductory section provides an initial, broad-brush look at the study. Imagine walking into an art gallery and spotting a picture hanging on the opposite wall. One gets a general impression of the frame and the subject of the picture. By approaching the picture gradually, the viewer notices more details and can see them in relation to the holistic image. When dissertation authors plunge too quickly into the details of the study, it is as though they have zoomed in on a small fragment of a large and complex picture without giving readers the benefit of an initial, overall impression. Several issues arise in the process of framing one's study.

## Searching for Voice

The notion that scholarly writing can be personalized often comes as a major surprise to students. Likewise, when students first start to write from this *stance* and *voice,* the results can be self-conscious and awkward. Faculty may be annoyed by excessive personal details or a confessional tone in the writing. In our experience, an excessive focus on this early writing—an intensive effort to make it sound more scholarly—can be counterproductive. Rather, it is more useful for students to elaborate on certain aspects of the background, such as the setting within which the idea for the study came to light. As such descriptions expand, they often contain clues to the "So what?" of the study and may also help to clarify a setting or context for the dissertation study itself. As a study begins to take shape and intent of the study becomes more explicit, students will often begin to see how to eliminate extraneous information. Exemplar 11.2.1 contains a series of paragraphs written by Melanie over eight months. In each case, she tries to write her way into the study, coming at it from slightly different angles.

## Bridging From Personal to Public

In practice-based, interpretive studies, an account of one's personal interest in the topic for the dissertation can be a useful first step in framing a study. Within a few paragraphs, however, it is important to begin establishing a conceptual bridge between one's personal interests and broader, public discourses. Without such a bridge, the writing might strike readers as naive or narcissistic. Integrating even a few key references into the account of one's personal interest gives a preliminary sense of which discourse communities would find the study of interest and why. This blending of the personal and the public is an example of experiential and discursive texts as they appear in the proposal.

Often, the introductory section ends with the statement of intent for the study and a list of the *guiding research questions.* These might, however, be incorporated into a section called "The Study."

---

### EXEMPLAR 11.2.1    A Case Study of Education and Welfare

#### Example of Evolving Introduction

- *August 1996:* While I was director of a job-readiness program at a community college, I had the opportunity of meeting and interacting with single moms who were receiving welfare. The purpose of this project was to assist the participants (the target population, single parents on welfare) in preparing for employment. For some of the students, the program provided the academic preparation needed to enroll in a job-training program. For others, it meant preparation for a successful job search. The goal of both groups was to obtain employment, become economically self-sufficient and leave the welfare system. My role in this program was very similar to that of a school principal.

- *January 1997:* It is necessary to consider the historical perspective of poverty and public assistance in order to get a sense of how the current welfare initiatives have evolved. There are several significant periods in the historical development of public assistance programs in the United States. As early as 1911, public assistance, known as *Mother's Pension Laws,* was created for the purpose of providing financial support for widows and wives with disabled husbands. Reinforcing the ideology of domesticity and motherhood, this financial assistance entitled women to remain in the home and care for their children.

*(Continued)*

- *April 1997:* More than eight years ago, I began working with women who were receiving Aid to Families with Dependent Children (AFDC), also known as *public assistance* or *welfare.* Until that time, in my position at the community college as an administrator of community services, I had the responsibility of creating and implementing vocational education programs to meet the learning needs of special populations (i.e., adults with mental disabilities; staff development for human service agencies). Because of my experiences with developing vocational curriculum in response to learning needs, I was asked to direct the demonstration project intended to serve single parents who are receiving public assistance.

*Authors' Commentary.* In each of the preceding paragraphs, the student tries to introduce her study. In the first draft, she plunges the reader directly into the situational details of a project she administered. In addition, she focuses on women who participated in the project, which implies that the women will be the centerpiece of her study and begs the question, "So what?" In other words, "Why is it important to study this group of women?"

The second draft plunges the reader into a historical account of welfare reform without indicating *why* it is "necessary to consider the historical perspective of poverty and public assistance." Further, no connection to education is made in this version.

In the third draft, the student begins to establish the context for her study by addressing the proverbial *who, what, when, where,* and *why* questions. In the process, she begins to link education, poverty, and welfare, as well as to connect herself as program director with a population of women who will become part of the study.

One of the noteworthy points about these drafts is that at no time did we give the student specific feedback that some revision was needed to help readers enter into her study. Rather, we focused on clarifying what was under study and her purpose for studying the program she administered. As the shape of the inquiry became clearer in the student's mind, she instinctively made changes that helped readers to enter into her study.

## THE STUDY

While we are discussing the importance of framing the study and providing an initial orientation to the inquiry, we want to address the notion of including a section called "The Study." This is a fairly straightforward description of the inquiry. It includes the intent of the study; flags the mode of inquiry; and concisely summarizes key procedural issues, including the *what, why, who, where, when,* and *how* of the study. Two major issues confront authors as they craft this part of their proposal: One is when to write this section, and the other is where to place it in the document.

When students first begin to talk about their study, they often ramble in a very unfocused way. Conversations often have a stream-of-consciousness quality as students skip from experiences related to their topic to questions about method to speculations about potential study participants or location to musings about outcomes. Early drafts of the proposal often have this same rambling quality.

Gradually, as the study comes into focus, oral descriptions become not only more focused but also more informative. What took 15 or 20 minutes to communicate now takes 5. What left others scratching their heads in bewilderment now elicits nods of understanding. By the same token, the document itself acquires a clearer focus and structure. Ideally, a coherent narrative flow emerges that invites readers into the world of the study. Unfortunately, over time, students may become so conversant with their study that they forget that others would welcome a short, to-the-point explanation.

For example, one student asked us to review and comment on the draft of his dissertation proposal. From the outset, we were plunged into discourses about learning disabilities interspersed with personal anecdotes about social and behavioral problems exhibited by students with certain types of disabilities. Juxtaposed to this information about the topic of the study was information about the student's anticipated mode of inquiry. As we waded through this material, we wondered, "Why are we reading all this stuff? What's the point of this study? Where's this leading?" The first glimmer of an overall description of the study came after 75 pages, when we encountered a set of guiding research questions. But even these did not give us a clear sense of the big picture.

Granted, a well-crafted proposal will include a great deal of detail. But if students plunge right into the detail, then readers, specifically committee members, can get lost. Incorporating a section called "The Study" can prevent readers' frustration and impatience. Essentially, this section functions like an abstract, describing in two or three paragraphs what is under study, why it is important to study, who will be involved in the study and who will be interested in the results, and when, where, and how the study will be conducted. In terms of conceptualization, this section is often written after the proposal has been completely drafted. In terms of placement, however, it needs to be incorporated toward the beginning of the document, often in the introductory section.

# STATEMENT OF INTENT

A well-crafted intent of the study flows logically from the *contextual background* and clearly communicates the purpose of the inquiry. A well-honed statement of intent can also signal the mode of inquiry and the audience to whom the study is aimed.

## Statement of Intent Versus Statement of Problem

Careful wording of the statement of intent is crucial to a well-conceptualized study. Yet students who are impatient to get on with the dissertation may be frustrated by the intensive deliberations associated with choosing the words and phrasing of the statement of intent. For example, students who have not yet come to grips with qualitative research often talk and write about the *Statement of the Problem,* a convention of science-based studies. We have abandoned this concept in favor of a *Statement of Intent* for the study.

This is more than semantic preference if one believes, as we do, that language is a manifestation of the ontological, epistemological, and axiological assumptions that underpin the study. The concept of *problem* implies that something has gone awry and must be fixed or corrected. The implication is that the right or correct way for something to function is already known, that deviations from this standard have been recognized, and that a solution must now be invented or found. In quasi-experimental studies, alternative solutions may have already been identified, and the researcher intends to demonstrate that one alternative is more effective than others.

This rational technical or functional view of stating and then solving problems is not particularly useful in critical or interpretive inquiries. Critical studies may aim to document or reveal systemic inequities that are far more pervasive (and pernicious) than technical or operational problems. Similarly, instead of demonstrating the efficacy of a particular intervention, interpretive or critical studies may try to problematize a phenomenon to reveal its complexity.

Interpretive studies in education typically do not aim at problem solution. Rather, they aim for deeper understanding—within a particular context—of some perplexing aspect of this complex human enterprise. For the most part, then, qualitative dissertations examine educational phenomena as they occur within somewhat small and circumscribed contexts.

## Practice-Focused Dissertations

As suggested throughout this book, many practitioners pursue doctorates not because they want to become full-time researchers or academicians, but rather because they want to better understand the theoretical and philosophical underpinnings of their practice. Often, these students are well-regarded teachers or administrators with a highly intuitive sense of what works. Yet they are hard-pressed to articulate the concepts and principles that guide their practice, especially in a way that can be helpful to others. Thus, another intent of interpretive studies can be to examine and explicate the nature of one's practice. Pam Krakowski (2004, 2006), for example, had instinctively enacted a narrative pedagogy in art education, almost since the beginning of her career. She knew that what she was doing differed from other traditions of art education, yet she had trouble explaining both the nature of and rationale for these differences. As she began to conceptualize her study, she entered into a recursive writing process that brought her ideas into clearer relief (see Exemplar 11.3).

Interestingly, Pam was somewhat reluctant to commit to the concept of *narrative pedagogy* for her dissertation because she did not understand the meaning of the concept. The nature of Pam's reluctance deserved careful consideration. On one hand, it might have signaled a case of commitment jitters, which would not be unusual for a first-time researcher. On the other hand, it might have reflected an intuitive sense that the focal point of narrative pedagogy did not quite reflect her true intent. Perhaps she needed to understand narrative pedagogy in order to align a statement of intent more appropriately with her professional and scholarly interests. Or it might have indicated that she had not yet grasped the purpose served by the statement of intent—to set the stage for an inquiry through which she could arrive at and articulate her understanding of narrative pedagogy in art education. Until Pam sorted through the nature of her reluctance, she had difficulty moving forward with crafting her proposal.

Marjorie, the student who saw herself as Henny Penny in Chapter 8 (Exemplar 8.1), crafted a slightly different type of qualitative study around her practice. As a graduate of and long-time teacher in a Catholic high school for girls, Marjorie was struggling to enact

*(Text continues on page 148)*

|  | March Draft | April Draft | August Draft |
|---|---|---|---|
| Working Title | *Entering the Child's World: A Narrative Study of Young Children's Art Making in an Integrated Art Setting.* OR | *Entering the Child's World: A Narrative Study of Studio Art as Pedagogy in Early Childhood.* | Same as April draft |
|  | *Entering the Child's World: A Narrative Study of an Art Teacher's Adaptation of the Reggio Emilia Approach.* OR |  |  |
|  | *Toward a New Paradigm: Finding the Balance Between Child-Centered and Subject-Centered Approaches to Teaching Art* |  |  |
| Intent of Study | To study my classroom to inform my pedagogy. (To find the most insightful, meaningful ways to teach art to young children.) | To delineate (portray) studio art as pedagogy in early childhood. To examine the pedagogy of studio art in early childhood. | To do a narrative study of my pedagogy, I would explore the use of narrative (as personal experience) in the teaching of art to children K–8 at a laboratory school. |
| Context | I hope to study one of my early childhood, multiage (K–2) art classes throughout the year. This would include once-a-week, 1-hour art classes; short- and long-term projects integrated with their teacher; small groups during and after school. | My K–3 students at the laboratory school. If needed, I could also include the 3- to 5-year-olds at the museum. | Consolidated into statement of intent |

*(Continued)*

**Exemplar 11.3 (Continued)**

|  | March Draft | April Draft | August Draft |
|---|---|---|---|
|  | This is a class where I have been collaborating with the classroom teacher in adapting the Reggio approach. |  |  |
| Importance of the Study | In the '50s and '60s, art education was dominated by a child-centered approach to the teaching of art, which focused on the child, creativity and self-expression. During the '60s, with the influence of Sputnik and a return to basics, the pendulum began to swing to a more subject-centered approach to teaching art. The subject-centered approach, commonly known as discipline-based art education, focused on teaching the art contents or disciplines—studio production, aesthetics, art criticism, and art history. The leading researchers in these areas were theorists primarily working with adults. They influenced curriculum development, leaving out the importance of understanding child development and how young children think and learn. Currently, there is beginning to be a call for a balance between subject-centered and child-centered approaches. | Children in the early childhood years present developmental and cognitive challenges vastly different from those of older children. How do we design art education programs for young children that have characteristics and patterns uniquely their own? In the '50s and '60s, a child-centered approach to art, emphasizing creativity and self-expression, dominated the field of art education. Over the last 20 years the emphasis has changed to a focus on the disciplines, or contents, of art education—studio production, aesthetics, art history, and art criticism. Each of these disciplines has pedagogical practices of its own. The theorists writing about these disciplines are often writing for adults or older children and have overlooked the importance of | Rationale: Part of the "so what" of this study is that art teachers who are being trained with content-based curriculum models often are not prepared to understand what is really meaningful to children in the art-making process. They are taught to plan curriculum even before they meet the children and know their interests. Curriculum is often imposed upon the children instead of emerging from the children's developmental and personal interest and experiences. Listening to children, watching their play, hearing their stories, observing their art making, and taking note of their personal narrative themes in their art and play can assist the art teacher in planning curriculum and designing art experiences that are meaningful for the children. |

|  | March Draft | April Draft | August Draft |
|---|---|---|---|
|  | Note: I am not sure if child-centered is the word that I am looking for. I would certainly have to define it—but it also is a "loaded" word with lot of negative connotations in art education, so maybe another word or phrase would be better. It also may be too narrow for what I want to cover. | understanding the young child—how he/she thinks, learns, and so on—when designing curriculum. In my field, there is a need to find a more child-centered approach to teaching the young child. |  |
| My Background Interest | *Authors' Commentary.* Pam's first draft did not include a personal background section. She did, however, talk quite a bit about her teaching experiences—usually referencing her time at the school for blind children. Often she related quite lengthy anecdotes about the children and the lessons she taught. It was difficult, however, to see in the many details what issue might be worthy of study. | Seventeen years ago, I taught art to blind children. Many of my art classes were with children 3–8 years old. During those years, my pedagogy began to be defined, it was important to listen carefully to the children and to understand the world from their point of view.<br><br>After teaching at this school for 11 years, I left to take a job at a private school, teaching art to children, K-8. | I've always been interested in the narrative quality of children's artwork. I've been interested in the stories that they tell and in the stories that they act out in their play. It seems that whatever art lessons I've done with children, I have always ended up tapping their own personal narratives. Most often these lessons were based on the themes that I observed in their art making, storytelling, and play. |

*(Continued)*

| March Draft | April Draft | August Draft |
|---|---|---|
| In the April draft, Pam begins to bring these anecdotes into her writing and as she does so their significance begins to take more focus. | I found myself frustrated that I could not do many of the things I had done with the blind students. My class size was 24 instead of 4. I had no assistant . . . The children were disruptive and much of my initial time was spent on classroom management.<br><br>After I had been teaching there for five years, I began to hear about the Reggio Emilia preschools. As I studied their philosophy and pedagogy, I discovered that many of my beliefs were consistent with theirs. I was inspired to understand and incorporate many of their principles in my own pedagogy. | To me, this has been the key to entering their worlds and finding out what was most meaningful to them. |

*Authors' Commentary:* Notice the overlap of ideas among the three drafts. A superficial reading could give the impression that Pam is merely reshuffling the same information, and to a certain extent, this is the case. Beyond that, however, each draft not only includes bits of new information but also shows different relationships among recurring concepts—personal narrative, pedagogy, entering the child's world, and child-centered versus subject-centered art education. Personal narrative, for example, appears as a mode of inquiry in all three drafts, but the subject of the narrative shifts as different possibilities are laid out—young children's art-making; an art teacher's adaptation of a particular art approach; child-centered and subject-centered approaches; studio art as pedagogy. Early on, Pam worried a great deal about where she could or should do her study and with what age group, as though these details were decisive elements of her study. This concern with context is reflected in the first two drafts, but it recedes in the third. Attention to context also appears in the background section, but an important shift occurs between the second and third drafts. In April, Pam gives a chronological description that emphasizes the situational aspects of her work history. The August draft focuses on a pedagogical concept, "The narrative quality of children's artwork." This phrase probably holds the conceptual key to Pam's study, a key that was foreshadowed in the second sentence of the intent for the study when Pam says, "I would explore the use of narrative in teaching." Previously, Pam had been talking and writing about the use of narrative as a mode of inquiry. In the August draft, however, there is a glimmer of narrative as a core pedagogical modality. Suddenly, the phrase "entering the child's world" no longer seems like an attempt to have a catchy title but rather, has pedagogical significance. Pam's continual recounting of her experience in teaching blind children no longer has the feel of romanticized nostalgia; instead, it represents the experiential foundation of her pedagogical philosophy. Her enthusiasm for Reggio Emilia seems less like cheerleading and more like a shorthand phrase for describing the type of pedagogy and curriculum she strives to enact. The decreased concern with context becomes understandable because listening with an "enlightened ear" to her students' stories about their artwork is not restricted to one classroom or age group.

The August draft represents a pivotal point for Pam. Now that the role of narrative in her own pedagogy has come more clearly into focus, she can intensify her immersion in the discourses related to narrative in education, art education, and educational research. She can begin to build a rationale for her study that draws more appropriately from these discourses. She can also begin to think more specifically about the procedures for her study, considering how she will capture the narrative aspects of her teaching.

a feminist pedagogy within a patriarchal system. The struggle was fraught with dilemmas, and Marjorie's intent was not to "solve" the dilemmas, because dilemmas are, by definition, irresolvable. Rather, she aimed to elucidate the nature of the dilemmas so that she could make more conscious and deliberate choices about her teaching practice. Hence, an early articulation of Marjorie's title was, *Through a Feminist Lens: An Autobiographical Study of Educational Dilemmas,* and her preliminary statement of intent read

> In this autobiographical study, I interpret how I came to name myself a feminist and how I narrate my struggle to enact a feminist pedagogy in a Catholic, all-girl high school. Coming to name this school as patriarchal and identifying the dilemmas that arise because of my evolving beliefs and how I am transforming my teaching practice are constructed as an emerging portrayal of what it means to me to be a woman and feminist teaching girls in an urban American high school setting.

This statement underwent several revisions as Marjorie entered more deeply into her study. This preliminary wording conveyed more of a sense of the thinking process that Marjorie intended to pursue in the study and less of a sense of how her dilemmas linked to a broader "So what?" But as worded, the statement helped Marjorie to organize her thinking and see the broad outline of her inquiry.

## Settling on an Intent
## Compatible With One's World View

As the deliberative process evolves, embryonic images for a study potentially can be shaped in a variety of ways. Making decisions about which avenue to pursue is part of crafting a viable proposal. For example, when we first met Rhonda, she was early in the deliberative process. The concept of *service learning at Christian colleges* continually surfaced in her musings about the dissertation, but each conversation seemed to take a slightly different perspective. Eventually, three possible intentions for the dissertation, each grounded in a different qualitative research tradition, began to emerge (see Exemplar 11.4).

---

### EXEMPLAR 11.4    Intent of the Study: Alternative Frames

*Authors' Commentary.* Rhonda is a highly motivated student with a strong background in quantitative research. Before, during, and after her participation in an introductory course on qualitative research, Rhonda and Maria engaged in email correspondence about her dissertation. Emerging from this discourse were three different ways of framing an intent for her study.

- *Qualitative/Empirical Intent:* To determine the status of teaching for "service to community" among Christian colleges.
- *Qualitative/Interpretive Intent:* To explicate the meanings of *service to community* and *servant leaders* within Christian colleges.
- *Qualitative/Critical Intent:* To critique the mission of Christian colleges to teach for "service to community" and to prepare "servant leaders."

Any of these studies is potentially worthwhile, but the wording indicates very different intentions for the study and modes of inquiry. Rhonda repeatedly expressed a desire to do a qualitative study even though she came from a very strong quantitative orientation. Had she, when presented with these possible statements of intent, gravitated to any one of them, she could have begun digging into the discourses that would allow her to flesh out a qualitative study within a particular tradition. Instead, none of these seemed to grab her, and she continued drafting ideas, such as the following, that are imbued with quantitative language:

> Maria, here are the new leanings for my dissertation. Compare five CCCU [Council for Christian Colleges and Universities] schools with five comparable (in size, location, etc.) from the CIC [Council of Independent Colleges] schools. Find out who has service learning, and if it is working. If it comes out that the CIC schools do and the CCCU schools don't, I can make recommendations. Final outcome will be Strategic Principles for Implementing a Service Component on your campus. I feel good about it because it gathers a lot of data and does comparisons. Also, I don't have to point my fingers at the CCCU schools that don't have service components—rather I can share ideas about how to start one up. Rhonda

*Authors' Commentary.* Implied in this framing for the study is an assumption that CIC schools have successful service learning and CCCU schools do not. If this is Rhonda's going-in assumption, a first step might be to state this as a hypothesis and then test the hypothesis through a comprehensive survey. A second assumption is that the CIC approach to service learning is "successful" and that principles of successful service learning can be distilled from these programs and disseminated to CCCU schools so that they, too, can have successful programs. To make this case, however, it would seem that more than five CIC schools would need to be studied and a research design that relates successful outcomes to particular pedagogical approaches would be needed. Establishing such a causal or correlational relationship would necessitate a quantitative approach.

As students struggle to clarify the intent of their study, they may initially state it as a question, trying to clarify what it is they really want to know. This is not necessarily a problem, but it does carry a potential danger—persistent lack of clarity about the "So what?" and "Who cares?" of the study. For example, the statement of intent for Melanie's study about women and welfare (Exemplar 11.2.2) evolved through three iterations as the purpose of her study came more clearly into focus. Look at Case Examples 1 through 5 in Section Four for examples of how concepts in the title flow into the statement of intent.

---

**EXEMPLAR 11.2.2    Evolution of a Statement of Intent**

- *First Iteration:* What are the educational implications of current welfare-reform policies?
- *Second Iteration:* To explore the educational implications of current welfare-reform policies for the impact/influence on women in poverty.
- *Third Iteration:* To make the case for education in welfare-reform policy.

*Authors' Commentary.* Notice how the first statement of intent does not offer any insight into the questions "So what?" and "Who cares?" It also does not indicate the inquiry tradition or research genre of the study. The concepts "impact/influence" in the second version suggest a more postpositivist cause-and-effect study. The third version addresses the "So what?" (i.e., policy formation), the "Who cares?" (i.e., policy makers), and the research genre (i.e., case study).

---

# GUIDING RESEARCH QUESTIONS

We are concerned that the following discussion of guiding research questions may be confusing in two ways. First, research questions are frequently thought of as data-collection questions. Second, on the surface, it appears as though guiding research questions pose issues that have already been addressed in the proposal. Hopefully, the following explanation will clarify these issues.

## Guiding Research Versus Data Collection Questions

We should begin by noting that not all faculty would agree with our way of thinking about the nature and purpose of guiding research questions. In a deductive, postpositivist study with a stated hypothesis, research questions flag sets of questions that will be used to gather the data needed to support or refute the hypothesis. In this sense, they are closely aligned with data-gathering questions, and this is what many faculty expect to see in a proposal. However, in an inductive, interpretive study, it is not possible to specify in advance all of the questions one might ask in the course of the inquiry. Nor is it possible to state in advance all of the texts one might need to acquire and examine. Therefore, we see guiding research questions as flagging areas of thinking that the researcher will need to pursue in order to move from the preliminary texts of the proposal to the more tightly reasoned texts of the dissertation.

Generally, no more than three to six guiding research questions are needed to structure a study. Usually, long lists of questions indicate that further deliberation on the intent of the study is needed. Well-formulated guiding questions can help the researcher to

- organize the wealth of information they have been amassing through their immersion in literature,
- recognize areas where additional information/thinking is needed,
- clarify the relationship between various bodies of discourse and specific facets of the study (e.g., topic, intent, context, genre),

- lay out a progression of thinking that constitutes the totality of the inquiry,
- provide a focal point for thinking through and organizing the research procedures, and
- visualize the nature and organization of texts that will compose the final dissertation.

Typically, a great deal of groundwork needs to occur before a solid set of guiding research questions can be formulated. Nevertheless, thinking about guiding questions from the outset is one way to bring the conceptual structure into clearer and clearer focus. Case Example 2, Parts 3 and 4 illustrate this point. In addition, review the guiding questions in Case Examples 1, 4, and 5 to see the ways in which guiding questions flag areas of intellectual work that will be undertaken to fulfill the intent of the study.

## Guiding the Movement
## From Proposal to Dissertation

Students in our introductory course on qualitative research often ask, "The proposal is the first three chapters of the dissertation, isn't it?" In a deductive, postpositivist study, this is likely to be the case. But in an inductive, interpretive study the answer is, "Maybe—sort of." The proposal is at best an approximation of the parameters of the inquiry. When well conceptualized, much of the experiential, discursive, and theoretic text constructed for the proposal is likely to have a place in the final dissertation. However, where and in what form this text appears is likely to undergo revision as new texts are gathered, interpreted, and constructed. So, for example, the introductory chapter of the proposal begins to contextualize the intent of the inquiry, often drawing from the researcher's recollections of professional experience. These recollections may be sufficient as a starting point, but a great deal more raw text will be needed to construct a persuasive experiential text in the final dissertation. Similarly, the second chapter of the proposal is likely to comprise quite an extensive discursive text, which argues the need for the study. But as the study progresses, additional information that can strengthen the rationale for the study is likely to surface. Integrating new information into the existing discursive text often entails more than simply plugging in a few references or adding a sentence or two. Because the core thesis is becoming clearer and clearer, major revisions may be required to construct or reconstruct the lines of reasoning that support the thesis. For these types of reasons, the guiding research questions may appear to flag issues that have already been addressed in the proposal. Realistically, however, they underscore the recursive nature of the reading, writing, and deliberation that continues throughout the inquiry process.

# RATIONALE FOR THE STUDY

In traditional proposals and dissertations, Chapter 2 is often labeled "Review of Literature" or "Literature Review." Much to the frustration of many faculty, these chapters often read like a laundry list of everything that the student has read on his or her topic.

One student described this approach as "genuflecting to the gods"—i.e., showing (and perhaps showing off) one's awareness of the "big names" in the field. Such laundry list reviews tend to read like annotated bibliographies in quasi-narrative form. They are neither interesting nor informative because they do little to explain how these references have informed the student's thinking or why the student thinks the study is worth doing.

When it comes to using literature to argue persuasively for an interpretive study, two words of caution are in order. Simply stating that all or most of the studies on a topic are quantitative and therefore a qualitative study is needed does not constitute a persuasive rationale. If the quantitative studies have already provided sufficient understanding of a phenomenon, then a small-scale qualitative study is not likely to add much of value to the discourse. Similarly, simply stating that a qualitative study will provide insight into the nuances of a phenomenon does not constitute a persuasive rationale. It is incumbent upon the student to provide a cogent rationale for why such nuanced understanding is necessary and important. To make this case, a major discursive text must be carefully constructed by drawing from the wealth of references the student has studied. It is also worth noting that one line of reasoning needs to take into account the type of knowledge that is valued in one's field. Literature that addresses these axiological and epistemological premises of professional, disciplinary, and practice-based knowledge may be different from literature that addresses the topic itself.

## Discursive Text Versus Review of Literature

We use the concept of *discursive text* rather than *review of literature* to underscore the interpretive moves entailed by constructing a persuasive rationale for the intent of the study. Accomplishing this complex intellectual task involves making careful decisions about many issues, including

- where to turn for relevant information related to one's topic in relation to one's field of study,
- what information to include and exclude as the discursive text is crafted,
- what organizing principle or principles can be used to make the discourses comprehensible, and
- how discourses can be used to frame the "What?" "So what?" and "Who cares?" of the study.

Attending to these questions involves more than simply summarizing what is in the literature. It also involves more than passing judgment on the ideas of other scholars—indicating whose ideas are right or wrong or with whom one agrees or disagrees. Far more useful is thinking carefully about the key concepts that appear in both the title of the proposal and the statement of intent. Each of these concepts needs to be elaborated and explained. (This is why it is so important to work diligently to craft these facets of one's study.)

In a postpositivist study the aim of elaborating on concepts may be to develop and support operational definitions as precursors to testing relationships among variables. In interpretive studies, however, the aim is to portray the richness of discursive exchanges through which the meanings associated with important concepts are tested and contested. All too often, we read proposals in which students lament, "There is no agreed-upon definition of this concept in the literature." To encourage students to let go of a definitional mode of thinking and enter into a discursive mode, we often respond, "Why would you expect there to be?" The challenge of crafting compelling discursive text is to find ways in which to represent the diversity of thinking associated with key concepts in one's study, not to winnow out those that are "extraneous." Potential strategies for organizing such representations include

- tracing the historical evolution of relevant discourses, showing the historical flow or development of key ideas (this is more than a simple chronological summary of who wrote what when);
- tracing conceptual threads (e.g., themes and subthemes, issues, or questions) within a discourse;
- mapping various schools of thought or ideological positions related to the topic being reviewed;
- mapping disciplinary perspectives of a topic; and/or
- mapping the positions of various stakeholder groups, such as practitioners, academics, scholars, policymakers, and consumers.

These organizing principles are not mutually exclusive. For example, Brenton Prosser (1999) traced the historical evolution of discourses on attention deficit disorder by comparing and contrasting medical, psychological, sociological, educational, political, and economic perspectives on this syndrome. Micheline, in reviewing discourses on educational inclusion, not only laid out different ideological positions but also related them to various stakeholder groups.

Seeing examples of well-written reviews of literature can provide ideas for organizing one's own approach. One of our colleagues, William Ayers, who teaches Introduction to Qualitative Research at the University of Illinois at Chicago, advises students to read *The New York Times* book review section to get a sense of how to organize a review along conceptual lines. Resources such as *Review of Research in Education* and *Review of Educational Research* (journals published by the American Educational Research Association) also provide useful examples of conceptual or issue-oriented reviews. The key point to keep in mind is how the multiple forms and sources of information can be woven together to create a well-reasoned and persuasive response to the following questions:

- How does the intent of the study emerge from and contribute to significant discourses?
- What is the potential significance of the study and to whom?
- Why is the study worth doing?

The Authors' Commentary in Case Example 2, Part 5 flags an example of a discursive text that was structured to situate the topic of the study—creative dramatics—within a complex set of discourses. In contrast, the chapter structure in Kathy's dissertation (Case Example 4, Part 3) emerged to accommodate discursive texts that represented very different discourses and discourse communities. The structure of Jean's dissertation (Case Example 5, Part 3) echoes the language and organization of the theater.

Reflective Interlude 11.1

### How Can I Construct a Persuasive Rationale for My Study?

- What are the major reasons I think my study is worthwhile?
- What information do I need to warrant these reasons?
- Where am I likely to find this information?
- How do I draw upon this information to develop well-supported lines of reasoning?
- In what order should I lay out my lines of reasoning so that they build upon each other?
- How do I interconnect these lines of reasoning to make the case that the proposed study is worth doing?
- How do I demonstrate my understanding of the ideas of other scholars?
- How do I explain the ways in which my understanding of my topic has been informed by the work of others?
- In what ways can I demonstrate the relationship between my question or questions about the topic and questions that are important to my field of study and/or practice?

## RESEARCH GENRE AND PROCEDURES

As mentioned in this Chapter's opening remarks, one purpose of the proposal is to assure the dissertation committee that the student is capable of conducting the study. Because the quality of interpretive inquiry rests upon the construction of insightful and well-reasoned experiential, discursive, and theoretic texts, the quality of writing in the proposal is often more reassuring than detailed research procedures. In other words, if the proposal is thinly conceptualized, poorly organized, rife with grammatical and syntactical errors, filled with inappropriate word choices, and jarring in voice and stance, a committee will be hard pressed to believe a student is prepared to conduct an interpretive study no matter how much procedural detail is included. That said, the research genre and procedures section of the proposal accomplishes a twofold purpose. First, it provides an explanation of and rationale for the research genre that is guiding the study. Second, it provides a careful explanation of the procedures that will be followed to address each guiding research question. When well conceptualized, these two facets of the proposal lay out at least a preliminary logic-of-justification for the inquiry. It is likely that the logics can be refined as the study progresses and the student has a much clearer sense of how the procedures are actually playing out. One student, for example, explained how she planned to recruit participants whose children might have a variety of developmental disabilities. In the end, all the parents who responded had children with similar disabilities. In the final dissertation, she needed to explain this difference between what she had planned and what happened. In addition, she needed to account for how she thought about this difference.

## Preparing to Construct a Logic-of-Justification Within a Research Genre

The Reflective Interludes in Chapters 5 through 9 are meant to encourage the thinking needed to identify one's own research proclivities. In this section, we flag several points to keep in mind as one explores literature related to research genres and procedures.

First and foremost, it is important that the student begins explorations early enough to allow time to become familiar with the traditions and language of various forms of educational research. St. Pierre (2002b) calls attention to the danger of summarily dismissing forms of research before understanding what they represent:

> One of the problems we've found in these critiques—and we certainly do not claim that post work does not deserve critique—is that those who protest the loudest seem to be those who have not read much in the literature. Like any other bodies of knowledge and practice, postmodernism, poststructuralism, postfoundationalism, deconstruction, and so forth, have their own complex histories, their own languages, their own contradictory and competing discourses, their own structures of intelligibility. (pp. 2–3)

As St. Pierre's comment suggests, any research tradition and genre will be subject to vigorous debate among certain communities of scholars. The significance of various discourses might seem quite obscure and consequently off-putting to some newcomers, while others might find them quite intriguing. The caution for doctoral students is not to pass judgment on the merits of these various discourses on genres (especially before they have studied them) but to use one's reaction as an indicator of one's worldview. In short, who are the scholars with whom one would like to deliberate? This question is relevant for general discourses on research traditions, genres, and procedures as well as for discourses within a field of study. It is less productive to expend energy lamenting the "marginal status" of qualitative research in one's field than to search for the pockets of discourse where scholars are engrossed in discussions that one finds meaningful.

Connecting with discourses where scholars are exploring what constitutes a particular form of qualitative research helps to avoid a potential pitfall. Too often, we read proposals where students create a negative logic-of-justification. In other words, they explain that they are not carrying out some sort of quantitative study or procedure, rather than explaining what they will be doing. Such "rationales" often indicate a lack of familiarity with the discourses related to a research tradition or genre. The passage in Exemplar 11.5, excerpted from a student's dissertation, was used as a lead-in to the dissertation's chapter on research methods. It serves to illustrate several ways in which a student's writing can reveal a less than persuasive logic-of-justification for both the purpose and genre of a study.

## EXEMPLAR 11.5    A Defensive Approach to Justifying a Qualitative Study

Because of the dominance of the technical, rational model in education, why would someone undertake an autobiographical and narrative inquiry with preservice teachers on the topic of dreams and goals? What value would a longitudinal study of this sort serve?

Although statistics are useful to portray a succinct picture on a given issue, they are unable to present the participants' values and beliefs. In this study, the "insider's point of view" (Glesne & Peshkin, 1992, p. 52) during their preservice experience was given primary consideration through the use of autobiographical inquiry, narrative inquiry, action research, and case study.

To complement quantitative research, a study of this sort provided "a place for teachers to tell and retell their stories of teaching."

*Authors' Commentary.* The questions in the opening paragraph *might* be a useful rhetorical device in an introductory chapter. Coming after a major discursive text that should have mapped the discourses on preservice teacher preparation, these questions set a defensive tone for the entire passage. By the time the student is writing a rationale for her research method, she should be able to state in positive terms what contribution a qualitative study will make to the existing discourses. Furthermore, within almost any field of education, robust discourses exist that are not dominated by rational, technical models; certainly, this is true in teacher education. Using the rational technical discourses as a point of departure suggests that the student is not familiar with these other discourse communities within her field of study.

In the second paragraph, the student falls into the trap of justifying a qualitative approach in terms of the limitations of statistics. It does not explain what a more experientially based study would contribute to an understanding of preservice teacher education, especially since a number of narrative studies are already available in the literature.

The phrase in the third paragraph, "To complement quantitative research," suggests that the student sees qualitative research as a secondary approach to quantitative research. The depth of discourses on qualitative research establishes the legitimacy of this inquiry tradition as separate from but equal to a quantitative tradition. Although some educational scholars may not value qualitative research, one makes a contribution to the scholarly communities that do value it. So a more positively structured rationale might lay out the following lines of reasoning:

1. Given the discourses on preservice teacher education, here is what we know through postpositivist and interpretive studies.

2. Left unanswered is the issue of _____ and the meanings that preservice teachers make of this issue.

3. An interpretive study provides an opportunity to examine more closely the meanings that preservice teachers make of this issue.

4. Within the discourses on preservice teacher education is a growing tradition of narrative inquiry that explores the stories that teachers construct about their lives.

5. This study is situated within that narrative tradition and aims to contribute to the body of literature on the issue of _____.

Points 4 and 5, when developed, can provide a logic-of-justification for a narrative inquiry.

Another red flag is raised by the student's referencing autobiographical inquiry, narrative inquiry, action research, case study, and longitudinal study. We consider each of these a distinct research genre, so this strikes us as an example of the "kitchen sink syndrome." Autobiography suggests that the author is telling her own life story. If she wants to claim the stories of other teachers as autobiographical, she might serve as the editor of a text to which teachers contribute life stories they write about themselves. If the dissertation author is representing the life stories of teachers, then it might be more appropriate to claim biography. Yet autobiography and biography both have conventions that call for in-depth analysis and representation of an individual's life. Within teacher education, however, there is already a long-standing tradition of narrative inquiry, which offers a rather robust logic for that genre.

It is not clear why the student would feel a need to include references to case study, action research, or a longitudinal study. By claiming narrative, the student could establish the parameters of the story—a setting, a particular number of characters (i.e., teachers to be interviewed), and a time frame. Suppose, for example, she threw in the idea of a longitudinal study because she wants to study preservice teachers' reaction to their last two years of preparatory coursework. She could simply build this timeframe into her description of a narrative study indicating that she would ask her participants to construct a story about that two-year experience.

In this brief passage, then, the student conveys an impression of a naive researcher who has little understanding of the concept of genre in general or the specifics of her genre in particular. This lack of self-conscious method is likely to undermine her dissertation committee's confidence that she is ready and able to carry out a study.

By the same token, reading only one or two authors on a particular research approach can also result in a flimsy logic-of-justification. For example, since the publication of *The Discovery of Grounded Theory* (Glaser & Strauss, 1967), a great deal has been published about the genre. Students intending to conduct a grounded theory study for their dissertation would do well to read as much of this literature as possible. This would give them a sense of how the genre has evolved over time as well as different points of view about the conventions associated with the genre. Rather than relying somewhat blindly upon the limited advice of one or two authors, students would have a richer context for constructing their logic-of-justification. Just as grounded theory has over a 40-year history, so too do other research genres such as narrative, ethnography, case study, and action research. Understanding how the discourses have evolved over time can help students understand thorny epistemological and methodological issues associated with a genre.

A final suggestion for preparing for the dissertation proposal is to practice procedures one might be imagining for one's study. For example, if one has little or no experience conducting interviews, running focus groups, collecting stories, or doing field observations, it would be important to try out these procedures to see what conceptual and practical issues arise. For example, students who think that focus groups are an expeditious way to gather multiple perspectives on an issue might be surprised to discover how difficult it is to make sense of a multifaceted conversation or how the group setting is not conducive to probing individual experiences. Similarly, it might be disconcerting to realize one is uncomfortable raising emotionally charged issues in an interview. Or a system for recording observations may not be capturing the most significant aspects of a situation. Discovering such issues before committing to a particular course of action in the dissertation proposal allows time for developing requisite skills or refining one's procedures.

It should come as no surprise at this point that our strongest suggestion is to begin writing and interpreting texts. We have met too many students who assert with great vehemence that they want to do a qualitative study in which they will collect stories from participants and write narratives. Yet they are brought up short when they realize that many participants are not able to tell compelling stories. Or that they as the researcher are unable to discern meanings beneath the surface of raw texts. Or as narrator of the dissertation, they are unable to craft an engaging or insightful narrative. The more one works with texts—collecting, interpreting, and constructing them—the more one will realize what genre and procedures one can and should commit to carrying out in the dissertation.

## Rationale for Research Genre

As students are drawn to particular modes of inquiry, they begin to acquire a language for discussing not only the topic of their study but also the mode of inquiry. This is an important step forward. However, the level of understanding gained through academic coursework, reading, and talking is only preliminary to the depth of understanding gained through the process of actually writing the rationale for one's research genre and procedures. Ongoing deliberation with one's research advisor (and ideally within a deliberative community) promotes the depth of thinking needed to develop a sound logic-of-justification.

When situating a study within a particular research genre, it is not enough to name the genre—that is, to say, "I am doing a case study"; "I am doing a narrative"; "I am doing an arts-based study." Such general statements do little to convey a student's awareness of the discursive histories and complexities associated with a genre. While it is not necessary to write a detailed review of all discourses associated with one's chosen genre, it is important to indicate which discourses underpin one's study. For example, if one is working within a narrative genre, is one drawing from sociological conceptions of narrative, from literary conceptions of narrative, or from the extensive discourses of teacher narrative? Is one claiming to write narratives about others or about oneself? In the words of Barone (1995) or McMahon (2000, 2006), does one anticipate writing mildly or wildly fictive narratives? Or in the frame of Richardson (1990), is one planning to work with everyday, autobiographical, biographical, cultural, or collective narrative, or some combination of the five? Similarly, in claiming to write a case study, is one drawing from the traditions in law, medicine, business, or education? Or, in Stake's (1995) words, is one proposing an intrinsic, instrumental, or collective case study? Is one planning to do a descriptive case *of* something or develop a rhetorical case *for* something? These are the types of questions it is important to anticipate and sort through no matter what genre one is claiming.

Again a cautionary note is in order. Students often think that the rationale for "choosing" one genre over another lies either in the nature of question they are posing or in some technical difference between genres. As suggested in Chapter 7, one's own proclivities for making meaning may be the most salient criterion upon which to claim a genre. This is the reason we strongly encourage students to reflect on their own talents as well as ways of knowing they may have cultivated through their undergraduate and master's level coursework. Without such introspection, it is possible to overlook the strengths one can bring to the dissertation. For example, we have met students who are formally trained in journalism but never thought to claim investigative journalism as their genre. And we have met students with extensive experience in film and video production who never considered documentary as a genre. Situating one's study within a particular research genre sets the stage for discussing the conventions that will guide the procedures of one's inquiry.

---

**Reflective Interlude 11.2**

**How Am I Refining My Understanding of Genre?**

- What did I write in response to the questions in Reflective Interlude 7.1? What changes do I want to make in these responses?
- As I read examples of various research genres, which genre suits my way of thinking and my abilities as a writer?
- As I read references about various research genres, which make the most sense to me? Which authors write about the genre in a way that I can relate to?
- Have I been bogged down in a search for the "ideal" genre for my study? If so, how can I begin to narrow my options and focus on a genre that fits with my talents, skills, and ways of knowing?
- As I imagine conducting my study within a particular genre, what procedures come to mind?

---

## Rationale for Research Procedures

In proposing procedures for an intimate, context-specific, practice-based, interpretive dissertation, it is useful to think about the conceptual moves needed to theorize from idiosyncratic experience. Although the procedures of specific studies may vary, the overall movement can be conceptualized in a series of questions:

- What phenomenon or issue is under study?
- How will I find individuals who have had experience with this phenomenon or issue or locate artifacts of it?
- How will I gather raw texts?
- How will I go about interpreting the meanings of these raw texts?
- How will I portray the experiential text in order to convey the nuances of the phenomenon or issue under study?
- How will I move from the experiential text to a theoretic text?

Addressing these questions within the conventions of a particular research genre allows a researcher to begin crafting his or her logic-of-justification. Consider, for example, an intent to study a prolonged and bitter teachers' strike. The geographic setting of the event is fairly straightforward—that is, a specific school district—but the chronological parameters of the event are more amorphous and could be framed in a variety of ways—for example, beginning with the first negotiations related to the expiring teachers' contract and continuing until the ratification of the new contract; beginning with the date of the teachers' walk out and continuing until their return to the classroom; beginning with the ratification of the contract and continuing for the remainder of the school year. The logic for setting the time frame is not inherent in the genre, but rather in what the researcher wants to understand (e.g., precursors to the strike, the aftermath of the strike). Similarly, whose experience of the strike is the researcher interested in understanding—the teachers', the administrators', the school board's, the parents', the students', the union negotiators', or some combination of these? As the researcher considers these types of questions, issues of genre come into play. A narrative study would logically call for eliciting stories from individuals who experienced the strike. A case study might logically focus on a careful analysis of the old and new contracts. (Because contracts are legal documents, the researcher might further claim to be drawing from case study procedures in law.) A grounded theory study might concentrate on media coverage of the strike—for example, newspaper editorials, letters to the editor, or interviews with various school personnel, parents, and students. It is also possible that within any one of these genres, various combinations of information might be gathered—negotiator interviews and contracts, media coverage and interviews with school board members, contracts and records of negotiation sessions, and so on. We can imagine students asking, "If any of these approaches allows for leeway in what information to gather from what sources, then what really is the difference between genres?" It is in the next conceptual move of the study where the conventions of the genre come more fully into play.

If, for example, one claims intrinsic case study as one's genre, then the mass of raw texts would be reviewed for descriptive information about the *where, what, when,* and *who* of the case. Doing a "content analysis" or "coding" would make little sense if one can go directly to a school district's Web site and obtain all the information necessary to describe its geographic location, size of student body, number and categories of personnel, composition of the school board, and so on. Conversely, if one claims a narrative genre to understand the effects of the strike on first-year teachers, then conventions of literary interpretation could be used to probe the surface and subtext of their stories for meanings. In literary interpretation, one often looks for major and minor themes but also for story structure, metaphors, and characters (e.g., the embattled school board, the victimized students, the beleaguered administrators, the self-sacrificing teachers). What one notices in the storied accounts of the strike cannot be specified in advance, nor can the most compelling or salient features of the stories. Rather, the researcher must live with the raw texts, reading and rereading them, noticing intriguing features of the story, cross checking these features across all the stories to see if they shed light on the nature of the experience. If students propose a narrative genre but have no understanding of these conventions of literary interpretation, they will be hard pressed to explain how they will make the conceptual move from gathering raw text to interpreting it. Repeatedly, we see claims for narrative studies that describe "data analysis" procedures embedded in postpositive techniques of deductive content analysis. Often, it seems that this mismatch of genre and procedure arises from a romanticized notion of telling stories. To further illustrate how the conventions of a genre come into play, students proposing a grounded theory of the strike would explain procedures for inductive coding of experiential text to identify concepts, constantly comparing, clustering and reclustering the conceptual codes, and generating a hierarchy of increasingly abstract codes until a core concept emerges. Hopefully, these brief comparisons of case study, narrative, and grounded theory illustrate the way in which the conventions of the genre help explain how the researcher anticipates moving from accounts or artifacts of an experience toward a theoretic interpretation.

The conventions of a genre also offer guidance for the next conceptual move of the inquiry—how the multiplicity of raw texts will be woven into a coherent experiential text. In claiming narrative, for example, students may collect 10, 15, 20, 40, or more individual stories or personal accounts. For several reasons, all of these individual stories cannot be incorporated directly into the dissertation. Even a relatively small number of narratives can be quite unmanageable in terms of the overall length of the dissertation. Beyond that logistical consideration, individual stories may vary in richness. Further, some individuals may tell a compelling story that can stand almost as is; others tell fairly boring stories in a rambling or disjointed fashion. So the narrative researcher faces the challenge of attending carefully to all of the stories, but finding a way to construct a composite narrative that portrays the variation and richness of individual responses to a seemingly similar experience. This is where the researcher's narrative sensibilities come into play. Is the researcher capable of telling a good story; what coherent composite story is he or she able to weave from the threads of meaning in the individual stories; what will be the structure, themes, characters, metaphors, and so on of this composite narrative? All too often, we see students who have equated narrative inquiry to simply collecting stories. Having little proclivity for a narrative mode of thinking, they flounder when facing the conceptual move from idiosyncratic experience to theoretic meanings. Regrettably, the resulting portrayal may consist of decontextualized snippets of information extracted almost randomly from raw interview texts.

A similar challenge faces those claiming grounded theory and planning to conduct interviews as a major source of raw text. At the proposal stage of the dissertation process, the apparently straightforward procedures of coding and constant comparative analysis seem reassuringly clear cut. Receiving less attention is the process of memoing, which is the grounded theory convention for making the conceptual move from myriad concepts to coherent theory. Even a relatively small number of interviews (say, 10 to 15) can yield hundreds, if not thousands, of codes. Neither the interviews per se nor all of the codes can be transferred directly into the dissertation. So a grounded theorist faces a challenge of portraying the variation and richness of individual responses to an experience. What constitutes the ground of the study; what goes into the background; what should be foregrounded; what constitutes the figure, and how can it be distinguished from the background; from the myriad concepts generated through coding and comparison, which should be incorporated into the ground to eventually warrant the theory? Without considering how the conventions of grounded theory will guide these conceptual decisions, students often resort to the snippet approach, what Laurel Richardson (2003) calls the insertion of "human filler" to illustrate abstract concepts. Or it leads to a laundry list of general themes, which several grounded theory scholars have begun to decry as eroding the very essence of the method (see, for example, Stern, 1994).

Those claiming case study do not escape the challenges of moving from the idiosyncratic to the conceptual or theoretic. Routinely, we meet practitioners who propose doing a case study of their classroom, school, district, or similar setting chosen, it seems, for convenient access to information. The illusion of convenience rapidly disappears when confronted with the question, "In what way does this idiosyncratic setting offer any useful insight into other settings that might be equally idiosyncratic?" Stake's (1995) distinction between *intrinsic* and *instrumental* case study, as well as his notion of *naturalistic generalization,* offers the key to making a conceptual shift from situational details to theoretic meaning. But if the dissertation proposal focuses narrowly on techniques for gathering information about the case (frequently described as "interviewing a random handful of stakeholders"), conceptual paralysis can occur when the limitations of studying a single case set in, or when one is inundated with highly disparate information from multiple sources.

## Potential Pitfalls

When students do not explicitly understand the research genre that guides their study, they run the risk of stumbling upon several pitfalls. Indeed, several of these pitfalls are worth flagging because they shed further light on issues related to genre and logic-of-justification.

*Pitfall—The Kitchen Sink Syndrome.* The kitchen sink syndrome seems to arise when students throw a number of buzzwords into the study, apparently in a desperate attempt to justify the rigor of the research methods. Ironically, the level of thought can be so superficial that the resulting impression is of a novice whose study is totally beyond his or her control. Students who fail to grasp the significance of *research tradition* and *research genre,* as well as students who think of *method* only as *technique,* can be especially susceptible to this pitfall. They are also susceptible to the next pitfall.

*Pitfall—The Fishing Expedition.* In this pitfall, students attend to the details of data collection in the research proposal, write vaguely about analyzing data to uncover significant themes or issues, but say virtually nothing about how they will derive meaning from the analysis. In short, the logic-of-justification is virtually absent from their proposal. The dysfunctional notion that bias can be avoided by taking the blank-slate approach contributes to this pitfall.

*Pitfall—The Rumpelstiltskin Syndrome.* This pitfall is often flagged by comments that go something like this:

> My advisor has a major grant and has been studying X for the past few years. She's already done a lot with the quantitative data, that's her main interest. But there's a lot of qualitative data that she doesn't have time to work with. It seems pretty interesting, and she says I can use it for my dissertation. She's not a qualitative researcher herself, although she is interested in learning more about that method.

The prospect of jumpstarting one's dissertation by making use of precollected data is highly seductive. So, too, is the notion that a sizable mass of qualitative data from a large pool of "subjects" surely contains useful insights and should not go to waste. In our experience, students who succumb to this seduction are likely to find themselves striking a bad bargain and ending up like the fairytale princess trying to spin straw into gold. Constructing meaning from masses of data—whether collected by the student or someone else—is extremely difficult in the absence of a well-formulated intent for the study.

To safeguard against these potential pitfalls, we contend that each proposal must be custom crafted so that the structural relationships between the intent of the inquiry, the mode of inquiry, and the anticipated form of the dissertation document are clearly laid out.

Well-conceived procedures typically require intricate and extensive discussions that cannot be excerpted easily from a proposal or dissertation. However, to give a sense of how these issues are addressed, review the Case Examples in Section Four.

# ANTICIPATED PORTRAYALS AND TENTATIVE OUTLINE OF DISSERTATION CHAPTERS

The traditional dissertation, conforming to the conventions of a five-chapter, scientific report, is only one form in which an inquiry might be represented. Accounts of qualitative inquiries, particularly those grounded in interpretive or critical traditions, might be more appropriately conceived of as a scholarly book.

The overall structure of the dissertation is likely to emerge as a student thinks through the relationships among the intent of the study, each guiding question, and the research procedures. This section of the proposal describes how the student envisions laying out the dissertation document. Often, it is fairly short, listing the anticipated title and purpose of each chapter. Although these points may have been addressed in earlier sections of the proposal, summarizing them in one place brings into sharper focus the form and format of the research report.

Students often worry that departures from the traditional science-report format will not be accepted by their schools. This is an important consideration and needs to be checked with one's advisor. It is our contention, however, that the form and format of the dissertation document must be epistemologically congruent with the nature of the inquiry being described. When a sound logic-of-justification for the inquiry has been developed, and when students engage in deliberation with their advisors and other committee members, support for alternative *dissertation formats* may be garnered.

In crafting such a proposal, students face a twofold challenge. One is to explain the anticipated results before knowing what will emerge from an inductive inquiry; the other is to describe the dissertation format before knowing what form of representation can best convey the process and results of the inquiry. The key to meeting these challenges is to have a clear enough sense of the inquiry tradition, research genre, and logic-of-justification to explain how the inquiry will be conducted and, subsequently, reported. For example, students working in a postpositive tradition may have a study that looks and reads like a science report. Students working in an interpretive tradition may have a study that looks and reads more like a scholarly book. A study within an arts-based genre of interpretive inquiry may look and read like a piece of literature. Studies within a critical tradition may take the form of a polemic.

Thus, the proposal foreshadows the format and style of the dissertation. When we say that the dissertation process is recursive, we mean that each draft brings into clearer focus the final form and content of the dissertation. The proposal is a pivotal iteration in that the student sees more clearly than before the intimations of the form that will emerge from the shadows of the puddle. The nature of the study is captured and conveyed in several key facets of the proposal: the title, the intent of the study, the guiding research questions, and the research procedures. All of these are shaped in concert with the research tradition and genre of the study.

## Reflective Interlude 11.3

### What Is the Reasoning Behind Each Procedure of My Study?

- What sources will I draw upon for my raw text? How will I gain access to these sources? Why am I choosing these sources?
- What makes me think I can conduct interviews, field observations, document analysis, or other techniques for obtaining experiential texts? What practice have I had or do I need to enhance my capacity to carry out these techniques for gathering raw texts?
- How do the techniques I intend to use fit within the genre I am proposing?
- What makes me think I can write compelling narratives, insightful conceptual frameworks, or other forms of experiential text? What practice have I had or do I need to enhance my capacity for the form of writing and thinking associated with the genre I am proposing?
- If I am planning to conduct my study within a particular setting, do I have a more compelling rationale than mere convenience?

# 12

## *Proposing the*
## *Dissertation Study*

---

**Key Concepts**

Ethical Sensibility

Institutional or Internal Review Board (IRB)

---

Once a proposal has been drafted, it is ready to be moved into a more public arena for formal approval. Typically, this entails a twofold review. One, conducted by an *internal review board* (IRB) or human subjects committee, safeguards the rights of study participants. The other, conducted by the student's dissertation committee, is meant to determine whether a viable study has been conceptualized and whether the student is able to carry out the study. Because each university has specific procedures for initiating and completing these reviews, we encourage students to obtain and read carefully any manuals or guidelines provided by their institution. Rather than providing procedural advice in this chapter, we explore the ways in which the proposal extends deliberation.

The issues raised in this chapter are meant to counterbalance a mind-set that we encounter all too often among students who see the relationship between doctoral candidate and reviewers as adversarial. From this perspective, committee members function as harsh and unforgiving critics, seeking out even the smallest flaws as an excuse to fail the proposal. This image of powerlessness seems to be fueled by dissertation folklore rife with horror stories about students whose work has fallen victim to faculty infighting or committee politics. Although such unfortunate situations may occur, we have never personally witnessed any. What we have noticed is the titillating sense of high drama with which such stories are passed from student to student (often in a tone of righteous indignation). Yet on more than one occasion, when students have launched into an "ain't it awful" anecdote, the comments attributed to malevolent intent often seem to us to be quite reasonable and responsible concerns about an inquiry.

We speculate that the shift from more private to more public deliberation may engender a heightened sense of vulnerability. More than one student has remarked in so many words, "I'm scared I'll be found out—that I'm an intellectual fraud. I'm afraid they'll decide I shouldn't have been accepted into the doctoral program. They're going to see that I'm here under false pretenses, that I'm not nearly as smart as everyone thinks I am." To cope with the anxiety spawned by such self-doubts, students may assume that the best defense is a good offense. This, in turn, may prompt an adversarial posture.

In this chapter, we attempt to reframe issues related to the proposal, suggesting that they are integral to the ongoing process of deliberation. To organize the discussion, five facets of proposing a qualitative study are considered.

- Forming a dissertation committee
- Obtaining approval from an internal review board
- Holding a meeting to review the proposal
- Dealing with meeting outcomes
- Moving forward with the study

## FORMING A DISSERTATION COMMITTEE

The following passage, written by a doctoral student as part of a think piece, raises questions about the role and purpose of the committee as well as concerns about committee composition:

> Since dissertation committees, for the most part, are the educational gatekeepers and guardians of academic traditions, the choice of a committee seems to be critical to the success of having a proposal approved. Most of the faculty at my school come from a tradition of empirical/quantitative research and do not "understand," "appreciate," or in some cases "approve of" qualitative approaches. (This may be a personal perception!) Should I seek a committee composed of faculty with quantitative or qualitative backgrounds? If I choose those faculty with qualitative experience, do I need to be concerned about the significant diversity within the qualitative paradigm? One of the reasons I am taking this course is to learn more about the qualitative approach to research since my previous research experiences and methods courses have been empirically based. An even more fundamental question may be whether a doctoral student like myself should be playing what Donmoyer calls the "paradigm-matching game"? Should I choose a committee composed of faculty with both qualitative and

quantitative biases, then have confidence in my ability to develop a research proposal that will be acceptable to both or, alternatively, should I develop the research proposal in such a way that the make-up of the committee is irrelevant?

The connotation of "educational gatekeeper" and "guardians of academic traditions" may vary depending upon the student's view of the dissertation. For students who see the dissertation as the last and largest "academic hoop or hurdle," the connotation is likely to be negative. The committee may be cast in the role of obstacle, whose purpose is to make completion of the study as difficult as possible. Conversely, students who see the dissertation as a potentially meaningful contribution to their field of study may have a more positive view. The committee can function in the role of mini-discourse community. Here, in a relatively protected and supportive environment, the novice scholar can hone the skills of deliberation. Implications of various lines of reasoning can be explored and fine-tuned. Connections between personal deliberations and formal or public discourses can be identified and strengthened. From this perspective, the committee serves as an important resource for the student.

Conceiving of the dissertation committee as a resource provides insight into its composition. Notice how the student in the above passage tends to frame selection of committee members as either/or and all-or-nothing alternatives. Also notice how the alternatives are posed in the abstract, as though there is some right or wrong way to form a committee. This decontextualized approach to choosing committee members can lead to a great deal of circular thinking. Further exacerbating such quandaries is a focus on faculty politics and personality conflicts.

It is more useful to think through the specific contribution each committee member can make to the study. This helps to clarify which faculty might serve as a resource for various dimensions of the study, such as the field of study to which the dissertation will contribute, the discipline that underpins the study, the research tradition and genre that guide the inquiry, and the form of representation the dissertation is likely to take. Drawing upon knowledge of faculty interests and expertise, and building upon existing relationships, students can create a deliberative community supportive of their efforts.[1]

We are reminded of a student who approached us about doing an interpretive study and who kept asking, with a great sense of urgency, who she should have on her committee. When asked why she was so anxious to settle this issue, she replied, "I want to get my proposal meeting scheduled." But upon further probing, it became increasingly apparent that she did not have a firm grasp on the intent of her study, its significance, or the research genre she professed to use. Choosing committee members within such a conceptual vacuum runs several risks. Committee members may not be able to provide the necessary guidance as the study moves forward. Or they may unconsciously begin to push the study in a direction where their expertise can be of assistance. At some point down the road, the student or committee members may begin to regret their premature commitment to each other and wonder uncomfortably if a "divorce" is possible.

This situation can be especially awkward for students who, understandably, do not want to offend or alienate faculty. Particularly sensitive is a situation in which it becomes increasingly clear that the student's advisor and committee chair is not appropriate given the emerging shape of the dissertation. Although we can understand a student's concerns about offending a faculty member, in reality most faculty are over-extended and do not mind having one less dissertation to guide. This may be especially true when the faculty member is also sensing that there is a mismatch of interest and/or deliberative compatibility.

To forestall the development of such awkward dynamics, we suggest that as students begin to think seriously about their dissertation, they write a three- to five-page description of their study. This short description provides a context for mutually exploring whether there is a fit among faculty, student, and study. It is also an excellent way to begin honing ideas for the proposal as responses to the short document can point to issues that require elaboration and clarification.

---

**Reflective Interlude 12.1**

### How Shall I Go About Forming My Committee?

- What is my reputation among faculty as a student, thinker, and scholar? What have I done throughout my doctoral work to establish my credibility as a thoughtful and capable student?
- In what ways have I explored whether my academic advisor is willing and able to guide or chair my dissertation?
- What faculty member or members know me, my work, and the issue or topic I am interested in studying?
- What faculty member or members know me, my work, and the research genre I am interested in using?
- What are my university's and program's requirements for committee composition?
- Am I required to have a committee member who is outside my program, school, university, or field of study? If so, what are the procedures for identifying such a committee member?
- How will I begin to talk with prospective committee members to ascertain their level of interest in serving on my committee?
- What are committee members' expectations for our working relationship? How frequently and to what extent do they want to be involved; what sort of updates do they expect; what is their process for reviewing documents and providing feedback?
- In what format do committee members want to receive preliminary drafts and the official copy of my proposal—for example, electronic copy via e-mail attachment, printed hard copy?
- How can I let committee members know that I have attended to comments and suggestions for my study?

---

## OBTAINING APPROVAL FROM AN INTERNAL REVIEW BOARD

The proposal often looms so large that it eclipses another important review of the dissertation proposal—an institutional review to protect the rights and welfare of study participants. Although students may see this as yet one more hurdle to be surmounted, in actuality, this review is rooted in ethical principles to which all educational professionals should be committed. In essence, such reviews focus on procedures for (a) obtaining informed consent from prospective study participants, (b) ensuring privacy and confidentiality, and (c) safeguarding against unnecessary risks or potentially harmful practices. Of particular concern to reviewers are studies involving children and other vulnerable populations.[2]

Whereas all doctoral students must be aware of their university's requirements for internal review, those who are conducting a study in another institution (e.g., a school or hospital) must also check to see if an additional review and approval is required by that organization. Larger school districts and health care facilities are likely to have an office of research that can receive and process a student's proposal. Smaller organizations, such as not-for-profit human service agencies, may have no established policy or procedure for granting access to clients. When this is the case, students may need to work with an agency administrator to secure cooperation and approval. In any event, these human-subject reviews have their own time frames and deadlines that students need to factor into their overall schedule for moving toward the proposal meeting.

Typically, internal review boards (IRBs) have a specific set of forms that must be completed. Much of the information will already be spelled out in the proposal and may require only a change in format. The challenge is to convey the essence of the study, often in a limited space, so that a group with little or no context for the study understands its intent, significance, genre, and procedures. Reaction from an *institutional review board* can serve as a valuable reality check on how clearly one is able to explain one's study. For example, one student who submitted a vaguely conceived proposal received the letter in Exemplar 12.1. Therein, the questions raised by the school district's office of research help to illustrate the risk one runs by rushing ahead without due deliberation.

> **Criterion for Judging Interpretive Dissertations**
>
> **Ethics**—Has the researcher attended to requirements of all relevant internal review boards? Does the language of the dissertation adhere to the principles of nondiscrimination? Does the description of research procedures demonstrate an ethical sensibility?

---

**EXEMPLAR 12.1    Response From a School District Office of Research to a Doctoral Student Request to Gather Dissertation Data From Students**

---

Dear Ms. Reilly:

The Internal Review Board considered your request for a clearance to conduct your research study within our school district. The Internal Review Board deferred making a decision on your request and asks that you provide additional information. Specifically, please respond to the following:

1. What is the rationale for your study?

2. What is the focus of your study?

3. What do you expect to learn?

*(Continued)*

###### EXEMPLAR 12.1 (Continued)

4. What is a *community of writers*?

5. What type of key information do you expect your study to provide?

6. What are the structure, process, and purpose of your students' journals?

7. What are your hypotheses?

8. What is your research design?

9. What do you mean by a *narrative research design*?

10. How will you systematically study student writings and videotapes and your writings and teacher journal?

11. What is the purpose of this systematic study in regard to each source of information?

12. What are your anticipated measurement procedures, measures, and analyses?

13. How will your study enhance knowledge and understanding of students' journals and the development of a community of writers?

Please send me a written response to this letter. After I receive your response, I will arrange for the Internal Review Board to give you additional consideration.

Sincerely . . .

*Authors' Commentary.* Questions 1, 2, 3, 5, 7, and 13 are related to the "So what?" of the study. The student has not made a convincing case that the study will contribute in some meaningful way to the field of education. Questions 8 and 9 press for clarification of the overall design of the study. Merely stating that she would follow a narrative research design did not communicate clearly enough the student's intent. In a quest for clarification, the review board then raises Questions 7 and 12, which are not germane to a narrative study being conducted within an interpretive paradigm. The student might argue that the review board was operating with too narrow a conception of *research*. Yet Questions 4, 5, 6, 10, and 11 suggest that the student did not adequately lay out the logic-of-justification for her research procedures. Two key concepts in the research design—*community of writers* and *student journals*—are not explained, nor is a rationale provided for their role in the study. Questions 10 and 11 point to a vagueness in procedures for analyzing or interpreting the data.

We include this example to illustrate two points. First, the student did not adequately consider the audience for her proposal. Given the role of the internal review board—to safeguard the students within their district and protect personnel from intrusive and time-wasting activities—the student misjudged how much information was needed to demonstrate that the study was meaningful.

Second, the student's reaction to the letter illustrates how a thoughtful response to a vaguely conceived proposal can evolve into a dissertation horror story. The student, having read the letter, sent it to the chair of her dissertation committee with a handwritten note,

"How can I respond to this guy and/or get him off my back!" Rather than using the district's response as a reality check and taking responsibility for her own lack of due diligence, the student seemed both resentful and dismissive of the questions about her study. We can imagine hearing about this incident in the future, with the school district cast in the role of villain for not understanding or supporting qualitative dissertation research.

From our perspective, the district's response strikes us as quite kind, given that the document submitted by the student apparently was so thinly conceptualized that it did not provide the most basic forms of information. The fact that the district would be willing to devote attention to a revised proposal is quite supportive. It is our contention, however, that students who submit this type of flawed proposal do much to undermine the credibility of qualitative research.

We contend that regardless of the type of research being proposed, it is the researcher's obligation to make the purpose and procedures of the study clear to others. Ill-conceived studies of any tradition or genre do not merit support. Qualitative researchers, especially those working with institutions that are unfamiliar with this type of inquiry, carry a special obligation to present their studies in a well-reasoned, credible, and ethical fashion. Requests for additional clarification or information should be viewed not as another arbitrary hurdle, but as a signal for additional deliberation.

# ETHICAL SENSIBILITIES BEYOND IRB APPROVAL

Underlying federal mandates for the establishment of IRBs is concern for the protection of human rights and welfare when individuals agree to participate in a study. Agreement or consent to be a "human subject" must be based on the individual's understanding of the risks and benefits associated with participation. The greater the potential risk to the individual's safety, health, and well being, the more closely the proposed research must be scrutinized by the IRB. Quite logically, biomedical research, in which unproven diagnostic and treatment procedures are being tested, is a major concern. Consequently, a great deal of attention has been given to clarifying definitions of risk, establishing guidelines for review, and developing training resources for researchers within the biomedical arena. Virtually all of this information is grounded in the postpositivist tradition of scientific research. Studies that involve minimal risk as defined within this tradition qualify for expedited or exempt review. Thus, educational research grounded in an interpretive tradition of inquiry often qualifies for exemption.

Graduate students in education often breathe a sigh of relief when their thesis or dissertation proposal receives exemption from scrutiny by their university's IRB. They feel at liberty to proceed with their study, perhaps assuming that they have attended in a responsible manner to the ethical issues associated with their research. Such an assumption would not be unreasonable given that almost all of the guidelines and information they have considered have little to do with the type of study they are about to conduct. Yet experienced qualitative researchers have begun to recognize that ethical issues as identified and defined within a postpositivist, scientific tradition do not adequately raise or address ethical issues associated with interpretive inquiries in education. In recent years, a growing body of discourse on the subtle and thorny ethical issues of qualitative research has emerged (see Sample Reference List 12.1).

---------------------------------- ❧ ----------------------------------

### Sample Reference List 12.1

**Ethical Issues in Qualitative Research**

American Educational Research Association, 1992

Ayers & Schubert, 1992

Blumenfeld-Jones, 2003

Boser, 2007

Bullough & Pinnegar, 2001

Campbell & Groundwater-Smith, 2007

Cannella & Lincoln, 2007

Christians, 2007

Clark & Sharf, 2007

Connolly & Reid, 2007

Dash, 2007

Denzin & Giardina, 2007

Dimitriads, 2001

Douvanis & Brown, 1995

Elliott, 1992

Fine & Weis, 1996

Fisher, 2007

Gunsalus et al., 2007

Halpin & Troyna, 1994

Halse & Honey, 2007

Harrison, MacGibbon, & Morton, 2001

Holland, 2007

Huber & Clandinin, 2002

Johnstone, 2000

Koro-Ljungberg, Gemignani, Brodeur, & Kmiec, 2007

Liberman, 1999

Lincoln, 1995, 1998

Lincoln & Guba, 1989

Lincoln & Tierney, 2004

Marzano, 2007

Mun Wong, 1998

Nespor, 2000

O'Connor, Netting, & Thomas, 2008

Patterson, 2008

Pritchard, 2002

Punch, 1994

Rambo, 2007

Schrum, 1995

Sharf, 1999

Taylor, 1992

Tierney & Corwin, 2007

Tilley & Gormley, 2007

Tunnell, 1998

Waldrop, 2004

Weisberg & Duffin, 1995

Zeni, 2001

One of the issues of concern in biomedical research is helping novice researchers to understand the line between accepted standards of quality care and clinical procedures that are undergoing careful evaluation for their efficacy and safety. In education, the line between events and activities inherent in classroom practice and those being undertaken as part of an interpretive inquiry can be fuzzy at best. This is particularly true when the inquiry is undertaken by educators within the context of their own practice. Illustrative of ethical issues that might be of concern in qualitative or interpretive inquiries are the following:

## Awareness of and Respect for the Cultural Context of One's Study

This example came from a colleague in Australia who was conducting a study on the experience of spirituality in daily life.

> My particular interlocutor in this instance is an Aboriginal Elder of the Nyungah Tribe. She is mid fifties, an artist, and highly regarded for her work, her interest in the environment and her contacts within and beyond her tribe, even internationally. Her sharing with me took up nearly three hours, and I drove five hours to gather her story. I was clear that I had to show absolute respect for her tradition, her tribal situation, her culture. I was careful and caring not to transgress, by my questions, any area that was taboo, or "men's business" in which case she could not know, or "women's business" in which case, she may not be able to tell. It would all depend on the particular questions that I asked as to what she was free to share with me . . . an interesting and highly valuable experience for me. In the last year though, this lady has passed on. According to the traditions of the Aboriginal people of Australia her name and experiences as they apply to my research may not be mentioned in print or any other form of media without breaking sacred taboos. I am bound to the university ethics committee guidelines, as are all official governmental and non-governmental departments and organisations of my country with regard to Aboriginal Australians. As a result I could not use her story.

## Understanding for Whom One Has the Right to Speak; Understanding the Ownership of Life Stories

With the emergence of narrative as a major form of interpretive inquiry, two catch phrases have become popular among many well-meaning, but naive, novices. They say their research will "give voice to" or "tell the story of" economically disadvantaged, socially marginalized, and/or politically disenfranchised individuals (e.g., those with a mental illness, migrant workers, homeless individuals). Unquestionably, it is important for educators to attend to the perspectives and experiences of individuals and groups. It is presumptuous, however, to suggest that individuals have no voice until it is bestowed by a researcher or that a research report conveys the stories of anyone but the researcher. Some might dismiss such concerns as quibbling over mere semantics, but issues of voice, stance, and authorship lie at the heart of ethical interpretive inquiry. Consequently, they demand thoughtful, sensitive, and careful attention.

## Constructing "Other"—
## Constructing Truth Claims About "Other"

Ethical interpretive inquiry requires sensitivity to issues of representing others and of making knowledge claims based on one's representation of others. Interpretive inquiries proceed on the assumption that researchers are putting forward their own interpretations of others and that these interpretations cannot be claimed as the truth or reality of someone else's experience, life, personality, character, and so on. This is an ontological and epistemological issue that lies at the heart of the difference between postpositivist and interpretive research, and is, perhaps, the aspect of interpretive research that gives novices the most trouble.

## Consent in Autobiographical Inquiries

Interpretive inquiries typically have an autobiographical quality because the researcher is telling the story of his or her research. This autobiographical quality intensifies when professionals conduct their studies within their context of practice. Inevitably, they are an actor within that context and must be portrayed as such. Beyond that, some researchers set out to write an autobiography or memoir to illuminate the question under study. While individuals have a right to make public the details of their own lives, they do not necessarily have the right to expose others to public view. This adds complexity to the ethical principles of "do no harm," informed consent, and anonymity of participants.

## Sensitivity to Power Differentials

Using one's work organization as the context for a study requires a heightened sensitivity to issues of power. One principal, for example, wanted to gain insight into why teachers in his elementary school were so resistant to his efforts at educational reform. He framed the teachers as the source of his problem and wanted them to participate in his study. He seemed oblivious to the fact that he held power over the teachers in terms of assignments, promotions, and performance evaluations and could coerce their participation. Another researcher was acutely aware of the fact that some of her colleagues were highly critical of her school system's policy on educational inclusion. In sharing their views with her, these colleagues made themselves vulnerable. Fortunately, this particular researcher recognized the need to be sensitive to this issue. A teacher who wants to study a pedagogical or curriculum approach may need input from her students. Again, will their participation be coerced because of the teacher's power over their grades or a desire to please an authority figure?

The scenarios in Exemplar 12.2 are drawn from an unpublished paper written by a student at the Flinders Institute for the Study of Teaching in South Australia (Prosser, 1998). They emerged during the course of a critical theory study of attention deficit hyperactivity disorder (ADHD) and help to illustrate the point that *ethical sensibility* goes beyond simply obtaining a signed consent to participate form. It is possible that some readers might think that the questions posed at the end of each scenario are somewhat simplistic or naive. What they serve to illustrate, however, is a heightened consciousness of oneself in the inquiry process, a stance of introspective reflection, and a willingness to pause long enough to consider what course of action or response might be ethically responsible.

## Reflective Interlude 12.2

### What Have I Done to Cultivate My Ethical Sensibilities?

- What are my university's requirements and procedures for internal review of dissertation proposals in education?
- What resources are available to help me understand internal review procedures?
- In what ways have I prepared myself to understand the ethical principles of qualitative and interpretive research?
- What ethical issues might arise in the course of my study? How can I respond to these issues in an ethically responsible way?
- What power differentials exist between me and those I might want to have as participants in my study? Can sufficient safeguards be established to protect participants, or do I need to rethink who I should ask to participate in my study?

### EXEMPLAR 12.2    Ethical Dilemmas and the Need for Ethical Sensibility

One school requests a presentation about the project to the staff outlining my aims and methods. Further, they request notification to all teachers of which students will be absent from each lesson. Most teachers are unaware of who has ADHD in the school. What should I tell them?

In the same school, most students who have agreed to participate keep forgetting to attend interviews, and my schedule is way behind. The school suggests that I go into classrooms and remove the students. Should I do this?

I discover among my cohort a student who is not diagnosed ADHD but the school believes should be. The student knows nothing about ADHD and struggles to participate. Further, his mother calls to complain about the emphasis on ADHD. What do I do?

I discover three students who have been labeled ADHD by the school, who are on medication "because it helps," but whose parents deny an ADHD diagnosis. Is it illegal to be on medication without an ADHD diagnosis? What do I do with this information?

During my time in one school, a journalist approached me for an interview asking for access to data on geographical distribution of ADHD. As the interview progressed, it became apparent that she was trying to get the name of a practitioner of whom overprescription is suspected, and get me to make a stance on medication use. Even though all my participants are supporters of medication, part of my concern is medicalization of ADHD. How do I respond?

A teacher that had been really helpful approached me to tell a story of a friend who was desperate for advice. Her child had been out of control since she was two, but several psychologists said it was not ADHD. However, her school is pushing for a medical diagnosis, and the mother wants to know what help is out there, if I think it is ADHD, and if I could refer her to any good pediatricians. What do I say?

*(Continued)*

A student in one school calls me professor and is trying to use my supposed authority to convince teachers he should get benefits under the guise of ADHD. What do I do?

The students in one school decided that the medical community unfairly represents them and they want to make their own documentary. They want to show they are not all out of control. One student wants to take himself off medication and film on videotape the difference between his behavior and teachers' responses in a classroom. How do I approach this?

## MEETING TO REVIEW THE PROPOSAL

The proposal meeting is often treated as a major milestone by students. Even those who have accepted the recursive nature of the dissertation process may see it as getting permission "to start" their study. Ideally, however, the meeting should be one more iteration of deliberation among the student's mini-discourse community. Even though students may have kept committee members informed of progress on the study, this may be the first opportunity for all committee members to meet with the student and each other to discuss the inquiry.

### Purpose of the Meeting

As mentioned above, students may assume that the purpose of the meeting is to find flaws in the proposal or to "rip the document to shreds." The committee's intent, however, is to make certain that they understand the study and to assure themselves on three points. One relates to topic—Is there a study here? The second relates to the inquiry process—Is the student prepared and able to conduct the inquiry? The third is determining the student's capacity to enter into deliberation—Is the student willing and able to engage in deliberation? As these issues are explored, committee members may offer suggestions for strengthening the conceptualization of the study. This does not necessarily mean that the study is flawed. Sometimes, students are so immersed in the details of the study that they have difficulty pulling back and describing it in more general terms. Committee members with a bit more distance are often able to suggest words or phrasing that sharpen the clarity of ideas.

### Structure and Process of the Meeting

The structure and process of the proposal meeting are shaped by the customs, culture, and rituals of each institution, school, or even program. Students who may never have attended a proposal meeting sometimes see it as shrouded in mystery. Not knowing what to expect and assuming they are not supposed to ask about this mysterious rite of passage, students can begin to stew in anxiety. In reality, the proposal review is a semipublic meeting that is announced so that interested parties can attend. Our own experience with this issue may not be typical of other schools, but it does illustrate the dynamic nature of customs surrounding the proposal (see Exemplar 12.3).

### EXEMPLAR 12.3    The Dynamic Nature of Customs and Rituals Surrounding the Proposal

Within our school of education, it was not customary for students to sit in on proposal meetings. Although meeting dates and places are posted in the school, members of our study group never realized that this meant that the meetings were open to interested parties.

With great timidity, one student finally asked if it would be all right for another study group member to come to her meeting. When this caused no consternation among faculty, group members began to invite each other to their proposal meetings. At one meeting, guests outnumbered committee members almost by a two-to-one ratio. Students were amazed when the committee chair first invited them to sit at the table and later asked if they wanted to add anything to the conversation. "Can you believe it?" they later shared with a sense of awed excitement. "They actually seemed pleased that we were there. Joe even said we made the discussion more meaningful."

Joe's inclusion of the students and his heartfelt remark about their contribution to the deliberation brought to light the other side of the coin. Over the years, some faculty seem to have been lulled into the assumption that students would have neither the time nor inclination to attend each other's meetings. Joe made explicit a change that had been occurring gradually as study group members involved each other in their meetings.

Lest we imply that all school cultures are the same, we relate the following anecdote. As a courtesy to a professional acquaintance who was trying to conceptualize a grounded theory study, Maria agreed to serve as an informal sounding board. When it came time for the proposal meeting, the student asked her advisor if Maria could attend. Permission was granted on the condition that Maria sit away from the table and serve as a silent note taker for the student.

Despite variations in school culture, advisors commonly ask students to give some introductory remarks and a short summary of their study. The intent is often to see if the student is able to (a) concisely describe the study and (b) explain his or her current thinking about the study. This is not meant to be a formal presentation, as some students assume. Nor is the student expected to walk the committee through the proposal or restate what is in the document. Rather, the student's remarks should establish a shared context for initiating a substantive conversation about the inquiry. It is important to note that committee members often look forward to this opportunity to exchange views with each other as well as to explore the study with the student. Students may erroneously assume that they are obliged to be on center stage for the entire meeting. One student, for example, had prepared an extensive PowerPoint presentation and tediously began to read each slide to the committee. Thirty minutes later, the student was still going strong, and the advisor had to interrupt this monologue to create space for discussion.

Worried that they will not be able to fill their allotted time or concerned about forgetting important details of the study, students may also prepare handouts or outlines from which to talk. Repeatedly, we have seen students misjudge the amount of time it takes to distribute and review the handouts. Although the advisor had in mind no more than a 10-minute introduction, the student monopolized a major portion of the meeting.

In most cases, we see this as an unfortunate by-product of the student's anxiety. Occasionally, however, a student seems to think that this is a clever strategy to control the meeting and thereby forestall annoying or intrusive questions. Such attempts to subvert the deliberative purpose of the meeting are likely to evoke impatience, frustration, and irritation. Beyond that, it risks compromising the quality of the dissertation.

To safeguard against such pitfalls, students might keep in mind the multifaceted nature of the discussion. By the time of the proposal meeting, students may have attained a heightened state of self-absorption, making it difficult for them to sort out the multiple layers of conversation.

## Listening to the Deliberations

The text and subtexts of the discussion may be accomplishing several purposes simultaneously. Most explicitly, the discussion gives the student an opportunity to educate faculty about the study. Students often fail to realize that they may now have more knowledge about the subject of their inquiry than faculty do. Certainly, they have the most intimate knowledge about the inquiry. Although students may feel as though they are being quizzed (or even grilled) about their proposal, it is more likely that the questions are meant to generate among all committee members a common understanding of the study. In the process, various perspectives can be brought together in ways that support the study and, in turn, reduce the potential for contradictory and fragmenting advice.

Beyond this dissertation-focused purpose, proposal meetings provide faculty with opportunities to meet new colleagues and to build relationships and networks. Likewise, faculty often welcome the opportunity to learn from each other and engage in intellectual discussions. Students may have given little consideration to the fact that faculty at a large university may not know each other and may welcome a connection with those who share similar scholarly interests. Furthermore, faculty who are caught up in teaching courses and serving on administrative committees may relish an all-too-rare moment for exchanging points of view on an intriguing subject. In several instances, faculty have agreed to serve on the committees of our study group members because of a mounting interest in qualitative research, and they see this as a way to become more familiar with the intricacies of such a dissertation.

In short, committee discourses are multilayered, and students are cautioned not to automatically equate faculty comments with criticisms of the proposal or with expectations for revisions. Audiotaping the meeting is valuable for capturing the discussion and having a record to review once the stress and anxiety have abated. Here, too, customs vary among institutions and individual faculty, so students are cautioned to discuss audiotaping with their committee chair and to obtain permission before proceeding.

Bringing the meeting to closure entails another set of issues. Although customs vary, it is more usual than not to ask the candidate to leave the room while faculty confer. Some students take offense at being excluded, or they see this as an intentional manipulation to increase the anxiety and drama of the meeting. Such negative views hearken back to the assumption of an adversarial relationship between student and committee. In actuality, this break in the conversation gives faculty a chance to sort through points that have been raised, collect their thoughts, and formulate the outcomes of the meeting.

# DEALING WITH MEETING OUTCOMES

Students often think in terms of passing or failing the proposal. In reality, a continuum of potential outcomes may result. Naturally, the outcome that every student hopes for is an acceptance of the proposal document as written and approval to proceed with the study. At the other end of the continuum is the outcome that students dread—having to rewrite major portions of the document and schedule another committee meeting. This latter outcome is more likely to occur when students have shortchanged the deliberative process and submitted a vaguely conceptualized proposal. When students have engaged in ongoing deliberations with their advisor and committee members, they are less likely to jump the gun and circulate an unacceptable proposal.

It is not uncommon for proposals to fall somewhere between totally adequate or totally inadequate. In the event that some revisions are needed, faculty might use one of several options for handling the process. For example, if committee members want to confirm the student's grasp of concerns raised in the meeting, the student might be asked to write and submit an addendum to the proposal. The addendum describes the student's understanding of issues that need to be addressed as the study proceeds. Because the proposal serves as a contract between the student and committee, the addendum can spell out major expectations or understandings that have emerged from the discussion without necessitating a major rewrite of the proposal.

Another option that may be exercised by a committee is relying upon the student's advisor to oversee and sign off on requested revisions. With this approach, the committee does not review the proposal or meet again. This option might be used when the conceptual structure of the study is sound, but procedural issues need some fine-tuning, or some aspect of the formal discourses needs to be incorporated.

Still another option entails asking the student to proceed with the study but to schedule an interim meeting to report on progress. This approach can be especially helpful when students have not yet begun to gather and work with the raw texts of the study. The committee may believe that the student will come to a deeper conceptualization of the study only after he or she has proceeded to this phase of the inquiry. We are reminded of one student who clung to a set of rather simplistic preconceptions about his topic—organizational learning—despite repeated prompting to consider alternative points of view. His committee requested an interim meeting in order to see if he was able to gain deeper insights as he heard from study participants.

The committee's rationale for choosing a particular option may appear arbitrary or mysterious to students. To understand the reasoning behind the various outcomes, it is useful to remember the three questions that underpin the purpose of the meeting: (1) Has a worthwhile and viable study been proposed? (2) Does the student have a firm enough grasp of the research genre and procedures to carry through with the study? (3) Has the student demonstrated a capacity for deliberation? In making a judgment on these three issues, committee members draw upon not only the written proposal but also their interactions with the candidate during the meeting and their knowledge of the student's scholarly capacities.

In both the proposal and the discussion during the meeting, committee members are looking for indicators that the student "owns" the study. This is a delicate balance point in the ongoing process of deliberation. On one hand, students need to internalize the intent and procedures of the study so that the committee's suggestions do not undermine the conceptual integrity of the inquiry. On the other hand, students must remain open to committee input. In short, students need to have a firm enough grasp of the study to take in information and weigh its value in refining the inquiry. For example, if a committee member with an empirical worldview raises questions about reliability, objectivity, and validity that are not epistemologically germane to an interpretive study, the student must be prepared to recognize that and respond appropriately.

This may engender a sense of anxiety in students who feel that they will never be prepared to handle the range of questions that might crop up in the committee meeting. Two advantages to being part of a deliberative community (even if it is comprised of only the student and his or her chair) are (a) having a chance to practice responding to a variety of questions and (b) gaining a sense of when one is ready for a formal review. In addition, students must keep in mind that they are not in the process alone. Here again, seeing the committee members as resources, not adversaries, is important. Through the committee's deliberations with the student, candidates can gain a clearer sense of which suggestions help to hone the study and which might subvert it.

In addition to the document and the student's conduct during the committee meeting, faculty's history with the student can play a role in shaping the outcomes of the meeting. The anecdote in Exemplar 12.4 raises several issues related to this point.

---

**EXEMPLAR 12.4    Student Credibility and the Myth of the "Sweetheart" Committee**

During a session of an introductory course on qualitative research, we asked Pat McMahon to share her experience of doing a narrative study. As Pat described various aspects of planning her study, it was quite clear that she had immersed herself in the discourses of composition theory and reflection. She had written and discarded numerous drafts of the proposal. She had engaged in substantive discussions about her ideas both with our dissertation study group and with various faculty. By the time of her proposal meeting, Pat had solidified her reputation with committee members as a thoughtful and conscientious doctoral candidate, a capable writer, and a disciplined thinker.

At some point during the class conversation, Pat was trying to make the point that in a highly interpretive study, the proposal is a best guess of what will emerge from the inquiry. Within this context, she said, "I feel very fortunate that my committee gave me well—not quite carte blanche—but a great deal of leeway in how I would proceed with my study."

Upon hearing this, one student blurted out, "How do I get those faculty on my committee?"

The implication was that somehow Pat was lucky enough to have a "sweetheart committee" that had taken it easy on her. In one short sentence, the student demonstrated a stunning failure to grasp not just Pat's dissertation experience but much of what we had been stressing throughout the semester.

The notion of the *sweetheart committee* seems deeply embedded in dissertation folklore. In this approach, students hope to trade on perceived friendships with faculty in order to gain a sympathetic and kindly review of their proposal. Instead, when faculty give a thoughtful critique, students may at best be surprised and at worst feel betrayed. This can fuel more horror stories about the arbitrary nature of committees and proposal meetings where some students "get off easy" and others are forced to "jump through more hoops." What may not be obvious are the different reputations that students may bring to the dissertation process. When students have a demonstrated record of credible work and scholarly deliberation, committee members may place their faith in the student's integrity, trusting that the student will keep them apprised of progress and seek assistance when necessary. Students who have earned such trust and respect are unlikely to misuse or abuse it in the interest of "getting by."

## MOVING FORWARD INTO THE STUDY

Before turning to the process of living with the study, we feel that a few words are in order about the aftermath of the proposal meeting. Over the years, we have noticed that a number of study group members have experienced "downtime" after the meeting, even when it has gone very well. In one sense, this downtime is associated with a lull in moving to the next phase of the inquiry. Students who had been impatient to get the go-ahead suddenly find themselves procrastinating. We speculate that students may have invested so much psychic energy in conceptualizing the proposal and gearing up for the meeting that they are exhausted. The realization that quite a bit of work still lies ahead may be daunting. Practitioners who put work on the back burner while they finished the proposal may become reimmersed in the demands of their work setting. This may provide a convenient excuse for not reorganizing their energy and getting started again.

In a few instances, students have experienced downtime in the form of feelings of depression. Several students have reported going home and crying for several days after the meeting. Such a reaction would certainly be understandable if the committee had not "signed on the dotted line." But some students describe feelings of profound disappointment even when their proposal was approved. We speculate that in at least some cases, students experience a letdown because they did not receive unqualified praise from their committee. Those who are used to receiving high grades and compliments about their work may feel that their proposal is not good enough because it did not elicit accolades. It is important to remember that the proposal—no matter how well conceived—is only an interim iteration of the study and is, inevitably, not good enough. What may be seen as grudging acceptance on the part of committee members may in fact be a tempered response in recognition of the work that lies ahead.

Another possible source of hesitation may arise when novice researchers equate everything prior to the proposal meeting as "planning the study" and everything after it as "implementing the study." The full force of doing a dissertation may hit home at this point and trigger a crisis of confidence. We are reminded of one student who decided that he needed a desk before he could proceed with his study. Rather than visiting an office furniture store, he set about designing a desk that he would subsequently build. We are not sure if he ever finished the desk. We know he did not finish his dissertation. Fortunately, such extreme reluctance to proceed with the study is the exception rather than the rule. For many students, digging into the information that informs their inquiry brings the study to life.

---

**Reflective Interlude 12.3**

### How Am I Preparing for My Proposal Meeting?

- What advice does my dissertation advisor have about preparing for the meeting?
- What type of presentation, if any, am I expected to make?
- How public is the meeting? How familiar will the audience be with the topic and genre of the study? What information is most meaningful to communicate in the time available?
- What are the university's requirements for announcing the proposal meeting and submitting an official copy before the meeting?
- What are the university's and/or program's customs around taping the meeting?

---

## NOTES

1. Again, we stress the point that each university and school has its own policies related to committee composition and procedures for having a dissertation committee approved. Students are encouraged to work closely with their advisor to make certain they understand and follow these institutional requirements.

2. Many universities, especially those who rely a great deal on federal grants, have instituted courses on the ethical conduct of research. In some institutions, successful completion of these courses may be mandatory prior to the submission of a dissertation proposal. We urge students to check with their university to determine what requirements they are expected to meet. Again, the earlier these requirements are understood and met, the better.

# 13

---

# *Living With the Study*

---

## Key Concepts

| | |
|---|---|
| Aha Moment | Vitality |
| Authorial Right | Immersing Oneself in the Inquiry |
| Criteria for Judging Interpretive Dissertations | Living With the Study |
| Aesthetics | Original Contribution |
| Rigor | Portrayal |
| Utility | Representation |
| Vérité | Theoretic Perspective |
| | Warranting One's Thesis |

---

In Chapter 3, we likened the dissertation process to running a marathon in order to raise the issue of pacing. Although pacing is important from start to finish, it is particularly crucial during the time one is *living with the study*. We use this phrase to connote the messy, and inevitably daunting, time between approval of the proposal and submission of the dissertation document to one's committee. We see this phase as punctuated by a pivotal *aha moment* when the researcher finally sees the theoretic interpretation—core thesis—he or she wants to put forward. In a sense, all the hard work leading up to the aha moment is only preparation for the hardest work of all—that is, crafting the experiential, discursive, and theoretic texts to *warrant the thesis*.

Some might see this as a phase of "doing the study" in which the researcher "implements" the plan laid out in the proposal. For us, *implementation* connotes a level of control over the completion of discrete action steps. In our experience, this impression of control is misleading in two ways. First, interpretive research is an inductive process in which the researcher is obliged to follow lines of inquiry as they emerge during the course of the study. How many of these avenues will open up and how long it will take to pursue them cannot be anticipated at the outset of the study. Second, the aha moment occurs when the researcher makes a conceptual leap—having an insight that puts the myriad individual, idiosyncratic, and situational details into a meaningful, coherent, *theoretic perspective.* It is not possible to predict, control, or schedule an aha moment. So rather than implementing a study, we see students immersing themselves in their inquiry. Those who embody a stance of study are willing to let their inquiry take on a life of its own and, in turn, to take over the student's life. Thus, *living with the study* is meant to connote the messiness of a process that includes

- immersing oneself in the inquiry;
- amassing and resonating with raw texts;
- drafting and redrafting preliminary experiential, discursive, and theoretic texts;
- coming to a conceptual leap; and
- recrafting the experiential, discursive, and theoretic texts to provide a coherent representation of the inquiry and to warrant one's thesis.

In this chapter we look at several issues associated with these aspects of living with one's study.

## IMMERSING ONESELF IN THE INQUIRY

Occasionally, we meet students who assert, "I don't have time to do a qualitative study. My job and/or family responsibilities are just too demanding." Such concerns are well taken, and if this is, in fact, the situation, then an interpretive dissertation may not be feasible. We offer for consideration, however, a student who taught full time, cared for an infant son, and nursed her sister through a terminal illness while she completed her dissertation. When we asked, "How can you do this?" she explained that concentrating on the dissertation provided a haven from the other stresses in her life. Although this student's situation was extreme, many students do continue to work, and most must attend to family obligations even while completing a qualitative dissertation. Yet once the dissertation proposal has been approved, the study tends to consume not just students' time but also their intellectual (and often emotional) energy. In our experience, the intensity of this work frequently comes as a sobering surprise, even to the most well-prepared students. Monique, for example, was an avid golfer and planned to sandwich the dissertation in between rounds of weekend golf. She made little progress until she relinquished her time on the links to immersion in her study.

The phrase *immersing oneself in the inquiry* connotes a sense of action. Because qualitative research in education has strong roots in sociology and anthropology, this sense of action is often described as "going into the field." Some novices, operating with a simplistic caricature of ethnography, infer that *field research* entails going to an unfamiliar (perhaps exotic) geographic location and gathering data about that place. But Eisncr (1991), in discussing this field-focused feature of qualitative research, cautions against an overly narrow conception of the field as a place:

> Researchers go out into the schools, visit classrooms, and observe teachers, places where humans interact in educational events. The field focus, however, is not limited to places in which humans interact. It also includes the study of inanimate objects such as school architecture, textbooks, classroom arrangement, the design of playgrounds. In short, anything that is related to education is a potential subject matter of qualitative study. (p. 32)

Eisner's point that the field can be more than a geographic location is well taken. Yet novice researchers might infer that the study of inanimate objects is the purpose of their fieldwork. From our perspective, too literal an emphasis on place or object as the subject matter of qualitative study can obscure the phenomenon that underpins the conceptual intent of an inquiry.

## Preparing for Immersion

Action-oriented practitioner-researchers sometimes have a difficult time explaining in advance the nature of the experience they will be trying to capture in their study. As "doers," they want to jump into an experience and through reflection figure it out as they go. To some extent, this may be necessary to get a feel for the context, the types of information that is most useful to gather, and the methods for managing all of the information. There are, however, potential pitfalls with this approach. Novice researchers may erroneously conceive of reflection as randomly jotting down notes and haphazardly thinking about whatever aspect of the experience catches their attention. This lacks the systematic *rigor* necessary for crafting the texts of the final dissertation. Furthermore, jumping into a context without some type of plan may be prompted by the naive assumption that the totality of any experience can be captured. Inevitably, the recollection and recording of experience—no matter how extensive—will be selective. Therefore, we suggest that such unstructured immersion be viewed as preliminary preparation for an inquiry.

Because educational phenomena are elusive and educational settings are complex and fluid, novice researchers can quickly become disoriented as they immerse themselves in the inquiry. This is the reason we stress the importance of carefully thinking through not only the experiential context of the study but also the conceptual context as well. This preparation is another aspect of developing oneself as an *instrument of inquiry.* Having a firm grasp of "where" they will be immersed and why that "place" has been chosen allows researchers to resonate more sensitively with what they find in "the field."

The quotation marks in the preceding sentence serve as a reminder that *context* is not necessarily a geographic location. For example, books and other written artifacts might comprise the context of historical, legal, or policy-related dissertations. For such studies, *going into the field* might mean going to a repository of documents.

## Keeping Focused

For many inquiries, immersion does involve entering an actual setting. It goes beyond the purpose and scope of this book to address practical strategies for gaining access to field sites, establishing rapport, gaining trust, and other issues commonly associated with field research. Rather, our focus remains on issues related to *self as instrument*.

Because interpretive inquiries study phenomena within particular contexts, novice researchers run the risk of getting lost in the specific events, activities, relationships, experiences, and so on that comprise the context. When students fashion their dissertation around some aspect of their practice, living with the study often keeps them immersed in their own work. Although this provides a rich context for the inquiry, it also blurs the boundary between practitioner and researcher. This is not necessarily a problem unless unwary practitioners become so enmeshed in concerns of practice that they lose sight of their study. Greta, for example, was studying the educational needs of nursing home administrators at a time when many individuals had moved into these positions with little formal preparation. Repeatedly, Greta found her research interviews turning into miniconsulting sessions as administrators, hungry for information, began to solicit her advice. Greta, being a teacher at heart, and having a strong desire to improve the quality of nursing home administration, found it exceptionally difficult to pull back from these interactions and maintain a focus on her inquiry. It is not as though the two were mutually exclusive. But without self-discipline, Greta ran the risk of sacrificing her dissertation to the needs of her study participants.

Classroom teachers and school administrators can be especially susceptible to the demands of practice. The immediate needs of students, the ever-present fires to be put out, are tremendously compelling to committed practitioners who are juggling job responsibilities and the dissertation. Thus, for practitioners, living with the study requires vigilance against losing sight of their study. Engaging in all three forms of reflection (recollective, introspective, and conceptual) can help practitioner-researchers step back from their context and refocus attention on their inquiry. A productive tension arises as researchers recollect the details of the context, resonate introspectively with the potential meanings of those details, and make conceptual connections with the phenomenon under study.

While some students choose to research an aspect of their own practice, others may prefer to investigate a phenomenon within a less familiar setting. The dissertation may provide an opportunity to examine an issue that has always troubled them, explore an arena of practice in anticipation of a career move, or grapple with the demands of a new professional role or position. In such cases, immersing oneself in the inquiry may require what Bill Ayers (1997) calls "hanging out." In describing his own experience in writing *A Kind and Just Parent*, Ayers talks about hanging out in the juvenile justice system for two years—listening, watching, talking, and reading. Through hanging out, the researcher develops the sensitivity necessary to understand the significant aspects of the context. Two years is not an unusual length of time to hang out in order to develop the capacity to resonate fully with a previously unfamiliar context and phenomenon. For example, when Maria reached the dissertation stage of her doctoral work, she accepted a position at an urban teaching hospital with the idea of doing her dissertation on the role of an educator in such a setting. It took her 18 months of living in that context before she was able to shape the intent of her study (Piantanida, 1982). Looking back on this situation several years later, Maria realized that the learning she had been doing during those first 18 months could have constituted her study. At the time, however, her understanding of qualitative research was not strong enough to guide her efforts.

# AMASSING AND RESONATING WITH RAW TEXTS

In Chapters 8 and 9, we tried to alert readers to a number of issues that arise as one amasses and resonates with raw texts, especially the difficult task of crafting richly descriptive and evocative experiential text. Here, we want to underscore the point that this aspect of living with the study is often prolonged, disorienting, and discouraging. To a certain extent, the disorientation and discouragement arise as elusive images emerge from the raw texts and then slip away. One student likened this to the little plastic toys she used to find in boxes of Cracker Jack. Held at one angle, one picture appeared; held at another angle, a second picture appeared. Holding the piece of plastic steady enough for either image to remain fixed for any length of time was virtually impossible. In qualitative research, the shifting images often arise from a figure-ground dilemma. Organized in one way—held at one angle—the text forms a figure that stands out against the background. Organized another way, the same text recedes into the background, allowing a different figure to emerge. Those with a low tolerance for ambiguity may seize too readily upon early impressions, prematurely bringing closure to the theorizing process. Thus, living with the study means trying out various configurations for juxtaposing situational detail with conceptual points in order to get in touch with the major ideas to be conveyed as a result of the inquiry.

Many members of our study group have described this as a time of darkness, pain, and despair (see Garman & Piantanida, 2006). Nothing seems to make sense. They are wracked with doubts about their intellectual capabilities, the merits of their studies, and the possibility of ever finishing the dissertation. Long-distance marathoners talk about "hitting a wall," often when they are within a couple of miles from the finish line. The capacity to endure complete exhaustion, to reach deeper into some unsuspected reservoir of strength, and to persist to the finish contributes to the integrity, rigor, and intellectual *vitality* of the study. Mentioning this difficult time is not meant to discourage students from undertaking the race. Rather, it is meant to acknowledge the angst that accompanies acts of creativity and to encourage students to keep writing their way toward an aha moment and beyond.

## The Fine Art of Task Avoidance

Some students seem to believe that it is a waste of time and effort to start writing before they have figured out what they want to say. In our experience, this is a mistake. It is often through the act of writing that researchers find their way out of the conceptual morass. That said, the difficulty of resonating for a prolonged period of time can lure even the most conscientious student into some subtle—and not so subtle—task-avoidance behaviors. Perhaps because all study group members have been women, the telltale behaviors manifest themselves in unexpected acts of domesticity. We beg our male readers' forbearance and urge them to watch for masculine equivalents.

The very earliest behavior to surface in our awareness was an unaccountable need to clean house. Career women with a self-confessed aversion to dusting, vacuuming, washing windows, and tidying up suddenly found themselves immersed in these homey pursuits. "My house hasn't been this clean since my mother's last visit," one woman reported. "I've been getting up in the middle of the night with an uncontrollable urge to organize my closets," said another. "I know I should be working at the computer," lamented a third, "but I keep drifting toward the basement to find stuff to donate to Goodwill." Our favorite variation on this domestic theme came from a woman who thought she would "knock off" her dissertation during her newborn son's naptime. Two years later, when she finally returned to the dissertation, she was overcome by a need to sew her toddler a Halloween costume. The snapshot of Will in his colorful clown suit is a classic study group artifact, cherished all the more because our friend never again plied a needle through a piece of fabric.

Initially, these activities seemed to be the crassest form of task avoidance. The consistency with which the behaviors recurred, however, began to make us wonder. Did these manual tasks play some important role in the process of resonating with texts? Perhaps the need to bring order and neatness to one's external environment made tolerable the hopeless jumble of thoughts and ideas. Perhaps breaks from the grueling efforts of resonating and writing were necessary, but truly fun diversions would offer too seductive an alternative to the confines of one's desk. Perhaps the calming effect of routine tasks allowed for a subliminal reprocessing of information. Over the years, we have come to believe that such activities—within reason—are an essential aspect of doing a qualitative dissertation.

Because cleaning and sewing seem to be so blatantly task avoidant, even the most novice researcher can generally pull back and resume the intellectual work of the inquiry. Yet there are several more subtle forms of task avoidance that can waylay the unwary student. Some students find it very energizing to be out in the field, talking to people, collecting more raw texts. It looks like they are right on task and working productively. And so they are, up to a point. When running out to gather more information supplants the more demanding task of making meaning of what has already been amassed, the researcher is engaged in a sophisticated form of task avoidance. Similarly, when researchers find themselves going to the library to search for the meaning of their data, an alarm should sound. As much as we stress the importance of immersing oneself in the discourses, there comes a time when more reading diverts attention from the painstaking work of grappling with the meaning of the raw texts. Our Halloween seamstress likened this form of task avoidance to reading cookbooks all afternoon when the dinner guests are scheduled to arrive at 5:00 and no food has been prepared.

Knowing when more raw text is needed, knowing when it is time to revisit the literature, knowing when it is time to generate iterative and theoretic interpretations, knowing when it is time to write—no matter how crudely conceived the ideas are— these are issues of pacing that novice researchers may be hard-pressed to monitor for themselves. For this reason, we urge student-researchers to remain engaged in deliberation with others who have either been through the process or who are further along in it. Whether this deliberation is with one's advisor, other committee members, a study group, or an electronic community, it is extremely helpful to receive feedback from those who can help one maintain a productive pace.

# COMING TO A CONCEPTUAL LEAP

In resonating with raw texts, researchers are trying out various iterative and theoretic interpretations as well as various forms of *representation*. At issue is far more than a neat or clever organization of the material. Inherent in this conceptual grappling is the process of generating knowledge, of interpreting the phenomenon under study, of struggling to create text to portray and warrant those meanings. The aha moment represents a conceptual leap in which the researcher sees the essence of the study and how the pieces fit into a larger, coherent *portrayal* of the phenomenon under study. This moment of insight allows researchers to concentrate on the intellectual task that dominates the latter half of living with the study—that is, carefully crafting the final experiential, discursive, and theoretic texts that compose the dissertation document. Exemplar 13.1 offers an example of an aha moment that Maria came to when she was working on her dissertation. The essence of this moment centers not on the content of her study but on what it means to generate knowledge in an interpretive study.

For us, the mosaic metaphor gives a gestalt of the interpretive knowledge-generating process. The piles of pebbles represent all of the raw texts that researchers amass as they live with the study. Resonating with these texts occurs as researchers continually sort and sift the pebbles. As researchers become intimately familiar with the texture, color, size, and shape of the pebbles, they can begin to see possibilities for creating mosaics that address the intent of the study. In any given pile of pebbles, an almost limitless variety of mosaics can potentially be created. In the end, each researcher must own his or her responsibility for deciding what mosaic is most compelling or meaningful to create. Coming to this decision is not a linear process. Rather, it entails a going back and forth between the details represented by the pebbles and the larger meanings that might be drawn from the details. It is, as we have said, a movement from the particular to the general, from the concrete to the abstract, from the idiosyncratic to the universal, from the situational to the conceptual. This is the intellectual work of living with the study. It is the most intensively demanding work of an interpretive inquiry.

---

**EXEMPLAR 13.1     Owning the Study—Owning the Knowledge-Generating Process**

During one phase of my research, I carried with me a binder containing transcripts of the interviews I had done with directors of hospital-based education and printouts of coded transcripts. For weeks, I had been sorting and resorting the codes, trying to find some meaning or pattern in them. Despite hours at the computer, everything I wrote seemed incredibly superficial. So when asked how my project was going, I would point to the binder and respond, "Well, I have all this—this stuff I've been gathering." I was hard put to explain what I was researching and the nature of my results.

*(Continued)*

One summer evening as we sat on Noreen's back porch, Joan brought to the study group, not a neatly organized binder, but a large cardboard box crammed full of folders with student papers, printouts with test scores and other demographic profiles, and, most intriguing to me, imaginative collages created by her students. "What am I going to do with all this?" Joan echoed my own frustration. "I know it means something, but I can't figure out what." (See Case Example 6 for Joan's final resolution of this question.)

As Joan talked, I had the image of gathering colorful pebbles from a variety of beaches and then fussing endlessly to sort the pebbles into piles of comparable size, color, texture, beach of origin, and so on. Despite the volumes of pebbles I had gathered, it was banal to talk about the various piles as though they somehow meant something. Suddenly, I realized that I could use the pebbles in a very different way. I could stop trying to maintain the identity of each separate pebble, and could instead use them selectively to create a colorful mosaic. In a flash of insight, I realized that the significance of the codes did not lie in accounting for the individual pieces of "data," but rather in using the pieces to create a meaningful picture of hospital-based education as *I understood it.* With this realization, I finally understood a constructivist view of theory put forth by George Kelly (1970): A theory

> is not a collection of information, regardless of how carefully catalogued it may be. Nor is it an account of a sequence of events, no matter how well authenticated. In essence a theory is simply a way of highlighting events so they may be viewed in some kind of perspective. (p. 260)

It was my theoretical sensitivity about hospital-based education that would allow for the movement from a collection of pebbles to a mosaic—from the codes to theory.

## OWNING THE STUDY

A crisis of confidence may occur with the dawning realization that it is *I,* the researcher, who generates a theoretic perspective to explain the meaning of phenomenon under study. How do I know which interpretation is the right one? What gives me the right to make an interpretation? Suppose others don't agree with my interpretation? Suppose they say I just made the whole thing up? What difference does my understanding make, anyway? Who am I to say what all this means? Such questions bring the researcher face-to-face with the epistemological and ontological crux of interpretive research. There are no "findings" waiting to be discovered in the midst of all the raw texts. It is unlikely that only one lesson can be learned from a conscientiously conducted inquiry. There is no unassailable proof to be made. There is no sweeping generalization or causal relationship to be established. What then constitutes the *theoretic text* of an intimate, interpretive study? The profound (and often disquieting) answer is simply this—it is the researcher's right and obligation to decide what major message she or he believes is important to put forward. When researchers have inquired into a phenomenon with sensitivity, rigor, and integrity, then the way they have made sense of the phenomenon under study may have *utility* for others who are struggling with the phenomenon in similar contexts. As illustrated by Exemplar 13.2, dissertation authors are not offering some grand truth about the phenomenon under study. Rather, they are claiming *their authorial right* to put forward their understanding of the phenomenon. This interpretive understanding constitutes the thesis of the dissertation that is both represented and warranted by carefully interweaving experiential, discursive, and theoretic text.

---

### EXEMPLAR 13.2    Crafting Theoretic Text

I began this journey with the idea of leaving my practitioner's hat behind momentarily in order to try to make sense of the very turbulent dynamics that have taken my educational world by storm over the last few years. My expectation was that as a student researcher, I could in some way escape the quick-paced, demanding world of a school practitioner, where vision is often limited to only fleeting glimpses, in order to capture and hold the concept of *education inclusion* [in special education] to the light for scrutiny. My intent was to work my way through numerous documents and a voluminous body of literature in search of understandings that could enlighten me and my colleagues as we attempt to meet the complicated, often contradictory, demands of this movement.

In retrospect, I think I had the simplistic impression that I would grow to understand the different "sides" of "the" debate in very much a two-dimensional, "pros and cons" kind of way, and that by so doing I would adopt a solid position of my own. Instead, what I grew to understand was the limitations of a two-sided metaphor.

In my attempts to "shed light" on this intricate educational concept, I came to think of it as more like a multifaceted cut stone that, when held before the eye, catches and reflects light differently with each subtle turn. And in a similarly complex arrangement of interconnectedness, the carefully polished planed surface of each individual side is yet also a part of another. So I have come to appreciate the many facets of educational inclusion.

What I did not know at the onset was that through the many voices of my fellow participants I would become enabled to "see" and experience the obscured complexities of educational inclusion beyond the face of it. Their discourses paved my way, allowing me to step inside and journey to the heart of the matter.

---

In reading Exemplar 13.2, notice how Micheline is not just describing what she did but is making clear how her thinking evolved. Her shift from a "pros and cons" mentality to the metaphor of a multifaceted stone is a representation of her theorizing process. She develops both the multifaceted stone metaphor and the metaphor of journeying to "the heart of the matter" to construct, represent, and warrant her theoretic understanding of educational inclusion.

## CONSTRUCTING, REPRESENTING, AND WARRANTING A THESIS

Interpretive researchers live with the phenomenon and context of the study, immersing themselves in it and striving to know it as deeply and intimately as possible. As they resonate with what they are seeing, hearing, saying, doing, experiencing, thinking, and feeling, they begin to discern salient features of the phenomenon and the context within which it is embedded. As suggested above, discernment comes through a recursive process of collecting raw texts, drafting alternative experiential texts, trying out theoretic interpretations, consulting literature to elaborate and extend tentative theoretic interpretations, and reweaving experiential text with discursive text to see if one's insights are holding up. Throughout this process, the push is toward clarifying the major messages that are worth conveying to others. As the importance of various messages comes in and out of focus, the researcher presses toward a conceptual insight that ties the pieces of the study into a coherent whole. It is this conceptual insight that constitutes the researcher's theoretic perspective of the phenomenon. And it is this theoretic perspective that constitutes the dissertation author's *original contribution* to the discourses.

The theoretic text comprises the researcher's representation of his or her theoretic perspective. Case Example 6 offers an example of this press toward a more insightful, theoretic perspective. Although she had a number of reasonably useful frameworks for characterizing her gifted female students, Joan was not satisfied until she made the conceptual leap from thinking about the students' behaviors and discrete characteristics to visualizing their way of being. In constructing portraits that conveyed her sense of the students' being, Joan was crafting theoretic text that offered a different approach to planning science curriculum for gifted adolescent females.

Inherent in the struggle toward a conceptual leap and theoretic perspective is a struggle toward a form of representation that can convey the complexity of the phenomenon clearly and persuasively. As Eisner (1991) contends:

> Qualitative inquiry . . . is ultimately a matter of persuasion, of seeing things in a way that satisfies, or is useful for the purpose we embrace. The evidence employed in qualitative studies comes from multiple sources. We are persuaded by its "weight," by the coherence of the case, by the cogency of interpretation. . . . In qualitative research there is no statistical test of significance to determine if results "count"; in the end, what counts is a matter of judgment. (p. 39)

This brings us back to the concept of *phronesis* as a capacity for wise judgment. The dissertation document as a whole is the researcher's evidence of his or her capacity to make wise judgments about both the process of the inquiry and the phenomenon under study. Once the researcher understands the theoretic perspective to be offered, he or she is in a position to explain the movement from the situational to the conceptual. It is likely that the inquiry process has played out in a slightly different fashion than had been imagined in the dissertation proposal. Thus, the experiential and discursive texts related to the inquiry process will probably need to be fine tuned to portray key methodological decisions that the student faced and the way in which these decisions were handled. When these texts are crafted with verisimilitude and offer evidence that methodological challenges were resolved with wisdom, the persuasiveness of the dissertation document is enhanced.

Similarly, understanding the theoretic perspective to be offered allows the researcher to sort through all of the pebbles (raw texts) to create a compelling mosaic (coherent dissertation). In other words, the interpretive researcher faces countless major and minor decisions about what to include and exclude about the phenomenon. The wisdom with which these decisions are made also contributes to the persuasiveness of the dissertation. The only evidence that committee members (and broader audiences) have of the student's wisdom is that which is contained in the document. In the next section, we offer a working list of criteria that can help students gauge the persuasiveness of the evidence they present in the form of carefully crafted experiential, discursive, and theoretic text.

## CRITERIA FOR JUDGING INTERPRETIVE DISSERTATIONS

Writing in 1996 as a newly appointed features editor of *Educational Researcher,* Donmoyer pondered his responsibility for passing judgment on manuscripts:

> Diverse recommendations from [manuscript] reviewers reflect, in part at least, the fact that ours is a field characterized by paradigm proliferation and, consequently, the sort of field in which there is little consensus about what research and scholarship are and what research reporting and scholarly discourse should look like. (p. 19)

One might think that after more than a decade such concerns had been laid to rest. But, if anything, the debates are being pursued with a renewed vehemence precipitated in part by No Child Left Behind and the National Research Council's (2002) report on the scientific nature of educational research. Given the nature of academic discourse and political debate, it is unlikely that any neat set of criteria will gain universal acceptance. That said, however, those who are committed to qualitative research are evolving an important discourse regarding *criteria for judging* the merits of such dissertations. (See Sample Reference List 8.1 for an illustrative list of references.)

In Chapter 7, we offered *self-conscious method* as one criterion for judging interpretive dissertations. This criterion underscores the importance of understanding the conventions of the research genre within which one is working so that one can offer a cogent logic-of-justification for each methodological and conceptual decision. Flaws in the logic-of-justification can potentially occur anywhere in the inquiry process. The nature of such flaws and where they occur can jeopardize the persuasiveness of the dissertation in any number of ways. This is why we

stress the necessity of revisiting one's description of genre and research procedures to make sure that each interpretive move is defensible within the conventions of the genre.

In Chapter 9, we suggested a criterion of *coherence* for judging the conceptual structure of experiential text. The criterion of *integrity* refers more broadly to the conceptual structure of the dissertation document as a representation of the entire inquiry. In a structurally sound dissertation, the experiential, discursive, and theoretic texts support each other and flow together conceptually. The logic-of-justification provides well-reasoned connections between how the inquiry was conducted and the knowledge generated from it. Knowledge claims are supportable given the ontological and epistemological assumptions that are inherent in the genre and are guiding the inquiry. The voice and stance of the dissertation author are congruent with the inquiry tradition and convey the researcher's relationship to the study and study participants.

> **Criterion—Integrity (as in Architecture)**
>
> Is the work structurally sound? Does it hang together? Is the research rationale logical, appropriate, and identifiable within an inquiry tradition? Is the proper persona (or voice) used for the author and other participants?

The criterion of *vérité* has several connotations related to the intellectual honesty and authenticity of the study. One connotation of *vérité* relates most directly to the quality of discursive text. This speaks to the way in which the dissertation author has been able to portray multiple and possibly contested ideas within relevant bodies of discourse. Vérité is compromised when only a few references about the phenomenon or the genre of the research have been sampled. Likewise, vérité is lacking when a skewed body of literature is treated as though it represents the totality of scholarly thinking about a topic. Vérité is enhanced when the student is able to explain his or her position on issues relative to the position of scholars in the field. Another hallmark of vérité is a capacity to draw from relevant literature, not to prove one's thesis, but to elaborate on concepts in ways that can enrich an understanding of the phenomenon under study.

> **Criterion—Vérité**
>
> Does the work ring true? Is it consistent with accepted knowledge in the field? Or if it departs, does it address why? Does it fit within the discourses in the appropriate literature? Is it intellectually honest and authentic?

Another connotation of *vérité* relates to the notion of *self as instrument of inquiry*, calling attention to the authenticity of the researcher. Contributing to the vérité of the study is evidence that the researcher has taken pains to cultivate a mind-set conducive to an authentic inquiry. For example, tendencies toward cheerleading or the vendetta mentality have been recognized, and efforts have been made to shift to a posture of deliberative curiosity. There is a heartfelt desire to learn from the inquiry rather than to promote oneself or one's pet theories. Red flags about authenticity can be triggered when the researcher conveys an inability to handle large masses of raw text, a limited capacity for tolerating cognitive dissonance and ambiguity, or a willingness to settle for premature closure as evidenced by overly simplistic or facile interpretation. Conversely, a sense of the researcher's authenticity is conveyed when time and energy have been invested in understanding the discourses that underpin both the subject of the inquiry and the research genre. Also contributing to authenticity are conscientious efforts to move from naiveté to theoretical sensitivity, from narrow and superficial understanding to deeper, richer conceptualizations. This sense of authenticity is often conveyed as the researcher describes the procedures used to gather, document, and make sense of raw texts about the phenomenon and context under study.

A third connotation of *vérité* and *authenticity* relates to the researcher's account of his or her reactions and thinking throughout the inquiry process. This connects with the researcher's capacity for reflection, with the self-discipline to engage systematically in a reflective process, and with a willingness to document the process. Authenticity in this sense of the word is communicated in two ways. One is through the written account of procedures provided in the dissertation document. The other is through an ongoing engagement in deliberation with one's research advisor, committee members, or other relevant parties.

The criterion of *rigor* speaks to the quality of thought that goes into the inquiry and is intricately connected to the criteria of integrity and vérité. At issue is the carefulness and thoroughness with which the researcher pursues information needed to fulfill the intent of the study. To gain a sense of this criterion, review the types of raw text that Micheline (Case Example 1) and Lynn (Case Example 2) gathered for their studies. See also the carefulness with which Pat worked with her students' portfolios (Case Example 3) and the multiple layers of interpretation that Joan pushed for (Case Example 6).

> **Criterion—Rigor**
>
> Is there sufficient depth of intellect rather than superficial or simplistic reasoning? Are the conclusions carefully crafted from sufficiently thick and rich raw texts? Does the researcher avoid solipsistic reasoning? Was reflection done in a careful and systematic, rather than haphazard, fashion? Has the interpretation of the experiential text been thorough and exhaustive? Is the theoretic text insightful?

The criterion of *utility* speaks to the significance of the inquiry and the extent to which the researcher has connected the situational aspects of the study to the theoretic text and, in turn, to broader discourses. Particularly indicative of the dissertation's utility is the extent to which the theoretic text helps others to discern important nuances of an educational phenomenon that may have previously gone unnoticed. Or the theoretic text may offer a heuristic framework that allows others to discern important connections among previously fragmented or isolated issues. When these implications address the intent of the study and are presented in ways that are useful to the intended audience, the dissertation has accomplished its purpose.

> **Criterion—Utility**
>
> Is the inquiry useful and professionally relevant to an identifiable discourse community? Does it make a contribution to a recognized field of study or established bodies of discourse? Does the piece have a clearly recognized professional and/or scholarly audience? Is it educative?

The titles of two sessions conducted at the 1996 annual meeting of the American Educational Research Association help to underscore an issue that we consider vital to the criterion of utility. One session was titled "Yes, But Is It Research? The Conversation Continues: Should a Novel Count as a Dissertation in Education?" (Saks, 1996).[1] An educational dissertation in the form of a novel was used symbolically to raise issues about the legitimacy of knowledge generated and portrayed through artistic, rather than scientific, modalities. If a dissertation could not be judged on its scientific merits, could it, in fact, count as research?

A day later, the reverse side of the issue was debated in a session titled "Yes, But Is It Art? A Critical Examination of Artistic Research From an Aesthetic Perspective." [2] Here, the concern focused on the issue, "Should the results of arts-based educational research be held to the same aesthetic standards as works created by artists?" If not, then is it appropriate to claim such studies as arts-based?

Both sides of the issue raise intriguing, thorny, and substantive concerns about dissertations that are pushing the edges of tradition and convention. Yet we contend that the debate as it played out at AERA overlooked an equally key question: "Does the research contribute in a meaningful way to one or more discourses in education?" From our perspective, students earning degrees in education have an obligation to conduct dissertation research that contributes to the field of education. Therein lies the utility of such inquiries to educational discourse communities.

At first glance, this point may seem too obvious to belabor. Yet repeatedly, we have seen students express ideas for their dissertations in psychological or sociological terms. Confounding the situation is the history of educational researchers drawing their methods from the social sciences. Novices concerned with the credibility or legitimacy of their research may focus on meeting the criteria embodied within those research traditions. More recently, as research methods have been drawn from the arts and humanities, concerns may focus on meeting the criteria of artistry. In either scenario, the obligation to be educative may be lost.

Good qualitative dissertations meet the criterion of *vitality* in several ways. A sense of vitality arises from the verisimilitude of the experiential text (see discussion in Chapter 9). When a text succeeds in creating a vicarious sense of the phenomenon and context of the study, readers often feel a sense of immediacy and identification with the people and events being described. The study comes alive for the reader.

By the same token, vitality alludes to the sense of vibrancy and intensity that accompanies an inquiry that is genuinely meaningful to the researcher. Earlier in this chapter, we talked about the study taking on a life of its own. In a well-conceived, well-written dissertation, this sense of aliveness shines through in the story of the study.

As researchers press for deeper meanings in their texts, the emerging ideas often become more and more robust. Insightful (as opposed to banal) interpretations bring concepts to life. At the same time, researchers may incorporate powerful metaphors and vivid images into the text. This, too, gives the study a sense of vitality and an aesthetic quality as well.

When the dissertation has been conducted within an arts-based research genre, a criterion of *aesthetics* is expectable. Indeed, as mentioned in the discussion of

---

**Criterion—Vitality**

Is the inquiry important, meaningful, and nontrivial? Does it have a sense of vibrancy, intensity, and excitement of discovery? Do metaphors and images communicate powerfully?

---

**Criterion—Aesthetics**

Is the dissertation enriching and pleasing to anticipate and experience? Does it give insight into some universal part of my educational self? Are connections between the particular and the universal revealed in powerful, provocative, evocative, and moving ways? Does the work challenge, disturb, or unsettle? Does it touch the spirit?

utility, some scholars would argue that arts-based studies should be judged, at least in part, on the aesthetic merits of the portrayals.

It is worth making the distinction between aesthetic qualities that are inherent in the portrayals and "artistic" touches that are added for their own sake. As arts-based research has gained momentum, the danger of such poesy has become more apparent as novices strive for a cleverness of form at the sacrifice of substance.

Yet even when qualitative dissertations are not conducted within an arts-based modality, they often have an aesthetic, sometimes spiritual, quality. We speculate that this quality arises, in part, when meaningful connections are made between the idiosyncrasies of individual circumstances and more universal conditions of the human experience. This is an effect of good art and good inquiry. Penetrating insights into the essence of the phenomenon under study can also give rise to an aesthetic simplicity. Furthermore, when the logic-of-justification is clearly laid out and the resulting texts support one another, the study can embody a conceptual elegance.

## INTERPRETIVE INQUIRY AS CREATIVE ENGAGEMENT

Hopefully, the preceding discussion of criteria underscores a point we have been trying to make since introducing the concept of *text* in Chapter 8. Namely, there is not one section of the dissertation labeled "Experiential Text," another labeled "Discursive Text," and a third labeled "Theoretic Text." Rather, these texts intertwine in ways that warrant the thesis being offered. Ultimately, the way in which the dissertation author weaves together these three forms of text is unique to each qualitative study. Thus, engaging in an interpretive study is a creative act, and therein lies its potential for transformation of both researcher and those who read the research. Whether the study fulfills this potential comes to light as the dissertation moves from the realm of the private writing to the realm of public deliberation.

## NOTES

1. See Saks, 1996. This session was an outgrowth of an exchange between Elliott Eisner and Howard Gardner at the 1994 Annual Meeting of the American Educational Research Association. Saks edited a transcript of the session into an article that gives a brief summary of the 1994 exchange and then offers an account of the 1996 symposium that also included Cizek, Donmoyer, Gough, Tillman, Stotsky, and Wasley.

2. Participants in this symposium included Robert Donmoyer, Maxine Greene, Elliott Eisner, Thomas Barone, and Cynthia Dillard.

# 14

# *Entering Into Public Discourse*

*The Dissertation Meeting*

**Key Concepts**

| | |
|---|---|
| Dissertation Defense/Meeting | Judgment of Merit |
| Dissertation Story | *n*-Minus-1 Draft |

At some point, the dissertation document is ready for distribution to the student's committee for formal review. Faculty, as representatives of a broader scholarly community, have an opportunity to judge whether the study is good enough to stand on its own merits and to be entered into the formal, public discourses.

The phrase *judgment of merit* often carries ominous overtones. As one student commented, "The dissertation is the culmination of all the work I've been doing. There's tremendous anxiety. It's terrifying." Often, it seems to us, a recurring image in the dissertation folklore—the defense as an inquisition—can exacerbate normal and expectable anxiety into debilitating terror or dread. Therefore, we begin this chapter by challenging the view of the defense as inquisition, reframing the *dissertation meeting* as one more iteration in an ongoing process of deliberation. We then explore a complex mix of issues that may influence the nature of candidate-committee deliberations. These include the quality of the dissertation, the congruence of perspectives about the quality, and the role of the dissertation in the candidate's professional life.

With this as a backdrop, we consider several practical issues. Because each university has specific policies, procedures, customs, and rituals associated with the dissertation meeting and bringing closure to the dissertation process, the points presented in this section of the chapter are not prescriptive. Rather, they are meant to help doctoral candidates know what to anticipate as they wrap up the dissertation. In concluding the chapter, we touch on several issues that can emerge as graduates begin to adjust to life after the dissertation.

# CHALLENGING THE STEREOTYPE OF "DEFENSE AS INQUISITION"

## The Inquisition Image

Embedded in dissertation folklore is an image of the defense as a grueling inquisition aimed at revealing all of the flaws and weaknesses in both the study and the candidate. This trial-by-fire image frames the *dissertation defense* as one last, arbitrary exercise of faculty power. If the candidate survives this grilling and clears this final hurdle, then she or he is rewarded with the degree. It would be pointless to argue that there are no instances in which the defense has occasioned faculty misuse or abuse of power. But it is even more pointless to cast committee members in the role of enemy and assume that they operate with malevolent intent. Such dysfunctional distortions of the dissertation committee's role and responsibility serve only to undermine the deliberative process.

The quality of the dissertation reflects on the candidate, the faculty who worked with the candidate, and the university that grants the doctoral degree. A dissertation that does not meet at least a minimum threshold of acceptable scholarship is a grave disservice to all three. In a sense, the committee's review safeguards the novice scholar from prematurely subjecting his or her work to broader (and probably far more critical) scrutiny.

When candidates have established a deliberative relationship with their committee, the dissertation meeting can be an integral part of an ongoing and evolving process. The defense does not have to be an all-or-nothing test in which the student irrevocably passes or fails. Rather, it can serve as a collective look at the most recent iteration of the evolving inquiry. Granted, by this time, candidates are hoping that this iteration is good enough to bring closure to the dissertation process. But conscientious student-researchers would consider it no favor for their committee to rubber-stamp a dissertation before it is ready.

Students caught up in the high drama of the dissertation defense as inquisition seem to assume that they have no say in the decision to schedule the meeting, nor are they privy to what will happen during this mysterious rite of passage. Looking at the meeting within the context of ongoing relationships can help to dissipate potentially debilitating anxiety.

## Continuity of Process and Relationships

Sometimes, candidates seem to imbue the dissertation defense with so much special significance that it is treated as a completely new and isolated event. Remembering that the meeting has evolved from an ongoing process and within a context of established relationships can help candidates to know what to expect. If the relationship with committee members is based on mutual trust and respect, is there any realistic reason to expect a sudden change in demeanor or behavior?

Perhaps some students believe that the ritual of the defense demands a harsh, adversarial stance from committee members. To determine whether this is a realistic concern, candidates can talk with their advisors about the purpose and tenor of the meeting. In addition, they can attend several dissertation meetings to observe firsthand what happens. Those who act on this latter suggestion are cautioned not to over generalize from the events of only one meeting. Each committee probably has its own unique personality, each candidate has a particular history with his or her committee, and each meeting probably unfolds in a different way. A single observation is likely to yield a narrow, and perhaps skewed, perspective. Again, discussing one's observations with one's advisor provides a good check and balance.

We can imagine some students groaning in despair as they read the preceding paragraphs. Reflecting on the relationship with their committee chair or particular committee members may evoke a deep sense of dread if there has been a history of less than satisfactory interactions. We are in no position to second-guess the roots of such relationships. Indeed, some faculty may be extremely difficult to work with. It is regrettable if students have inadvertently or of necessity chosen such faculty to be on their committee, because that detracts from the dissertation experience. Yet in our experience, such unsatisfactory interactions arise far less often than the folklore might imply. Our point is to caution candidates against automatically assuming the worst.

Conversely, some students might think, "I've got it made. My chair is a good friend and will get me through this." Counting on friendship, especially in the case of questionable scholarship, can lead to a rude awakening when committee members seriously critique the dissertation. Such a turn of events could feel like a betrayal, especially if students have trivialized the significance of the dissertation and the meeting. For conscientious, responsible faculty, critiquing the dissertation is not about friendship; it is about scholarship.

One other issue is worth flagging at this point. Students should not automatically assume that faculty bring a wealth of experience and wisdom to the dissertation meeting. Junior faculty receive virtually no formal orientation to or preparation for their role as dissertation advisors. As a result, they are likely to draw upon their own limited experience with the dissertation process. Depending upon their satisfaction with the process, they may either try to re-create the experience for their advisees or reject a model that was distasteful. Inexperienced faculty may also be surprised to discover that each university has its own dissertation culture. Norms assimilated at the institution where they completed their doctoral work may not readily fit into the culture of the university where they embark on their faculty career. This may precipitate a period of readjustment for beginning faculty.

Senior faculty may face a slightly different dilemma. Those schooled in the quantitative or empirical mode of research often sense that guiding a qualitative study is somewhat different. Yet they are not quite sure of where the difference lies. Faculty in this position may be groping to understand how to best help their advisees, even as they are struggling to understand a new epistemological ballpark.

Developing one's own style of guiding the dissertation process and conducting the meeting grows with time and experience. Certainly, our own understanding of the process has deepened as a result of working with a wide range of students with very different needs and abilities. Serving on committees with other faculty also broadened our appreciation for different styles of advising students and conducting meetings. Again, our best advice to all students is to enter into substantive conversations with committee members about their views of the dissertation. It is hoped that portions of this book can help students frame their concerns in ways that promote productive explorations for everyone involved.

### Reframing the Defense

We hope that the preceding discussion helps to dispel the image of the dissertation meeting as an inquisition of hapless doctoral candidates. Before leaving this image, however, one other point is worth mentioning. Underlying the trial-by-fire mentality is an assumption that it is the pressure of the dissertation meeting itself that "makes or breaks" the candidate. This suggests that the ultimate criterion for earning the doctoral degree is how well one responds under fire. Perhaps, for some students and faculty, this represents a test of the candidate's capacity for tough discourse and rigorous deliberation. From our perspective, this parodies the real rigors of the dissertation—completing an intellectually sophisticated, conceptually sound inquiry. As mentioned throughout the book, we believe deeply in the transformative power of the dissertation, the journey from student to scholar. In our experience, the transformation occurs incrementally throughout the journey, rather than instantaneously as a result of grilling at the meeting. The ultimate test lies in the scholarship evidenced in the dissertation.

If, as we suggest, the dissertation meeting is not a ritualistic inquisition or trial by fire, how might the nature of deliberation among candidate and committee members be better understood? There is, of course, no simple answer to this question, because the deliberations are shaped by a complex constellation of issues. At the heart of this constellation is the dissertation document itself, providing an account of the inquiry. A core issue, then, is the quality of the dissertation from the committee's and candidate's perspective. Intertwining with this issue is a second issue—what the dissertation process itself represents to candidate and faculty. Both of these are connected with the issue of public discourse, most immediately within the meeting and then over time. The interplay among these issues underpins the deliberations occurring during the dissertation meeting.

## QUALITY OF THE DISSERTATION

In earlier chapters, we set forth criteria (self-conscious method, verisimilitude, coherence, integrity, vérité, rigor, utility, vitality, aesthetics, and ethics) that, from our perspective, constitute hallmarks of a conceptually sound interpretive dissertation. In our own meetings with candidates, deliberations are shaped in large part by the extent to which the dissertation provides evidence that the inquiry has met these criteria. Given this, dissertations might fall anywhere along a continuum from unacceptable to exemplary.

## Unacceptable Quality

At one end of the continuum is a dissertation with pervasive conceptual flaws. In some instances, gaps may actually exist in the inquiry itself; for example, insufficient raw texts were collected, interpretations of raw and experiential texts were cursory and facile, or implications may be trivial or perfunctory. In other instances, the inquiry itself may have been adequate, but the representation of the inquiry in the dissertation document may call its credibility into question. Although the document does not meet a minimum threshold of acceptability, the exact nature or source of the problems may be elusive. In a sense, scheduling a formal review is premature. Yet the candidate, advisor, and/or committee members may feel a need to meet in order to sort through the troubling aspects of the inquiry or document. Such a meeting might better be planned as a working session rather than an official review.

During such deliberations, the candidate is not a passive spectator awaiting orders on how to fix the flaws. Rather, he or she is an active participant in the deliberations, grappling along with faculty for a clearer vision of what is missing and what needs to be done. What often makes these deliberations so difficult (and frustrating) for all concerned is the inextricable connection between the content of the experiential, discursive, and theoretic texts and the logic-of-justification used to generate and interconnect them. In essence, the conceptual soundness of an interpretive dissertation lies in the quality of thinking that the student-researcher brings to bear on the inquiry. "Fixing" the conceptual flaws is not simply a matter of revising portions of the text, but rather of the candidate gaining a new or heightened awareness of where his or her thinking missed the mark. For example, when a student never quite grasps the intricate connections between research genre and logic-of-justification, the dissertation may have all the hallmarks of the kitchen sink syndrome. To "fix" the study, the inquiry would need to be reframed within a particular genre and the texts of the inquiry would need to be warranted through a more coherent logic-of-justification. Although specific passages in the dissertation could be used to illustrate the problem, merely changing those would not address the deeper structural inconsistencies in the inquiry.

## Marginally Acceptable Quality

Less extreme, and more common, are dissertations that hover near the threshold of acceptable scholarship but contain one or more significant flaws. Often, these are more readily resolvable because they arise from more contained problems. The final chapter of Jake's dissertation, for example, had a somewhat rambling discussion of the implications of the study. Committee members suggested including a summary chart that would highlight the implications and thereby make them more readily accessible to readers. The procedural chapter in Ruth's dissertation did not describe how she had obtained a set of documents that were central to her thesis. In the process of living with the study, Ruth had come to take this piece of information for granted and had forgotten that readers would not automatically understand this aspect of the study. In such situations, committee members are often able to suggest changes to fine-tune unclear aspects of the inquiry or additions to address gaps. Deliberations may call attention to aspects of the study that the candidate is too close to see. Or exhausted candidates might be reenergized by seeing more specifically what revisions are needed to reach closure. The discussion in these meetings takes on more of a problem-solving flavor as committee and candidate come to a common agreement on changes that will result in an acceptable document.

## Acceptable Quality

When student-researchers have conscientiously engaged in deliberation throughout the inquiry process, they may come to the dissertation meeting with a document that meets or exceeds the minimum threshold of acceptability. The focus of deliberation in such meetings might take a couple of different turns. On one hand, the deliberations might focus on the meaning of the dissertation to the candidate, exploring what she or he has learned from the inquiry and future plans for pursuing the ideas generated by the study. Committee members who have read the document independently may welcome the opportunity to exchange their reactions with each other as well as with the candidate. To a great extent, such deliberations may serve to affirm what the candidate has come to know or believe as a result of the inquiry. Over the years, however, we have experienced a slightly different twist on these deliberations. In essence, committee members agree that the dissertation is acceptable as is, but also see the potential for its being exemplary. Deliberation, in these cases, might explore the candidate's interest in taking the document to a more polished and sophisticated level.

## Exemplary Quality

At times, committees are privileged to receive a dissertation draft that is truly exemplary. In our experience, two types of students seem to produce exemplary documents—those with a strong need for conceptual clarity and coherence, and those with an exquisite narrative sensibility. Often, these two attributes come hand in hand. In short, these students seem unable to rest until they can tell a coherent, well-crafted story. For them, the essence of the story is a fully developed conceptual picture that flows seamlessly from concrete, lived experience to a significant theoretic "So what?"

Candidates who produce such fine pieces of scholarship might wonder, "What will we talk about for 2 hours?" It is just as likely, however, that they may experience a feeling much like Pat McMahon expressed.

> I looked forward to my dissertation meeting. I had done all this work. This was a chance to really discuss it with others. Sure, the adrenaline was flowing; I was psyched for the meeting. But I wouldn't call it fear. I was ready.

Indeed, the committee as well as the candidate is ready for generative discussion. The candidate's work serves as a springboard for deliberation in which all participants can explore the implications of the study and extend their thinking about the phenomenon that has been so insightfully illuminated. Committee members might also suggest avenues for entering the dissertation into the public discourses—not only through its addition to the university's library and dissertation abstracts, but through articles, presentations, or even a monograph or book. Possibilities for further research may also be explored.

Such meetings are a pure pleasure for faculty and represent some of the finest moments of scholarly discourse that the academy offers. More common, however, are meetings in which candidate and committee deliberate together to ensure a document that will hold up to external, scholarly scrutiny. Complications can arise, however, when the candidate and faculty have different perspectives on the quality of the document that is being reviewed.

# PERSPECTIVES ON THE QUALITY OF THE DISSERTATION

## Congruence of Perspective

The preceding discussion is predicated on the notion that the candidate and committee share a common ground for deliberating about the dissertation document. Ideally, the candidate and committee members have congruent assessments of the quality of the dissertation. Or if they have different perspectives, they all value deliberation as a way of achieving mutual understanding and, if necessary, reasonable compromises.

When this is the case, candidates, seeing themselves as co-participants in the meeting, are less likely to attribute differences of perspective to faculty power plays or a failure of committee members to "get their act together." Nor is there an expectation that the committee will provide a neat to-do list explaining what must be done so that the dissertation will "pass." Students who have cultivated a capacity for deliberation understand that a meeting of the minds can evolve from the discussion. As a result, they can enter into the discussion with an openness to input, a capacity to listen carefully, a willingness to explore the implication of questions and comments, and a readiness to articulate their perspective and the rationale behind that perspective. When committee members come with a similar readiness to explore, the meeting can be highly productive and satisfying even if the starting point was something less than an acceptable dissertation.

## Disparity of Perspectives

Problems tend to arise when faculty see the dissertation as having major flaws, and the candidate believes the document is at least acceptable, if not good. This tends to create a tension from the outset of the meeting. In a worst-case scenario, this can result in a stalemate, with the committee asking for revisions that the candidate resists making. Several factors can fuel such an unfortunate situation. If candidates believe that the dissertation is merely an academic exercise, the request for revisions may be interpreted as an arbitrary hurdle. In essence, candidates with a marginal investment in the dissertation may take the position, "I've jumped through all the hoops you wanted me to. Enough is enough. So approve the dissertation and let me get on with my life." A less extreme variation of this theme can arise if students have little sense of ownership in the inquiry. They see themselves as victims of "not being told the right information" or of not receiving the right help. Help is construed as detailed instructions for completing a task rather than guidance and support for developing their capacity for scholarly deliberation.

Ironically, an adversarial dynamic can also emerge when students see themselves as highly creative, free-spirited individuals whose talents are misunderstood or unappreciated. In a sense, they put themselves outside (or even above) the deliberative process, refusing to compromise their vision of the dissertation document. Here, the student's sense of owner-ship is so strong that committee members are pushed to take it or leave it. Although we concede that some extraordinarily creative geniuses may produce dissertations that cannot be appreciated or fairly evaluated by faculty, in most cases, this posture serves only to demonstrate the candidate's failure to grasp the significance of deliberation.

## Working Toward a Shared Perspective

Hopefully, such extreme mismatches in candidate and committee perspectives are rare. More typical may be candidates who do not have a clear sense of their own work. Having little personal experience from which to draw, these novice researchers lack a context for realistically assessing the merits of what they have produced. We have seen both sides of this coin—one where students think their dissertation is more complete than it actually is, and the other where students underestimate the quality of their work. In either situation, the meeting provides a forum through which candidates may gain a more explicit understanding of how their work meets (or does not meet) the criteria for sound dissertation research. The meeting offers another opportunity for learning what it means to be a researcher and scholar and for judging scholarly products with an enlightened eye.

Another scenario emerges when candidates are well grounded, have an accurate sense of their work, and agree with committee members that the dissertation is adequate but not exceptional. In such cases, extenuating circumstances may come into play as the candidate and/or the committee must decide whether to push for another, more polished draft or settle for what is essentially an *n-minus-1 draft,* meaning one draft away from a fully formed dissertation. For example, Magdalena realized that her dissertation would benefit from the revisions being suggested, but not required, by her committee. Yet she had been studying in the United States on a grant from her government. The grant was due to expire, and she was expected to return to her homeland and assume her teaching responsibilities. With some regret, Magdalena decided to let the dissertation stand as written.

## Necessary Compromises

Implicit in much of what we have said throughout the book is an assumption that dissertation research can be a compelling part of real life. Yet realistically, we know that at times other real-life circumstances such as Magdalena's necessitate bringing the dis-sertation process to closure when the document itself is still one draft away from being conceptually complete. The imminent birth of a child, relocation because of a spouse's change of job, or financial exigencies are all examples of situations that may impose a somewhat arbitrary closure on the dissertation. Both the candidate and advisor may know full well that the dissertation could benefit from one final edit to pull all the pieces together. Yet both may need to compromise and live with an acceptable, rather than exemplary, document in the face of such compelling realities.

An exceptionally uncomfortable extenuating circumstance arises occasionally when a committee concludes that the dissertation is as good as it is going to get. Having worked exhaustively (and exhaustedly) to help a candidate understand how the study needs to be strengthened and having seen only marginal improvement over a prolonged period of time, the committee may decide that closure is in order. Some may wonder, "If the work isn't up to par, shouldn't the student fail?" Perhaps in an ideal world or in the purest sense, this is true. Yet circumstances are rarely that uncomplicated, and when students have put forth considerable effort, withholding the degree may not be legally or ethically defensible.

Our intent in laying out these various scenarios is to flag two points. First, congruity or incongruity of perspectives about the quality of the dissertation helps to shape the nature of committee-candidate deliberations during the meeting. Second, for many reasons, not all completed dissertations are of equal quality. Latching onto the first qualitative dissertation one encounters and assuming that it is a model to be emulated is extremely risky. Ongoing deliberation with one's chair and committee members is the best safeguard against this potential pitfall. This latter point leads to another issue that comes into play during the dissertation meeting—faculty and the candidate's views on the relationship between the dissertation and the graduate's future role.

## THE ROLE OF THE DISSERTATION IN THE CANDIDATE'S PROFESSIONAL LIFE

Throughout this book, we have challenged the view of the dissertation as primarily an academic exercise. This challenge is rooted in our own beliefs about the personal and professional meaning of the dissertation. These beliefs, in turn, are grounded in the experience of doing our own dissertations.

At the time Noreen did her dissertation, qualitative inquiries were not really an option at our university. This was not a matter of deliberate policy but rather a reflection of the prevailing empirical paradigm. Consequently, Noreen engaged in a study of clinical supervision that did not ring true to her own, more interpretive proclivities. Dissatisfied with the end result of her efforts, Noreen often quips, "I wanted the dissertation bound on all four sides before it was put in the library." Naively, she consoled herself with the idea that "nobody reads dissertations anyway." Three years later, much to her chagrin, she began to see her study cited in articles about clinical supervision. "This was mortifying," she explained to the advisees who formed the first dissertation study group. "But I didn't have any help. There was no collaborative deliberation. I was left to work on my own." This dissertation experience gave rise to Noreen's belief in deliberation, her passionate advocacy of interpretive research as a credible option for dissertation research, her commitment to support student learning about interpretive research, and her belief that dissertations have a public presence that cannot and should not be minimized.

Maria, having attended to Noreen's message about the public nature of the dissertation, set out to write a dissertation that could ultimately be published as a book (Piantanida, 1982). Her aim was not only to contribute insights into the practice of education in hospitals but also to promote practice-based research by other hospital-based educators. Although neither of these goals was achieved in a way she had hoped, the methods chapter of Maria's dissertation proved helpful to other students who were grappling with a rationale for qualitative research—in particular, grounded theory. At the time, the concept of logic-of-justification had not yet entered the discourses on qualitative methods. This was, in essence, what she created as she struggled to understand the legitimacy of her research procedures. From this experience came Maria's passionate belief that grappling with one's logic-of-justification fosters a transformation from a vendetta or cheerleading mentality to a posture of deliberative and scholarly curiosity.

Through our encounters with various faculty and students, however, we have come to recognize a range of perspectives about the role of the dissertation in relation to the candidate's professional role. When teaching the introductory course on qualitative research, we encounter students who see no relationship between the dissertation and their professional life outside of the academy. The dissertation may be treated merely as an extra long paper to be read only by committee members (and perhaps one's spouse or mother). If this view persists, it can translate into a perspective that the quality of the dissertation does not really matter. Deliberations during the dissertation meeting can feel like a tug-of-war as faculty push the candidate to see the public ramifications of a document that the student is treating like a glorified term paper.

In professional schools, some faculty emphasize the role of students as practitioners. Doctoral study serves to enhance professional competence through the acquisition of more sophisticated techniques, skill sets, and models. Doctoral students, especially those who have already earned a reputation as excellent practitioners, may be seen as contributing in action-oriented arenas of professional practice. The title of *doctor* may open doors and provide such practitioners with access to new arenas where they can strive to effect change. Within this frame, the contribution to scholarly discourses in one's field of study may be seen as less compelling than contributions in one's arena of practice.

Other faculty may view the doctoral degree as an "entrance card" to the academy, assuming that graduates will pursue careers as university faculty. From this perspective, greater weight might be given to a highly theoretical study and to mastering sophisticated research skills. The dissertation allows the candidate to develop in-depth expertise in a concentrated area of study and serves as a training ground where future academicians learn how to guide dissertation research. Committee members, knowing the pressures and requirements for tenure, may judge the dissertation in terms of its potential for spin-off articles suitable for publication in scholarly journals, a substantive foundation for a long-range research agenda, and perhaps a leverage point for acquiring grant funds.

As suggested throughout this book, our own view lies somewhere between these two points. What matters to us is the candidate's evolution as a scholarly practitioner with a demonstrated capacity for deliberation. This view is predicated on the notion that, regardless of the professional role or arena that the graduate pursues, a deliberative orientation will serve him or her in good stead. Indeed, as the highest degree in the land, the doctorate carries an expectation that graduates will contribute in writing to the discourses of their field. Students who think, "Once I get through this, I'm never going to write again" overlook the obligation for scholarship inherent in the degree. Ideally, graduates who have developed a capacity for deliberation are better able to build bridges between the world of practice and the world of research.

The point for doctoral candidates to keep in mind is simply that any dissertation committee may be composed of faculty operating with differing perspectives. Although the differences are not mutually exclusive, they are likely to influence the concerns that faculty raise during the dissertation meeting. In part, deliberations about the dissertation may include faculty reconciling their different perspectives about the role of the dissertation within the scheme of the candidate's professional development and the university's requirements.

The purpose of the preceding discussions has been, first, to dispel the inquisitional image of the dissertation meeting, and second, to suggest a number of issues that influence the deliberative nature of the meeting. With this context in mind, we now turn to several practical considerations that also come into play.

## ANTICIPATING PRACTICAL CONSIDERATIONS

### Scheduling the Meeting

Embedded within the inquisition mentality is an erroneous ready-or-not assumption that candidates have no say about when the dissertation is ready for formal committee review. Typically, however, this is a joint decision of the candidate and his or her advisor. As the student-researcher sees an end to living with the study, it is possible to begin projecting a date for the dissertation meeting. After the aha moment, candidates seem better able to gauge both the amount of work and the time required to complete a draft of the entire dissertation.

Even so, candidates may get caught in a time warp. On one hand, they may be working feverishly to complete their study in order to meet deadlines for graduation. They may be so engrossed in writing that other deadlines may be overlooked. For example, we have worked with several candidates who scheduled the meeting, assuming that they could give the dissertation to their committee a few days before the meeting. Panic ensued when they discovered that the university requires that the document be available to the university community at least two weeks prior to the meeting. Keeping in mind that submission dates are similar to those for the dissertation proposal can help to forestall such problems in timing. It is also important to anticipate the time required after the meeting to make any final changes prior to submitting the approved dissertation to the university to meet the deadline for graduation. Even minor corrections or revisions can be time consuming.

The sense of time pressure often arises from these logistical concerns rather than from any command performance dictated by the committee. Candidates are encouraged to work closely with their advisors, using two key dates as anchor points for establishing a realistic time line. If the candidate hopes to graduate in the same semester that the dissertation is completed, then one nonnegotiable date is the university's deadline for applying for graduation. The other is the desired date for the committee meeting. Working backward and forward from these two dates allows candidates to develop a feasible work schedule. At this stage of the process, preparing the dissertation document for public review is a key aspect of the work to be accomplished.

## Preparing the Dissertation
## Document for Public Review

Scheduling the dissertation meeting entails making a copy of the document available for public review—potentially by any member of the university community. Each university has specific procedures for officially submitting the document that will be discussed at the meeting and for announcing the date, time, and location of the meeting. Students who assume that they can get their document to obliging faculty at the last minute may have overlooked this more public aspect of the dissertation process. The dissertation defense is open to the entire university community, and the formal posting of the dissertation gives interested parties an opportunity to review the document prior to the meeting. Customs surrounding the number of faculty and students who attend dissertation meetings varies among programs. Understanding the customs of one's own program is part of knowing what to anticipate.

Getting the dissertation ready for submission refers to both the form and the conceptual content of the document. A few words serve to highlight issues related to readiness of form. Readiness of content is a bit more complicated.

In terms of the dissertation document itself, a balance must be struck between a document that appears to be a rough draft versus one that appears finished. A document riddled with typographical mistakes or having incomplete or inconsistent citations can come across as intellectually sloppy. In addition, committee members may feel freer to request substantive changes when the document appears to be a work in progress. On the other hand, submitting a highly polished, even professionally bound document can convey an impression that the candidate expects to do no more work on it. Unless such a formal document is required by the university, candidates who take this approach run the risk of incurring additional expense for reprinting and rebinding a document as well as annoying committee members who may feel constrained about suggesting revisions. Another point to consider is the way in which committee members prefer to receive their review copy. Some prefer hard copy so that they do not have to print out a large document. Others prefer receiving the file as an email attachment. Students should check with faculty to determine their preferences.

In terms of content, the candidate's dissertation advisor usually has an opportunity to review the document prior to its official distribution to committee members. This provides a checkpoint for catching any major problems or glaring gaps in the document. The candidate and his or her advisor determine when the document is good enough for formal review. Ideally, of course, both the candidate and advisor will feel that the dissertation is ready to move into the public eye of the committee. As discussed above, however, extenuating circumstances may result in a decision to move forward with a rougher draft than the advisor and/or candidate prefers. For example, nonnegotiable graduation deadlines may necessitate scheduling the dissertation meeting a bit earlier than the candidate and/or advisor would prefer. Either or both know that revisions are likely to be needed. Meeting about a less-than-finished document can allow the candidate to address committee concerns while polishing the document. This may save some time, making it possible to meet university deadlines.

A conceptual impasse is another reason for scheduling a committee meeting even though the candidate and/or advisor senses that something is missing. The conceptual intricacies of well-crafted dissertations often slip in and out of focus—even at this late stage in the process. Sometimes, the candidate is just too close to the inquiry to pull back and see either gaps in the text or places where the conceptual arguments are not quite in focus. Entering into deliberation with the full committee can provide new, more distanced perspectives that help to resolve the impasse. In our own experience, a frequently missing piece is a well-crafted portrayal of the overall *dissertation story.* The last vestiges of the science report stereotype may result in a rather sterile account of the research. On more than one occasion, the committee's "permission" for candidates to "put themselves into the study" has finally freed novice researchers to fully embrace an interpretive stance and find their scholarly voice.

In determining whether the dissertation is good enough, the advisor and candidate may also benefit from committee input. Occasionally, we have worked very intensively with a student-researcher who is pushing the edge of an interpretive research genre. Although the logic-of-justification and experiential, discursive, and theoretic texts make sense to us, we are not sure how other, less intimately involved committee members might view the dissertation. Scheduling a meeting before the dissertation is completely finished provides a good check and balance, forestalling the possibility of a candidate moving in a direction that would not pass muster with the committee.

More unusual are situations in which student-researchers have resisted our urging to develop deeper, more substantive interpretations. From our perspective, more work needs to be done; from the candidate's perspective, the study is good enough. Or they may not understand the points we are raising well enough to incorporate them into the document. In such cases, full committee input may help to strike a reasonable balance. A few words of elaboration are warranted here. Our preferred standard for qualitative dissertations, particularly interpretive studies, goes beyond good enough or acceptable to exemplary. Because issues of legitimacy are still subject to debate, it is important to represent this work as credibly as possible. When qualitative studies are flawed, skeptics can cite it as proof that interpretive research has little merit. When more traditional, quantitative dissertations are flawed, the tendency is to attribute the imperfections to a lack in the researcher's skills and abilities rather than to the mode of inquiry. Thus, we tend to believe that qualitative dissertations contribute not only to the field of study but also to the tradition of qualitative inquiry. Our press is to have those contributions reflect as well as possible on the value and merit of such research.

One final point about preparing the dissertation for formal committee review is worth mentioning. In the preceding comments, we have stressed the importance of candidates working closely with their advisors. This is not meant to imply that other committee members see nothing until the advisor approves circulating the document. Student-researchers who value deliberation and who skillfully draw upon the expertise of various committee members are likely to keep everyone apprised of their progress. Yet faculty preferences for involvement at this stage vary. Some committee members want to see work in progress or to receive progress reports. Others prefer to see only the final draft. Checking the preferences of individual committee members is prudent. Regardless of preference, however, at some point the document is ready for formal review. Less formal discussion with individual committee members gives way to collective, discursive deliberation of the dissertation meeting.

## Participating in the Dissertation Meeting

Actual procedures for conducting the dissertation meeting are likely to vary not only among universities but also among faculty. We know some faculty, for example, who tend to approach the meeting somewhat casually, perhaps hoping that this informal manner will allay candidates' anxiety. Others tend to be more formal, marking the significance of this milestone by rituals such as wearing academic robes.

To initiate the discussion, candidates are often asked to give a brief opening statement. Candidates are advised to check with their advisors regarding the expected purpose and length of these remarks. For example, some faculty might want to see if the candidate can give a concise summary of the study. Others might prefer an explanation of what the dissertation means to the candidate. Much has transpired for the candidate since the proposal was reviewed and approved. The account of the inquiry represented in the dissertation is formal and geared to a public audience of strangers. The committee, having a more personal connection with the candidate, may welcome some additional insight into what the dissertation experience has meant.

Whatever focus the candidate takes, it is wise to check with one's advisor on the approximate length of these introductory remarks. The caution we sounded for the proposal meeting holds for the dissertation meeting as well. An extended presentation with an excessive reliance on handouts, PowerPoint, overhead transparencies, or slides can actually be off-putting to faculty, who come to the meeting expecting to engage in substantive conversation with the candidate and each other. Irritation can arise if limited meeting time is consumed with a rehash of what faculty have already read.

We have seen candidates use visual aids quite effectively, so we do not mean to imply that such approaches should never be used. One candidate, for example, had studied nonformal education for women in Bangladesh. At the outset of the meeting, she used PowerPoint to extend the major theoretical themes embedded in her portrayals of these women. These ideas had occurred to her during the hiatus between submission of the dissertation and the meeting, when she had a breathing space for further reflection. This lull may yield new insights or better ways to articulate points in the dissertation.

As was the case with the proposal, the discussion during the dissertation meeting can evolve in many directions and on many levels. Automatically equating questions or comments with criticisms or faultfinding is an impoverished view of the meeting. Certainly, if the candidate and/or committee has concerns about the quality of the inquiry or the document, these will be a major focus of deliberation. If the study has been well done, however, it is likely that the deliberations will be educative as faculty exchange views on various aspects of the study. Some faculty, for example, may comment on the subject of the inquiry, suggesting contributions that the dissertation is making to their particular field of study. Other faculty might be more aware of the dissertation's methodological contribution to the field of qualitative research. Through such exchanges, the faculty have opportunities to extend their thinking in new directions. It is hoped that by understanding the complex mix of issues that influence the committee's deliberations, candidates will be better able to sort out the threads of conversation.

As the meeting draws to a close, candidates and guests are often asked to leave the room, affording the committee members privacy for their final deliberations about the dissertation. Prior to the meeting, committee members had their individual perspectives about the quality of the dissertation. Now, having heard each other's perspectives, they can assess to what extent their individual views are congruent with those of their colleagues and the candidate. The committee chair then has an opportunity to mediate among divergent viewpoints and determine what revisions, if any, the committee expects.

Depending on the quality of the dissertation and the agreements reached by candidate and committee, the meeting may conclude with one of several outcomes. What everyone hopes for, of course, is approval of the dissertation. What everyone dreads is the need for extensive revisions and another meeting. Typically, at least some revisions will be necessary. Often, committee members approve the document, relying on the chair to oversee the final corrections or revisions. Customs for informing candidates of the committee's decisions vary. If substantial work remains to be done, congratulations may not be in order. If the dissertation has been approved (with or without revision), the title of *doctor* may be conferred by the chair with varying degrees of pomp and circumstance. Some faculty, for example, make a point of taking the candidate around to faculty and introducing the new Dr. _____.

## BRINGING CLOSURE TO THE DISSERTATION PROCESS

Following the dissertation meeting, candidates may experience a rush of competing emotions: relief or joy that the dissertation has passed muster, disappointment that work still remains to be done, disbelief that it is "really over." In our experience, the full import of the meeting does not immediately sink in. Having time to debrief the meeting with one's advisor helps candidates process both the explicit outcomes and the more subtle nuances of the deliberation. At a purely practical level, candidates may need to review the revisions that are expected and to settle on a process for completing this work to their advisor's satisfaction. It is likely that candidates may be puzzled by comments that seemed so important during the meeting but played no apparent role in the final judgment of the dissertation.

Naomi stands out as a reminder of the importance of debriefing. The university where Naomi completed her degree has a policy of randomly assigning a faculty member to be an outside reviewer on each dissertation committee. In Naomi's case, this representative of the university-at-large came from a scientific discipline and asked a number of questions during the meeting that were not appropriate to an interpretive study in education. The chair of Naomi's committee felt that Naomi had done an excellent job of responding to the questions without compromising the integrity of her qualitative research genre. At the end of the meeting, the dissertation was approved by the committee, and shortly thereafter, Naomi graduated and returned to her own country. Two years later, during a social visit from her chair, Naomi confessed that she had left the meeting feeling like a complete failure. For two years, the specter of the outside reviewer and his questions had haunted her, leaching away any sense of pride and accomplishment that she very much deserved.

On a more positive note, when candidate and advisor have engaged in intensive deliberation throughout the dissertation process, both may welcome a time to sit back and reflect on the journey they have traveled together.

These professional wrap-ups are, of course, accompanied by more personal matters. Often, a priority for candidates is informing family and friends, who have been waiting with bated breath, for the meeting outcomes. Some type of informal celebration may be held to mark the occasion. (More extensive celebrations are typically planned around graduation. Parties, of course, are often the order of the day. Some students intend to treat themselves to an extra-special reward.)

In a day or two, this initial flurry of post-meeting excitement gives way to the more serious business of finishing the document. Candidates facing substantive revisions may experience a letdown and have difficulty finding the energy to engage in yet one more iteration of deliberation. Even if no major changes have been requested, final cleanup work (e.g., correcting typographical mistakes, double checking citations and bibliography, final formatting) requires time and attention. Universities are now typically requiring the final dissertation to be submitted in a specific electronic format. If this format has not been followed in drafting the dissertation, then some time will be required to convert the document. Thus, another sense of closure is gained when the dissertation is, at long last, officially submitted to the university. After the public nature of the dissertation meeting and the post-meeting celebrations, this milestone can seem anticlimactic. Noreen still remembers leaving the education building after turning in her dissertation and wondering, "What?! No church bells ringing; no people dancing in the streets?! No fireworks?!"

Public recognition of the candidate's accomplishment does occur during graduation. Sometimes, graduates see little point in attending what may be viewed as a long and perhaps boring ceremony. We strongly urge graduates to attend, because it is during this academic ritual that the individual is formally and officially acknowledged as a member of the doctoral community. The bestowing of the degree and the title of *doctor* marks an official passage and helps graduates assimilate their new identity as scholars and their families to celebrate their accomplishments.

## Reflective Interlude 14.1

### How Prepared Am I for My Dissertation Meeting?

- What are my university's and program's requirements around deadlines for submission of the document and scheduling the meeting?
- What are my university's requirements around deadlines for graduation?
- What are my university's and program's norms around structuring the meeting, expecting a formal presentation, and fostering deliberation among those in attendance?
- How is my document viewed by my dissertation chair and other members of my committee?
- Given the views of my committee members, what is the nature of the meeting (e.g., working session, formal defense), and what is the outcome likely to be?
- How will I remain open to the committee's deliberations and suggestions for improving the dissertation?

# 15

## *Life After the Dissertation*

**Key Concepts**

Life After the Dissertation

Narrative Desire

Postdissertation Disequilibrium

Postgraduation Malaise

Rebalancing Personal Life

Rebalancing Professional Life

We are reminded of a comment frequently made by our colleague, Larry Knolle: "The dissertation should change your life. If it doesn't, it hasn't done its job." We return to this rather sobering pronouncement and consider the question, "What is the nature of these changes?" Although specific changes depend upon the meaning of the dissertation within each individual's unique life circumstances, a sense of *postdissertation disequilibrium* often seems to follow its completion. This unsettled feeling may persist for weeks, months, or even years.

We still vividly remember our own sense of surprise when *life after the dissertation* did not suddenly return to normal. Doing the dissertation had irrevocably changed us in ways we had not anticipated and, at the time, could not fully articulate. Consequently, returning to "normal" was not simply a matter of resuming our lives as they had been before the dissertation. As we have journeyed along the postdissertation path with members of our study group, we have begun to suspect that this state of disequilibrium may be fairly common and therefore deserving of attention.

Initially, we attributed this sense of malaise to the effort expended in juggling routine personal and professional demands along with the dissertation. Just the sheer relief of being finished might precipitate an almost pervasive sense of exhaustion or lethargy. Some time might be needed to recoup one's energy.

Beyond this, however, another consideration emerged. When we talked about living with the study, we cautioned that the dissertation has a way of taking over one's life. Normal life activities may be sacrificed as the dissertation demands ever more attention. Hobbies or leisure activities may be the first to go. More mundane chores such as shopping, cooking, cleaning, or yard work may receive minimal effort. Time with friends may be reluctantly reduced or put off as one's focus becomes increasingly constricted to the study. After graduation, some of our study group members have described a dawning realization that they were, once again, at liberty to resume these normal pursuits.

Along with rebalancing the personal aspects of one's life, changes may also be occurring on the professional front as well. With the doctoral credential in hand, graduates may seek new positions within their current organization or begin a search for a new role in a new organization. Even those who do not change jobs may experience disequilibrium as they see their professional world differently, and/or colleagues see them differently. Thus, efforts to rebalance one's professional life may also contribute to the sense of being at loose ends.

Even in the process of rebalancing one's personal and professional life, however, a more subtle sense of loss may be operating. For so long, the dissertation has been an ever-looming presence, providing a focal point for organizing one's time and energy. Even when other personal and professional demands temporarily supersede work on the dissertation, this dominating force consumes attention. Graduation, while bringing a welcome release from this obligation, also leaves a void. Those who gave themselves up to the discursive and deliberative nature of the dissertation may experience this void as a loss of meaningful intellectual engagement. Coping with this sense of loss can also be part of regaining a sense of equilibrium.

In this chapter, we explore issues related to these three areas of adjusting to life after dissertation—rebalancing one's personal life, rebalancing one's professional life, and refocusing one's intellectual life.

# REBALANCING PERSONAL LIFE

Throughout the book, we have argued that the researcher's sensibilities lie at the heart of meaningful inquiries. Honing one's self as an instrument of inquiry is crucial to the completion of a quality dissertation, particularly when one is working in the interpretive tradition. Nowhere is this more evident than in the prolonged process of living with the study. An extraordinary degree of concentration is needed as one becomes immersed in the phenomenon and context of the study, amasses and slogs through mounds of raw texts, struggles toward an aha moment, and crafts well-warranted experiential, discursive, and theoretic texts. Sustaining this intensity of concentration necessitates not only major blocks of uninterrupted time for deliberation but also freedom from distractions.

Carving out the space for intensive deliberation is not easy for adults who are likely to be running a household, parenting children, maintaining a quality relationship with a spouse or significant other, and supporting friendships. Although it seems crass to characterize commitments to family and friends as distractions, in terms of living with the study, they do divert attention from the inquiry.

Under such circumstances, completing a quality dissertation often entails making difficult choices and uncomfortable compromises. Just recognizing that something has to give in order to finish the dissertation may be tremendously disconcerting for those who believe they can and should "do it all." Those who are highly competent and independent may find it difficult to ask for and accept help. Receiving patience, understanding, and support from one's children, spouse, extended family, and friends may engender conflicting feelings of gratitude and guilt.

Accommodating these various pressures may occur subtly as the candidate and those closest to him or her slowly make more time and space for the dissertation. By the time the dissertation is finished, unrecognized realignments may have been forged in relationships, responsibilities, priorities, and the structuring of daily and weekly routines.

Maria often quips, "I forgot how to cook while I was working on my dissertation. For the life of me, I can't remember fixing dinner. I finally agreed that a microwave might be useful. We must have lived on reheated leftovers from the huge meals my mother fixed on the weekends."

More wrenching are decisions that alter long-standing family traditions and rituals: "I'm not hosting Thanksgiving dinner this year." "I've already told my family I won't be coming for the holidays." "This year we're not going to the beach. The children are really bummed out. But I need the time to write." Even smaller adjustments in family routines can be stressful: "I feel like an absentee parent. As soon as dinner is over, I disappear. There's time for quick 'good nights' and then I'm back to writing."

Upon graduation, those who have made sacrifices and offered support throughout the dissertation process may experience a tremendous sense of both pride and relief. This initial elation, however, may give way to a sense of disorientation as the time and energy allocated to the dissertation are suddenly available for other pursuits. Unexpected tensions can arise as the new graduate and those closest to him or her sort through how this recaptured time and energy will be used. Some may have assumed that life would return to a predissertation norm, with everyone picking up the pieces where they had left off. Others may have assumed that the doctorate would launch them into a new lifestyle or status. Neither of these extremes is realistic. Rather, some negotiations and tradeoffs are likely to occur as everyone touched by the dissertation process expresses his or her wishes and needs.

We do not mean to suggest that this period of readjustment must inevitably be troublesome. Our intent is to flag this initial time after the dissertation as an opportunity for reflection. The void left when the dissertation is no longer a dominant presence can be filled in many ways. This may be one of life's rare opportunities to deliberately and deliberatively reassess and rebalance one's priorities, interests, and needs as one moves forward from the dissertation.

## REBALANCING PROFESSIONAL LIFE

### Coping With Career Changes

Even as one is adjusting to life after the dissertation in the personal realm, changes are likely to be occurring in one's professional world. Many students enter doctoral programs with the express purpose of earning a degree that will enable them to attain a specific professional goal. Teachers may want to move into administration. Educators in public schools may want to become university faculty. Practitioners may have planned a shift from one field of study to another. Thus, finishing the dissertation can initiate a phase of career transition as graduates are now positioned to actively pursue such goals. The disequilibrium associated with these anticipated changes is probably not disconcerting. Repeatedly, however, we talk with graduates who experience a sense of disequilibrium that goes deeper than the unsettled and anxious feelings normally associated with a job search.

Virginia, for example, had been an excellent principal in a small Catholic girls' school. Upon completing her dissertation, she accepted a principalship in a suburban public district. Although the substantial increase in salary was welcome, Virginia's primary motivation for changing jobs was to make a contribution in a larger educational arena. Within a few months, the frustrations and stresses of this job resulted in health problems that were severe enough to warrant a medical leave of absence.

Alex's long-standing goal had been to teach at a university. The salary differential between secondary and higher education positions came as a sobering, even shocking, test of Alex's career aspirations. After much soul searching (and careful budget review), Alex decided to accept a university position and a considerable reduction of income.

Hazel's reality shock was not rooted in concerns of salary but of culture. Hazel completed her doctoral work at a university that evinced at least gender sensitivity, if not gender equity. As the first woman hired to teach in a program of administrative studies at a less cosmopolitan university, she was disconcerted (actually outraged) by her colleagues' assumption that she, as one of the girls, would fetch the coffee for faculty meetings.

Again, our intent is not to paint a gloomy or pessimistic picture. Indeed, we know a number of graduates who go on to make highly exciting and satisfying career moves by changing roles, organizations, or both. Being alert to the possibility of a more disquieting sense of disequilibrium, however, may facilitate rebalancing one's professional life.

## Coping With the Perceptions of Others

A variation of professional disequilibrium has come to our attention in more recent years as several study group members have remained in their same role and organization. For these committed teachers, doctoral study had never been a "ticket out of the class-room." Rather, their motivation had been to enrich their knowledge and understanding of teaching. This had raised exciting possibilities from our perspective, especially in light of the calls for teachers to participate more fully in scholarly pursuits. Disparities between the rhetoric and reality of being what Lynn Richards calls "a doctor in the classroom" can yield a profoundly disturbing disequilibrium.

Kathy Ceroni, for example, related a small but rather telling anecdote indicating that teachers achieving the status of doctor are not even acknowledged, let alone valued, by her school district. At an open house to mark the start of the new school year, a program was prepared listing all of the district's personnel. Whereas the superintendent's doctoral title was listed, the academic credentials of the district's three teachers who also hold doctor-ates were omitted. Perhaps this was simply a clerical oversight; we suspect that it signals a deeper lack of recognition and respect.

Such small slights might seem rather innocuous. At times, the lack of recognition for one's accomplishments can even be amusing, as in the anecdote from Lynn Richards recounted in Exemplar 15.1.

---

**EXEMPLAR 15.1    Where Is That Dr. Richards Anyway?
Or, Not a Doctor in Sight**

On the first day of this school year, I was welcoming my new class of second graders at our classroom doorway. As I mentally matched each young face with the previous year's school pictures, which I had carefully studied on their official files, one sweet, freckle-faced brunette handed me a legal-sized envelope. In her best first-day-of-school printing, she had carefully penciled, "Dr. Richards." "Why thank you!" I said to her in my friendliest elementary teacher voice. "So, you're Haley. Your cubby and desk are right over here." Distracted by other newly arriving children, I held onto the envelope as I greeted and seated other apprehensive-looking young children. As I walked by Haley's desk, her hand shot up as she simultaneously gestured toward the envelope I still carried. "That's for Dr. Richards," she reiterated. Looking toward a timid face in the doorway, I replied absently, "I know, Hon. I'll read it as soon as I have a chance." Not to be deterred, Haley's small hand once again surfaced. "You know that letter I gave you?" she persisted. "Uh huh," I said, beginning to wonder if my middle-aged patience would last the day, much less the school year. "Well, it's for *Dr.* Richards." "I *know;* you told me before," I replied with some emphasis. "Well," said Haley with a puzzled and pained expression, "do you know where *he* is?"

I hesitated only a second and then burst into a laugh, "Oh—*I'm* Dr. Richards, did you think I would be a man?" "Well, yeah," she answered nonplussed. "Then I guess it's OK—you can read it now." Inside, she had printed

Dear Dr. Richards
I am looking fored to se you from
Haley
XOXOX

At sharing time later that day, I asked the children if they knew why I was called *doctor.* A handsome little towhead, who had obviously discussed this titled-teacher phenomenon with his parents, volunteered, "Because you went to school longer than any other teachers in this school!" I asked Haley if I minded if I shared our "morning mix-up" with the class. She was quite good-natured about the joke on herself and willingly reiterated her version of our initial encounter. I asked how many others thought I would be a man because *Dr.* was written at the top of our classroom roster. About 7 out of 21 hands were raised.

The next day, Haley brought me a longer note and a drawing. It read

This is about 2nd grade by Haley. I wok up very very early and then I got dressed sould I go to school or sould a not. and then I wot up to the busstop and then it sprisd me my Best frend cam running to me. and sprisding me ugen I thot

> Dr. Richards was a man. and I met this little grel named Kelly. and I got yoos to it and I like my class.
>
> I like my class, too, and that is definitely one of the benefits of staying a doctor in the elementary classroom.

A darker, more pernicious form of devaluing comes through in the following excerpt from a think piece that Lynn also wrote called "Is There a Doctor in the Classroom?":

As a bargaining member of the Pennsylvania State Educational Association, I completed my Doctoral Degree in the last year of a contract that fortuitously included a Doctoral column on the salary schedule. This meant that I was entitled to a three thousand dollar increase in my yearly salary. That salary increase was a cause of consternation during the next round of negotiations as the Doctoral column was eliminated from the proposed new contract and would have required that I pay back thousands of dollars to the district each year. Some of my colleagues were sympathetic to my "holding an earned doctoral degree" dilemma while others clearly resented the fact that my "portion of the pot" might impact on their salaries. "Why should we pay for her degree?" they implied.

The attitude that I had overstepped the boundaries of the elementary classroom and that I was no longer "one of them" revealed itself through other avenues as well. My elementary school building has a Building Fund whose stated purpose is: "To acknowledge staff members and their immediate families in times of joy and sorrow." Events which are outlined in the Fund to be "acknowledged" include weddings, births, deaths, surgery, Secretary's Day, Christmas gifts (for secretaries, support staff and principal), PTO Chairs and Retirements.

The "event" of completing a doctoral degree is not covered in the guidelines (perhaps I should have seemed more "joyous"), so a vote was cast and the majority ruled that no funds were to be expended as "that degree was something that she wanted to do" (perhaps becoming a parent isn't?). Later on, my closer building teammates revealed their fury at "educators refusing to celebrate an educational doctoral degree." In retrospect, I wonder if people in the building could have better understood my "retirement" from the classroom to teach elsewhere than my remaining as a doctor in one of their classrooms.

We hope that these anecdotes represent isolated incidents rather than a widespread attitude toward classroom teachers who "overstep their place." Our intent is not to burst anyone's vision of finishing the doctorate and living happily ever after. We include these stories to illustrate a potential source of disequilibrium in the professional realm: Holding a doctorate may alter the ways in which one is seen and treated by one's colleagues. Responding to these altered perceptions may not always be easy. In part, it calls for an integration of doctoral status into one's identity. Noreen's advice to new graduates is, "You have earned the highest degree in the land. Wear the title of doctor proudly."

This is not meant as a suggestion to flaunt the title in self-serving or self-aggrandizing ways. Rather, it encourages graduates to recognize and internalize their accomplishments as scholars. The following postdissertation reflections of Pat McMahon, Kathy Ceroni, Lynn Richards, and Marilyn Llewellyn provide insight into the complexity of integrating this sense of scholar into one's image.

## Internalizing One's Identity as Scholar

During a conversation about life after the dissertation, Pat commented, almost off-handedly, "I don't really feel like a scholar." This comment came as a shock. For us, Pat's dissertation represented a turning point in the evolution of our own understanding of qualitative research, bringing into the foreground the power of personal narrative as a mode of research. During her dissertation meeting, one committee member repeatedly referred to Pat's dissertation as "stunning," and all committee members approved the document without revision. It was a masterful piece of scholarship, and in many ways, the quality and credibility of Pat's dissertation gave us the confidence to work with other study group members as they shaped more explicitly narrative inquiries. Because our perception of Pat's scholarly ability and contributions did not, apparently, match hers, we pursued this issue further. As Pat explained,

> I'm not sure. I guess I had in mind sort of a stereotype of scholars and scholarly research. What I did for my dissertation didn't match that image. Since finishing my dissertation, I've become very excited about arts-based educational research and story as a form of knowledge. Looking back, I think the dissertation helped to bring out my artistic side. The work I've been doing since then has strengthened this sense of myself as an artist. This didn't match with my stereotype of traditional academic scholars. But now, I've begun to see more clearly how my natural inclination to reconstruct experience through stories is a form of inquiry. This has helped me to integrate these two sides of myself, the storyteller and the researcher, into my sense of being a scholar.

Pat's comments raise three important issues. First, completing the dissertation or receiving the degree does not magically transform one's sense of self. It is not as though one day a person isn't a scholar and the next day he or she is. Rather, it is an evolutionary process that is likely to begin with doctoral study, continue with the dissertation, and extend beyond graduation. Second, gaining some distance from the dissertation experience affords new opportunities for deliberation. From a different vantage point, perspectives can emerge that might have been lost when one is in the thick of the dissertation. The third issue is not as apparent but relates to the importance of discourse communities.

Coinciding with Pat's work on her dissertation was an increasingly robust discourse on the role of story, storying experience, and narrative in educational research. But there was no clearly identified discourse community with which Pat could connect. In short, it is difficult to see oneself as a member of a scholarly community when such a community does not exist. This changed a couple of years later when two groups of artistically and narratively inclined scholars began to coalesce within the American Educational Research Association—that is, one special interest group on arts-based educational research and another on narrative inquiry.

Kathy Ceroni's postdissertation deliberations offer additional insights into internalizing a scholarly identity. For us, Kathy's dissertation raised important and thorny epistemological questions, questions with which we have been able to grapple far more cogently because of her work. Even the committee member who most vigorously challenged the highly personal quality of Kathy's dissertation came to a clearer understanding and greater openness toward interpretive inquiry because of her carefully crafted logic-of-justification. Yet Kathy periodically comments,

> I didn't really understand a lot of the implications of my study at the time. When I hear you talk about it, I think, "Wow, did I really do that?" It's strange, but you saw more in my study at the time than I did. I feel like I'm just beginning to understand what I did with the dissertation. How could that be?

While richly evocative dissertations often allow outsiders to gain different insights from those of the researcher, Kathy's postdissertation reflections suggest that something far more complicated was taking place. For Kathy, the dissertation brought to the surface previously unnamed and unfaced fears. The deliberations of her dissertation inquiry led to a profound yet disturbing transformation in Kathy's understanding of herself in the world. As she wrote in the final chapter of her dissertation:

> The journey I have taken as I have engaged in this study has been a journey into self. It is a journey that has brought me to a place where I feel compelled to pause and reflect on the contradictions and dilemmas inherent in my life as a teacher and as a female. It has been a solitary journey, as journeys into self tend to be, but I have not experienced loneliness. For along the way I have met and engaged with others, who like me, are struggling to deal with the complexities of their work and struggling to give voice to those complexities . . .
>
> The journey has been painful, and the wisdom I have come to is a bitter wisdom, yet paradoxically, it has liberated me from the technocratic mindlessness that imbues our culture, and it is, therefore, a cause for celebration. Through study and reflection I have come to "see" and develop an understanding not only of the ways in which the dominant ideology functions to oppress my class and gender, but also of the ways in which I have acted in complicity with the very forces I am struggling to combat . . .
>
> To entertain this reconceptualized view has involved a degree of intellectual risk-taking, creating in me a sense of fear analogous to the experience of finding oneself swimming in waters of unknown depth. (Ceroni, 1995, pp. 227–228)

Swimming in waters of unknown depth can be both frightening and disorienting. For some scholars like Kathy, completion of the dissertation may precipitate a period of more introspective reflection. Our encouraging Kathy to write articles and to submit proposals for presentations would have focused her attention outward. As the reflection in Exemplar 15.2 illustrates, Kathy had a far deeper need to find a renewed sense of grounding and direction for her deliberations.

We find it interesting that the concept of *voice* plays a pivotal role in giving Kathy a renewed direction for her deliberations and writing. As Kathy became immersed in her dissertation, she was exquisitely tuned to nuances of voice and stance. These served, in fact, as key structural elements for the layers of portrayals that comprise her dissertation. What appeared externally to be a hiatus from scholarly endeavors was, for Kathy, a time in which the lessons learned from the dissertation could incubate. Kathy is now ready to claim a more overtly feminist stance and voice, something she did not feel prepared to do during the dissertation. This has, in turn, allowed her scholarly self to reemerge from the background.

---

### ⁄⁄⁄ EXEMPLAR 15.2    A Search for New Direction

When I actually finished writing my dissertation, I felt *tired*—fatigued might be a more accurate word—the kind of fatigue a traveler would feel when she comes to the end of an arduous journey. But the spent feelings I experienced did not give me peace. At first, I thought this was just because the knowledge I had come to was a *bitter wisdom,* one that called upon me to abandon my former beliefs and accept a disempowering view of teacher professionalism, one that forced me to recognize and accept that I had been as White and White (1986) describe it, "blinkered," and because of being blinkered, I had deceived myself by allowing myself to be deceived. This confrontation was not celebratory. In the last section of my final chapter, which was subtitled "Reconciling the Grief," I wrote:

> Reflecting on the dilemmas of my life as a female teacher in the modern world has afforded me both pleasure and pain. As I have made discoveries and connections through the process of reflection, I have felt a sense of intellectual energy and creativity that has been exhilarating, yet paradoxically, I have also experienced paralyzing feelings of melancholy, alienation and ambivalence. (Ceroni, 1995, p. 230)

The negative feelings I describe in this passage stayed with me for a long time, because I "knew" that what I had confronted was much bigger, deeper, broader than the boundaries of my study. And the mystery around those bigger, deeper, broader boundaries frightened me. I did not know how to live, how to act on the knowledge I had gained because there were still "places" I had not yet traversed. I think now I can find those places in feminist theory. Dimen (1989) tells us,

> Perhaps the missing conceptual link in feminist theory is an engaged personal voice, saturated with feelings, values, and political protest, a voice such as emerges in feminist biography in which subject engages with subject. But this politics of autobiography and biography should not replace the received patriarchal voice; rather, it should juxtapose it. The point is to use the different power of both voices to generate a sense of opposition, difference, creative tension. The resultant third voice, retaining the personal power of the first and intersubjectivity of the second, might thereby open a window on as yet unimagined, ungendered possibilities of speaking, knowing, and living. (p. 35)

> For the first time since finishing my dissertation, I feel a sense of direction, that autobiography in this "third voice" could be a way for me to resume my journey, carrying with me the knowledge I have come to in my dissertation while at the same time providing me with a hope in the possibility of speaking, knowing, and living authentically in the world.
>
> *Authors' Commentary.* Kathy began to explore this new direction in her chapter in Garman and Piantanida's (editors) *The Authority to Imagine* (Ceroni, 2006.)

Each time we give students in the introductory course on qualitative research an opportunity to review completed dissertations, Lynn Richards's document evokes tremendous interest. She has served as an inspiration and model for other classroom teachers who suddenly see the possibility of crafting dissertations around their own pedagogy. Yet Lynn, too, expresses inner doubts, as the following excerpt from "Is There a Doctor in the Classroom?" illustrates:

> One of the professional devils that I am currently contemplating was foreshadowed in my dissertation. Although I have completed a study of the infusion of the creative dramatics process within all the elementary classroom content areas of the district, I find that I use the informal drama process less frequently than during previous years and that I am at a loss to explain why this is so since I value classroom drama highly as a personalized and "dynamic, fluid and continuous elementary classroom curriculum," and "perceive drama as an integral component of teaching, of learning, and of knowing" (Richards, 1996, p. 264). Deep inside, I feel like a pedagogical charlatan who fraudulently continues to use the title of Doctor of Education and who deliberately conceals her lack of scholarly impetus at home, at school, and within the study group conversations.

Lynn's comments evoke an interesting point about one's sense of scholarship. The intensity of an interpretive dissertation inquiry engenders an acute awareness of scholarly engagement. By comparison, the demands of routine teaching may seem unscholarly. However, since completing her dissertation, Lynn has cotaught a university course on creative dramatics; submitted articles for publication; written instructional materials; presented a workshop on creative dramatics for teachers in Bosnia; participated in a special project on the art of Bosnian children; and presented her research experience to other graduate students. Lynn faithfully attends study group meetings, carefully reads and comments on the evolving dissertations of other study group members, and, most recently, has become involved in teaching in an inquiry-centered master of arts program. This, it seems to us, is no trivial manifestation of Lynn's commitment to scholarship, especially because she, as an elementary teacher, is under absolutely no mandate to engage in these activities.

Throughout the book, we have alluded to the transformative power of the dissertation. From our vantage point, this transformative potential is affirmed when we contrast the Pat, Kathy, and Lynn we first met with the Dr. McMahon, Dr. Ceroni, and Dr. Richards who completed such exemplary dissertations. Yet their ongoing struggle to claim a well-deserved identity as scholar reminds us of the complexity of this transformation. It would be easy to explain away the discrepancy simply as their having few points of reference for judging the caliber of their own accomplishments. Or, in Kathy's and Lynn's case, we could fault the lack of organizational affirmation or valuing of their scholarly abilities. Yet these speculations seem too facile. We have come to a deeper appreciation of the subtleties and intricacies of the transformation. A postdissertation reflection by Marilyn Llewellyn (Exemplar 15.3) echoes the sense of genuine humility exhibited by Pat, Kathy, Lynn, and other study group members.

Perhaps when student-researchers look as carefully and deeply into themselves and their practice as these scholars have done, it brings one not to a place of prideful knowing but of respectful—and humble—questioning. This speculation leads to our consideration of another aspect of disequilibrium: the intellectual void that occurs once the dissertation is completed.

---

### ////  EXEMPLAR 15.3   Interior Transformations

As I approached the completion of my doctoral work, some persons advised me that life would be very different after I finished the dissertation. Others warned me to be prepared for the postdoctoral depression that would set in after I finished writing my dissertation. Although neither of these things happened as predicted, I have often wondered since finishing my degree, "What happens now? Will I ever find the time to engage in such an intense inquiry again? Will I ever write again? Where will I find the time?" My response to these ever-nagging questions is that I must continue to engage in the deliberative process and make the time for this in my life. I addressed aspects of this in the final chapter of my *Project Demonstrating Excellence* (dissertation), where I reveal what happened to me through engaging in my study and the transformative aspects that the deliberative inquiry process brought for me. Perhaps one of the most significant revelations for me has been that engaging in this process is not a one-time event. Rather, it is a way of being and living in the world.

My inquiry focused on spirituality, pedagogy, and education. In my writing, I articulated a personal understanding of spirituality as pedagogy and portrayed the transformative possibilities in being and learning together in such a way as to make them accessible to other educators interested in spirituality as pedagogy. My hope was to further the conversation related to spirituality and education within curriculum-theorizing discourse and to contribute to the field of curriculum studies.

The process of writing the *Project Demonstrating Excellence* was an integral part of my personal journey toward a fuller understanding of myself as an educator. Through this inquiry process, I learned about dimensions of my "self" that I might not otherwise have come to know and understand. This understanding has directed me to dwell in this world with more integrity. Richard Palmer (1969) describes Heidegger's conception of understanding as the "power to grasp one's own possibilities for being, within the context of the lifeworld in which one exists" (p. 131). Engaging in this inquiry process was significant in the lifelong journey toward wholeness and selfhood, and my coming to terms with spirituality as pedagogy was pivotal in my ongoing transformation as an educator. Through conversation with other persons, the text of my life, and various discourse communities, spaces were opened up that shaped new understandings of spirituality, education, and pedagogy. I am no longer the same person that I was when I began the study. Through active engagement about the meaning of my life as a human being and who I am as an educator, I experienced a renewed integration of self and a recovery of the power in the spiritual in my life.

Through engaging in deliberative inquiry, I was able to enter into significant life experiences and arrive at new textures of meaning. I came to see the writing of my *Project Demonstrating Excellence* as an epiphany in my journey toward deeper awareness of myself. I experienced a great deal of vulnerability in committing to my study because of not knowing where my questions would lead me. As Gadamer says,

> To question genuinely means to "place in the open" because the answer is not yet determined. Consequently, a rhetorical question is not a true question, for there is no genuine questioning when the thing spoken of is never really "questioned." In order to be able to question one must will to know, and that means, however, to know that you do not know. When one knows he does not know, and when he does not therefore through method assume that he only needs to understand more thoroughly in the way he already understands, then he acquires that structure of openness characterizing authentic questioning. (quoted in Palmer, 1969, p. 198)

This study began with a question, one that required self-inquiry. (See Exemplar 7.2.) Through the study, I came to clearer understandings of the ways that my spirituality shaped my pedagogy. I believe that I engaged in authentic questioning in this study that invited me into a more authentic way of seeing myself as a teacher and opportunities for new ways of being. In the process, I was shaped by the story that I wrote. Ultimately, I was graced with a renewed desire and commitment to continue to struggle, to live, and to teach authentically.

# REFOCUSING ONE'S INTELLECTUAL LIFE

## A Loss of Focus

Conventional wisdom holds that the dissertation creates a foundation upon which one can build an ongoing research agenda. Indeed, one colleague, Helen Hazi, described exactly this outgrowth of her dissertation work:

> The dissertation was such an exciting time of learning for me. It became the basis for a career of research and for a process of continuous learning. As a university professor, research has been my vehicle for promotion and national recognition. I was able to build upon both the topic and design of my dissertation to continue a law and policy focus in my writing, teaching, and service. Doing research has also become the way that I now learn. The topics that I write on are those that I want to learn most about. Not only was the dissertation a time to learn skills and to discover new knowledge, but it was also a transformative experience that is still an important part of my professional life.

We often marvel at the energy, focus, and productivity with which our colleague has pursued the lines of inquiry established in her dissertation. However, as discussed above, we have been struck by the number of study group members who, in spite of doing excellent dissertations, seem to experience a prolonged sense of *postgraduation malaise.* The following passage from Lynn's think piece helped to crystallize the complex mix of issues that may contribute to an intellectual disequilibrium:

> In my postdoctoral reflections, I have come to realize that I have been grieving the loss of the study, which propelled me (and gave me administrative license) to create, personalize, and infuse my classroom with creative dramatics. I also have acknowledged that if I were sustaining the same intensity of application of the classroom drama process, I would have to be engaged in another doctoral dissertation. However, I have also considered the possibility that I have met my professional/status goals—having traversed the horizontal columns of the salary scale, becoming the highest paid teacher and the only doctor in the district's classrooms—and need to look to new educational horizons. Subsequently, I have coauthored creative dramatics modules/scripts for primary teachers, taught informal drama to graduate students at the University, presented sessions at local and national conferences, and continued my work with the Obnova Renewal Children's Art Gallery (an extended project with its roots in a four-day workshop which I presented with a university team to educators in Bosnia-Herzegovina). I have written articles for *Stage of the Art Magazine,* a publication of the American Alliance of Theatre Educators (Spring 1998, pp. 5–10). I continue in the scholarly discourses of the Study Group. And yet, I still remain professionally unfulfilled and feeling guilty. Another colleague and I attempted to initiate a Teacher Inquiry Group within the District—none of us was able to sustain the focused energies or consistent interest that the dissertation process provides.

The intensity of the dissertation process itself can be exceptionally meaningful. Without such intensity, it is possible to feel adrift, with no particular purpose or direction. Yet knowing the toll that such intense commitment takes may engender some ambivalence. On one hand, the sense of freedom is appealing. On the other hand, there may be a longing to recapture the heightened sense of intellectual engagement associated with the dissertation.

## Seeking Contexts and Direction for Deliberation

Sorting through this odd mix of feelings and deciding what to do with one's life after the dissertation may take some time. Just as Lynn has given presentations, written articles, and engaged in teaching, so, too, have Kathy, Pat, and Marilyn pursued these traditional modes of scholarly activity. Yet these episodic endeavors do not match the sustained intellectual effort of the dissertation, nor do they automatically provide an ongoing deliberative milieu. Lynn's attempt to create an inquiry group within her district parallels a similar effort that Maria made nearly 20 years ago. For both, the underlying intent was to create an intellectually stimulating context within their work environments. Lack of organizational support and the difficulty of identifying a critical mass of peers with the time or inclination for deliberation led to failure in both cases. In the end, Lynn and Maria, as well as Kathy, Pat, and Marilyn, have continued to participate in the dissertation study group because it provides a milieu of intense, discursive deliberation that has not been available to them elsewhere. Within this context, they can continue to make contributions by supporting the scholarly endeavors of others.

We have come to associate this longing for a deliberative context with the most fundamental transformation wrought by the dissertation. As expressed by Marilyn, deliberation is not merely something one does. Rather, it becomes a way of being in and relating to the world. Sue Goodwin, a former study group member, who went on to become a highly regarded school superintendent and later a university faculty member, found a way to integrate her deliberative capacity within her professional life:

> The fact I chose to conduct a conceptual study struck a part of how I go about doing whatever it is I do. I don't seem to be making conscious choices here, but I intuitively seem to end up where I belong. Such is the case with the dissertation. My study was an evolving study . . . one that changed course and grew as I gathered data. So is the superintendency . . . at least the way I best approach it. Each issue is dynamic, each destination has no map. I think this ties in closely with why I have been so opposed to functionalist models of staff development or planning throughout my career.
>
> The process of conducting a conceptual study may actually have helped me prepare for the superintendency. I tolerate well ambiguity, chaos, and change. Not knowing an answer or, better yet, not knowing exactly what I'm looking for serves to motivate me like a detective, to continue looking. I experience each day on the job the same emotions that I felt while conducting my study . . . at times frustration sometimes bordering on fear . . . fear of an unknown outcome, or fear that the outcome will stretch me beyond my limits.
>
> I have come to understand that to be a truly good superintendent I have to work with my context (the data!). I can't control it, or even direct it. I move in and out of it, listening to it and taking direction from all aspects of it (community, staff, culture, curriculum, students, etc.). Once I can do this, the context (data) seems to embrace me and allow me to move freely within it and become a part of its dynamic nature. I haven't yet figured out my importance. Maybe like the conceptual researcher, I collect data, synthesize it, and try to communicate some sense of it to our people.

## Refocusing a Writing Agenda

Writing, of course, is a traditional way in which young scholars capitalize on their dissertation research. Indeed, as mentioned above, several study group alumnae, particularly those who pursued faculty positions in research universities, have continued ambitious research and writing agendas. Of greater curiosity to us, however, is the number of study group members who have been slow to use this avenue for scholarly engagement. This has been especially puzzling because those who are drawn to qualitative research tend to have at least a proclivity, if not major talent, for writing.

For some time, we speculated that the structural integrity of qualitative dissertations made it difficult to dismantle them into shorter presentations or publishable articles. Maria, in fact, struggled a great deal with this issue in the years immediately following her graduation. As she explains,

> Looking back, I can now see several dysfunctional assumptions that kept me from writing. I thought I had to condense my entire dissertation into a short article. For the life of me, I couldn't figure out how to do that and authentically portray the inquiry. I also thought that I had to provide as much data in an article as I had in the dissertation. Without that, how could I warrant whatever argument I was making? So this kept me stuck for a long time. It was Pat's dissertation that really helped me break through this dysfunctional mind set. Integral to Pat's study was the notion of contrived ambiguity. This was very interesting to me, because of some curriculum consulting I was doing at the time. I desperately wanted Pat to write an article that I could give to several faculty with whom I was collaborating. At that point, I saw the possibility of taking a particular concept or issue from the dissertation and using it (rather than the entire dissertation) as the centerpiece for an article. This seems so obvious now, I'm almost embarrassed to say it.

Yet what became so obvious to Maria did not immediately catalyze a flurry of writing activity for Pat. A couple of years later, however, the two formed a small writing group. Discussions within that new forum have shed additional light on this puzzling reluctance to write about their dissertations. For both Pat and Maria, writing is their primary mode for grappling with perplexing aspects of experience. Indeed, both were instinctively drawn to qualitative research for precisely this reason. Thus, crafting the dissertation was a way in which to solve a complex and nagging conceptual puzzle. Once an amorphous and confusing jumble of experience was sorted out and put into perspective through writing, neither had much interest in revisiting these "old puzzles." For a while, they were satisfied to enjoy a time of "contentedly" resting in their practice (Rowan, 1981; Stabile, 1999).

The intriguing part is the way in which new intellectual puzzles were beginning to stir beneath the apparent calm of these surface experiences. It was only a matter of time before they were overcome by a renewed *narrative desire*. This desire, it seems, is more readily embraced and actualized in the service of inquiry than in the functional packaging or repackaging of written pieces simply for the sake of publication.

These observations have led to several final speculations about the role of writing in refocusing one's intellectual life after the dissertation. Crafting an interpretive dissertation seems to bring to more conscious awareness the power of writing as a mode of inquiry. The experience of the dissertation may allow for a more focused harnessing of one's proclivity and talents for writing. A postdissertation reflection by Pat provides an insightful account of the transformation wrought by coming to own one's narrative sensibility. Because this passage is more extensive, we have included it in Case Example 3.

Thus, filling the intellectual void left by completing the dissertation is not merely a matter of doing "some—any—writing." Rather, it entails slogging around in experiential puddles until a new embryonic image begins to take shape. The deliberative curiosity associated with bringing this shadowy image to light can provide a new focus for one's intellectual life and precipitate new cycles of deliberation.

# *Afterword*

One of our intentions in writing this book has been to demystify the dissertation experience—giving a clearer sense of issues that require attention, pitfalls that can hinder progress, and approaches that foster forward movement. This perspective does not paint an easy picture of the dissertation. Indeed, we believe it does students and the academy a grave disservice to imply that the dissertation should be made simple. We hope that the day never comes when we enter a bookstore and see, nestled among the piles of black and yellow self-instructional manuals, the title *Dissertations for Dummies.*

For us and for many of the students with whom we have been privileged to work, the transformative power of the dissertation cannot and should not be trivialized. Doctoral study offers the possibility of transformation from student to novice researcher to scholar. This, from our perspective, is the very essence of doctoral study.

Yet this personal transformation can be bittersweet. On one hand, earning the doctoral degree can bring the satisfaction of career advancement, professional recognition, and a sense of accomplishment. But for those who embrace the notion of deliberation and allow the dissertation to touch their hearts, the sweetness of these rewards can be intermingled with a sense of loss. A false, even arrogant, sense of certainty is traded for a more tenuous relationship with life's ambiguities. This is not an easy way of living in the world, nor may it be what many students bargained for when they entered a doctoral program. Our aim in sharing this challenging vision of the dissertation is not to dissuade novice researchers from taking the journey. Rather, it is to make more explicit both the difficulties and the rewards of choosing a deliberative path.

Several years ago, we hosted a gathering of past and present study group members. Approximately 25 women met and shared their dissertation experiences. Some were seasoned veterans from the first-generation group, and others were neophytes just beginning their journey. As we were socializing after the more formal portion of the meeting, one "old-timer" came up to us and said,

> They're standing on our shoulders. It's so exciting to hear what they're doing. Back when we were all struggling to understand qualitative research, I never dreamed where our work would lead—how other students could build on what we did. It's just so exciting.

Our colleague's comment brought home something we had been sensing but had not put into words. Indeed, members of the current study group were standing on the shoulders of earlier members and of each other. Cautious forays into the interpretive realm had blossomed into vigorous explorations of this epistemological terrain. The notion of embedding dissertation research in the context of one's practice had emerged from shadow into full light. Embryonic forms of stories and tales matured into sophisticated narratives. These are among the legacies of deliberation within our own small discourse community.

In writing this book, we have tried to extend this legacy to others who might be drawn to interpretive dissertation research. It is our way of honoring those who remain true to their own ways of knowing and of supporting those who are willing to temper their ideas and themselves in the crucible of deliberative inquiry.

Recently, a young man we will call Jeff was referred to Noreen for help in interpreting his dissertation data. It seems he had gathered quite a bit of qualitative data and was struggling to make sense of it without interjecting his own view into the interpretation. As the conversation evolved, he said, "You mean, I can offer *my* perspective on what all this means?" "Who else's perspective could you offer?" Noreen responded. This led to a further exploration of Jeff's dilemma. It seems that he was working in a broader, empirically oriented project where objectivity was a taken-for-granted value. As glimmers of interpretive possibility began to surface, Jeff offered,

> You know, what I really want to do is write biographies. In fact, I'm working on one now that is going to be published. As soon as I've got this dissertation behind me, I'm going to concentrate on writing biographies.

The irony, of course, was that Jeff and his dissertation were ideally suited to a biographical genre of interpretive research. Apparently, it had never occurred to Jeff that he might wed his penchant for biography with his dissertation.

Our hope in writing this book has been to forestall such wasted opportunities for others who, like Jeff, might have gladly followed an interpretive path had they just known it was possible. From our perspective, the dissertation experience is a journey rich with possibilities—the possibility of discovering one's scholarly self, the possibility of adding one's own voice to the evolving discourses of qualitative-dissertation research, and the possibility of forging one's own unique legacy through scholarly deliberation.

# SECTION FOUR

## *Case Examples of Interpretive Dissertations*

# *Introduction to Case Examples*

I n this section, we draw from six interpretive dissertations to illustrate various points about the process of conceptualizing and conducting a study. In reviewing these examples, it is not as crucial to understand the topic of the study or specific terms as it is to gain a sense of the interrelationships among intent, genre, and procedures. Through our author commentaries, we call attention to features and issues for reader consideration.

The first case example is drawn from Micheline Stabile's practice-based heuristic study of educational inclusion. At the time she did her dissertation, Micheline was a seasoned administrator in a large urban school district. She had responsibility for working with professional staff who worked in the district's special education program.

Lynn Richards and Patricia (Pat) McMahon are both experienced teachers. As they approached the dissertation, both were struggling with their own pedagogy, wanting to incorporate a new dimension into the teaching and learning that occurred in their classrooms. Lynn was drawn to the possibility of integrating creative dramatics throughout the second-grade curriculum she was expected to teach. Pat was intrigued with the possibility of using writing portfolios to cultivate reflection and discourse with her composition students at the community college where she taught at the time. Both gravitated toward personal narrative as their research genre.

The genre of narrative has attracted considerable interest among educational researchers in the past 20 or so years. In many ways, narrative—especially personal narrative—is ideally suited for professionals who want to examine issues embedded within their own practice. Newcomers to qualitative research may, however, simplistically assume that they are engaged in narrative inquiry merely because they are writing in a narrative style. This ignores the deeper epistemological underpinnings of narrative as a mode of generating knowledge by reconstructing the meaning of experience (Bruner, 1986, 1996; Coles, 1989; Dewey, 1938; Hopkins, 1994; Mitchell, 1981; Nash, 2004). We hope that the glimpses into Lynn's and Pat's studies illustrate the underlying process of personal narrative inquiry: starting with careful documentation of one's practice (not just the events, but the thinking behind the events); creating from the documentation an experiential text that portrays one's practice; interpreting the text for the embedded meanings; and finally creating a theoretic text of the embedded meanings. Lynn's and Pat's descriptions of their dissertations also give a flavor of the variety of raw text forms that can be used to support a narrative inquiry. Particularly striking in Lynn's dissertation is the table of contents, which clearly illustrates a point we made earlier—qualitative dissertations do not automatically follow the format of a science report.

Like Lyn and Pat, Kathleen (Kathy) Ceroni and Jean Konzal brought years of professional experience and expertise to the dissertation. Yet neither entered the dissertation process with an explicit understanding of their research genre. Rather, the genre emerged as they became more deeply immersed in their studies and struggled with what style and format would suit the nature of knowledge they were generating. Both of their studies serve to underscore the recursive nature of interpretive dissertations. Researchers working in scientific genres generally would not revise the title of their study, statement of intent, or guiding questions once the proposal was completed. In qualitative studies—especially in the interpretive tradition—such revisions are likely to occur as the core thesis comes more clearly into focus with each successive draft of the dissertation.

Kathy did not explicitly set out to do a literary study. Indeed, she had misgivings about the topic for her study—an examination of the Lead Teacher Initiative in Pennsylvania. Yet having participated as a research assistant in an earlier study on this topic (Ceroni & Garman, 1994), Kathy was intrigued at some level with notions of teacher empowerment, peer or collegial support of professional development, and the contributions that experienced teachers might make to their own districts' efforts at school reform.

As an educational administrator, teacher, and parent, Jean was able to look at the issue of school reform as both a provider and consumer of education. Troubled by resistance to and failure of many school reform initiatives, Jean began an in-depth study of one town's reform efforts. Given the amount of time Jean spent with school personnel and citizens of the town, as well as the 1,000 pages of interview transcripts she amassed, she might have framed her study as an ethnography or case study. Yet neither genre seemed to do justice to the passionate voices she was hearing. In a final section of her dissertation, Jean describes the process that led her to the arts-based genre of Readers Theater.

In a sense, these latter two studies contradict a major theme of this book—namely, the importance of thinking through the research genre in conjunction with the intent of the study in order to craft a conceptually coherent study. Neither Kathy nor Jean was in a position to act on this advice. Only by entering into their inquiries and struggling with the meanings encountered were they able to come to grips with the issue of genre. This was not ideal, but in the end, both women were able to complete credible studies because of the scholarly integrity and perseverance they brought to the process. In practical terms, Kathy and Jean invested an extra year in order to bring their dissertations to fruition.

The final Case Example is drawn from Joan Leukhardt's dissertation. Like Maria, Joan was a member of Noreen's initial dissertation study group, and neither had available to them the language of interpretive research. Nevertheless, Joan's genre of conceptual case study and her use of Shakespearean characters to portray her understanding of gifted adolescent girls' responses to science foreshadowed the interpretive work of later study group members.

# Case Example 1

• • • •

# *Problematizing Educational Inclusion*

## *A Practice-Based Heuristic Inquiry*[1]

Micheline Stabile, EdD

## PART 1: DISSERTATION TITLE

*Authors' Commentary.* Notice how the dissertation title contains key concepts that describe Micheline's study. *Educational Inclusion* flags what is under study. *Practice-Based Heuristic Inquiry* indicates the research genre. *Problematizing* signals the intended outcomes of the study (i.e., to lay out the complexities inherent in an educational phenomenon that is often discussed in overly simplistic and functional ways.) When *problematizing* and *heuristic* are considered together, they foreshadow the nature of the portrayal that Micheline aims to generate: a heuristic representation of the problematic aspects of educational inclusion.

As Micheline crafted this title, she debated for some time about using the term *practice-based* to qualify *heuristic inquiry.* As she reviewed the discourses on heuristic inquiry, she was uncomfortable with the intensively introspective and psychological nature of many dissertations that fell within this genre. This was not the embryonic image lurking in the shadows of her dissertation puddle. Yet she was hesitant to modify the notion of heuristic inquiry, saying, "Who am I to reframe the nature of this genre?" In the end, two perspectives persuaded her to take this step. One was our reminder that as a researcher, she has a right to add her perspective to the discourses on heuristic inquiry. The other was her own growing conviction that her title should explicitly indicate the practice-oriented nature of her study. In the body of her proposal, Micheline explains her view of the relationship between "practice-based" and "heuristic inquiry."

## PART 2: INTRODUCTION

*Authors' Commentary.* The following excerpt is taken from the first section of Chapter 1 of Micheline's proposal titled "Background" and is an example of an experiential text.

One of the most traumatic events of my professional career was the "failing" of one of my young second-grade students in my first year of teaching. I never realized how pivotal this event was until more than twenty-five years later when I wrote a narrative called *For Timmy.*

Thus I discovered that my professional path and studies in the field of education have been largely guided by my experiences within the profession as an elementary school teacher. When I reflect upon what brings me to this study of educational inclusion, I find that I must travel back to this beginning point. For in recalling my first year of teaching, I realize that from the start I became challenged by the group of students that was resistant to the typical traditional instructional practices and structures of our educational system.

Through the years I came to think of these students who fail within the system, as those whom the *system* fails, and to view the various labels created to classify "their" dysfunction as social constructions of questionable educational relevance. My interest in gaining an understanding of how our educational system might better serve the needs of this group of "unsuccessful" students has led me to seek and to advocate for alternative pedagogical approaches and policies throughout my professional lifetime. And so, it is all the more puzzling to me that when the educational inclusion movement swept into my professional world I was taken totally off guard, not by the addition of yet another reform initiative, but rather by my reaction to it. As a woman who personally stands to benefit from inclusion as a societal value and as a professional who considers herself to be an advocate for students, I was confused by my own immediate ambivalence to the movement, my concern about what it might mean for students, and my fear of the strong political rhetoric that characterized its onset.

*Authors' Commentary.* In the interest of brevity, we have not reproduced Micheline's story *For Timmy,* which appears in the proposal immediately after the first paragraph reprinted above. This story, however, was included in virtually every draft of every document that Micheline produced as she worked her way toward the proposal. Eventually, she became as bored with reading it as we were. Yet in the proposal (and ultimately the dissertation), the story fit well and served several purposes: It anchors the dissertation in Micheline's development as a professional, conveys a sense of her educational philosophy, signals the interpretive nature of her inquiry, and foreshadows a fundamental modality of reflective deliberation through which Micheline makes meaning of experience.

Notice the verbal and conceptual economy with which Micheline frames the study. In two relatively short paragraphs, she places the current inquiry within a personal context that spans 25 years of professional growth and intellectual development. She conveys not only her initial biases but also how these preconceptions were shaken—moving her to a more deliberative stance for the dissertation. Also woven into this background are information about her professional roles and her perspective on regular and special education.

*(Continued)*

(Continued)

From this personal opening, Micheline then provides a more formal frame for the study by linking her concerns to three discourses. Within the background section of Chapter 1, she includes three subsections titled:

"Special Education: Introductory Perspectives"

"Educational Inclusion: Introductory Perspectives"

"A World Divided: Perspectives of an Educational Administrator"

# PART 3: STATEMENT OF INTENT AND GUIDING RESEARCH QUESTIONS

*Authors' Commentary.* Following our commentary is a chart that Micheline used in her proposal to explain how she envisioned conducting the study and then representing it in the dissertation document. The chart is organized around the phases of heuristic inquiry that Micheline drew from the literature, and there is a guiding question for each phase. We have incorporated her statement of intent into the chart to make it easier to visualize how the guiding questions relate to the intent. A number of points are worth noting in reviewing the chart.

Notice how the concepts of problematizing and educational inclusion are carried forward from the title of the study into the intent. The consistency of language and wording begin to create a sense of conceptual coherence. When students vary the wording in the title and intent, sometimes it seems inadvertent, as though little thought has been given to the relationship between these two facets of the study. In other cases, the variations seem more deliberate—an attempt to make the writing "interesting" by changing words or sentence structure. We encourage students to be more straightforward, echoing key concepts from the title in the statement of intent.

Also notice the way in which the purpose—or "So what?"—of the study is made explicit. Also embedded in the purpose are the prospective audiences for the study—educational policymakers and administrators.

Both the title and intent convey Micheline's position that educational inclusion is viewed too simplistically and needs to be problematized. Rather than trying to pretend she has no position or trying to obscure it, she makes it explicit and subsequently provides a rationale for her position in the body of the proposal. One reason that Micheline could take this approach is the thoroughness with which she had immersed herself in the formal discourses on educational inclusion and the insightfulness of the discursive text she constructed for her comprehensive examination. In addition, she expanded the experiential text to portray not just her own experiences but also a range of perspectives she encountered in her practice setting. In this way, Micheline demonstrated her theoretical sensitivity, a capacity to resonate with raw texts, and an open-minded stance that engendered confidence in her ability to carry out the study.

Also, note the conciseness with which so much information is communicated—the "What?" "How?" and "So what?" of the inquiry—as well as Micheline's position toward the phenomenon under study, the discourses to which the study will contribute, and the audiences who are likely to find the results of her study of interest or use. Although each of these points required elaboration in the body of the proposal, the conceptual richness of the title and statement of intent convey the impression of someone who is in command of her study.

Drawing from discourses on heuristics dating back to Archimedes, Micheline laid out key phases of her inquiry. Unable to say in advance what heuristic would best portray the problematic nature of educational inclusion, Micheline used her guiding research questions to articulate the inquiry process. Each of the phrases set off in quotation marks (*engagement, immersion, acquisition,* etc.) relates to a specific facet of heuristic inquiry. Recognizing that these concepts might not be familiar to readers, Micheline provided a thumbnail sketch of the heuristic inquiry process as part of her introduction. Later, in the Procedures section of the proposal, she returned to these concepts and explained in more detail how she planned to carry out each process.

## PART 4: RESONATING WITH RAW TEXT

*Authors' Commentary.* In planning her study, Micheline anticipated having a number of planned and spontaneous encounters with parents, teachers, and administrators. Through storied conversations, she would try to capture the essence of the dilemmas, issues, concerns, and problematics embedded in these encounters. The following e-mail, written when Micheline was in the throes of this process, provides a glimpse into the messiness of resonating with the raw texts of the inquiry.

I'm at an interesting point in that I've written several stories and a few pieces in which I have used collections of vignettes that I've pulled out as I've reflected on the transcripts because they seem to hang together for one reason or another.

I have identified at least one dilemma, conflict, or major issue in most of the stories and collections of vignettes. On some, I've done a very preliminary first round of interpretation in relation to the identified issue.

What I'm finding is that some of these pieces themselves are beginning to loosely group together, mostly based on some more global literature and theory that speaks to the dilemma, conflict, or major issue that I identified. Which is kind of like a "one-layer-deeper interpretation."

But I'm feeling very scattered and at different points at the same time—i.e., story writing, and first and second layer of interpretation. I still haven't even finished transcribing AERA tapes and a few conversations.

Statement of Intent: The intent of my study is to "problematize" the concept of educational inclusion for the purpose of informing educational policy and administrative practice.

| Chapter | Phase of Heuristic Inquiry | Guiding Questions | Description of Heuristic Phase | Process/Product | Anticipated Dissertation Chapter Content |
|---|---|---|---|---|---|
| 1 | Initial Engagement: Unrest in Practice | What is the nature of my initial engagement with the concept of educational inclusion? | During this period of initial engagement, I see the challenge of the researcher/practitioner to identify within practice an intense interest, a concern that calls out, begging for attention—one that holds important social meanings and compelling personal and professional implications. | *Reflection, Dialogue, Indwelling Deliberation, Plans, Decisions.* Identification of topic; definition of terms; articulation of purpose, intent, rationale, and approach. | In Chapter 1, I will portray my initial engagement with this study. |
| 2 | Initial Engagement: Research Plan | What processes can I use to accomplish the intent of my study? | "At this time the investigator reaches inward for tacit awareness and knowledge, permits intuition to run freely, and elucidates the context from which the question takes form and significance" (Douglas & Moustakas, 1985, p. 27). | *Planning, Decision Making.* Detailed description of the heuristic inquiry process and articulation of its uses to develop my anticipated procedures for this study. | In Chapter 2, I will describe heuristic inquiry and the processes/procedures of this study. |
| 3 | Immersion/Acquisition: Meeting Other Realities | How do I move from initial engagement to immersion/acquisition through | During phases of immersion, I view the researcher/practitioner as adopting a stance of openness. He/she enters fully into life with others wherever the research topic is being expressed or talked about—in public settings, in social | Immersion/Acquisition Through Literature and Practice. Log of literature and practice encounters. | In Chapter 3, I will discuss my immersion through selected literature and |

| Chapter | Phase of Heuristic Inquiry | Guiding Questions | Description of Heuristic Phase | Process/Product | Anticipated Dissertation Chapter Content |
|---|---|---|---|---|---|
| | | discourses related to educational inclusion found in selected literature? | contexts, in professional gatherings. The heuristic inquirer is alert to all possibilities for meaning and is guided by tacit understandings to literature, to other people, to institutions, to nature, and to unanticipated places near and far. I see the immersion/acquisition of my inquiry as a time to gather information related to educational inclusion from practice and literature and then to create texts from different perspectives revealed in the discourses of various participants. | • Natural<br>• Deliberate<br>• Contrived<br><br>Observations, meetings, dialogue with self and others, videos, training materials, curricular materials, staff development sessions. | practice related to educational inclusion. |
| 4 | Immersion/ Acquisition: Learning Other Realities | How do I move from immersion within literature to immersion in the discourse of my administrative practice? | "Virtually anything connected with the question becomes raw material for immersion, for staying with, and for maintaining a sustained focused and concentration" (Douglass & Moustakas, 1985, p. 45). | *Immersion/Acquisition.* Creating acquisitions from immersion through *storied conversations.* | In Chapter 4, I will present and discuss my acquisitions in the form of *storied conversations.* |
| 5 | Realization: Making Meaning | How do I portray the problematic nature of | At some unspecified point, the heuristic researcher will resist the urge to rely upon methods and will, while considering the intent of the study and the | *Incubation, Deliberation, Illumination, Interpretation, Problematizing, Explication.* | In Chapter 5, I will present a narrative |

*(Continued)*

(Continued)

| Chapter | Phase of Heuristic Inquiry | Guiding Questions | Description of Heuristic Phase | Process/Product | Anticipated Dissertation Chapter Content |
|---|---|---|---|---|---|
| | | educational inclusion that I have come to "realize" through the processes of immersion and acquisition? | intended audience, resonate off the pieces and draw upon processes of imagination. In so doing, he/she will gain a clear sense of the issues in what Garman refers to as a "leap of insight" resulting in what is commonly described as an "Aha!" or, to use a word related to heuristic, a "Eureka!" Eisner (1991) maintains that in qualitative studies "the self is the instrument" that engages the situation and makes sense of it. He suggests that it is this ability to see and interpret significant aspects that provides unique personal insight into the experience under study. "At some unspecified point the heuristic researcher will have gained a clear sense of the direction in which the theme or question is moving and will know (tacitly) what is required to illuminate it" (Douglass & Moustakas, 1985, p. 48). | Portrayal of problematized aspects of educational inclusion. | portrayal of my interpretations. |
| 6 | Creative Synthesis: Generating | What heuristic can be "creatively synthesized" to | Through processes of imagination, intuition, self-reflection, and the tacit dimension, the educational inquirer will represent a synthesis of | The creation of a heuristic representation that problematizes the concept of | In Chapter 6, I will present my heuristic |

240

| Chapter | Phase of Heuristic Inquiry | Guiding Questions | Description of Heuristic Phase | Process/Product | Anticipated Dissertation Chapter Content |
|---|---|---|---|---|---|
| | New Realities | inform educational policy and administrative practice regarding educational inclusion? | understandings. The heuristic portrayal can take any number of forms and is meant to capture the essence of the understandings of the concept under study that has been gained through the inquiry process. With the creation of this heuristic representation, the educational researcher/practitioner culminates the research process by fulfilling what Eisner articulates as an obligation of the educational researcher to be educative in a public way. "In synthesis the searcher is challenged to generate a new reality, a new monolithic significance that embodies the essence of the heuristic truth" (Douglass & Moustakas, 1985, p. 52). | educational inclusion that can be used by an educational administrator/practitioner/leader to<br>• Evoke reflection<br>• Invite substantive conversation<br>• Engender an appreciation for the complexities involved as attempts are made to transform this value into practice | representation, problematizing the concept of educational inclusion. |
| 7 | "Resting" in Practice | What are the implications of my study? | Rowan (1981), in his discussion of a cycle of research that characterizes what he calls "alternative research paradigms," describes a period of contentment that begins and ends each new research cycle. Rowan refers to this time as "resting in his own experience" (p. 98). | *Reflection.* Discussion of Implications. | In the final chapter, I will discuss the implications of my study. |

*Authors' Commentary.* Notice the variety of activities in which Micheline was engaged as she lived with her study. She was transcribing interviews, storying spontaneous conversations, experimenting with various representations of experiential text, and speculating about tentative interpretations and meanings. She was also writing e-mails as one way of engaging in deliberation with others as she struggled to sort through her own thoughts about where she was in the inquiry process and about the texts she was collecting. Hopefully, this reinforces the point that interpretive studies do not proceed in a linear fashion. Rather, the researcher is constantly working back and forth among various conceptual tasks.

Anyway, I feel like I've hit a snag about the notion of problematizing. I went back and looked at the section from my overview [proposal] in which I describe what I mean by problematizing. While it hangs together with what I'm doing (which feels purely by chance/blind instinct), I feel an uncomfortable dissonance when I see how some others like Popkewitz [1984] or even Peshkin [2000] use the term.

Tomorrow night I'd like to give the study group an idea of where I am and give them a few of the storied conversations to take home to read in order to converse with them at a later time about the major issues that I've identified from them. And if there is time, I would find a discussion of the notion of problematizing useful.

When I get to feeling insecure I go back and read through parts of my overview document. I think I'm in the transition period between the immersion and realization phases of heuristic inquiry. In the process I think it is referred to as "acquisition," but now that I'm here I'm not sure that I like that word to describe it. I feel like I have been on a roll, but I'm beginning to feel the need for reassurance that I'm not off on a very interesting, time-consuming tangent as I am sometimes wont to do.

*Authors' Commentary.* In reading this passage, notice two strategies that Micheline used to keep her bearings, even as she felt lost in the mounting texts. First, she kept checking back to her proposal, revisiting key concepts in both her statement of intent (i.e., problematizing) and research procedures (i.e., acquisition). Second, she reached out to the study group and engaged in deliberation with other members—even though she wasn't sure of herself or her ideas. Micheline sensed that she was at a critical juncture in living with the study. When some students hit this phase, they withdraw, believing that they must figure everything out by themselves. This withdrawal may be prompted by a dysfunctional notion that "real" researchers generate results on their own, and it would be "cheating" to draw upon insights gained through interaction with others. Withdrawal might also be prompted by a desire to hide a sense of intellectual inadequacy that seems to accompany this phase of the research. Entering into deliberation at this juncture often feels risky. Yet in our experience, it is students' willingness to be vulnerable that helps them to tolerate the ambiguities of living with the study, to forestall premature closure, and to avoid overly simplistic interpretations and representations.

Notice also how Micheline returned to the formal discourses, pushing her own thinking by comparing and contrasting her concept of *problematizing* with that of others. This illustrates our point about the way in which formal literature comes into play throughout the study, not just at the proposal writing stage. It also exemplifies the recursive nature of the inquiry process. Micheline's proposal contained her best understanding of the concept in the abstract. As she lived through the study, she brought an experiential understanding to it as well, allowing her to think more deeply about its meaning. Depending upon the insights she came to, she could go back and revise her explanation of this procedure. This type of conceptual fine-tuning lies at the heart of crafting persuasive theoretic text.

# Case Example 2

## *Pictures in Our Minds*

*A Narrative Study of the Incorporation of Creative Dramatics as Pedagogy in Elementary Classroom Content Areas*

Lynn A. Richards, EdD

## PART 1: TITLE

*Authors' Commentary.* As Lynn's title indicates, she is working in a narrative genre. Therefore, a major procedural and conceptual challenge was transforming almost a school year's worth of multimedia raw texts into a coherent narrative. Because so many of the creative-drama activities were visual, an added challenge was creating vivid visual images with words. The first half of Lynn's title, *Pictures in Our Minds,* alludes to the visual quality not only in the narrative but also in the nature of the learning engendered by creative dramatics. This phrase came from one of Lynn's students as he tried to explain why he liked creative-drama activities. It did not appear in the title of her proposal but was added to the dissertation to convey the nature of the knowledge generated through the inquiry.

## PART 2: DISSERTATION ABSTRACT

*Authors' Commentary.* To give an overall picture of Lynn's study, we include verbatim the abstract from her dissertation. With this as background, we then offer additional information about the work Lynn did to conceptualize her intent and later her representation of the study.

This narrative study represents one elementary educator's search for pedagogical insight. I begin by describing my initial professional orientation toward the field of creative dramatics and my interest in how an elementary classroom could be infused with drama activities across the curriculum. Throughout the study, I connected my personal experiences with the thoughts of other researchers, drama theorists, teachers, and especially with the voices of my own students.

Over a span of six months, I document my second-grade classroom practices through the multiple lenses of teacher journal, lesson plans, and audio/videotapes. I also include those modes of student response, which informed my thinking: learning logs, essay writings, journals, audio/videotape transcriptions, and drama debriefing field notes. Through narrative vignettes, I explore the implicit contradictions in the varied roles and generic responsibility of the elementary classroom teacher, especially in how the boundaries of Teacher and Student become blurred as drama activities are incorporated into each content area. My examination of the ongoing drama activities and debriefings are further guided by two questions: "What are my intentions as Teacher?" and "What are the Children's Perceptions?"

Within this instructional context, I portray how my pedagogic philosophies, the connections between home and school life, and daily classroom events collide with, meld into, and transform the prescribed language arts, social studies, mathematics, and science curricula. I then synthesize these portrayals into broader pedagogic contexts by construing drama as four analogies: "Drama as Knowing," "Drama as Discourse," "Drama as Narrative," and "Drama as Synectics." These categories are described through classroom examples of the children's diverse ways of making meaning, extended student-to-student discussions, contextualization of drama experiences through shared narrative discourse, Teacher-Student sharing of role and life stage synergy, and how creative drama is embedded within the teaching-learning process. I conclude this study with some broad observations for other elementary educators who are committed to incorporating drama as pedagogy within their own classroom life.

# PART 3: INITIAL ARTICULATION OF QUESTIONS FOR A STUDY OF CREATIVE DRAMATICS

*Authors' Commentary.* Notice how Lynn's abstract concisely conveys a great deal of information as well as an impression of someone in command of her study. Contrast this impression with her initial uncertainty and misgivings about undertaking the dissertation, which she recounted after finishing her doctorate. (See Chapter 4.) This ability to articulate the nature of one's study illustrates the concept of self-conscious method. Coming to this point entailed many recursive turns as illustrated by the following list of questions that Lynn began to brainstorm when she first began thinking about what she wanted to study. Lynn's initial lists often had more than 20 or 25 questions. Gradually, she began to narrow her focus and generated the following 14 questions. While this number of questions is unwieldy, posing them was an important step in helping Lynn bring her intent and final guiding questions into focus.

1. How does creative drama contribute to a cooperative classroom climate? Do consistent, warm, and "nonjudgmental" school experiences impact on self-esteem?

2. Does creative drama help students to connect specific content knowledge to real-world experiences?

3. Does creative drama promote a young child's awareness of and empathy with others? Can drama activities expedite "decentering"?

4. Do creative-drama activities and learnings transform into emerging literacy and emergent student writing?

5. Can "gaps" in readers' prior knowledge be instantiated through participation in creative-drama activities? Do "active classrooms develop active readers"? (or learners?)

6. How can holistic learning be facilitated by the creative-drama process? How does creative drama address the idea of extending educational equity for all students?

7. What effect does participation in creative-drama activities have on oral language development?

8. Does creative drama significantly promote student-to-student interactions as opposed to traditional "teacher asks and one student responds" classroom dialogue?

9. How does the role of the teacher adjust as the structure of drama in the classroom leads from diminished teacher direction to more loosely structured, child-developed activities?

10. How does the leader's ability to ask searching, skillful, and reflective questions contribute to the quality of drama and learning experiences of the children?

11. What are the understandings of the participants involved in the drama experiences? How does the debriefing process make visible the child's perceptions of the teacher' intended plan or objectives of the lesson? What reciprocal learning processes (student-to-teacher as well as teacher-to-student) are facilitated?

12. What features of the classroom setting (physical, social, temporal, and spatial) are changed as the children are engaged in creative-drama experiences? How are the interactions and behaviors of the participants instigated, sustained, and developed?

13. Do intermediate-age school children and primary-age elementary-school children exhibit different patterns of learning in their creative drama participation? Is drama applicable across age levels in all instructional applications? Are some content areas more "teachable" for different drama stages and cognitive ages?

14. What are the implications for the elementary classroom practitioner and/or the teacher educator?

*Authors' Commentary.* The mix of questions in the preceding list suggests a variety of potential avenues for a study. Questions 1, 3, and 13, for example, tend to have a more psychological thrust, looking for cause-and-effect relationships between creative drama as an instructional intervention and self-esteem, empathy, and student learning. Some questions (e.g., 4 and 7) focus more specifically on student acquisition of literacy and oral language skills. Still others (1, 6, 8, 9, 10, and 12) are more pedagogically oriented but tend to be framed in terms of cause and effect. When Lynn revised this list a few weeks later, most of the questions remained the same except for a few minor changes in wording. Of significance, however, was the following question that Lynn added to the above list—"What happens when a teacher facilitates creative-drama activities in the classroom?" This additional question, when coupled with Question 14, eventually led to the central focus of Lynn's study and helped her to recraft the statement of intent and final guiding research questions.

# PART 4: STATEMENT OF INTENT AND GUIDING RESEARCH QUESTIONS

The intent of this research is to delineate creative dramatics as pedagogy. This narrative study also investigates how primary-school children's content-area learning is shaped by the classroom-drama process.

1. How can creative drama be construed as pedagogy?

2. What happens when a teacher uses drama as pedagogy in an elementary classroom?

3. How are the narratives of the classroom interpreted?

4. What are the pedagogical implications of using creative drama in the elementary classroom?

# PART 5: GATHERING RAW TEXTS

*Authors' Commentary.* Lynn chose to study an educational phenomenon—the integration of creative dramatics into an elementary curriculum—within the context of her classroom. To fulfill the intent of her study, Lynn felt that it was crucial to amass raw texts throughout an entire school year. The following passage, excerpted from pages 35–41 of her dissertation, describes the variety of raw texts she collected. Notice the structures and processes that Lynn created to gather a thick, rich set of raw texts. Also notice how she engaged in recollective and conceptual reflection as she worked with these texts.

The following passage is an example of an experiential text in that it recounts Lynn's experience of doing the study. Lynn supported this narrative explanation of her procedures for collecting raw texts with a series of appendices that detailed questions and protocols that she used to guide the discourse and deliberations with students and other adults. Take a look at the way in which Lynn was able to summarize her research process in the Abstract for her dissertation and her more full-blown representation of the process in her procedures chapter. Knowing how much detail to share in various sections of the dissertation document is part of the writerly decisions facing the doctoral candidate.

In order to construct a rich and comprehensive narrative, which was also consistent with narrative research method, documentation of the students' oral, nonverbal, and written responses to varied curricular topics and drama activities through teacher- and student-generated classroom experiences was gathered on a daily basis. Specific attention was given to my initial lesson planning, my subsequent content-area instruction, and to the children's interactions with and reactions to the subject-area material.

In addition to the weekly written lesson plans required by the school district, I maintained a second lesson plan book specifically outlining daily creative-drama activities. These lesson plans detailed the upcoming day's drama activities and outlined which subject-area concepts that I anticipated each planned classroom-drama process would address. At the end of each school week, I summarized the drama activities which were actually used within our classroom, recorded which drama activities were added or deleted (and why) and delineated the various curricular areas with which drama was integrated.

Ongoing classroom observations and research reflections were recorded through daily writings in my teacher journal. This journal was based on field note observations, which I had written during the regular school day. . . . The descriptive portion of my field notes was jotted into several small composition notebooks as I observed the children participate in daily drama activities. Depictions of student and teacher dialogue, the physical arrangement of the classroom, the actions of the children, and the general ambiance of each school day were recorded in as much written detail as I could humanly capture.

The reflective portion of the field notes was written after the school day. While reading and rewriting my daily observations into my teaching journal, I speculated on recurring patterns, emerging themes, aspects of classroom relationships, curriculum connections, the affective environment, and pedagogical perspectives. The journal-writing process allowed me to examine my initial drama planning in more detail, to study the connections of the drama applications with the prescribed district curriculum, and to more fully articulate my thoughts surrounding my classroom teaching and the children's reactions to my content-area instruction. I was also able to reflect on our dramatic actions and pedagogic processes over the extended period of time.

The voices of the children are woven throughout this narrative study. I recorded both their verbal responses and nonverbal actions in my field notebooks in as much detail as possible during our daily debriefings. Because of the children's age and the difficulty they have in expressing themselves through extended writing, the children's points of view and narratives about creative drama were also documented through semi-weekly audiotaped interviews. All 24 students were audiotaped on individual cassette tapes at least twice during the study process. . . . In order to capture the individual inflections, tonal qualities, and nuances of the children's dialogue, I personally transcribed the audiotape interviews and organized them for later review and analysis. . . . The children were encouraged to share their audiotapes within the classroom. Add-on responses and reflections were then solicited through the children's routine "question and comment" conversations with each other.

The children were also asked to interview each other about their participation in creative-drama activities. . . . In order to solicit the children's more elaborated thoughts and to provide a forum for those questions, which I had noted as I transcribed the children's audiotapes, I decided to also videotape the children in small groups as we listened to and discussed their audiotapes. . . . During the first few discussions, I simply placed the video camera on its tripod and let it run. Later on, the children took turns running the video camera and focusing in (sort of) on the person who was speaking.

Videotapes of selected drama activities were also incorporated into the study. The simultaneous enactments of the children during various drama activities were recorded on a semiweekly basis. Most videotaping sessions were predetermined as an integral part of my lesson planning. . . . Factors such as the nature of the drama activity, the daily schedule, video camera accessibility, and the requests of the children also influenced videotaping times. The use of videotape allowed me to study the temporal, nonverbal, and social aspects of the drama activities more systematically. The video camera also allowed me to view myself in my roles as classroom manager, drama leader, and small-group discussion participant. In order to compare the children's perceptions of learning with drama, some drama debriefings were simultaneously videotaped as the children viewed the initial videotape of their drama activities on a VCR and commented on their taped drama actions. This gave the children (and myself) the opportunity to view ourselves "in dramatic classroom action." This type of video debriefing provided one basis of comparison of the children's point-of-view about learning and my pedagogical perceptions.

Approximately eighteen hours of videotape were collected by the children and myself over the course of the study. . . . I formatted a general application of Erickson's [1992] "Five Stages of Ethnographic Microanalysis of Interaction" to provide a framework for detailed elaboration of my field notes and journal descriptions, to highlight the nuances of nonverbal communications, to define speaker-to-speaker relationships, as well as to become an outside observer of my own actions and teaching behaviors. By following this adapted format, I transcribed 61 pages of video commentary and was able to construct detailed narrative portrayals of the creative-dramatics process.

I also gathered other modes of student response through the study of varied classroom artifacts. A learning log was used as a source of description of the ways in which the children thought about their own subject-area learning and their creative-drama experiences. The children were encouraged to express their thinking through both illustrations and writings. I also examined the extended writing portions of content-area assessments as required through the district's grading policies and "Focused Correction Areas" and documented when and how the children's learning through drama activities was evident.

Two student teachers, one parent volunteer aide, and two other elementary classroom teachers were asked to observe selected drama activities within our classroom. The selection of the adult observers was primarily based upon mutual compatibility of our teaching/aiding schedules. . . . I audiotaped all five of the adult discussions after each drama observation. . . . Although most adults seemed "nervous" about supplying the "right answers" during our interview, our discussions barely touched on the format for the drama-observation protocol. Instead, we tended to focus on the observer's perceptions of the children's involvement in the drama activity, the children's verbal discussions of the topics under study, my roles as drama leader and classroom manager, and the learning atmosphere of the classroom as accented through the creative drama process. I transcribed these audiotapes and gave a copy of each transcription to the individual adult. These interviews informed and elaborated my own thinking concerning the direction and situation of my guiding questions within this unfolding study.

# PART 6: STRUCTURE OF THE DISSERTATION AND A NOTE ON DISCURSIVE TEXT

*Authors' Commentary.* Having the mass of raw texts described above, Lynn faced the challenge of crafting a coherent dissertation that would represent the complexity of her study as well as the pedagogical insights she had derived from it. Here is the chapter outline from her final dissertation, which illustrates the point that narrative studies often cannot be adequately represented within the traditional format of the five-chapter dissertation.

In reviewing the chapter outline, take a moment to look at the structure of Chapter II, in which Lynn draws upon formal literature first to explain various conceptions of and terminology for drama and then to link creative dramatics to pedagogy, elementary curriculum, and classroom practice. By the end of Lynn's second chapter, a reader with no prior knowledge of creative dramatics will have gained an orientation to this discourse as well as an understanding of the importance of the study.

Chapter I. Introduction

Intent of the Study

Guiding Questions

Importance of the Study

Chapter II. Drama Definitions: A Selected Review of the Literature

Definitions of Drama in Education

Drama as Subject and as Process

Types of Educational Drama

Classroom Drama Situated in Educational Context

Chapter III. Drama Data: The Study Process

Narrative Inquiry

Description of the School Setting

The Children

Duration of the Study

The Data Collection Process

## Case Example 3

# *A Narrative Study of Three Levels of Reflection in a College Composition Class*

## *Teacher Journal, Student Portfolios, Teacher-Student Discourse*

Patricia L. McMahon, PhD

## PART 1: DISSERTATION ABSTRACT

*Authors' Commentary.* Because of her narrative proclivities, Pat worked intuitively within a highly interpretive tradition and implicitly built her logic-of-justification by tacitly drawing upon her literary background. At the time Pat began to work on her study, narrative inquiry was just beginning to enter the discourses of educational research. Often, however, narrative inquiry was framed in one of two ways. One was the collecting of "stories" from research participants as data for the study of a particular issue or question. The stories were subsequently analyzed to extract information related to the issue or question. Often, the original stories never appear in the research account, or at most, snippets of the stories are used to illustrate a particular point. This approach to narrative often entailed the collection of enough stories to warrant empirical knowledge claims about a population under study within a social-science perspective. The other approach to narrative inquiry was to collect data about the lives of individuals in a more empirical fashion (e.g., observation, interviews) and then represent the data through a crafted story. Pat's study represents a third meaning of narrative: an inchoate way of coming to know. As Pat says, "I always think in stories."

For us, Pat's study represents an interesting and pivotal point in the evolution of qualitative dissertations within our study group. Prior to her work, dissertations of group members had become increasingly interpretive, and many were, in essence, personal narratives, but we had not thought to explicitly name this a dissertation genre. With her background in English literature and her practice as a composition teacher, Pat was the first study group member to draw upon the discourses about narrative that had been growing among educational researchers. Looking back from her study, we now recognize that prior dissertations had been fairly conservative, still attending to epistemological issues embedded in a more postpositive tradition. Pat moved us into a new ballpark, a change that we did not fully comprehend until two years later, when Kathy Ceroni defended her study (Case Example 4).

This is a narrative study, which focuses on the struggles of a composition teacher wishing to create a more personally meaningful learning experience for students and teacher alike. In Chapter I, I introduce my desire to involve students more rigorously in their own writing process and in the life of the class. In Chapter II, I begin to think about reflection in the composition curriculum and devise an educational encounter to engage my students in the process of reflection.

The centerpiece of this curriculum is the requirement of a writing portfolio, for which I provide no specific guidelines or model. Purposely problematizing the learning experience, I ask my students to capture their thinking both in the form of the reflective content of their portfolio and in negotiating for themselves a reflective procedure which allows them to create the structure of the portfolio itself.

Chapter III, my reflective journal, is the story of what occurs in the classroom as a result of this task. Here, I explain what transpires during the course of one semester when students are asked to construct knowledge for themselves, and I describe our work as a discourse community as we attempt to understand how knowledge is made and what it means to reflect.

In Chapter IV, I am faced with the task of analyzing 65 student portfolios in order to reach conclusions about the nature of reflection exhibited within them. Struggling to envision a conceptual framework to capture the range of material before me, I realize I am working to make meaning, trusting the same inductive process in which I had placed my students. Eventually, I see my students' writing as their means of making sense of the portfolio experience itself.

Four categories of response to the portfolio emerge: "Searching for Boundaries," "Finding a Voice," "Pursuing Connections," "Making Discoveries." I describe each mode of interpretation in Chapter V, where I present individual portrayals of students' reflection as it is represented in their writing and in their discourse.

## PART 2: RESONATING WITH RAW TEXTS—COMING TO INTERPRETATIONS

*Authors' Commentary.* In the following passage, Pat describes her process for dealing with the 65 portfolios she had collected from her students. Her description helps to illustrate several important points about resonating with raw texts. First, notice that Pat kept each portfolio intact, making notes about her observations of each text. This is consistent with her background in literary criticism and

*(Continued)*

(Continued)

with the concept of *close reading* of original texts. It is also consistent with a literary conception of narrative. Others, working in more analytic modes, might have fractured the raw texts into words or phrases and then worked with the fragments. Second is Pat's multiple readings of the portfolios. One of the most common mistakes we see students make is to stop at a point similar to Pat's second reading. They have noted some similarities in the raw texts and begin to write about these as "the findings" of their study. Not knowing what to do with the differences within and among texts, they begin to ignore the nuances and in the process subvert their original intent to "understand the lived experiences of individuals." Third, Pat mentions the inductive nature of the process—not knowing what might ultimately be important to say about the portfolios. Reading even this brief account of her process can help to allay concerns that she was just looking to confirm what she already believed about portfolio making.

My review of the 65 portfolios consisted of reading each portfolio several times, at the end of which I had filled six legal-sized notebooks. The first time I read, I did so quickly, taking very general notes on what each of the portfolios included. This initial reading was my way of getting acquainted with the range of material and writing in those portfolios. There was just so much to absorb, and I didn't know what I was looking for, so I felt it necessary to take many notes on each of the portfolios in order to give myself a stable record of what I had been able to notice.

My second review of the portfolios entailed a much closer reading of my students' work. During this time, my note taking grew much more detailed, as I began to detect general patterns among the portfolios. My note taking in this phase allowed me to keep track of portfolio "families." In other words, I was able to see similarities emerging among the students' work, and I took note of why some of these portfolios looked alike. In addition to recognizing and recording the overall similarities, I also had to record the differences within these portfolio families. In the process of this second reading, I was also able to note which portfolios did not seem to fit in any family or grouping. These portfolios, and there seemed to be many, caused me to take more notes than the others, because I was working to discern a "wholeness" to each of them, and I couldn't at this point. Because I couldn't be sure which information would be relevant, I could not afford to be selective about what I recorded. I wrote as much detail as possible about what was in those portfolios. One of the benefits of note taking at this stage was that it forced me to attend to the detail of what each student had done.

By the third time I read the portfolios, I knew I had to pay even more attention to detail. I had to capture specific moments from each one of the portfolios in my notes. By this I mean I was recording verbatim my students' language as they attended to what they were thinking and feeling about the portfolio requirement as well as how they explained their reasoning for including the material they chose to write about in their portfolios. I found myself highlighting certain statements or passages of writing that would in some way, I thought, enable me to get even more focused.

I had to be extremely vigilant during each of these three readings because I was never sure what material would turn out to be important to my study. My note taking was an absolutely vital part of my dissertation process. It enabled me to see what was in those port-folios and what wasn't, and in the process of recording my notes, I gradually was able to envision the possibilities. By the end of the third round of close reading and note taking, I was able to start thinking about a conceptual framework for my study.

# PART 3: POSTDISSERTATION REFLECTIONS

It is difficult for me to consider how my life has changed since I became a Doctor without embracing the moments along the way that helped me reach my goal. The idea of "becom-ing" reminds me of Eudora Welty (1984), specifically her elegant autobiography, *One Writer's Beginnings,* in which she marks the unfolding stages of her development as a writer with chapters titled "Listening," "Learning to See," and "Finding a Voice." Although Welty is describing the process of becoming a writer of fiction, I believe I moved through this same pattern of consciousness while writing my dissertation. Of course, the narrative nature of my dissertation lends itself to Welty's philosophy, but I am inclined to say that all good inter-pretive research comprises these stages of awareness in the journey to become a scholar, and these stages are amorphous and reflexive.

Long before I actually began writing my dissertation, I was listening. Soon after I began my doctoral studies, I realized that at least part of the inherent drama of being a doctoral student was knowing how to listen and to whom. One of my professors, eventu-ally a member of my dissertation committee, was fond of saying, "Writing a dissertation should change your life!" His own dissertation had been reviewed in *The New York Times,* and its subsequent acclaim had indeed, I surmised, changed his life. I didn't think there was even a remote chance of my work finding its way to *The New York Times* or even the local gazette, but I did hold on to the possibility that writing a dissertation could change one's life. I think I heard what he wanted me to, and while the idea of writing a disserta-tion was still frightening, his mantra reaffirmed something I had only dared to wish: Writing a dissertation did not have to be the unpleasant obligatory conclusion to one's coursework. It was around this time in my studies that I vowed to stop listening to the var-ious horror stories of fellow graduate students who were further along in the program than I was. If I wanted to believe in possibilities that I could not yet even imagine, I knew I would have to listen to my own voice, a mere whisper of encouragement. But as faint as it was, I could hear it, and it made me a more careful listener. What I needed most as I approached the end of my coursework was someone else to hear me.

Someone did hear, and she is also the person who enabled me to enter another phase of my doctoral studies: learning to see. This professor offered me an alternative lens through which to see my world, and when I tried it on, the view was breathtaking. For the first time in my life, everything was in focus. This professor, eventually my dissertation chair and research advisor, Dr. Noreen Garman, introduced me to myself. As strange as this may sound, it is true. It is not enough to say that she introduced me to qualitative research. What I learned in her classes is that I cannot separate myself from my research. And so, the more I grew to under-stand my research stance, my worldview, the better acquainted I became with myself: the indi-vidual, the teacher, the writer, the interpretive researcher.

Now I could hear my voice; it was louder, and I thought it was the voice of a storyteller. What had been an unformed wish, that writing my dissertation would not be a sterile, uneventful undertaking, now became a promise: I could seize this opportunity to write a dissertation about something that really mattered to me. I saw my dissertation as an invitation to immerse myself in an extended inquiry. I would write to discover how I could become a better teacher, and I could use narrative as a means of coming to know. This is why writing my dissertation was one of the most meaningful events of my life. Through my writing, I found my voice, and a teacher-researcher emerged. This highly focused exploration of my teaching was the gift that my dissertation presented me.

Part of the gift of writing my dissertation was the hard work it required. It was an extended lesson in learning about my students, my teaching, and myself. It was also a lesson about thinking and writing. Eudora Welty (1984) states, "Learning stamps you with its moments. It isn't steady. It's a pulse" (p. 10). I believe this insight accurately reflects one's movement through the entire arc of the dissertation process, from the time a graduate student begins to imagine what she will study to the day she submits her document for review and defends her work. But certainly, Welty's description of the pulselike process of learning resonates most strongly with me when I think about the actual task of writing my dissertation. As I look back on the experience, I can feel the tempo of my own moments of discovery as I wrote. The rhythm of my writing was not always smooth, because my ability to make connections did not occur at a steady pace. Sometimes, there were long pauses between my beats of insight; I was still in the process of learning to see. Between these beats (sometimes labor-intensive episodes that seemingly yielded nothing), I would call to mind the advice of another of my teachers and dissertation committee members. His words enabled me to put the dissertation experience in perspective. He wanted me to see this time in my life for what it was, and so he used to say to me, "Remember, your dissertation is not the culmination of all you know or all you will ever be; it's your ticket into the conversation. It is the beginning of your life as a researcher, not the end." These were important words for me to hear, because they reminded me that I really was on my way to "becoming." My dissertation was not a destination; it was part of my journey to become a scholar. This meant that even the rough moments of writing (or not writing) were potentially significant opportunities for deepening my understanding not only of the focus of my study but also of my own conceptualizing and composing processes. There is such drama in this perspective! The dissertation imbues its writer with a heightened sense of awareness, a vigilance for discovering connections and making meaning. Again, I will refer to Eudora Welty (1984), who so artfully describes this experience:

> Connections slowly emerge. Like distant landmarks you are approaching, cause and effect begin to align themselves, draw closer together. Experiences too indefinite of outline in themselves connect and are identified as a larger shape. And suddenly a light is thrown back, as when your train makes a curve, showing that there has been a mountain of meaning rising behind you on the way you've come, is rising there still, proven now through retrospect. (p. 98)

Looking back on my dissertation journey, I can still feel the impact of its effect on me. The work of my dissertation—not only what I learned but also how I learned—is reflected in the goals I set for myself today. In this sense, my interpretive study is ongoing, dynamic, generative. It was the start of an adventure that has enriched my life in many ways, both personally and professionally. I believe I am a better person for having gone through the rigors of the dissertation experience; I have a deeper understanding of who I am and what I know and how I know, and this knowledge has made me a more effective teacher. I believe I wrote my way into understanding how to become a better teacher. I excavated and explored the ground of my practice, bringing to light and naming what had previously been intuitive and unnamed. In giving language to what it is I do in the classroom, I have come to see myself and my pedagogy more clearly, and this clarity has given me a foundation upon which I may continue to build the art and scholarship of my teaching.

So, when people ask me how my life is different now that I am a PhD, I tell them that there have been no great external changes. The real changes I carry within me every time I walk into a classroom or talk with a student or reinvent my curriculum. My dissertation is now part of me, and it was through writing my narrative that I came face to face with the story of who I am. When I speak now, I hear the voice of a more knowledgeable, understanding, and invigorated teacher. This was my goal from the start. Becoming a PhD was my reward for reaching that goal.

# Case Example 4

• • • •

# *Promises Made, Promises Broken*

## *A Literary Criticism of the Pennsylvania Lead Teacher Experience*

Kathleen Ceroni, PhD

## PART 1: ABSTRACT FROM DISSERTATION

*Authors' Commentary.* Kathy's formal abstract offers a concise and straightforward account of what was actually a study full of twists and turns. In this case example, we try to give a flavor of several issues that made the study particularly challenging both for Kathy and members of her dissertation committee. As described in her abstract, Kathy set out to study the Lead Teacher Initiative in Pennsylvania. In retrospect, however, we see Kathy's study as a coming-of-age literary narrative.

This study is a personal odyssey of my struggle to come to terms with some of the recurring events and conflicts I have experienced as a teacher. Using the Pennsylvania Lead Teacher Initiative as my context, I examine its roots in teacher development reform discourses and shape an official story of how it was conceived in Pennsylvania.

After interviewing lead teachers and non-lead teachers, I created a series of encounters, which I call "inner views storied." Using literary theory (narrative) as a rationale, I create texts that portray the stories of my encounters with my participants in a way that enables the reader to hear our conversations. Since all of the characters in the inner views storied are female, a feminine perspective is present. Interestingly, a disproportionate number of Pennsylvania leader teachers are women.

Using principles of literary and educational criticism, I interpret the texts of the inner views storied, focusing on the surface and embedded meanings in them. I interpret the themes that emerge from a critical theory perspective and convey the appearance/reality dualism within the texts by showing that the Lead Teacher Initiative represents a symbolic effort to "professionalize" teaching, while the lived experience of the teachers involved in the lead teacher programs (mostly women) reveals the effects of proletarianization.

Through this interpretive study, I developed an understanding not only of the ways in which the dominant ideology functions to oppress my class and gender but also of the ways in which I have acted in complicity with the very forces I have been struggling to combat. The journey has been painful and the wisdom I have come to is a bitter wisdom, yet paradoxically, it has liberated me from the rational technical mind-set that imbues our culture and has made me available for new beginnings.

## PART 2: STATEMENT OF INTENT AND GUIDING RESEARCH QUESTIONS

The intent of this study is to create texts generated within the Pennsylvania Lead teacher Initiative in order to interpret the surface and embedded meaning within those texts.

1. What are some of the texts generated within the Pennsylvania Lead Teacher Initiative?

2. What are surface and embedded themes that emerge from these texts?

3. How are the themes interpreted relative to the appearance/reality dualism inherent in the texts?

4. How can these interpretations broaden our understanding of the ways in which teachers respond to professional development plans?

*Authors' Commentary.* The guiding research questions speak of texts, surface and embedded themes, appearance, and reality dualism. One member of Kathy's committee challenged the nature of these questions. "They talk about the process of the inquiry," he contended, "more than they indicate how each piece contributes to the conceptual 'So what?' of the inquiry." His critique raises a good point, and one that we continue to ponder in our work with students. Yet the fidelity with which Kathy adhered to literary principles throughout her study and the clarity of her rationale for each facet of the inquiry created an intellectually rigorous and defensible dissertation.

## PART 3: STANCE AND VOICE

*Authors' Commentary.* Listed below are the titles of each chapter in Kathy's final dissertation, along with the stance she claims within each chapter. In five of her six chapters, Kathy wrote in a personal, narrative voice. In Chapter III, however, where she constructed a text from public documents about the Lead Teacher Initiative, she adopted a more formal, detached stance and voice. The explicit descriptors of stance signal the perspective from which Kathy was viewing the

*(Continued)*

(Continued)

Lead Teacher Initiative and crafting text about it. Kathy's dissertation offers another example of how various discourses can serve a study. In Chapter I, Kathy drew from formal literature about teachers as a resource for school reform. In Chapter II, she used formal literature to trace the evolution of various incentive plans aimed at encouraging teachers to assume leadership roles. Chapter III captured and conveyed a very different type of discourse. Using a variety of official and "fugitive" documents, Kathy portrayed the enactment of the Lead Teacher Initiative in Pennsylvania.

Chapter I. The Promise and the Caution: Teacher Leadership as Resource
    (Stance—Teacher as Researcher)

Chapter II. The Promise in Perspective: A View of Teacher Leadership Incentive Plans
    (Stance—Researcher as Inquirer)

Chapter III. The Promise Made: The Official Story of the Pennsylvania Lead Teacher Initiative
    (Stance—Researcher as Documenter)

Chapter IV. Teachers' "Inner Views" of the Pennsylvania Lead Teacher Experience
    (Stance—Researcher as Literary Theorist)

Chapter V. The Promise Revisited: An Interpretation of the Contradictions Embedded in the "Inner Views Storied" of the Pennsylvania Lead Teacher Experience
    (Stance—Researcher as Literary Critic)

Chapter VI. The Promise Abandoned: The Illusory Nature of Teacher Leadership Reform
    (Stance—Researcher as Teacher)

# PART 4: ISSUES OF ONTOLOGY AND WARRANTING KNOWLEDGE CLAIMS

*Authors' Commentary.* The text in this part of the case example represents our attempt to describe how Kathy's study challenged us and other members of her committee to reexamine our assumptions about objectivity, subjectivity, intersubjectivity, and the relational nature of understanding. Fearing that shading such a long passage would be visually distracting, we have highlighted only this brief introductory paragraph as our commentary. We want to make clear, however, that the following narrative is our representation of Kathy's dissertation experience. Were she to give her account of the experience, it could be quite different.

As part of her efforts to capture the lead teacher experience, Kathy interviewed more than 20 teachers, some of whom served in a lead teacher capacity and some of whom worked with lead teachers. As Kathy struggled with how to present more than 20 raw interview texts, she came to the realization that it would not be feasible to include verbatim transcripts of all the interviews. As Kathy reflected further, she was drawn to the stories of 8 teachers. Although she used all of the interviews to inform her thinking, it was these 8 stories that Kathy chose to represent as experiential text in Chapter IV of her dissertation. After drafting the first interview, Kathy shared it with us. Maria's immediate reaction was, "Good grief! She can't use these interviews. There's no semblance of objectivity or neutrality. She's put words in the teachers' mouths. She's finished sentences for them. She shared her own biases and experiences. This isn't legitimate interviewing."

Following this mental outburst was a second, more tentative reaction.

> Wait a minute. At the beginning of this chapter, she explained how she was going to present these interviews and why she was doing it that way. It made sense when I read it. She made a case for doing the interviews this way. Maybe I've got too narrow a view of interviewing. Maybe she's working from a different set of assumptions.

When we shared this response with Kathy, her initial reaction was to insist that the interviews did reflect the teachers' thinking, because she had audiotaped the interviews and transcribed them verbatim. She kept insisting, "But this is what the teachers really said. I was really careful with the transcription. I even included all the *ums, uh-huhs,* and pauses." This focus on procedure, however, missed the point. Because Kathy had not followed the conventions of social-science interviewing, she was hard-pressed to warrant the transcripts as the authentic experiences and thoughts *of the teachers.*[2] Yet the interviews were compelling and not easily dismissed.

As Kathy continued to think more deeply about what the interviews represented, she came to realize that the transcripts were an authentic account of her conversations with the teachers. And the conversations were, in turn, an authentic account of her own struggle to understand herself—her longing to be seen as a committed professional, her desire to make a positive contribution to school reform, and her evolving sense of betrayal when promises of teacher empowerment felt once again like a manipulative ploy. The interviews represented a dialectical process of coming to know herself. As she elaborated on her rationale for the interviews, she came eventually to the concept of *inner views storied.* Drawing from discourses on dialectic, dialectical knowing, narrative, and story, Kathy built a logic-of-justification for this concept. In the end, these interviews represented Kathy's mode for drawing out and examining her own tacitly held views of the Lead Teacher Initiative, professionalism, power, and trust between teachers and school administrators.

This became a major point of contention during the dissertation meeting, when one committee member asked in so many words, "If it is your intention to examine the lead teacher experience, how can you claim that these *inner views storied* accurately capture what is really happening with the initiative?" It is impossible to do justice to this question within the space limitations of this case example. The question, however, strikes at the heart of the issue of what is under study. In Kathy's study, the answer is multilayered.

Embedded in the title of Kathy's dissertation proposal were two major concepts: the Lead Teacher Initiative, and promises made and broken. As Kathy lived with the study, the Lead Teacher Initiative became the less compelling phenomenon to her. As she wrestled with the meaning of her raw texts, the initiative per se began to serve more and more as a context for looking at the phenomenon of teacher empowerment, or more to the point, disempowerment. This shift between what is the figure and what is the background is not uncommon in qualitative studies. Resonating with the study entails a willingness to live with the uncertainty of having the phenomenon and context fade in and out of focus, catching a glimmer of a picture only to have it blur into the masses of raw texts.

On the surface, Kathy's study is about the Lead Teacher Initiative. Beneath that, however, the Lead Teacher Initiative serves as a symbol of the never-ending parade of reform initiatives that tout empowerment and professionalism for teachers. In this regard, the Lead Teacher Initiative serves as a symbolic representation of Kathy's sense of professionalism and power (or, more to the point, powerlessness) in her role as committed teacher. Thus, Kathy herself becomes a symbol of other teachers who are asked to believe in and support various reform initiatives. Had Kathy embedded her study within an empirical tradition, the results she generated would not have been warranted by her inquiry process. By framing the inquiry within the genre of literary criticism, Kathy carefully created a logic-of-justification that warrants the study and the meanings she generates.

As long as Kathy insisted that the interviews were about the teachers and about the Lead Teacher Initiative, she was on shaky ontological ground. By claiming the interviews as *her* inner views storied and then building a logic-of-justification for this concept, Kathy provided ontological warrants for her way of coming to understand her reactions to school reform initiatives. The verisimilitude of her experiential text allows readers to share vicariously in Kathy's dawning realization of her own assumptions, vulnerabilities, blind spots, and values that contribute to her seduction by the promises made. This, in turn, sets the stage for her interpretation of the concept *promises broken.*

Through a literary criticism of the inner views storied, Kathy called attention to the nuances of language and experience that account for her feelings of betrayal. These interpretations ultimately led Kathy to the concept of *bitter wisdom,* which became the major message or lesson learned from the study.

As Kathy laid out what she meant by *bitter wisdom,* she connected her own idiosyncratic experience to a more universal human experience of professionals caught between promises made and promises broken. She did not claim that her experience corresponded in detail to the experiences of all or even some teachers. But in portraying the story of her dissertation inquiry, Kathy took readers on a journey from naiveté to bitter wisdom; from trust and hope to betrayal and despair; from the promise of making a difference in the nature of schooling to the "reality" of being a pawn in some larger organizational game. By sharing vicariously in this journey, readers may revisit similar experiences of their own and come to understand more deeply the nature of professional disillusionment.

# Case Example 5

● ● ● ●

# *Our* Changing *Town,*
# *Our* Changing *School*

## *Is Common Ground Possible?*[3]

Jean Konzal, EdD

*Authors' Commentary.* The case example contains several excerpts from Jean's dissertation. The first, taken from her abstract, sets the stage for the study. Next is the table of contents, which illustrates how distinctive a dissertation structure can be. The final excerpts, taken from her afterword, highlight some of the difficulties that arose from Jean's decision to claim Readers Theater as her genre.

## PART 1: ABSTRACT

Attempts to reform secondary-school classroom practices have been a focus for educators throughout this century. But each time changes have been attempted, they have been met with resistance and have eventually failed. Virtually unexplored among the reasons for failure has been the inability of the schools to engage the parents in the reform efforts and to create common understandings of "good" secondary schools. The purposes of this study are to uncover the complexities of today's reform efforts in secondary schools—especially as they relate to the difficulties faced by parents and educators as they attempt to come to common ground in defining classroom practices that are found in good secondary schools; to portray the dramas inherent in parent and educator relationships and the dilemmas facing them as they try to find common ground, using Readers Theater as a vehicle for portrayal; and to move educators and parents to think about these dilemmas and to take action toward resolving them.

## PART 2: STATEMENT OF INTENT AND GUIDING RESEARCH QUESTIONS

The last sentence of the abstract is a verbatim restatement of the intent of the study.

1. In what ways does using the metaphor of *research as art* rather than *research as science* influence the methodology and portrayal of research findings in this study?

2. Based on current literature concerning a parent's role in reform efforts and on the researcher's own personal and professional experiences as a parent and an educator, what societal and educational conditions influence parent/school relationships in the context of secondary school reform?

3. In terms of defining "good" secondary schools, is common ground possible among parents? And is common ground possible between parents and educators?

4. What are the dilemmas faced by parents and educators as they attempt to build common understandings about "good" secondary schools as interpreted by the researcher?

*Authors' Commentary.* Notice that the intent of Jean's study embodies not only the generation of knowledge but also a call to action. It was this latter intent that pushed Jean to find a vehicle for promoting dialogue that could create common understandings among parents and educators. Readers Theater eventually emerged as that vehicle that, in turn, led to the following format for the dissertation.

## PART 3: DISSERTATION FORMAT

*Authors' Commentary.* The organization of Jean's final dissertation serves to illustrate several important points. First, it is a good example of form following content. Jean uses the language of the theater to organize the major sections of her document. This allows her to present a great deal of complex information in an organized way. Second, Jean did not have this organizational structure when she wrote her proposal. It emerged as she resonated with the texts she had collected and wrestled with how to appropriately represent the experiential and theoretic text. Third, notice how Jean uses appendices to provide information about her research process. In addition, one appendix contextualizes her study within four settings. This is another way of connecting an intimate study to a broader audience.

Prologue

Readers Theater Scripts

Epilogue

Afterword: On Becoming a Researcher/On Becoming an Artist

Appendices

# PART 4: ISSUES OF ONTOLOGY, EPISTEMOLOGY, AND REPRESENTATION

*Authors' Commentary.* As mentioned in the opening notes to Section 4, Jean did not initially conceive of her study as an arts-based inquiry. Rather, she came to this idea gradually as she struggled with two fundamental issues: the "What?" and "So what?" of her study. As indicated in the intent of her study, Jean set out "to uncover the complexities of today's reform efforts in secondary schools—especially as they relate to the relationships among parents and between parents and educators engaged in reform efforts." Having amassed approximately 1,000 pages of interview transcripts, plus artifacts of a community's school-reform efforts, Jean faced the challenge of creating a picture of this complex and dynamic educational phenomenon. In terms of the "So what?" of her study, Jean came to believe that dialogue among parents and between parents and educators is crucial yet extremely difficult. She wanted to present the implications of her study in a way that could help others generate such dialogue. These concerns led her to the notion of *Readers Theater,* a fundamental reexamination of her ontological and epistemological assumptions, and a substantive reformulation of her guiding questions.

When Jean proposed her dissertation, it conveyed her thinking about parent involvement in school reform as she understood it at the outset of her study. Once she immersed herself in the phenomenon of school reform, she came to new and deeper understandings. At that juncture, she faced a pivotal decision in the inquiry. Should she adhere to her original conceptualization, or should she fine-tune her conceptualization now that the latent image in the dissertation puddle had finally come into focus?

At the heart of this decision were several dilemmas: (a) Did the rigor and legitimacy of her study lie in adhering to the original proposal or in following the line of thinking generated from the raw texts? (b) Did fidelity to the inquiry lie in systematically accounting for all of the raw tests or in an artistic rendering of an experiential text? (c) Did the "reality" of the study lie in the verbatim statements of individual participants or in the passionate spirit communicated by the collective voices that informed Jean's thinking? Such questions cannot be taken lightly, and Jean's integrity as a researcher came through as she engaged in deliberation with us, with the chair of her committee, and with those more knowledgeable about Readers Theater.

The preceding comments may have created the impression that Jean's decision to use Readers Theater was determined solely by the intent of her study. However, as the following excerpt from her afterword indicates, Jean's choice of genre was also influenced by an interest in theater that predated the dissertation.

*Afterword Excerpt 1.* When I made the decision to return to school to pursue a doctorate, I had to make another decision—to put my newly found passion for theater into a box and place it on the shelf for the time being. For the three years prior to returning to school I had given voice to the creative part of myself through theater. I thought the decision to return to school would force me to put that aside.

*Authors' Commentary.* Jean was well into the data-gathering phase of her disserta-tion when she attended an Arts-based Educational Research Institute sponsored by the American Educational Research Association. There, she met Robert Donmoyer and June Yennie-Donmoyer, who introduced her to the concept of *Readers Theater* (Donmoyer & Yennie-Donmoyer, 1995). As she indicates in the following excerpt, this artistic form for representing the results of her study was very seductive.

*Afterword Excerpt 2.* When I returned from the institute I debated with myself whether or not to commit to such a project. Readers Theater seemed to be the perfect medium for my work. Parent voices could be presented directly. Parents would, at long last, be heard unedited. But, I was afraid. I knew I could write a report of my findings in a traditional qualitative report—I had done that before. But could I actually write a script? The more I thought about it, though, the more seduced I became by the idea, and the easier it seemed to do. I started talking with others. "I'm going to write a script. I'm going to present my study in play form." The more I said this, the more I convinced myself that I could do it, that it wouldn't be that hard a task.

And then I began the process. Like most qualitative researchers, I found myself buried in data. Where should I begin? How should I begin? As I began to organize and reorganize my data, I began to realize that I had dug myself a very large hole. Not only had I committed myself to making sense out of this data in a way that would be credible in the research community, but I had also committed myself to do it in an aesthetically pleasing way. While I was a novice researcher, I soon discovered I was even more of a novice when it came to writing Readers Theater scripts.

I had none of the craft of scriptwriting available to me. I have to admit to a very naive view of the craft. All I had to do was piece together dialogue from the parent transcripts, and voila, a script would emerge. Wrong! The response to my first attempts was sobering.

Learning the craft of writing a Readers Theater script was a challenge for me. I came to the process with little understanding of what it takes to craft a script. Not only did I have no experience writing a script of any kind, I had to learn how to craft a Readers Theater script, which was significantly different from a traditional script. . . . When I think back to my glib pronouncements that I will write a script, I am embarrassed by my naiveté. Any art form, in addition to requiring an aesthetic sensibility, requires mastery of the techniques of the form.

*Authors' Commentary.* This passage from Jean's afterword underscores an important issue in crafting a study. When Jean came upon the idea of Readers Theater, it seemed to satisfy three converging needs: her growing affinity for the-ater, a desire to cultivate her aesthetic nature, and the intent of her study. As Jean points out, however, she had no experience in actually writing scripts, nor a real-istic appraisal of her capacity to create such artistic pieces. In the end, Jean strug-gled not only with the act of creating art but also with the tension between what constitutes research and what constitutes art. Jean had already completed a major

*(Continued)*

(Continued)

draft of her dissertation when her tacit epistemological assumptions about art and research not only emerged but also clashed. Coming to grips with these issues necessitated a rewriting of virtually the entire dissertation. To preserve the artistic integrity she was striving to create in the dissertation, and to satisfy strongly embedded assumptions of rigorous inquiry, Jean included four substantive appendices that described her inquiry process, the context for her study, and the results of two surveys in a more traditional, science-based style.

We offer this commentary, not to dissuade students from engaging in an arts-based genre of qualitative inquiry, but as a warning to proceed with caution. Arts-based genres, particularly the notion of telling stories that has become so popular in the past two decades, can be extremely seductive, especially to those with an aversion to statistics. Yet the mere attraction to such genres is not enough. Through the Reflective Interludes, students are encouraged to carefully weigh the talents and skills that they might bring to such an inquiry. As Jean's experience illustrates, lack of preparation can be overcome if students are willing to commit to the intensive learning process that extends the time for completing the dissertation. Without such commitment—and integrity—students run the risk of completing a conceptually flawed dissertation and undermining the credibility of such studies within the university and field of study.

# Case Example 6

# *A Special Program for Gifted Female Adolescents*

## *A Conceptual Case Study for Planning Curriculum*

Joan Leukhardt, PhD

*Authors' Commentary.* Joan Leukhardt wanted to understand why gifted female students tended not to take advantage of programs in math and science once they reached adolescence. She decided to investigate this phenomenon within a gifted program at her school called the Experience Excursion. This Case Example contains Joan's account of her thinking process as she tried to come to grips with her sense of what was going on with the 48 female participants in the program. Particularly noteworthy in Joan's account are four points. First, as a teacher of math and science, Joan came to the dissertation inclined to believe that quantitative data would be informative. Indeed, she drew upon quite a bit of quantitative data in her quest to understand the students. Yet as she resonated with the data and her own experiences with the gifted students, she knew that the numbers did not tell the whole story. Second, in one effort to create a manageable, stable record, Joan drew upon a framework in the literature on gifted students. Interestingly, this framework fit—sort of—and she was able to draw some meaningful insights from this iteration of interpretation. All too often, we see students stop at this point, satisfied that they have something to present in the results and conclusions section of the dissertation. Frequently, these students are operating with vague stereotypes of how data are supposed to be analyzed and presented. Joan, however, was not satisfied with what she perceived to be a rather thin and sketchy interpretation. Her persistence in resonating more deeply with the raw texts is the third point worth noting. In trusting her own impressions and observations, Joan exemplifies the notions of *self as instrument, resonating with texts,* and *reflection.* Fourth, the final frame for understanding the gifted adolescents came from outside the study, but not

*(Continued)*

(Continued)

from a preexisting theory of gifted students. Rather, Joan's theoretic representation came from her knowledge and love of Shakespeare. This illustrates Eisner's (1991) notion of *seeing with an enlightened eye* and Glaser and Strauss's (1967) notion of *theoretical sensitivity* or *theoretical wisdom*. It also illustrates the point that the meanings derived from the study are not contained in the raw texts per se, but rather in what sense the researcher makes of them.

The following passage is excerpted from pages 56 through 62 of Joan's study. Although this dissertation was completed in 1983, Joan's description of her struggle to make sense of her "data" foreshadows many of the issues inherent in arts-based, interpretive research. Joan organized this passage into several subsections that lay out the progression of thinking that brought her to an aha moment.

## A. BACKGROUND INFORMATION

My search for a useful way to group the multitude of data on participants was a long and difficult process. In some ways, such as family background and intelligence quotients (IQ), the participants were quite homogenous, and facts can be succinctly stated. They were from white, middle-class, suburban families with traditional structures; multiple children; mothers as full-time homemakers or in the clerical, nursing, or teaching fields; fathers in the manager/administrator, professional/technical, or craft/shop-work fields. IQ scores ranged from 122 to 148, with only three scores lower than 130; the mean IQ was 135. . . .

After noting that the above characteristics were to be expected in the conservative community and in the school's gifted program, I had the task of sorting the myriad of other details I had gathered in order to discern meaning from them.

## B. TWO ATTEMPTS AT GROUPING PARTICIPANTS

A logical grouping of students was according to grade levels. That grouping did produce results, which showed some similarities among participants within the same grade and some difference between participants in different grades. Those differences along grade-level lines have program implications . . . , but they did not help me determine characteristics that would give a sufficient picture of the participants.

I next made an attempt to analyze participants according to their observed orientation toward traditional values. Details emerged from the analysis, but the personalities of the participants did not come alive. My understanding of them as individuals did not increase in meaningful ways, but I did arrive at another recommendation for educational programs.

*Authors' Commentary.* Joan's description of these two potential ways of grouping participants illustrates her avoidance of a pitfall that we commonly see among students who are trapped in a scientific or scientistic way of thinking. In short, they display the data according to such obvious and simplistic characteristics, which affords them very little to say beyond a restatement of the "facts." Joan's intuitive sense that this would not be meaningful kept her pushing deeper into her raw texts.

## C. HIGH ACHIEVERS, SOCIAL LEADERS, CREATIVES, AND REBELS

Still feeling the need to describe participants more clearly, I grappled with another frame work for perceiving gifted students. My and others' experiences in the field of education of the gifted . . . had resulted in a neat way of categorizing gifted students: High Achievers, Social Leaders, Creatives, and Rebels. Using these four examples of gifted students, I found it easy to relate their characteristics to inservice and preservice teachers. Knowing that gifted students range from "the shiny-faced cherub thirsting for knowledge" to "the sullen, smirking fighter parrying for advantage" helps teachers develop realistic expectations and teaching strategies for each type.

I now hoped I might be able to group the Experience Excursion participants into these rubrics, perhaps adding to the existing profiles by further delineating the characteristics inherent in each behavior type. . . . There were many High Achievers within the group [of study participants]; there were many Social Leaders; there were several Creatives; there were no Rebels. That distribution of the four types of gifted students was not surprising. It has been my experience that the first two categories usually comprise the largest group within our total gifted program, and because the Experience Excursion participants were self-selected, it was unlikely that Rebels would be among those who would join an "establishment" group.

However, I was troubled by the fact that the three types represented within the Experience Excursion did not appear to be exclusive of each other. Although there were participants who fit distinct definitions, there were many others who fit into two or all three of the categories, such as the cheerleading captain who had a grade point average (GPA) of 4.3, the varsity swimmer who had a GPA of 3.6, and the poet-painter–newspaper editor who had a GPA of 4.2.

Whereas this classification system advanced my thinking in regard to describing the Experience Excursion participants, it proved inadequate by itself. There were other, as yet intangible, qualities that cut across those four behavior types, blurring the lines between them and not giving a clear picture of the participants.

*Authors' Commentary.* Joan's description in this passage points to another common pitfall of the unwary interpretive researcher. Overwhelmed by the volume of raw texts and unable to readily see a way to represent the range of experiences

*(Continued)*

(Continued)

reflected in the texts, students find a framework in the literature and present their results as though that further confirms the validity of the framework. This, however, is not what they had set out to do when they argued that the existing literature did not sufficiently probe the nuances of a particular experience. Joan shows a discursive sensibility by recognizing a framework in the gifted education literature and acknowledging its usefulness. But she also shows a theoretic sensitivity in her intuitive feeling that there was more to say about her participants.

## D. FINDING A FRAMEWORK

High Achievers differed from each other in ways I had not yet discerned. I wanted to capture the nuances of their behavior that would give me clues to their unfathomed characteristics. Setting aside the boxes of collages, the rolls of charts, and the stacks of transcripts, forms, and computer printouts, I closed my eyes and created mental pictures of my participants. There was one with a direct gaze, another with a pinched face, another with wide eyes and a ready smile, and a fourth with downcast eyes. Eventually, all 48 paraded before me, projecting images of confidence, competitiveness, innocence, or concern.

I began to conceptualize a new model, a second four-factor category system—this one based on evidence of *being* rather than of *behavior.* It appeared that the demeanor I had envisioned for each participant stemmed from some inner quality of each, perhaps her will or motivation. There were differences in the reasons participants achieved well and differences in the reasons participants were active socially. It seemed to me that exploring those differences within a construal derived from the four modes of bearing that I "saw"—certain attitudes, deportment, and carriage—could produce vivid pictures of the participants.

*Authors' Commentary.* Joan's press to go beyond behaviors to being exemplifies a point we made in relation to worldview and one's ontological assumptions about ways of being in the world. Although Joan did not discount the usefulness of understanding patterns of behavior, she did not feel this gave her a meaningful way of thinking about and relating to her students. It was this drive for an ontological understanding that seemed to push Joan further into conceptual reflection toward a theoretic interpretation.

## E. SHAKESPEARE'S WOMEN

At this point in my thinking, I leapt from my visualization of participants to Shakespeare's characterization of women: There was Portia, self-assured and purposeful; Cordelia, sweet and obedient; Miranda, naive and emotional; Desdemona, self-abasing and fearful.

These character types "clicked" with my overall impressions of the Experience Excursion participants. Their outward signs of motivation seemed to parallel the parts of Portia, Cordelia, Miranda, or Desdemona. I studied my list of participants and was encouraged that I could identify most of the students as one of the types. The fit became stronger as I sorted interview transcripts and other documents into the four categories. Profiles of each type emerged: facial expressions, body language, choice of dress, reaction to authorities, interactions with friends, locus of control . . . and interplay with the previously mentioned category system for gifted students. . . . These prototypes—Portia, Cordelia, Miranda, and Desdemona—would provide a meaningful characterization (an educational construal) of the participants and insight into some of their educational needs.

## F. INTERPRETIVE PROFILES OF FOUR TYPES OF GIFTED FEMALE ADOLESCENTS

The Interpretive Profiles of the four types of gifted female adolescents are divided into two parts. The script, appearing on the left-hand side of the pages, can be used in the classroom to generate discussion and to aid students in self-analysis. The notes on the script for educators, printed as a gloss in the right-hand margin, elaborate on the script with details from the study and with my conclusions as to each type's educational needs.

## NOTES

1. Recipient of the 2000 Mary Catherine Ellwein Award for Outstanding Qualitative Dissertation of the American Educational Research Association; Recipient of the 1999 University of Pittsburgh School of Education Outstanding Dissertation Award.

2. Some scholars, such as Heshusius (1994), would argue the impossibility of objectivity regardless of the procedures employed to distance researcher from participants.

3. Recipient of the 1997 Outstanding Dissertation Award of the Families as Educators Special Interest Group of the American Educational Research Association and the 1997 Mary Catherine Ellwein Outstanding Dissertation Award of the American Educational Research Association Qualitative Research Special Interest Group and Division D.

# References

Abrams, M. H. (1989). *Doing things with texts: Essays in criticism and critical theory* (M. Fischer, Ed.). New York: Norton.

Adams, M. (1984). *The writer's mind: Making writing make sense.* Lanham, MD: University Press of America.

Alasuutari, P. (1995). *Researching culture: Qualitative method and cultural studies.* London: Sage.

Allison, B., & Race, P. (2004). *The student's guide to preparing dissertations and theses.* New York: Routledge.

Almy, M., & Genishi, C. (1979). *Ways of studying children: An observation manual for early childhood teachers* (2nd ed.). New York: Teachers College Press.

Altrichter, H., Feldman, A., Posch, P., & Somekh, B. (2007). *Teachers investigate their work: An introduction to action research across the professions.* New York: Routledge.

Alvermann, D. E., O'Brien, D. G., & Dillon, D. R. (1996). On writing qualitative research. *Reading Research Quarterly, 31*(1), 114–120.

American Educational Research Association. (1992). Ethical standards of the American Educational Research Association. *Educational Researcher, 21*(7), 23–26.

Anderson, E. (2007). Feminist epistemology: An interpretation and a defense. In A. E. Cudd & Robin O. Andreasen (Eds.), *Feminist theory: A philosophical anthology* (pp. 188–209). Victoria, Australia: Blackwell.

Anderson, G. L. (2002). Reflecting on research for doctoral students in education. *Educational Researcher, 31*(7), 22–25.

Anderson, G. L. (2007). *Studying your own school: An educator's guide to qualitative practitioner action research* (2nd ed.). Thousand Oaks, CA: Corwin.

Anderson, G. L., & Herr, K. (1999). The new paradigm wars: Is there room for rigorous practitioner knowledge in schools and universities? *Educational Researcher, 28*(5), 12–31, 40.

Anderson, W. T. (1990). *Reality isn't what it used to be: Theatrical politics, ready-to-wear religion, global myths, primitive chic, and other wonders of the post-modern world.* San Francisco: Harper & Row.

Andrews, R., & Haythornthwaite, C. (Eds.). (2007). *The Sage handbook of e-learning research.* Thousand Oaks, CA: Sage.

Anfara, V. A. (Ed.). (2007). *The handbook of research in middle level education.* Charlotte, NC: Information Age.

Anfara, V. A., & Mertz, N. T. (Eds.). (2006). *Theoretical frameworks in qualitative research.* Thousand Oaks, CA: Sage.

Angrosino, M. V. (2007). *Naturalistic observation.* Walnut Creek, CA: Left Coast Press.

Angrosino, M. V., & Mays de Perez, K. A. (2003). Rethinking observation: From method to context. In N. K. Denzin & Y. S. Lincoln (Eds.), *Collecting and interpreting qualitative materials* (2nd ed., pp. 107–154). Thousand Oaks: Sage.

Angus, I., & Langsdorf, L. (Eds.). (1993). *The critical turn: Rhetoric and philosophy in postmodern discourse.* Carbondale: Southern Illinois University Press.

Annells, M. (1996). Grounded theory method: Philosophical perspectives, paradigm of inquiry, and postmodernism. *Qualitative Health Research, 6*(3), 379–393.

Asamen, J. K., Ellis, M. L., & Berry, G. L. (Eds.). (2008). *The SAGE handbook of child development, multiculturalism, and media.* Thousand Oaks, CA: Sage.

Atkinson, P. (1990). *The ethnographic imagination: Textual constructions of reality.* New York: Routledge.

Ayers, W. (1997). *A kind and just parent: The children of juvenile court.* Boston: Beacon.

Ayers, W., & Schubert, W. (1992). Do the right thing: Ethical issues and problems in the conduct of qualitative research in the classroom. *Teaching and Learning, 6*(2), 19–24.

Ball, D. L., & Forzani, F. M. (2007). What makes education research "Educational"? *Educational Researcher, 36*(9), 529–540.

Banks, J. A. (1995). The historical reconstruction of knowledge about race: Implications for transformative learning. *Educational Researcher, 24*(2), 15–25.

Banks, J. A., & McGee Banks, C. A. (1995). *Handbook of research on multicultural education.* New York: Macmillan.

Barone, T. E. (1992). A narrative of enhanced professionalism: Educational researchers and popular storybooks about school people. *Educational Researcher, 21*(8), 15–24.

Barone, T. E. (1995). The purposes of arts-based educational research. *International Journal of Educational Research, 23*(2), 169–180.

Barone, T. E. (2000). *Aesthetics, politics, and educational inquiry: Essays and examples.* New York: Peter Lang.

Barone, T. E. (2001). Science, art, and the predisposition of educational researchers. *Educational Researcher, 30*(7), 24–28.

Barone, T. E., & Eisner, E. W. (1997). Arts-based educational research. In R. M. Jaeger (Ed.), *Complementary methods for research in education* (pp. 71–98). Washington, DC: American Educational Research Association.

Barthes, R. (1976). *The pleasure of the text* (R. Miller, Trans.). London: Cape.

Barthes, R. (1979). From work to text. In J. Harari (Ed.), *Textual strategies: Perspectives on post-structuralist criticism* (pp. 73–82). Ithaca, NY: Cornell University Press.

Bartholomae, D., & Petrosky, A. (1999). *Ways of reading: An anthology for writers* (5th ed.). Boston: Bedford/St. Martin's.

Belth, M. (1965). *Education as a discipline: A study of the role of models in thinking.* Boston: Allyn & Bacon.

Berliner, D. C. (2002). Educational research: The hardest science of all. *Educational Researcher, 31*(8), 18–20.

Berliner, D. C., & Calfee, R. C. (1996). *Handbook of educational psychology: A project of Division 15, the Division of Educational Psychology of the American Psychological Association.* New York: Macmillan.

Bessant, J., Hil, R., & Watts, R. (2003). *"Discovering" risk: Social research and policy making.* New York: Peter Lang.

Best, J. W., & Kahn, J. V. (2006). *Research in education.* Boston: Allyn & Bacon.

Beverley, J. (2003). *Testimonio,* subalternity, and narrative authority. In N. K. Denzin & Y. S. Lincoln (Eds.), *Strategies of qualitative inquiry* (2nd ed., pp. 319–335). Thousand Oaks, CA: Sage.

Biklen, S. K., & Casella, R. (2006). *A practical guide to the qualitative dissertation.* New York: Teachers College Press.

Birmingham, P., & Wilkinson, D. (2003). *You and your action research project* (2nd ed.). New York: Routledge.

Blackford, J. (1997). *Cultural colonisation: Exploring the cultural frameworks of nursing practice.* Bundoora, Victoria, Australia: LaTrobe University.

Blake, D., & Hanley, V. (1995). *The dictionary of educational terms.* Aldershot, UK: Arena.

Blumenfeld-Jones, D. S. (2003, April). *Curricular thinking toward a "ground of ethics": Social imagination, relational authority and the teacher.* Paper presented at the meeting of the American Association for the Advancement of Curriculum Studies, Chicago.

Bochner, A. P. (1997). It's about time: Narrative and the divided self. *Qualitative Inquiry, 3*(4), 412–438.

Bochner, A. P. (2000). Criteria against ourselves. *Qualitative Inquiry, 6*(2), 266–272.

Bodone, F. (2005). *What difference does research make and for whom?* New York: Peter Lang.

Boehm, A. E., & Weinerg, R. A. (1997). *The classroom observer: Developing observations skills in early childhood settings* (3rd ed.). New York: Teachers College Press.

Bogdan, R. C., & Biklen, S. K. (1992). *Qualitative research for education: An introduction to theories and methods* (5th ed.). Boston: Allyn & Bacon.

Boote, D. N., & Beile, P. (2005). Scholars before researchers: On the centrality of the dissertation literature review in research preparation. *Educational Researcher, 34*(6), 3–15.

Boote, D. N., & Beile, P. (2006). On "Literature Reviews of, and for, Educational Research": A response to the critique by Joseph Maxwell. *Educational Researcher, 35*(9), 32–35.

Booth, W. C., Colomb, G. G., & Williams, J. M. (2003). *The craft of research* (2nd ed.). Chicago: University of Chicago Press.

Boser, S. (2007). Power, ethics, and the IRB: Dissonance over human participant review of participatory research. *Qualitative Inquiry, 13*(8), 1060–1074.

Bové, P. A. (1990). Discourse. In E. Lentricchia & T. McLaughlin (Eds.), *Critical terms for literary study* (pp. 50–65). Chicago: University of Chicago Press.

Brazziel, W. F. (1992). Older students and doctorate production. *Review of Higher Education, 15*(4), 449–462.

Bresler, L., & Ardichvili, A. (2002). *Research in international education: Experience, theory, and practice.* New York: Peter Lang.

Brickman, W. W. (1982). *Educational historiography: Tradition, theory, and technique.* Cherry Hill, NJ: Emeritus.

Brizuela, B. M., Stewart, J. P., Carrillo, R. G., & Berger, J. G. (Eds.). (2000). *Acts of inquiry in qualitative research.* Cambridge, MA: Harvard Educational Review.

Brodsky, C. (1987). *The imposition of form: Studies in narrative representation and knowledge.* Princeton, NJ: Princeton University Press.

Brown, A., & Dowling, P. (2007). *Doing research/reading research: A mode of interrogation for education.* New York: Routledge.

Bruner, J. (1985). Narrative and paradigmatic modes of thought. In E. Eisner (Ed.), *Learning and teaching the ways of knowing: Part H. 84th NSSE yearbook* (pp. 97–115). Chicago: University of Chicago Press.

Bruner, J. (1986). *Actual minds, possible worlds.* Cambridge, MA: Harvard University Press.

Bruner, J. (1996). *The culture of education.* Cambridge, MA: Harvard University Press.

Brunner, D. D. (1994). *Inquiry and reflection: Framing narrative practice in education.* Albany: SUNY Press.

Bryant, M. T. (2004). *The portable dissertation advisor.* Thousand Oaks, CA: Corwin.

Bullock, A., Stallybrass, O., & Trombley, S. (Eds.). (1988). *The Fontana dictionary of modern thought* (2nd ed.). London: Fontana.

Bullough, R. V. (2006). Developing interdisciplinary researchers: What ever happened to the humanities in education? *Educational Researcher, 35*(8), 3–10.

Bullough, R. V., & Pinnegar, S. (2001). Guidelines for quality in autobiographical forms of self-study research. *Educational Researcher, 30*(3), 13–21.

Burdell, P., Swadener, B. B. (1999). Critical personal narrative and autoethnography in education: Reflections on a genre. *Educational Researcher, 28*(6), 21–26.

Burgess, H., Sieminski, S., & Arthur, L. (2006). *Achieving your doctorate in education.* Thousand Oaks, CA: Sage.

Burkhardt, H., & Schoenfeld, A. H. (2003). Improving educational research: Toward a more useful, more influential, and better-funded enterprise. *Educational Researcher, 32*(9), 3–14.

Burnaford, G. E., Fischer, J., & Hobson, D. (Eds.). (2001). *Teachers doing research: The power of action through inquiry* (2nd ed.). Mahwah, NJ: Lawrence Erlbaum.

Cahnmann-Taylor, M., & Siegesmund, R. (2007). *Arts-based research in education: Foundations for practice.* New York: Routledge.

Campbell, A., & Groundwater-Smith, S. (Eds.). (2007). *An ethical approach to practitioner research: Dealing with issues and dilemmas in action research.* New York: Routledge.

Cannella, G. S., & Lincon, Y. S. (2007). Predatory vs. dialogic ethics: Constructing an illusion or ethical practice as the core of research methods. *Qualitative Inquiry, 13*(3), 315–335.

Caputo, J. D. (1987). *Radical hermeneutics: Repetition, deconstruction, and the hermeneutic project.* Bloomington: Indiana University Press.

Carson, T. R., & Sumara, D. J. (Eds.). (1997). *Action research as a living practice.* New York: Peter Lang.

Carter, K. (1993). The place of story in the study of teaching and teacher education. *Educational Researcher, 22*(1), 5–12, 18.

Casey, K. (1995–1996). The new narrative research in education. In M. W. Apple (Ed.), *Review of research in education* (pp. 211–253). Washington, DC: American Educational Research Association.

Castetter, W. B., & Heisler, R. S. (1984). Developing and defending a dissertation proposal (4th ed.). Philadelphia: University of Pennsylvania Press.

Ceroni, K. M. (1995). *Promises made, promises broken: A literary criticism of the lead teacher experience in Pennsylvania.* UMI ProQuest Digital Dissertation #AAT 9529124.

Ceroni, K. M. (2006). Coming to know through the text of talk: From interview to inner views storied to interpretation. In N. B. Garman & M. Piantanida (Eds.), *The authority to imagine: The struggle toward representation in dissertation writing* (pp. 113–125). New York: Peter Lang.

Ceroni, K. M., & Garman, N. B. (1994). The empowerment movement: Genuine collegiality or yet another hierarchy? In P. Grimmett & J. Neufcld (Eds.), *Teacher development and the struggle for authenticity* (pp. 141–161). New York: Teachers College Press.

Charmaz, K. (2003). Grounded theory: Objectivist and constructivist methods. In N. K. Denzin & Y. S. Lincoln (Eds.), *Strategies of qualitative inquiry* (2nd ed., pp. 249–291). Thousand Oaks, CA: Sage.

Cherryholmes, C. (1988). *Power and criticism: Poststructural investigations in education.* New York: Teachers College Press.

Christensen, P., & James, A. (Eds.). (2008). *Research with children: Perspectives and practices* (2nd ed.). New York: Routledge.

Christians, C. G. (2003). Sexualities, queer theory, and qualitative research. In N. K. Denzin & Y. S. Lincoln (Eds.), *The landscape of qualitative research: Theories and issues* (2nd ed., pp. 208–243). Thousand Oaks: Sage.

Christians, C. G. (2007). Cultural continuity as an ethical imperative. *Qualitative Inquiry, 13*(3), 437–444.

Clandinin, D. J., Huber, J., Huber, M., Murphy, M. S., Orr, A. M., Pearce, M., & Steeves, P. (2006). *Composing diverse identities: Narrative inquiries into the interwoven lives of children and teachers.* New York: Routledge.

Clark, C., Moss, P. A., Goering, S., Herter, R. J., Lamar, B., Leonard, D., Robbins, S., Russell, M., Templin, M., & Wascha, K. (1996). Collaboration as dialogue: Teachers and researchers engaged in conversation and professional development. *American Educational Research Journal, 33*(1), 193–231.

Clark, M. C., & Sharf, B. F. (2007). The dark side of truth(s): Ethical dilemmas in researching the personal. *Qualitative Inquiry, 13*(3), 399–416.

Clarke, A., & Erickson, G. (Eds.). (2003). *Teacher inquiry: Living the research in everyday practice.* New York: Routledge.

Cleveland, D. (2004). *A long way to go: Conversations about race by African American faculty and graduate students.* New York: Peter Lang.

Clough, P. T. (1998). *The end(s) of ethnography: From realism to social criticism* (2nd ed.). New York: Peter Lang.

Clough, P. T. (2000). Comments on setting criteria for experimental writing. *Qualitative Inquiry, 6*(2), 278–291.

Clough, P., Goodley, D., Lawthom, R., & Moore, M. (2004). *Researching life stories: Method, theory and analyses in a biographical age.* New York: Routledge.

Cochran-Smith, M., Feiman-Nemser, S., McIntyre, D. J., & Demers, K. (Eds.). (2008). *Handbook of research on teacher education* (3rd ed.). New York: Routledge.

Cochran-Smith, M., & Lytle, S. L. (1999). The teacher research movement: A decade later. *Educational Researcher, 28*(7), 15–25.

Coffey, A., & Atkinson, P. (1996). *Making sense of qualitative data: Complementary research strategies.* Thousand Oaks, CA: Sage.

Coghlan, D., & Brannick, T. (2004). *Doing action research in your own organization* (2nd ed.). Thousand Oaks, CA: Sage.

Cohen, D. H., Stern, V., & Balaban, N. (1997). *Observing and recording the behavior of young children.* New York: Teachers College Press.

Cohen, L., Manion, L., & Morrison, K. (2007). *Research methods in education* (6th ed.). New York: Routledge.

Coles, R. (1989). *The call of stories: Teaching and the moral imagination.* Boston: Houghton Mifflin.

Colwell, R. (1992). *Handbook of research on music teaching and learning: A project of the Music Educators National Conference.* New York: Macmillan.

Conlan, M. D. (2006). *The spirituality of everyday life: An heuristic phenomenological investigation.* Unpublished doctoral dissertation, University of South Australia, Underdale.

Conle, C. (2001). The rationality of narrative inquiry in research and professional practice. *European Journal of Teacher Education, 24*(1), 1–13.

Connelly, F. M., & Clandinin, D. J. (1990). Stories of experience and inquiry. *Educational Researcher, 19*(5), 2–14.

Connelly, F. M., & Clandinin, D. J. (1991). Narrative inquiry: Storied experience. In E. C. Short (Ed.), *Forms of curriculum inquiry* (pp. 121–153). Albany: SUNY Press.

Connelly, F. M., He, M. F., & Phillion, J. I. (Eds.). (2007). *The SAGE handbook of curriculum and instruction.* Thousand Oaks, CA: Sage.

Connolly, K., & Reid, A. (2007). Ethics review for qualitative inquiry: Adopting a values-based, facilitative approach. *Qualitative Inquiry, 13*(7), 1031–1047.

Conrad, C., & Serlin, R. C. (Eds.). (2006). *The SAGE handbook for research in education: Engaging ideas and enriching inquiry.* Thousand Oaks, CA: Sage.

Cooper, C. (2000). The use of electronic mail in the research process. *Nurse Researcher, 7*(4), 24–30.

Corbin, J. M. (1998). Alternative interpretations: Valid or not? *Theory & Psychology, 8*(1), 121–128.

Corbin, J. M., & Morse, J. M. (2003). The unstructured interactive interview: Issues of reciprocity and risks when dealing with sensitive topics. *Qualitative Inquiry, 9*(3), 335–354.

Corbin, J., & Strauss, A. (1990). Grounded theory research: Procedures, canons, and evaluative criteria. *Qualitative Sociology, 13*(1), 3–21.

Covino, W. A. (1994). *Magic, rhetoric, and literacy: An eccentric history of the composing imagination.* Albany: SUNY Press.

Crabtree, B. F., & Miller, W. L. (Eds.). (1992). *Doing qualitative research.* Newbury Park, CA: Sage.

Creswell, J. W. (2002). *Research design: Qualitative, quantitative, and mixed methods approaches.* Thousand Oaks, CA: Sage.

Creswell, J. W. (2007). *Qualitative inquiry and research design: Choosing among five approaches* (2nd ed.). Thousand Oaks, CA: Sage.

Cresswell, J. W., & Plano-Clark, V. L. (2007). *Designing and conducting mixed methods research.* Thousand Oaks, CA: Sage.

Crockett, D. K. (2006). *Action research and critical action research.* New York: Peter Lang.

Crosby, A. W. (1997). *The measure of reality: Quantification and Western society 1250–1600.* Cambridge, UK: Cambridge University Press.

Crossley, M., & Watson, K. (2003). *Comparative and international research in education: Globalisation, context and difference.* New York: Routledge.

Crotty, M. (1996). *Phenomenology and nursing research.* South Melbourne, Australia: Churchill Livingstone.

Crotty, M. (2003). *The foundations of social research: Meaning and perspective in the research process.* Thousand Oaks, CA: Sage.

Dalute, C., & Lightfoot, C. (Eds.). (2004). *Narrative analysis: Studying the development of individuals in society.* Thousand Oaks, CA: Sage.

Daly, K. (1997). Re-placing theory in ethnography: A postmodern view. *Qualitative Inquiry, 3*(3), 343–365.

Dana, N. F. (2003). *The reflective educator's guide to classroom research: Learning to teach and teaching to learn through practitioner inquiry.* Thousand Oaks, CA: Corwin.

Dash, L. (2007). Journalism and institutional review boards. *Qualitative Inquiry, 13*(6), 871–874.

Davies, B., & Gannon, S. (Eds.). (2006). *Doing collective biography (Conducting educational research).* New York: McGraw-Hill.

Davis, G. B., & Parker, C. A. (1979). *Writing the doctoral dissertation: A systematic approach.* Woodbury, NY: Barron's Educational Series.

Davis, O. L., & Ponder, G. (Eds.). (2007). *Handbook of curriculum inquiry.* Charlotte, NC: Information Age.

Dei, G., & Johal, G. S. (2005). *Critical issues in anti-racist research methodologies.* New York: Peter Lang.

DeLorme, D. E., Zinkhan, G. M., & French, W. (2001). Ethics and the Internet: Issues associated with qualitative research. *Journal of Business Ethics, 33,* 271–286.

deMarrais, K. (Ed.). (1998). *Inside stories: Qualitative research reflections.* Mahwah, NJ: Lawrence Erlbaum.

deMarrais, K., & LeCompte, M. D. (1999). *The way schools work: A sociological analysis of education* (3rd ed.). New York: Addison Wesley Longman.

Denzin, N. K. (1997). *Interpretive ethnography: Ethnographic practices for the 21st century.* Thousand Oaks, CA: Sage.

Denzin, N. K. (2000). Aesthetics and the practices of qualitative inquiry. *Qualitative Inquiry, 6*(2), 256–265.

Denzin, N. K., & Giardina, M. D. (Eds.). (2006). *Qualitative inquiry and the conservative challenge.* Walnut Creek, CA: Left Coast Press.

Denzin, N. K., & Giardina, M. D. (Eds.). (2007). *Ethical futures in qualitative research: Decolonizing the politics of knowledge.* Walnut Creek, CA: Left Coast Press.

Denzin, N. K., & Lincoln, Y. S. (Eds.). (1994). *Handbook of qualitative research.* Thousand Oaks, CA: Sage.

Denzin, N. K., & Lincoln, Y. S. (Eds.). (2003a). *Collecting and interpreting qualitative materials* (2nd ed.). Thousand Oaks, CA: Sage.

Denzin, N. K., & Lincoln, Y. S. (Eds.). (2003b). *The landscape of qualitative research: Theories and issues* (2nd ed.). Thousand Oaks, CA: Sage.

Denzin, N. K., & Lincoln, Y. S. (Eds.). (2003c). *Strategies of qualitative inquiry* (2nd ed.). Thousand Oaks, CA: Sage.

Denzin, N. K., & Lincoln, Y. S. (Eds.). (2005). *The SAGE handbook of qualitative research* (3rd ed.). Thousand Oaks, CA: Sage.

Denzin, N. K., Lincoln, Y. S., & Smith, L. T. (Eds.). (2008). *Handbook of critical and indigenous methodologies.* Thousand Oaks, CA: Sage.

Derrida, J. (1989). Structure, sign and play in the discourse of the human sciences (A. Bass, Trans.). In P. Rice & P. Waugh (Eds.), *Modern literary theory: A reader* (176–191). London: Edward Arnold.

Dewey, J. (1916). *Democracy and education.* New York: Macmillan.

Dewey, J. (1997). *Experience and education.* New York: Touchstone. (Original work published 1938)

Diamond, C. T. P., & Mullen, C. A. (Eds.). (1999). *The postmodern educator: Arts-based inquiries and teacher development.* New York: Peter Lang.

Dimen, M. (1989). Power, sexuality, and intimacy. In A. M. Jaggar & S. R. Bordo (Eds.), *Gender/body/knowledge: Feminist reconstructions of being and knowing* (pp. 34–51). New Brunswick: Rutgers University Press.

Dimitriads, G. (2001). Coming clean at the hyphen: Ethics and dialogue at a local community center. *Qualitative Inquiry, 7*(5), 578–597.

DiStefano, A., Rudestam, K. E., & Silverman, R. (Eds.). (2004). *Encyclopedia of distributed learning.* Thousand Oaks, CA: Sage.

Dixson, A. D., Chapman, T. K., & Hill, D. A. (Eds). (2005). Portraiture methodology [Special issue]. *Qualitative Inquiry, 11*(1).

Donmoyer, R. (1996). Educational research in an era of paradigm proliferation: What's a journal editor to do? *Educational Researcher, 25*(2), 19–25.

Donmoyer, R., & Yennie-Donmoyer, J. (1995). Data as drama: Reflections on the use of readers theater as a mode of qualitative data display. *Qualitative Inquiry, 1*(4), 402–428.

Douglas, J. D. (1985). *Creative interviewing.* Beverly Hills, CA: Sage.

Douglass, B. G., & Moustakas, C. (1985). Heuristic inquiry: The internal search to know. *Journal of Humanistic Psychology, 25*(3), 39–55.

Douvanis, G., & Brown, J. (1995). Privileged communication in educational research: The case for statutory protection. *Educational Researcher, 24*(5), 27–30.

Duke, N. K., & Beck, S. W. (1999). Education should consider alternative formats for the dissertation. *Educational Researcher, 28*(3), 31–36.

Edwards, C., Gandini, L., & Forman, G. (Eds.). (1998). *The hundred languages of children: The Reggio Emilia approach—advanced reflections* (2nd ed.). Norwood, NJ: Ablex.

Edwards, R., Nicoll, K., Solomon, N., & Usher, R. (2004). *Rhetoric and educational discourse: Persuasive texts.* New York: Routledge.

Eisenhart, M. (2001). Educational ethnography past, present, and future: Ideas to think with. *Educational Researcher, 30*(8), 16–27.

Eisenhart, M., & DeHaan, R. L. (2005). Doctoral preparation of scientifically based education researchers. *Educational Researcher, 34*(4), 3–13.

Eisenhart, M., & Towne, L. (2003). Contestation and change in national policy on "scientifically based" educational research. *Educational Researcher, 32*(7), 31–38.

Eisner, E. W. (1991). *The enlightened eye: Qualitative inquiry and the enhancement of educational practice.* New York: Macmillan.

Eisner, E. W. (1993). Forms of understanding and the future of educational research. *Educational Researcher, 22*(7), 5–11.

Eisner, E. W. (1997). The new frontier of qualitative research methodology. *Qualitative Inquiry, 3*(3), 249–273.

Eisner, E. W., & Day, M. D. (2004). *Handbook of research and policy in art education.* Mahwah, NJ: Lawrence Erlbaum.

Eisner, E. W., & Peshkin, A. (Eds.). (1990). *Qualitative inquiry in education: The continuing debate.* New York: Teachers College Press.

Elam, D., & Wiegman, R. (Eds.). (1995). *Feminism beside itself.* New York: Routledge.

Elliott, C. (1992). Where ethics comes from and what to do about it. *Hastings Center Report, 22*(4), 28–35.

Ellis, C. (2000). Creating criteria: An ethnographic short story. *Qualitative Inquiry, 6*(2), 273–277.

Ely, M., Anzul, M., Friedman, T., Garner, D., & McCormack Steinmetz, A. (1991). *Doing qualitative research: Circles within circles.* London: Falmer.

Ely, M., Vinz, R., Downing, M., & Anzul, M. (1997). *On writing qualitative research: Living by words.* London: Falmer.

English, F. W. (2000). A critical appraisal of Sara Lawrence-Lightfoot's *Portraiture* as a method of educational research. *Educational Researcher, 29*(7), 21–26.

English, F. W. (2006). *Encyclopedia of educational leadership and administration.* Thousand Oaks, CA: Sage.

Ercikan, K., & Roth, W.-M. (2006). What good is polarizing research into qualitative and quantitative? *Educational Researcher, 35*(5), 14–23.

Erickson, F. (1992). Ethnographic microanalysis of interaction. In M. D. LeCompte, W. L. Milroy, & J. Preissle (Eds.), *The handbook of qualitative research in education* (pp. 201–225). New York: Academic Press.

Erickson, K., & Stull, D. (1997). *Doing team ethnography: Warnings and advice.* Thousand Oaks, CA: Sage.

Evans, R. (2007). Existing practice is not the template: Comments on Shulman, Golde, Bueschel, and Garabedian. *Educational Researcher, 36*(9), 553–559.

Fahnestock, J., & Secor, M. (1991). The rhetoric of literary criticism. In C. Bazerman & J. Paradis (Eds.), *Textual dynamics of the professions: Historical and contemporary studies of writing in professional communities* (pp. 76–96). Madison: University of Wisconsin Press.

Farmer, T. (2002). *Using the Internet for primary research data collection: Understanding this thing we call the Internet.* Retrieved March 2, 2004, from http://infotekonline.com

Fay, B. (1987). *Critical social science: Liberation and its limits.* Oxford, UK: Polity.

Fetterman, D. M. (1998). *Ethnography: Step-by-step.* Thousand Oaks, CA: Sage.

Fine, M., & Weis, L. (1996). Writing the "wrongs" of fieldwork: Confronting our own research/writing dilemmas in urban ethnographies. *Qualitative Inquiry, 2*(3), 251–274.

Finley, S., & Knowles, J. G. (1995). Researcher as artist/artist as researcher. *Qualitative Inquiry, 1*(1), 110–142.

Finn, J. (2005). *Getting a Ph.D.: An action plan to help manage your research, your supervisor and your project.* New York: Routledge.

Firestone, W. A., & Riehl, C. (Eds.). (2005). *A new agenda for research in educational leadership.* New York: Teachers College Press.

Firth, G. R., & Pajak, E. F. (Eds.). (1998). *Handbook of research on school supervision.* New York: Macmillan.

Fischer, C. T. (Ed.). (2006). *Qualitative research methods for psychologists: Introduction through empirical studies.* Boston: Elsevier.

Fish, S. (1980). *Is there a text in this class? The authority of interpretive communities.* Cambridge, MA: Harvard University Press.

Fisher, J. A. (2007). "Ready-to-recruit" or "ready-to-consent" populations? Informed consent and the limits of subject autonomy. *Qualitative Inquiry, 13*(6), 875–894.

Fitzpatrick, J., Secrist, J., & Wright, D. J. (1998). *Secrets for a successful dissertation.* Thousand Oaks, CA: Sage.

Flood, J., Jensen, J. M., Lapp, D., & Squire, J. R. (1991). *Handbook of research on teaching the English language arts: A project of the International Reading Association and the National Council of Teachers of English.* New York: Macmillan.

Flood, R. (1979). *An introduction to quantitative methods for historians* (2nd ed.). Bungay, Suffolk, UK: Richard Clay.

Flyvbjerg, B. (2001). *Making social science matter: Why social inquiry fails and how it can succeed again.* New York: Cambridge University Press.

Fontana, A., & Frey, J. H. (2003). The interview: From structured questions to negotiated text. In N. K. Denzin & Y. S. Lincoln (Eds.), *Collecting and interpreting qualitative materials* (pp. 6–106). Thousand Oaks, CA: Sage.

Fontana, A., & Prokos, A. (2007). *The interview: From formal to postmodern.* Walnut Creek, CA; Left Coast Press.

Fosnot, C. T. (Ed.). (2005). *Constructivism: Theory, perspectives, and practice* (2nd ed.). New York: Teachers College Press.

Freeman, M., deMarrais, K., Preissle, J., Roulston, K., & St. Pierre, E. A. (2007). Standards of evidence in qualitative research: An incitement to discourse. *Educational Researcher, 36*(1), 25–32.

Gabel, D. (1994). *Handbook of research on science teaching and learning: A project of the National Science Teachers Association.* New York: Macmillan.

Gall, M. D., Gall, J. P., & Borg, W. R. (2007). *Educational research: An introduction* (8th ed.). Boston: Allyn & Bacon.

Gamson, J. (2003). Sexualities, queer theory, and qualitative research. In N. K. Denzin & Y. S. Lincoln (Eds.), *The landscape of qualitative research: Theories and issues* (2nd ed., pp. 540–568). Thousand Oaks: Sage.

Garman, N. B. (1985). Andragogy and professional education: When adults come together to learn about practice. *Australian Administrator, 6*(1), 1–5.

Garman, N. B. (2006). Imagining an interpretive dissertation: Voice, text, and representation. In N. B. Garman & M. Piantanida (Eds.), *The authority to imagine: The struggle toward representation in dissertation writing* (pp. 1–15). New York: Peter Lang.

Garman, N. B., & Piantanida, M. (Eds.). (2006). *The authority to imagine: The struggle toward representation in dissertation writing.* New York: Peter Lang.

Garratt, D., & Hodkinson, P. (1998). Can there be criteria for selecting research criteria? A hermeneutical analysis of an inescapable dilemma. *Quality Inquiry, 4*(4), 515–539.

Geertz, C. (1973). *The interpretation of cultures.* New York: Basic Books.

Geertz, C. (1983). *Local knowledge.* New York: Basic Books.

Geiger, R. (1997). Doctoral education: The short-term crisis vs. long-term challenge. *Review of Higher Education, 20*(3), 239–251.

Genishi, C. (Ed.). (1992). *Ways of assessing children and curriculum: Stories of early childhood practice.* New York: Teachers College Press.

Gergen, K. (1988). If persons are texts. In S. B. Messer, L. A. Sass, & R. L. Woolfolk (Eds.), *Hermeneutics and psychological theory* (pp. 28–51). New Brunswick, NJ: Rutgers University Press.

Given, L. M. (2008). *The SAGE encyclopedia of qualitative research methods.* Thousand Oaks, CA: Sage.

Glaser, B. G. (1978). *Theoretical sensitivity: Advances in the methodology of grounded theory.* Mill Valley, CA: Sociology Press.

Glaser, B. G. (1992). *Basics of grounded theory analysis: Emergence vs. forcing.* Mill Valley, CA: Sociology Press.

Glaser, B. G. (1994). *More grounded theory methodology: A reader.* Mill Valley, CA: Sociology Press.

Glaser, B. G. (1998). *Doing grounded theory: Issues and discussions.* Mill Valley, CA: Sociology Press.

Glaser, B. G., & Strauss, A. L. (1967). *The discovery of grounded theory: Strategies for qualitative research.* Hawthorne, NY: Aldine.

Glatthorn, A. A. (2005). *Writing the winning dissertation: A step-by-step guide* (2nd ed.). Thousand Oaks, CA: Corwin.

Glesne, C., & Peshkin, A. (1992). *Becoming qualitative researchers: An introduction.* New York: Longman.

Golde, C. M. (2000). Should I stay or should I go? Student descriptions of the doctoral attrition process. *Review of Higher Education, 23*(2), 199–237.

Golde, C. M. (2006). Preparing stewards of the discipline. In C. M. Golde & G. E. Walker (Eds.), *Envisioning the future of doctoral education: Preparing stewards of the discipline. Carnegie essays on the doctorate* (pp. 3–20). San Francisco: Jossey-Bass.

Golde, C. M. (2007). Signature pedagogies in doctoral education: Are they adaptable for the preparation of education researchers? *Educational Researcher, 36*(6), 344–351.

Golde, C. M., & Walker, G. E. (Eds.). (2006). *Envisioning the future of doctoral education: Preparing stewards of the discipline. Carnegie essays on the doctorate.* San Francisco: Jossey-Bass.

Golden-Biddle, K., & Locke, K. D. (2006). *Composing qualitative research: Crafting theoretical points from qualitative research.* Thousand Oaks, CA: Sage.

Goodman, J. (2003). *Mapping civic debate following September 11th, 2001: Civic courage, social cartography and curriculum theorizing.* UMI ProQuest Digital Dissertation. #AAT 3104731.

Goodman, J. (2006). Confronting authority and *self:* Social cartography and curriculum theorizing for uncertain times. In N. B. Garman and M. Piantanida (Eds.), *The authority to imagine: The struggle toward representation in dissertation writing* (pp. 49–63). New York: Peter Lang.

Goodwin, S. P. (1983). *An explication of human resources supervision: A grounded theory study of a public alternative high school.* UMI ProQuest Digital Dissertation #AAT 8327738.

Gordon, J. (2002). *Beyond the classroom walls: Ethnographic inquiry as pedagogy.* New York: Routledge.

Gott, R., & Duggan, S. (2004). *Understanding and using scientific evidence: How to critically evaluate data.* Thousand Oaks, CA: Sage.

Green, J. L., Camilli, G., & Elmore, P. B. (Eds.). (2006). *Handbook of complementary methods in education research.* Mahwah, NJ: Lawrence Erlbaum.

Greenwood, D. J., & Levin, M. (2007). *Introduction to action research: Social research for social change* (2nd ed.). Thousand Oaks, CA: Sage.

Grouws, D. A. (1992). *Handbook of research on mathematics teaching and learning: A project of the National Council of Teachers of Mathematics.* New York: Macmillan.

Grubs, R. E. (2002). *Living with shadows: Contextualizing the experience of being at-risk and reaching a decision about prenatal genetic testing.* University of Pittsburgh. UMI ProQuest Digital Dissertation #AAT 3078844.

Grubs, R. E. (2006). Reimagining grounded theory: Moving toward an interpretive stance. In N. B. Garman and M. Piantanida (Eds.), *The authority to imagine: The struggle toward representation in dissertation writing* (pp. 81–96). New York: Peter Lang.

Guidici, C., Krechevsky, M., & Rinaldi, C. (Eds.). (2001). *Making learning visible: Children as individual and group learners.* Reggio Emilia, Italy: Reggio Children.

Gunsalus, C. K., Bruner, E. M., Burbules, N. C., Dash, L., Finkin, M., Goldberg, J. P., et al. (2007). The Illinois white paper: Improving the system for protecting human subjects: Counteracting IRB "mission creep." *Qualitative Inquiry, 13*(5), 617–649.

Haggerson, N. L. (1988). Reconceptualizing inquiry in curriculum: Using multiple research paradigms to enhance the study of curriculum. *Journal of Curriculum Theorizing, 8*(1), 81–102.

Halpin, D., & Troyna, B. (Eds.). (1994). *Researching education policy: Ethical and methodological issues.* London: Falmer.

Halse, C., & Honey, A. (2007). Rethinking ethics review as institutional discourse. *Qualitative Inquiry, 13*(3), 336–352.

Hamel, J. (1993). *Case study methods.* Newbury Park, CA: Sage.

Hamilton, R. J., & Bowers, B. J. (2006). Internet recruitment and email interviewing in qualitative studies. *Qualitative Health Research, 16*(6), 821–835.

Hammersley, M. (1989). *The dilemma of qualitative method: Herbert Blumer and the Chicago tradition.* London: Routledge.

Hammersley, M. (1997). Qualitative data archiving: Some reflections on its prospects and problems. *Sociology, 31*(1), 131–142.

Hancock, D. R., & Algozzine, B. (2006). *Doing case study research: A practical guide for beginning researchers.* New York: Teachers College Press.

Hanninen, V. (2004). A model of narrative circulation. *Narrative Inquiry, 14*(1), 69–85.

Harding, S. (2007). Rethinking standpoint epistemology: What is "strong objectivity"? In A. E. Cudd & Robin O. Andreasen (Eds.), *Feminist theory: A philosophical anthology* (pp. 218–236). Victoria, Australia: Blackwell.

Hargreaves, A. (1996). Revisiting voice. *Educational Researcher, 25*(1), 12–19.

Harris, M. C. (1995). *Meanwhile, back at the ranch: A qualitative study of principals and school reform.* UMI ProQuest Digital Dissertation #AAT 9529127.

Harrison, J., MacGibbon, L., & Morton, M. (2001). Regimes of trustworthiness in qualitative research: The rigors of reciprocity. *Qualitative Inquiry, 7*(3), 323–345.

Hart, C. (1999). *Doing a literature review: Releasing the social science research imagination.* Thousand Oaks, CA: Sage.

Hatch, T., Ahmed, D., Lieberman, A., Faigenbaum, D., White, M. E., & Mace, D. H. P. (2005). *Going public with our teaching: An anthology of practice.* New York: Teachers College Press.

Hayden, M., Thompson, J., & Levy, J. (Eds.). (2007). *The SAGE handbook of research in international education.* Thousand Oaks, CA: Sage.

Hazi, H. M. (1980). *Analysis of selected teacher collective negotiation agreements in Pennsylvania to determine the legal control placed on supervisory practice.* UMI ProQuest Digital Dissertation #AAT 8028105.

Hazi, H. M. (1982). A grounded theory study using a cache of documents to explicate legal control of supervisory practice in Pennsylvania. *The Researcher, Annual Journal of the Norteastern Educational Research Association, 1*(1), 12–15.

Hendricks, C. C. (2006). *Improving schools through action research: A comprehensive guide for educators.* Boston: Allyn & Bacon.

Herr, K., & Anderson, G. L. (2005). *The action research dissertation: A guide for students and faculty.* Thousand Oaks, CA: Sage.

Heshusius, L. (1994). Freeing ourselves from objectivity: Managing subjectivity or turning toward a participatory mode of consciousness? *Educational Researcher, 23*(3), 15–22.

Heshusius, L., & Ballard, K. (1996). *From positivism to interpretivism and beyond: Tales of transformation in educational and social research.* New York: Teachers College Press.

Hesse-Biber, S. N. (Ed.). (2006). *Handbook of feminist research: Theory and Praxis.* Thousand Oaks, CA: Sage.

Hesse-Biber, S. N., & Leavy, P. L. (2005). *The practice of qualitative research.* Thousand Oaks, CA: Sage.

Hesse-Biber, S. N., & Leavy, P. L. (2006). *Feminist research practice: A primer.* Thousand Oaks, CA: Sage.

Hinds, P. S., Vogel, R. J., & Clarke-Steffen, L. (1997). The possibilities and pitfalls of doing a secondary analysis of a qualitative data set. *Qualitative Health Research, 7,* 408–424.

Hine, C. (2004). *Social research methods and the Internet: A thematic review.* Retrieved September 26, 2007, from http://www.socresonline.org.uk/9/2/hine.html

Hitchcock, G., & Hughes, D. (1989). *Research and the teacher: A qualitative introduction to school-based research.* London: Routledge.

Hodder, I. (2003). The interpretation of documents and material culture. In N. K. Denzin & Y. S. Lincoln (Eds.), *Collecting and Interpreting Qualitative Materials* (2nd ed., pp. 155–175). Thousand Oaks: Sage.

Holland, K. (2007). The epistemological bias of ethics review: Constraining mental health research. *Qualitative Inquiry, 13*(6), 895–913.

Holland, P. (1983). *A hermeneutic study of educational myth: Implications for clinical supervision.* UMI ProQuest Digital Dissertation #AAC 8411689.

Holland, P. E., & Garman, N. B. (1992). Macdonald and the mythopoetic. *JCT: An Interdisciplinary Journal of Curriculum Studies, 9*(4), 45–72.

Holly, M. L. (1989). *Writing to grow: Keeping a personal-professional journal.* Portsmouth, NH: Heinemann.

Holstein, J. A., & Gubrium, J. F. (1995). *The active interview.* Thousand Oaks, CA: Sage.

Holt, J. (1976). *Instead of education: Ways to help people do things better.* New York: Dutton.

Hopkins, R. L. (1994). *Narrative schooling: Experiential learning and the transformation of American education.* New York: Teachers College Press.

Hostetler, K. (2005). What is "good" educational research? *Educational Researcher, 34*(6), 16–21.

Howe, K. R. (1998). The interpretive turn and the new debate in education. *Educational Researcher, 27*(8), 13–20.

Howe, K. R., & Eisenhart, M. (1990). Standards for qualitative (and quantitative) research: A prolegomenon. *Educational Researcher, 19*(4), 2–9.

Huber, J., & Clandinin, D. J. (2002). Ethical dilemmas in relational narrative inquiry with children. *Qualitative Inquiry, 8*(6), 785–803.

Huebner, D. (1995). Education and spirituality. *Journal of Curriculum Theorizing, 11*(2), 13–34.

Husen, T., & Postlethwaite, N. (1985). *The international encyclopedia of education* (Vol. 1). London: Pergamon Press.

Jackson, B. (1987). *Fieldwork.* Urbana: University of Illinois Press.

Jacob, E., & White, C. S. (Issue Editors). (2002). Scientific Research in Education [Special issue]. *Educational Researcher, 31*(8).

Jacobson, W. (1998). Defining the quality of *practitioner* research. *Adult Education Quarterly, 48*(3), 125–138.

Jaeger, R. M. (Ed.). (1997). *Complementary methods for research in education* (2nd ed.). Washington, DC: American Educational Research Association.

Jalongo, M., & Isenberg, J. (1995). *Teachers' stories from personal narrative to professional insight.* San Francisco: Jossey-Bass.

Janesick, V. J. (1997, April). *Journal writing as a qualitative research technique: History, issues, and reflections.* Paper presented at the annual meeting of the American Educational Research Association, San Diego, CA.

Janesick, V. J. (1998). *"Stretching" exercises for qualitative researchers.* Thousand Oaks, CA: Sage.

Jensen, L. A., & Allen, M. N. (1996). Meta-synthesis of qualitative findings. *Qualitative Health Research, 6*(4), 553–560.

Johns, M. (2003). *Online social research: Methods, issues, and ethics.* New York: Peter Lang.

Johnson, B., & Christensen, L. B. (2007). *Educational research: Quantitative, qualitative, and mixed approaches.* Thousand Oaks, CA: Sage.

Johnson, R. B., & Onwuegbuzie, A. J. (2004). Mixed methods research: A research paradigm whose time has come. *Educational Researcher, 33*(7), 14–26.

Johnstone, D. B. (2000). The special ethicality of the academy: A review essay. *Review of Higher Education, 23*(2), 229–236.

Jonassen, D. H. (1995). *Handbook of research for educational communications and technology: A project of the Association for Educational Communications and Technology.* New York: Macmillan.

Jones, S. G. (Ed.). (1998). *Doing Internet research: Critical issues and methods for examining the net.* Thousand Oaks, CA: Sage.

Josselson, R., & Lieblich, A. (1993). *The narrative study of lives: Vol. 1. The narrative study of lives series.* Newbury Park, CA: Sage.

Juhl, P. D. (1980). *Interpretation: An essay in the philosophy of literary criticism.* Princeton, NJ: Princeton University Press.

Kamberelis, G., & Dimitriadis, G. (2005). *On qualitative inquiry.* New York: Teachers College Press.

Kamler, B., & Thomson, P. (2006). *Helping doctoral students write: Pedagogies for supervision.* New York: Routledge.

Kelly, A. E., Lesh, R. A., & Baek, J. Y. (Eds.). (2008). *Handbook of design research methods in education: Innovations in science, technology, engineering, and mathematics.* New York: Routledge.

Kelly, G. A. (1970). Behavior is an experiment. In D. Bannister (Ed.), *Perspectives in personal construct theory* (pp. 255–269). London: Academic Books.

Kelly, G. J., Luke, A., & Green, J. (Eds.). (2008). What counts as knowledge in educational settings: Disciplinary knowledge, assessment, and curriculum. *Review of Research in Education, 32*(1), vii–x.

Kemmis, S., & McTaggart, R. (Eds.). (1988). *The action research planner* (3rd ed.). Geelong, Australia: Deakin University Press.

Kerdeman, D. (1998). Hermeneutics and education: Understanding, control, and agency. *Educational Theory, 48*(2), 241–266.

Kezar, A. (2003). Transformational elite interviews: Principles and problems. *Qualitative Inquiry, 9*(3), 395–415.

Kilbourn, B. (1999). Fictional theses. *Educational Researcher, 28*(12), 27–32.

Kilbourn, B. (2006). The qualitative doctoral dissertation proposal. *Teachers College Record, 108*(4), 529–576.

Kincheloe, J. L. (1991). *Teachers as researchers: Qualitative inquiry as a path to empowerment.* London: Falmer.

Kincheloe, J. L. (2005). *Critical constructivism primer.* New York: Peter Lang.

Kincheloe, J., & McLaren, P. (2003). Rethinking critical theory and qualitative research. In N. K. Denzin & Y. S. Lincoln (Eds.), *The landscape of qualitative research: Theories and issues* (2nd ed., pp. 433–488). Thousand Oaks, CA: Sage.

Kleinman, S. (2007). *Feminist fieldwork analyses.* Thousand Oaks, CA: Sage.

Knapp-Minick, B. (1984). *A study of dysfunctional stereotypes regarding women and promotion: Implications for educational remedy.* UMI ProQuest Digital Dissertation #AAT 8511002.

Knoeller, C. (1998). *Voicing ourselves: Whose words do we use when we talk about books.* Albany: SUNY Press.

Konzal, J. (1995). *Our changing town, our changing schools: Is common ground possible?* UMI ProQuest Digital Dissertation #AAT 9614203.

Koro-Ljungberg, M., Gemignani, M., Brodeur, C. W., & Kmiec, C. (2007). The technologies of normalization and self: Thinking about IRBs and extrinsic research ethics with Foucault. *Qualitative Inquiry, 13*(8), 1075–1094.

Koshy, V. (2005). *Action research for improving practice: A practice guide.* Thousand Oaks, CA: Sage.

Krakowski, P. G. (2004). *Balancing the narrative and the normative: Pedagogical implications for early childhood art education.* University of Pittsburgh. UMI ProQuest Digital Dissertation #AAT3139692.

Krakowski, P. G. (2006). Chapter 5: A search for balance: Representing a narrative pedagogy. In N. B. Garman & M. Piantanida (Eds.), *The authority to imagine: The struggle toward representation in dissertation writing* (pp. 67–80). New York: Peter Lang.

Kridel, C. (Ed.). (1998). *Writing educational biography: Explorations in qualitative research.* Levittown, PA: Garland.

Krueger, R. A., & Casey, M. A. (2000). *Focus groups: A practical guide for applied research.* Thousand Oaks, CA: Sage.

Kuhn, T. S. (1970). *The structure of scientific revolution* (2nd ed.). Chicago: University of Chicago Press.

Kvale, S. (1996). *InterViews: An introduction to qualitative research interviewing.* Thousand Oaks, CA: Sage.

Labaree, D. F. (1998). Educational researchers: Living with a lesser form of knowledge. *Educational Researcher, 27*(8), 4–12.

Labaree, D. F. (2003). The peculiar problems of preparing educational researchers. *Educational Researcher, 32*(4), 13–22.

Ladson-Billings, G. (2003). Feminisms and qualitative research. In N. K. Denzin & Y. S. Lincoln (Eds.), *The landscape of qualitative research: Theories and issues* (2nd ed., pp. 398–432). Thousand Oaks, CA: Sage.

Ladson-Billings, G. (2005). *Beyond the big house: African-American educators on teacher education.* New York: Teachers College Press.

Ladson-Billings, G., & Tate, W. F. (Eds.). (2006). *Education research in the public interest: Social justice, action, and policy.* New York: Teachers College Press.

Lancy, D. F. (1993). *Qualitative research in education: An introduction to the major traditions.* New York: Longman.

Lather, P. (2004a). Scientific research in education: A critical perspective. *British Educational Research Journal, 30*(6), 759–772.

Lather, P. (2004b). This IS your father's paradigm: Government intrusion and the case of qualitative research in education. *Qualitative Inquiry, 10*(1), 15–34.

Lather, P. (2007). *Getting lost: Feminist effort toward a double(d) science.* Albany: SUNY Press.

Lather, P., & Moss, P. (2005). Introduction: Implications of the *Scientific Research in Education Report* for qualitative inquiry. *Teachers College Record, 107*(1), 1–3.

Lawrence-Lightfoot, S., & Hoffmann Davis, J. (1997). *The art and science of portraiture.* San Francisco: Jossey-Bass.

LeCompte, M., Milroy, W., & Preissle, J. (Eds.). (1992). *The handbook of qualitative research in education.* San Diego, CA: Academic Press.

Leonard, T., & Willis, P. (2008). *Pedagogies of the imagination: Mythopoetic curriculum in educational practice.* Secaucus, NJ: Springer.

Lester, F. K. (Ed.). (2007). *Second handbook of research on mathematics teaching and learning.* Charlotte, NC: Information Age.

Leukhardt, J. C. (1983). *Students in a special program for gifted female adolescents: A conceptual case study for planning curriculum.* UMI ProQuest Digital Dissertation #AAT 8327694.

Levstik, L. S., & Tyson, C. A. (Eds.). (2008). *Handbook of research in social studies education.* New York: Routledge.

Liberman, K. (1999). From walkabout to meditation: Craft and ethics in field inquiry. *Qualitative Inquiry, 5*(1), 47–63.

Lichtman, M. (2006). *Qualitative research in education: A user's guide.* Thousand Oaks, CA: Sage.

Lincoln, Y. S. (1995). Emerging criteria for quality in qualitative and interpretive research. *Qualitative Inquiry, 1*(3), 275–289.

Lincoln, Y. S. (1998). The ethics of teaching in qualitative research. *Qualitative Inquiry, 4*(3), 315–327.

Lincoln, Y. S., & Guba, E. G. (1985). *Naturalistic inquiry.* Beverly Hills, CA: Sage.

Lincoln, Y. S., & Guba, E. G. (1989). Ethics: The failure of positivist science. *Review of Higher Education, 12*(3), 221–240.

Linclon, Y. S., & Tierney, W. G. (2004). Qualitative research and institutional review boards. *Qualitative Inquiry, 10*(2), 219–234.

Llewellyn, M. (1998). *Bringing forth a world: Spirituality as pedagogy.* UMI ProQuest Digital Dissertation #AAT 9825673.

Llewellyn, M. (2006). Embracing a language of spiritual inquiry. In N. B. Garman & M. Piantanida (Eds.), *The authority to imagine: The struggle toward representation in dissertation writing* (pp. 97–109). New York: Peter Lang.

Locke, L. F., Silverman, S. J., & Spirduso, W. W. (2004). *Reading and understanding research* (2nd ed.). Thousand Oaks, CA: Sage.

Locke, L. F., Spirduso, W. W., & Silverman, S. J. (2007). *Proposals that work: A guide for planning dissertations and grant proposals* (5th ed.). Thousand Oaks, CA: Sage.

Logsdon, M. B. (2000). *A pedagogy of authority: Speculative essays by an English teacher.* University of Pittsburgh. ProQuest Digital Dissertation #AAT 99–98630.

Logsdon, M. B (2006). Writing essays: Minding the personal and theoretic. In N. B. Garman & M. Piantanida (Eds.), *The authority to imagine: The struggle toward representation in dissertation writing* (pp.155–166). New York: Peter Lang.

Longino, H. E. (2007). Can there be a feminist science? In A. E. Cudd & R. O. Andreasen (Eds.), *Feminist theory: A philosophical anthology* (pp. 210–217). Victoria, Australia: Blackwell.

Lopez, G. R., & Parker, L. (2003). *Interrogating racism in qualitative research methodology.* New York: Peter Lang.

Lowe, M. (2006). *Beginning research: A guide for foundation degree students in education.* New York: Routledge.

Lunenburg, F. (2007). *Writing a successful thesis or dissertation.* Thousand Oaks, CA: Corwin.

Lyons, N., & LaBoskey, V. K. (2002). *Narrative inquiry in practice: Advancing the knowledge of teaching.* New York: Teachers College Press.

Macdonald, J. B. (1995). A vision of a humane school. In B. J. Macdonald (Ed.), *Theory as a prayerful act: The collected essays of James B. Macdonald, Vol. 2* (pp. 49–67). New York: Peter Lang.

Macey, D. (2000). *The Penguin dictionary of critical theory.* New York: Penguin.

Madriz, E. (2003). The interpretation of documents and material culture. In N. K. Denzin & Y. S. Lincoln (Eds.), *Collecting and interpreting qualitative materials* (2nd ed., pp. 363–388). Thousand Oaks, CA: Sage.

Manheimer, M. L. (1973). *Style manual: A guide for the preparation of reports and dissertations.* New York: Marcel Dekker.

Mann, C., & Stewart, F. (2000). *Internet communication and qualitative research.* Thousand Oaks, CA: Sage.

Manus, M. B., Bowden, M. G., & Dowd, E. T. (1992). The purpose, philosophy, content, and structure of doctoral comprehensive/qualifying exams: A survey of counseling psychology training programs. *The Counseling Psychologist, 20*(4), 677–688.

Maranhao, T. (Ed.). (1990). *The interpretation of dialogue.* Chicago: University of Chicago Press.

Marshall, C., & Rossman, G. B. (2006). *Designing qualitative research* (4th ed.). Thousand Oaks, CA: Sage.

Marzano, M. (2007). Informed consent, deception, and research freedom in qualitative research: A cross-cultural comparison. *Qualitative Inquiry, 13*(3), 417–436.

Mason, J. (2002). *Qualitative researching* (2nd ed.). Thousand Oaks, CA: Sage.

Mathison, S. (1998). Why triangulate? *Educational Researcher, 17*(2), 13–17.

Mathison, S. (Ed.). (2005). *Encyclopedia of evaluation.* Thousand Oaks, CA: Sage.

Mauch, J. E., & Birch, J. W. (1983). *Guide to the successful thesis and dissertation—Conception to publication: A handbook for students and faculty.* New York: Marcel Dekker.

Maxwell, J. A. (2004). Causal explanation, qualitative research, and scientific inquiry in education. *Educational Researcher, 33*(2), 3–11.

Maxwell, J. A. (2005). *Qualitative research design: An interactive approach* (2nd ed.). Thousand Oaks, CA: Sage.

Maxwell, J. A. (2006). Literature reviews of, and for, educational research: A commentary on Boote and Beile's "Scholars before Researchers." *Educational Researcher, 35*(9), 28–31.

Maxwell, N. (1992). What kind of inquiry can best help us create a good world? *Science, Technology, & Human Values, 17*(2), 205–227.

May, R. (1975). *The courage to create.* New York: W. W. Norton.

Mayer, R. E. (2000). What is the place of science in educational research? *Educational Researcher, 29*(6), 38–39.

Mayer, R. E. (2001). Resisting the assault on science: The case for evidence-based reasoning in educational research. *Educational Researcher, 30*(7), 29–30.

Maykut, P., & Morehouse, R. (1994). *Beginning qualitative research: A philosophic and practical guide.* London: Falmer.

Maykut, P., & Morehouse, R. (2004). *Beginning qualitative evaluation.* New York: Routledge.

Mazzei, L. A. (2007). *Inhabited silence in qualitative research: Putting poststructural theory to work.* New York: Peter Lang.

McCall, M. M. (2003). Performance ethnography: A brief history and some advice. In N. K. Denzin & Y. S. Lincoln (Eds.), *Strategies of qualitative inquiry* (2nd ed., pp. 112–133). Thousand Oaks, CA: Sage.

McClintock, R. (1971). Toward a place for study in a world of instruction. *Teachers College Record, 73*(20), 161–205.

McCracken, G. (1988). *The long interview.* Newbury Park, CA: Sage.

McCullough, G. (2004). *Documentary research in education, history and the social sciences.* New York: Routledge.

McGinty, S. (2000). *The politics and machinations of education and research: International case studies.* New York: Peter Lang.

McLaughlin, C., & McIntyre, D. (2006). *Networking practitioner research: The effective use of networks in educational research.* New York: Routledge.

McMahon, P. L. (1993). A narrative study of three levels of reflection in a college composition class: Teacher journal, student portfolios, teacher-student discourse. UMI ProQuest Digital Dissertation #AAT 9329582.

McMahon, P. L. (2000). From angst to story to research text: The role of arts-based educational research in teacher inquiry. *Journal of Curriculum Theorizing, 16*(1), 125–145.

McMahon, P. L. (2006). Narrative yearnings: Reflecting in time through the art of fictive story. In N. B. Garman & M. Piantanida (Eds.), *The authority to imagine: The struggle toward representation in dissertation writing* (pp. 183–199). New York: Peter Lang.

McMillan, J. H., & Schumacher, S. (1997). *Research in education: A conceptual introduction* (4th ed.). New York: Longman.

McMillan, J. H., & Schumacher, S. (2006). *Research in education: Evidence based inquiry.* Boston: Allyn & Bacon.

McNiff, J., Lomax, P., & Whitehead, J. (2003). *You and your action research project.* New York: Routledge.

McNiff, J., & Whitehead, J. (2006). *All you need to know about action research* (2nd ed.). Thousand Oaks, CA: Sage.

McTaggart, R. (Ed.). (1997). *Participatory action research: International contexts and consequences.* Albany: SUNY Press.

Meloy, J. M. (2002). *Writing the qualitative dissertation: Understanding by doing* (2nd ed.). Mahwah, NJ: Lawrence Erlbaum.

Merriam, S. B. (1997). *Qualitative research and case study applications in education.* San Francisco: Jossey-Bass.

Mertens, D. M. (2005). *Research and evaluation in education and psychology: Integrating diversity with quantitative, qualitative, and mixed methods* (2nd ed.). Thousand Oaks, CA: Sage.

Mertler, C. A. (2006). *Action research: Teachers as researchers in the classroom.* Thousand Oaks, CA: Sage.

Metz, M. H. (2001). Intellectual border crossing in graduate education: A report from the field. *Educational Researcher, 30*(5), 12–18.

Metz, M. H., & Page, R. N. (2002). The uses of practitioner research and status issues in educational research: Reply to Gary Anderson. *Educational Researcher, 31*(7), 26–27.

Mienczakowski, J. (1995). The theater of ethnography: The reconstruction of ethnography into theater with emancipatory potential. *Qualitative Inquiry, 1*(3), 360–375.

Miles, M., & Huberman, M. S. (1994). *Qualitative data analysis: An expanded sourcebook* (2nd ed.). Thousand Oaks, CA: Sage.

Miller, P. W. (1990). Preparing for the comprehensive examination and writing the dissertation proposal: Advice for doctoral students. *Journal of Industrial Teacher Education, 27*(2), 83–86.

Miller, S., & Fredericks, M. (1996). *Qualitative research methods: Social epistemology and practical inquiry.* New York: Peter Lang.

Miller, S. I., & Fredericks, M. (1999). How does grounded theory explain? *Qualitative Health Research, 9*(4), 538–351.

Millman, J., & Darling-Hammond, L. (Eds.). (1990). *The new handbook of teacher evaluation: Assessing elementary and secondary school teachers.* Thousand Oaks, CA: Sage.

Milne, W. M. (2000). *Reflective artmaking: Implications for art education.* UMI ProQuest Digital Dissertation #AAT 9974457.

Milne, W. M. (2006). Imagining reflective artmaking: Claiming self as artist-teacher-researcher. In N. B. Garman & M. Piantanida (Eds.), *The authority to imagine: The struggle toward representation in dissertation writing* (pp. 127–137). New York: Peter Lang.

Mishler, E. G. (1986). *Research interviewing: Context and narrative.* Cambridge, MA: Harvard University Press.

Mitchell, C., O'Reilly-Scanlon, K., & Weber, S. (2004). *Just who do we think we are? Methodologies for autobiography and self-study in education.* New York: Routledge.

Mitchell, W. J. T. (Ed.). (1981). *On narrative.* Chicago: University of Chicago Press.

Mohr, M. M., Nocerino, M. A., Clawson, S., MacLean, M. S., Rogers, C., & Sanford, B. (2003). *Teacher researcher for better schools.* New York: Teachers College Press.

Montuori, A. (2005). Literature review as creative inquiry: Reframing scholarship as a creative process. *Journal of Transformative Education, 3*(4), 374–393.

Morgan, D. L. (1996). *Focus groups as qualitative research.* Thousand Oaks, CA: Sage.

Morgan, D. L. (1998). Practical strategies for combining qualitative and quantitative methods: Applications to health research. *Qualitative Health Research, 8*(3), 362–376.

Morse, J. A. (2006). The politics of evidence. *Qualitative Health Research, 16*(3), 395–404.

Morse, J. M. (1991). Approaches to qualitative-quantitative methodological triangulation. *Nursing Research, 40*(2), 120–123.

Morse, J. M. (1994). "Emerging from the data": The cognitive processes of analysis in qualitative inquiry. In J. M. Morse (Ed.), *Critical issues in qualitative research methods.* Thousand Oaks, CA: Sage.

Moustakas, C. (1990). *Heuristic research: Design, methodology, and applications.* Newbury Park, CA: Sage.

Moustakas, C. (1994). *Phenomenological research methods.* Thousand Oaks, CA: Sage.

Mullen, C. A. (2005). *Fire and ice: Igniting and channeling passion in new qualitative researchers.* New York: Peter Lang.

Mullen, C. A., & Finley, S. (Guest Eds.). (2003). Arts-based approaches to qualitative inquiry [Special issue]. *Qualitative Inquiry, 9*(2).

Mun Wong, L. (1998). The ethics of rapport: Institutional safeguards, resistance, and betrayal. *Qualitative Inquiry, 4*(2), 178–199.

Nash, R. J. (2004). *Liberating scholarly writing: The power of personal narrative.* New York: Teachers College Press.

National Research Council. (2002). Scientific research in education. R. J. Shavelson & L. Towne (Eds.), *Committee on Scientific Principles of Educational Research.* Washington, DC: National Academy Press.

Nespor, J. (2000). Anonymity and place in qualitative inquiry. *Qualitative Inquiry, 6*(4), 546–569.

Nielsen, H. B. (1995). Seductive texts with serious intentions. *Educational Researcher, 24*(1), 4–12.

Noblit, G. W. (1999). *Particularities: Collected essays on ethnography and education.* New York: Peter Lang.

Noblit, G., Flores, S. Y., & Murillo, E. G. (Eds.). (2004). *Postcritical ethnography: Reinscribing critique.* Cresskill, NJ: Hampton Press.

Norris, J. (2000). Drama as research: Realizing the potential of drama in education as a research methodology. *Youth Theatre Journal, 14,* 40–51.

O'Connor, C., Lewis, A., & Mueller, J. (2007). Researching "Black" educational experiences and outcomes: Theoretical and methodological considerations. *Educational Researcher, 36*(9), 541–552.

O'Connor, M. K., Netting, F. E., & Thomas, M. L. (2008). Grounded theory: Managing the challenge for those facing institutional review board oversight. *Qualitative Inquiry, 14*(1), 28–45.

O'Donoghue, T., & Punch, K. (Eds.). (2004). *Qualitative educational research in action: Doing and reflecting.* New York: Routledge.

Ogden, E. H. (2006). *Complete your dissertation or thesis in two semesters or less.* Lanham, MD: Rowman & Littlefield.

Oldfather, P., & West, J. (1994). Qualitative research as jazz. *Educational Researcher, 23*(8), 22–26.

Olson, D. R. (2004). The triumph of hope over experience in the search for "what works": A response to Slavin. *Educational Researcher, 33*(1), 24–26.

Opie, C. (2004). *Doing educational research.* Thousand Oaks, CA: Sage.

Page, R. (2000). Future directions in qualitative research. *Harvard Educational Review, 70*(1), 100–108.

Page, R. (2001). Reshaping graduation preparation in educational research methods: One school's experience. *Educational Researcher, 30*(5), 19–25.

Pallas, A. M. (2001). Preparing educational doctoral students for epistemological diversity. *Educational Researcher, 30*(5), 6–11.

Palmer, R. E. (1969). *Hermeneutics: Interpretation theory in Schleiermacher, Dilthey, Heidegger, and Gadamer.* Evanston, IL: Northwestern University Press.

Paltridge, B., & Starfield, S. (2007). *Thesis and dissertation writing in a second language: A handbook for supervisors.* New York: Routledge.

Patterson, D. (2008). Research ethics boards as spaces of marginalization: A Canadian story. *Qualitative Inquiry, 14*(1), 18–27.

Patton, M. Q. (2001). *Qualitative research and evaluation methods.* Thousand Oaks, CA: Sage.

Paul, J. L. (2005). *Introduction to the philosophies of research and criticism in education and the social sciences.* Upper Saddle River, NJ: Pearson.

Paulston, R. G. (1993). Mapping discourses in comparative education texts. *Compare, 23*(2), 101–114.

Paultson, R. G. (1995). Mapping knowledge perspectives in studies of educational change. In P. Cookson & B. Schneider (Eds.), *Transforming schools* (pp. 137–179). New York: Garland.

Paulston, R. G. (Ed.). (1996). *Social cartography: Mapping ways of seeing social and educational change.* New York: Garland.

Paulston, R. G., & Liebman, M. (1994). An invitation to postmodern social cartography. *Comparative Education Review, 38*(2), 215–232.

Peshkin, A. (2000). The nature of interpretation in qualitative research. *Educational Researcher, 29*(9), 5–9.

Petrey, S. (1990). *Speech acts and literary theory.* New York: Routledge.

Phenix, P. H. (1964). *Realms of meaning: A philosophy of the curriculum for general education.* New York: McGraw-Hill.

Phillips, D. C. (1994). Telling it straight: Issues in assessing narrative research. *Educational Psychologist, 29*(1), 13–21.

Phillips, D. K., & Carr, K. (2006). *Becoming a teacher through action research: Process, context, and self-study.* New York: Routledge.

Piantanida, M. (1982). *The practice of hospital education: A grounded theory study.* UMI ProQuest Digital Dissertation # AAT 8317299.

Piantanida, M. (2006). Speculations on the personal essay as a mode of curriculum inquiry. In N. B. Garman & M. Piantanida (Eds.), *The authority to imagine: The struggle toward representation in dissertation writing* (pp. 167–182). New York: Peter Lang.

Piantanida, M. (in press). Resonance. In L. M. Given (Ed.), *The SAGE encyclopedia of qualitative research methods.* Thousand Oaks, CA: Sage.

Piantanida, M., Tananis, C. A., & Grubs, R. E. (2004). Generating grounded theory of/for educational practice: The journey of three epistemorphs. *International Journal of Qualitative Studies in Education, 17*(3), 325–346.

Pinar, W. F. (2003). *International handbook of curriculum research.* Mahwah, NJ: Lawrence Erlbaum.

Pinar, W. F. (2006). *The synoptic text today and other essays. Curriculum development after the reconceptualization.* New York: Peter Lang.

Poland, B. D. (1995). Transcription quality as an aspect of rigor in qualitative research. *Qualitative Inquiry, 1*(3), 290–310.

Polkinghorne, D. E. (1988). *Narrative knowing and the human sciences.* Albany: SUNY Press.

Polkinghorne, D. E. (1997). Reporting qualitative research as practice. In W. G. Tierney & Y. Lincoln (Eds.), *Representation and the text: Reframing the narrative voice.* Albany: SUNY Press.

Popkewitz, T. S. (1984). *Paradigm & ideology in educational research.* New York: Falmer.

Preskill, H., & Catsambas, T. T. (2006). *Reframing evaluation through appreciative inquiry.* Thousand Oaks, CA: Sage.

Pritchard, I. A. (2002). Travelers and trolls: Practitioner research and institutional review boards. *Educational Researcher, 31*(3), 3–13.

Prosser, B. (1998). *Bitter sweet symphony: A research project presentation on ADHD in South Australian schools.* Unpublished manuscript, University of Pittsburgh.

Prosser, B. (1999). *Behaviour management of management behaviour? A sociological study of attention deficit hyperactivity disorder in Australian and American secondary schools.* Unpublished doctoral dissertation, Flinders University, Bedford Park—South Australia.

Punch, M. (1994). Politics and ethics in qualitative research. In N. Denzin & Y. S. Lincoln (Eds.), *Handbook of qualitative research* (pp. 83–97). Thousand Oaks, CA: Sage.

Rambo, C. (2007). Handing IRB an unloaded gun. *Qualitative Inquiry, 13*(3), 353–367.

Rasberry, G. W. (2001). *Writing research/researching writing: Through a poet's I.* New York: Peter Lang.

Ray, W. (1986). *Literary meaning: From phenomenology to deconstruction.* New York: Basil Blackwell.

Reason, P., & Bradbury, H. (Eds.). (2006). *Handbook of action research: Concise paperback edition.* Thousand Oaks, CA: Sage.

Reason, P., & Hawkins, P. (1988). Storytelling as inquiry. In P. Reason (Ed.), *Human inquiry in action: Developments in new paradigm research* (pp. 79–101). Newbury Park, CA: Sage.

Reed, J. (2007). *Appreciative inquiry: Research for change.* Thousand Oaks, CA: Sage.

Reinharz, S. (1993). Empty explanations for empty wombs: An illustration of secondary analysis of qualitative data. In M. Schratz (Ed.), *Qualitative voices in educational research* (p. 193). London: Falmer.

Rennie, D. L. (1998). Grounded theory methodology: The pressing need for a coherent logic of justification. *Theory & Psychology, 8*(1), 101–119.

Rhodes, C. (2000). Ghostwriting research: Positioning the researcher in the interview text. *Qualitative Inquiry, 6*(4), 511–525.

Richards, L. A. (1996). *A narrative study of the incorporation of creative dramatics as pedagogy in elementary content areas.* University of Pittsburgh. UMI ProQuest Digital Dissertation #AAT 9637875.

Richards, L. A. (2006). Pictures in my mind: Viewing images of dissertation authorities through process drama and narrative inquiry. In N. B. Garman & M. Piantanida (Eds.), *The authority to imagine: The struggle toward representation in dissertation writing* (pp. 19–34). New York: Peter Lang.

Richardson, L. (1990). *Writing strategies: Reaching diverse audiences: Vol. 1. Qualitative Research Methods Series.* Newbury Park, CA: Sage.

Richardson, L. (2000). Evaluating ethnography. *Qualitative Inquiry, 6*(2), 253–255.

Richardson, L. (2003). Writing: A method of inquiry. In N. K. Denzin & Y. S. Lincoln (Eds.), *Collecting and interpreting qualitative materials* (2nd ed., pp. 499–541). Thousand Oaks, CA: Sage.

Richardson, V. (1994). Conducting research on practice. *Educational Researcher, 23*(5), 5–10.

Richardson, V. (2006). Stewards of a field, stewards of an enterprise. The doctorate in education. In C. Golde & G. Walker (Eds.), *Envisioning the future of doctoral education: Preparing stewards of the discipline. Carnegie essays on the doctorate* (pp. 251–267). San Francisco: Jossey-Bass.

Ricoeur, P. (1981). *Hermeneutics and the human sciences: Essays on language, action and interpretation* (J. R. Thompson, Ed. and Trans.). UK: Cambridge University Press.

Ricoeur, P. (1984). *Time and narrative.* Chicago: University of Chicago Press.

Ricoeur, P (1991). *From text to action: Essays in hermeneutics, II* (K. Blamey & J. B. Thompson, Trans.). Evanston, IL: Northwestern University Press.

Riessman, C. K. (1996). *Narrative analysis.* Thousand Oaks, CA: Sage.

Ritchie, J. S., & Wilson, D. E. (2000). *Teacher narrative as critical inquiry: Rewriting the script.* Thousand Oaks, CA: Sage.

Roberts, C. M. (2004). *The dissertation journey: A practical and comprehensive guide to planning, writing, and defending your dissertation.* Thousand Oaks, CA: Corwin.

Roberts, R. H., & Good, J. M. M. (Eds.). (1993). *The recovery of rhetoric: Persuasive discourse and disciplinarily in the human sciences.* Charlottesville: University Press of Virginia.

Robinson, J. A., & Hawpe, L. (1986). Narrative thinking as a heuristic process. In T. R. Sarbin (Ed.), *Narrative psychology: The storied nature of human conduct* (pp. 111–125). New York: Praeger.

Robinson, V., & Lai, M. K. (2006). *Practitioner research for educators: A guide to improving classrooms and schools.* Thousand Oaks, CA: Corwin.

Rogers, R., Malancharuvil-Berkes, E., Mosley, M., Hui, D., & Joseph, G.O. (2005). Critical discourse analysis in education: A review of literature. *Review of Educational Research, 75*(3), 365–414.

Rose, G. (2007). *Visual methodologies: An introduction to the interpretation of visual methods* (2nd ed.). Thousand Oaks, CA: Sage.

Rossman, G. B., & Rallis, S. F. (2003). *Learning in the field: An introduction to qualitative research* (2nd ed.). Thousand Oaks, CA: Sage.

Rowan, J. (1981). A dialectical paradigm for research. In P Reason & J. Rowan (Eds.), *Human inquiry: A sourcebook of new paradigm research* (pp. 93–112). New York: John Wiley.

Rubin, H. J., & Rubin, I. S. (1995). *Qualitative interviewing: The art of hearing data.* Thousand Oaks, CA: Sage.

Rudestam, K. E., & Newton, R. R. (2007). *Surviving your dissertation: A comprehensive guide to content and process* (3rd ed.). Thousand Oaks, CA: Sage.

Runco, M. (Ed.). (2008). *The creativity research handbook.* Creskill, NJ: Hampton Press.

Sagor, R. (2005). *The action research guidebook: A four-step process for educators and school teams.* Thousand Oaks, CA: Corwin.

Saks, A.L. (1996). Viewpoints: Should novels count as dissertation in education? *Research in the Teaching of English, 30*(4), 403–427.

Salomon, G. (1991). Transcending the qualitative-quantitative debate: The analytic and systemic approaches to educational research. *Educational Researcher, 20*(6), 10–18.

Samaras, A. P. (2006). *Self-study of teaching practices.* New York: Peter Lang.

Sandelowski, M. (1991). Telling stories: Narrative approaches in qualitative research. *IMAGE: Journal of Nursing Scholarship, 23*(3), 161–166.

Sanida, K. V. (1987). *The legal responsibilities of the school psychologist as determined by appeal opinions of hearing officers' decisions in the state of Pennsylvania.* UMI ProQuest Digital Dissertation #AAC 8719321.

Scheurich, J. J. (1997). *Research method in the post modern.* London: Falmer.

Scheurich, J. J., & Young, M. D. (1997). Coloring epistemologies: Are our research epistemologies racially biased? *Educational Researcher, 6*(4), 4–16.

Schmuck, R. A. (2006). *Practical action research for change* (2nd ed.). Thousand Oaks, CA: Corwin.

Schön, D. A. (1983). *The reflective practitioner: How professionals think in action.* New York: Basic Books.

Schrag, F. (1992). In defense of positivist research paradigms. *Educational Researcher, 21*(5), 5–8.

Schram, T. H. (2003). *Conceptualizing qualitative inquiry: Mindwork for fieldwork in education and the social sciences.* Upper Saddle River, NJ: Pearson Education.

Schratz, M. (Ed.). (1993). *Qualitative voices in educational research.* London: Falmer.

Schrum, L. (1995). Framing the debate: Ethical research in the information age. *Qualitative Inquiry, 1*(3), 311–326.

Schubert, W. H. (1991). Philosophical inquiry: The speculative essay. In E. Short (Ed.), *Forms of curriculum inquiry* (pp. 61–76). Albany: SUNY Press.

Schwandt, T. A. (1999). On understanding understanding. *Qualitative inquiry, 5*(4), 451–464.

Schwandt, T. A. (2001, Winter). Responsiveness in everyday life. *New Directions for Evaluation, 73–88.*

Schwandt, T. A. (2003). Three epistemological stances for qualitative inquiry: Interpretivism, hermeneutics, and social constructionism. In N. K. Denzin & Y. S. Lincoln (Eds.), *The Landscape of qualitative research: Theories and issues* (2nd ed., pp. 292–331). Thousand Oaks: Sage.

Schwandt, T. A. (2007). *The SAGE dictionary of qualitative inquiry* (3rd ed.). Los Angeles: Sage.

Seale, C. (1999). Quality in qualitative research. *Qualitative Inquiry, 5*(4), 465–478.

Seidman, I. (2006). *Interviewing as qualitative research: A guide for researchers in educational and the social sciences* (3rd ed.). New York: Teachers College Press.

Shank, G., & Brown, L. (2007). *Exploring educational research literacy.* New York: Routledge.

Shapin, S. (1996). *The scientific revolution.* Chicago: University of Chicago Press.

Sharf, B. F. (1999). Beyond netiquette: The ethics of doing naturalistic discourse research on the Internet. In S. G. Jones (Ed.), *Doing Internet research: Critical issues and methods for examining the Net* (pp. 243–256). Thousand Oaks, CA: Sage.

Shavelson, R. J., & Towne, L. (Eds.). (2002). *Scientific research in education.* Report of the Committee on Scientific Principles for Education Research. Washington, DC: National Academy Press.

Shaver, J. (1991). *Handbook of research on social studies teaching and learning: A project of the National Council for the Social Studies.* New York: Macmillan.

Sherman, R. R., & Webb, R. B. (1988). *Qualitative research in education: Focus and methods.* London: Falmer.

Short, E. C. (Ed.). (1991). *Forms of curriculum inquiry.* Albany: SUNY Press.

Shulman, L. S. (2007). Practice wisdom in the service of professional practice. *Educational Researcher, 36*(9), 560–563.

Shulman, L. S., Golde, C. M., Conklin Bueschel, A. C., & Garabedian, K. J. (2006). Reclaiming education's doctorates: A critique and a proposal. *Educational Researcher, 35*(3), 25–32.

Sikula, J., Houston, W. R., & Haberman, M. (Eds.). (1990). *Handbook of research on teacher education: A project of the Association of Teacher Educators.* New York: Macmillan.

Sills, C., & Jensen, G. H. (Eds.). (1992). *The philosophy of discourse: The rhetorical turn in twentieth-century thought* (Vol. 1). Portsmouth, NH: Boynton/Cook.

Silverman, D. (2004). *Doing qualitative research: A practical handbook* (2nd ed.). Thousand Oaks, CA: Sage.

Singer, R. N., Murphey, M., & Tennant, L. K. (1993). *Handbook of research on sport psychology: A project of the International Society of Sport Psychology.* New York: Macmillan.

Sipe, L., & Constable, S. (1996). A chart of four contemporary research paradigms: Metaphors for the modes of inquiry. *TABOO: The Journal of Culture and Education, 1,* 153–163.

Slavin, R. E. (2002). Evidence-based education policies: Transforming educational practice and research. *Educational Researcher, 31*(7), 15–21.

Slavin, R. E. (2004). Education research can and must address "what works" questions. *Educational Researcher, 33*(1), 27–28.

Slavin, R. E. (2008). Perspectives on evidence-based research in education. What works? Issues in synthesizing educational program evaluations. *Educational Researcher, 37*(1), 5–14.

Smith, D. G. (1991). Hermeneutic inquiry: The hermeneutic imagination and the pedagogic text. In E. C. Short (Ed.), *Forms of curriculum inquiry* (pp. 187–209). Albany: SUNY Press.

Smith, J. K., & Heshusius, L. (1986). Closing down the conversation: The end of the quantitative-qualitative debate among educational inquirers. *Educational Researcher, 15*(1), 4–12.

Smyth, J., Hattam, R., & Shacklock, G. (1997). *Pursuing a qualitative/critical research thesis in education.* Adelaide, Australia: Flinders Institute for the Study of Teaching.

Snow, C. P. (1998). *The two cultures.* New York: Cambridge University Press.

Soltis, J. S. (1984). On the nature of educational research. *Educational Researcher, 13*(10), 5–10.

Somekh, B., & Lewin, C. (2005). *Research methods in the social sciences.* Thousand Oaks, CA: Sage.

Spindler, G. (Ed.). (1982). *Doing the ethnography of schooling.* New York: Holt, Rinehart & Winston.

Spindler, G., & Hammond, L. (Eds.). (2006). *Innovations in educational ethnography: Theories, methods, and results.* Mahwah, NJ: Lawrence Erlbaum.

Spodek, B. (1982). *Handbook of research on the education of young children.* New York: Macmillan.

St. Pierre, E. A. (2000). *Working the ruins: Feminist poststructural theory and methods in education.* New York: Routledge.

St. Pierre, E. A. (2002a). "Science" rejects postmodernism. *Educational Researcher, 31*(8), 25–27.

St. Pierre, E. A. (2002b, January). *Working the ruins: Qualitative research in the postmodern.* Keynote address presented at QUIG, Athens, GA.

Stabile, M. (1999). *Problematizing educational inclusion: A practice-based heuristic inquiry.* UMI ProQuest Digital Dissertation #AAT 9928088.

Stabile, M. (2006). Problemitizing educational inclusion through heuristic inquiry. In N. B. Garman & M. Piantanida (Eds.), *The authority to imagine: The struggle toward representation in dissertation writing* (pp. 35–47). New York: Peter Lang.

Stake, R. E. (1995). *The art of case study research.* Thousand Oaks, CA: Sage.

Stake, R. E. (2003). Case studies. In N. K. Denzin & Y. S. Lincoln (Eds.), *Strategies of qualitative inquiry* (2nd ed., pp. 134–164). Thousand Oaks, CA: Sage.

Stanley, C. A. (2007). When counter narratives meet master narratives in the journal editorial-review process. *Educational Researcher, 36*(1), 14–24.

Stay, B. L. (1996). *A guide to argumentative writing.* San Diego: Greenhaven.

Stephens, D. (2007). *Qualitative research in international settings.* New York: Routledge.

Stern, P. N. (1980). Grounded theory methodology: Its uses and processes. *IMAGE, 12*(1), 20–23.

Stern, P. N. (1994). Eroding grounded theory. In J. M. Morse (Ed.), *Critical issues in qualitative research methods* (pp. 212–223). Thousand Oaks, CA: Sage.

Sternberg, D. (1981). *How to complete and survive a doctoral dissertation.* New York: St. Martin's Press.

Sternberg, R. J., & Horvath, J. A. (1995). A prototype view of expert teaching. *Educational Researcher, 24*(6), 9–17.

Stewart, A. (1998). *The ethnographer's method.* Thousand Oaks, CA: Sage.

Stewart, D. W., Shamdasani, P. N., & Rook, D. W. (2007). *Focus groups: Theory and practice* (2nd ed.). Thousand Oaks, CA: Sage.

Stout, C. J. (Ed.). (2006). Arts-based Research in Art Education [Special issue]. *Studies in Art Education, A Journal of Issues and Research, 48*(1).

Strauss, A., & Corbin, J. (1998). *Basics of qualitative research: Techniques and procedures for developing grounded theory* (2nd ed.). Thousand Oaks, CA: Sage.

Street, A. (1990). *The practice of journalling for teachers, nurses, adult educators and other professionals.* Geelong, Australia: Deakin University Press.

Street, A. (1995). *Nursing replay: Researching nursing culture together.* Melbourne, Australia: Churchill Livingstone.

Stringer, E. T. (2007). *Action research* (3rd ed.). Thousand Oaks, CA: Sage.

Sullivan, G. (2005). *Art practice as research: Inquiry in the visual arts.* Thousand Oaks, CA: Sage.

Suter, W. N. (2006). *Introduction to educational research: A critical thinking approach.* Thousand Oaks, CA: Sage.

Szabo, V., & Strang, V. R. (1997). Secondary analysis of qualitative data. *Advanced Nursing Science, 20*(2), 66–74.

Tananis, C. A. (2000). *Discursive evaluation: The journey of an "epistemorph" toward an interpretive practice and inquiry.* University of Pittsburgh. UMI ProQuest Digital Dissertation #AAT 9974482.

Tananis, C. A. (2006). Imagining in the forest dark: The journey of an epistemorph in the land of ologies. In N. B. Garman & M. Piantanida (Eds.), *The authority to imagine: The struggle toward representation in dissertation writing* (pp. 139–152). New York: Peter Lang.

Tashakkori, A., & Teddlie, C. (Eds.). (2003). *Handbook of mixed methods in social and behavioral research.* Thousand Oaks: Sage.

Taylor, C. (1985). *Philosophy and the human sciences: Philosophical papers 2.* Cambridge, UK: Cambridge University Press.

Taylor, C. (1992). *The ethics of authenticity.* Cambridge, MA: Harvard University Press.

Taylor, C., Wilkie, M., & Baser, J. (Eds.). (2006). *Doing action research: A guide for school support staff.* Thousand Oaks, CA: Corwin.

Taylor, G. R. (Ed.). (2005). *Integrating quantitative and qualitative methods in research* (2nd ed.). Lanham, MD: University Press of America.

Tedlock, B. (2003). Ethnography and ethnographic representation. In N. K. Denzin & Y. S. Lincoln (Eds.), *Strategies of qualitative inquiry* (2nd ed., pp. 249–291). Thousand Oaks, CA: Sage.

Thomas, B., Stamler, L., Lafreniere, K., & Dumula, R. (2000). The Internet: An effective tool for nursing research with women. *Computers in Nursing, 18*(1), 13–18.

Thomas, R. M. (2003). *Blending qualitative and quantitative research methods in theses and dissertations.* Thousand Oaks, CA: Corwin.

Thomas, R. (2007). *Theses and dissertations: A guide to planning, research, and writing* (2nd ed.). Thousand Oaks, CA: Corwin.

Thompson, P. (2007). *Visual research with children and young people.* New York: Routledge.

Thorne, S. (1998). Ethical and representational issues in qualitative secondary analysis. *Qualitative Health Research, 8*(4), 547–555.

Tierney, W. G. (1994). Reframing the narrative voice in educational research. *Review of Education/Pedagogy/Cultural Studies, 16*(1), 87–92.

Tierney, W. G., & Corwin, Z. B. (2007). The tensions between academic freedom and institutional review boards. *Qualitative Inquiry, 13*(3), 388–398.

Tierney, W. G., & Lincoln, Y. S. (1994). Teaching qualitative methods in higher education. *Review of Higher Education, 17*(2), 107–124.

Tierney, W. G., & Lincoln, Y. S. (Eds.). (1997). *Representation and the text: Reframing the narrative voice.* Albany: SUNY Press.

Tilley, S., & Gormley, L. (2007). Canadian University ethics review: Cultural complications translating principles into practice. *Qualitative Inquiry, 13*(3), 368–387.

Tillman, L. C. (2002). Culturally sensitive research approaches: An African-American perspective. *Educational Researcher, 31*(9), 3–12.

Tillman, L. C. (Ed.). (2008). *The SAGE handbook of African American education.* Thousand Oaks, CA: Sage.

Tobin, K., & Kincheloe, J. (Eds.). (2006). *Doing educational research: A handbook.* Rotterdam, Netherlands: Sense Publishers.

Tripp, D. H. (1983). Co-authorship and negotiation: The interview as an act of creation. *Interchange, 14*(3), 32–44.

Tunnell, K. D. (1998). Interviewing the incarcerated: Personal notes on ethical and methodological issues. In Kathleeen Bennett deMarris (Ed.), *Qualitative research reflections: Inside stories* (pp. 127–137). Mahwah, NJ: Lawrence Erlbaum.

Tyson, C. A. (1998). A response to "Coloring epistemologies: Are our qualitative research epistemologies racially biased?" *Educational Researcher, 27*(9), 21–22.

Van Maanen, J. (Ed.). (1983). *Qualitative methodology.* Beverly Hills, CA: Sage.

Van Maanen, J. (Ed.). (1995). *Representation in ethnography.* Thousand Oaks, CA: Sage.

Van Maanen, J., Dabbs, J. M., & Faulkner, R. R. (Eds.). (1982). *Varieties of qualitative research.* Beverly Hills, CA: Sage.

van Manen, M. (1977). Linking ways of knowing with ways of being practical. *Curriculum Inquiry, 6*(3), 205–228.

van Manen, M. (1984). Doing phenomenological research and writing: An introduction. *Phenomenology and Pedagogy, 2*(1), 36–39.

Vidich, A. J., & Lyman, S. M. (1994). Qualitative methods: Their history in sociology and anthropology. In N. K. Denzin & Y. S. Lincoln (Eds.), *Handbook of qualitative research* (pp. 23–59). Thousand Oaks, CA: Sage.

Waldrop, D. (2004). Ethical issues in qualitative research with high-risk populations. In D. K. Padgett (Ed.), *The qualitative research experience.* Belmont, CA: Wadsworth/Thomson Learning.

Wallace, M., & Wray, A. (2006). *Critical reading and writing for postgraduates.* Thousand Oaks, CA: Sage.

Webster, L., & Mertova, P. (2007). *Using narrative inquiry as a research method.* New York: Routledge.

Weisberg, M., & Duffin, J. (1995). Evoking the moral imagination: Using stories to teach ethics and professionalism to nursing, medical, and law students. *Change, 27*(1), 21–27.

Welty, E. (1984). *One writer's beginnings.* New York: Warner.

Wexler, P. (Ed.). (1991). *Critical theory now.* London: Falmer.

White, J., & White, P. (1986). Teachers as political activists: Three perspectives. In A. Hartnett & M. Naish (Eds.), *Education and society today* (pp. 171–182). London: Falmer.

Whitehead, J., & McNiff, J. (2006). *Action research: Living theory.* Thousand Oaks, CA: Sage.

Whyte, W. F. (Ed.). (1991). *Participatory action research.* Newbury Park, CA: Sage.

Willis, J. W. (2007). *Foundations of qualitative research: Interpretive and critical approaches.* Thousand Oaks, CA: Sage.

Willis, P. (1998). *Inviting learning: An exhibition of risk and enrichment in adult education practice.* Unpublished doctoral dissertation. University of Technology of Sydney. Australia.

Willis, P., & Neville, B. (1996). *Qualitative research practice in adult education research.* Melbourne, Australia: David Lovell.

Willis, P., Smith, R., & Collins, E. (2000). *Being, seeking, telling: Expressive approaches to qualitative adult education research.* Flaxton, Australia: Post Pressed.

Wojecki, A. (2004). *Desert journal: Stories of whiteness and space in central Australia.* Unpublished doctoral dissertation. University of South Australia, Underdale.

Wolcott, H. F. (1994). *Transforming qualitative data: Description, analysis, and interpretation.* Thousand Oaks, CA: Sage.

Wolcott, H. F. (2001). *Writing up qualitative research.* Thousand Oaks, CA: Sage.

Woods, P. (1996). *Researching the art of teaching: Ethnography for educational use.* London: Routledge.

Yanchar, S. C., & Williams, D. D. (2006). Reconsidering the compatibility thesis and eclecticism: Five proposed guidelines for method use. *Educational Researcher, 35*(9), 3–12.

Yin, R. K. (1993). *Applications of case study research.* Thousand Oaks, CA: Sage.

Yin, R. K. (2003). *Case study research: Design and methods* (3rd ed.). Thousand Oaks, CA: Sage.

Young, L. J. (2001). Border crossings and other journeys: Re-envisioning the doctoral preparation of educational researchers. *Educational Researcher, 30*(5), 3–5.

Zeichner, K. (1999). The new scholarship in teacher education. *Educational Researcher, 28*(9), 4–15.

Zeni, J. (2001). *Ethical issues in practitioner research.* Thousand Oaks, CA: Sage.

Zinsser, W. (Ed.). (1995). *Inventing the truth: The art and craft of memoir* (2nd ed.). New York: Houghton Mifflin.

# Index

**CORWIN**

A SAGE Company

The Corwin logo—a raven striding across an open book—represents the union of courage and learning. Corwin is committed to improving education for all learners by publishing books and other professional development resources for those serving the field of PreK–12 education. By providing practical, hands-on materials, Corwin continues to carry out the promise of its motto: **"Helping Educators Do Their Work Better."**